Paul within Judaism

Paul within Judaism

Restoring the First-Century Context to the Apostle

Mark D. Nanos and Magnus Zetterholm,
editors

Fortress Press
Minneapolis

PAUL WITHIN JUDAISM

Restoring the First-Century Context to the Apostle

Cover design: Laurie Ingram

Cover image © Snark/Art Resource, NY

Library of Congress Cataloging-in-Publication Data is available

Print ISBN: 978-1-4514-7003-1

eBook ISBN: 978-1-4514-9428-0

The paper used in this publication meets the minimum requirements of American National Standard for Information Sciences — Permanence of Paper for Printed Library Materials, ANSI Z329.48-1984.

Manufactured in the U.S.A.

This book was produced using PressBooks.com, and PDF rendering was done by PrinceXML.

Contents

Contributors

Kathy Ehrensperger is Reader in New Testament Studies at Trinity St. David College, University of Wales. She is the author of *That We May Be Mutually Encouraged: Feminism and the New Perspective on Paul* (T & T Clark, 2004); *Paul and the Dynamics of Power: Communication and Interaction in the Early Christ-Movement* (T & T Clark, 2007); and *Paul at the Crossroads of Cultures: Theologizing in the Space Between* (T & T Clark, 2013).

Neil Elliott is Acquiring Editor in biblical studies at Fortress Press. He is the author of The *Rhetoric of Romans* (1990; Fortress Press edition, 2005); *Liberating Paul: The Justice of God and the Politics of the Apostle* (1994; Fortress Press edition, 2006); *The Arrogance of Nations: Reading Romans in the Shadow of Empire* (Paul in Critical Contexts; Fortress Press, 2008); and, with Mark Reasoner, *Documents and Images for the Study of Paul* (Fortress Press, 2010).

Paula Fredriksen is the Aurelio Professor of Scripture emerita at Boston University, and currently Distinguished Visiting Professor at The Hebrew University, Jerusalem. She is the author of *From Jesus* to Christ (2nd ed., Yale University Press, 2000); *Jesus of Nazareth, King of the Jews* (Knopf, 1999); *Augustine and the Jews: A Christian Defense of Jews and Judaism* (Yale University Press, 2010); and *Sin: The Early History of an Idea* (Princeton University Press, 2012). She also edited with Adele Reinhartz and contributed to *Jesus, Judaism, and Christian Anti-Judaism: Reading the New Testament After the Holocaust* (Westminster John Knox, 2002). Her latest book, *Paul, the Pagans' Apostle,* is forthcoming from Yale University Press.

Karin Hedner Zetterholm is Associate Professor in Jewish Studies at Lund University. She is the author of *Jewish Interpretation of the Bible: Ancient and Contemporary* (Fortress Press, 2012); *Portrait of a Villain: Laban the Aramean in Rabbinic Literature* (Peeters, 2002); and various articles on the impact of Jesus-oriented Judaism on rabbinic Judaism.

Caroline Johnson Hodge is Associate Professor at the College of the Holy Cross. She is the author of *If Sons, Then Heirs: A Study of Kinship and Ethnicity in the Letters of Paul* (Oxford University Press, 2007). Her essays include "Married to an Unbeliever: Households, Hierarchies and Holiness in 1 Corinthians 7:12-16," *Harvard Theological Review* 103, no. 1 (2010): 1–25; "A Light to the Nations: The Role of Israel in Romans 9-11," in *Reading Romans,* ed. Jerry L. Sumney (Society of Biblical Literature, 2011); "Paul and Ethnicity and Race," in the *Oxford Handbook of Pauline Studies,* ed. Barry Matlock (Oxford University Press, forthcoming); "Daily Devotions: Stowers's Modes of Religion Meet Tertullian's *ad Uxorem,*" in *"The One Who Sows Bountifully": Essays in Honor of Stanley K. Stowers,* eds. Caroline Johnson Hodge, Saul M. Olyan, Daniel Ullucci, and

Emma Wasserman (Brown Judaic Studies, 2013), 43–54; and "Mixed Marriage in Early Christianity: Trajectories from Corinth," in *Corinth in Contrast: Studies in Inequality*, eds. Steve Friesen, Dan Showalter, and Sarah James (Brill, 2014).

Mark D. Nanos is a Lecturer at University of Kansas. He is the author of *The Mystery of Romans: The Jewish Context of Paul's Letter* (Fortress Press, 1996); *The Irony of Galatians: Paul's Letter in First-Century Context* (Fortress Press, 2002); and the editor of *The Galatians Debate: Contemporary Issues in Rhetorical and Historical Interpretation* (Hendrickson, 2002) and "Paul between Jews and Christians," a special issue of *Biblical Interpretation* 13, no. 3 (2005). He has written many essays on the topic of reading Paul within Judaism, including "Paul and Judaism: Why Not Paul's Judaism?" in *Paul Unbound: Other Perspectives on the Apostle*, ed. Mark Douglas Given (Hendrickson, 2010), 117–60; "Romans" and "Paul and Judaism," for *The Jewish Annotated New Testament*, eds. Marc Brettler and Amy-Jill Levine (Oxford, 2011); and "Paul: A Jewish View," in *Four Views on the Apostle Paul* (Zondervan, 2012).

Anders Runesson is Associate Professor of New Testament and Early Judaism at McMaster University. He is the author of *The Origins of the Synagogue: A Socio-Historical Study* (Almqvist & Wiksell International, 2001); *O That You Would Tear Open the Heavens and Come Down! On the Historical Jesus, Jonas Gardell, and the Breath of God* (Libris and Artos, 2011; in Swedish); and *Divine Wrath and Salvation in Matthew* (Fortress Press, forthcoming 2015). In addition to numerous articles on Matthew's Gospel, Paul, and ancient Jewish-Christian relations, he is the co-editor of *The Ancient Synagogue: From*

Its Origins to 200 C.E.: A Source Book (Brill, 2008); two volumes on Mark and Matthew in comparative perspective (Mohr Siebeck, 2011 and 2013); *Purity, Holiness, and Identity in Judaism and Christianity* (Mohr Siebeck, 2013); and *Jesus and the First Christians* (Verbum, 2006, in Swedish; forthcoming in English, Eerdmans).

Magnus Zetterholm is Associate Professor in New Testament Studies at Lund University. He is the author of *Approaches to Paul: A Student's Guide to Recent Scholarship* (Fortress Press, 2009); *The Formation of Christianity in Antioch: A Social-Scientific Approach to the Separation between Judaism and Christianity* (Routledge, 2003); and the editor of *The Messiah in Early Judaism and Christianity* (Fortress Press, 2007).

Respondent

Terence Donaldson is Lord and Lady Coggan Professor of New Testament Studies at Wycliffe College at the University of Toronto and author of *Paul and the Gentiles: Remapping the Apostle's Convictional World* (Fortress Press, 1997); *Judaism and the Gentiles: Jewish Patterns of Universalism (to 135 CE)* (Baylor University Press, 2007); and *Jews and Anti-Judaism in the New Testament: Decision Points and Divergent Interpretations* (Baylor, 2010).

Introduction

Mark D. Nanos

A new perspective in Pauline scholarship is represented in this volume. This perspective is readily distinguishable from other interpretations of the apostle, including the collection of views now formally recognized as "*the* (!) New Perspective on Paul" and, all the more, the views mounted in opposition to it because of the New Perspective's challenge to major tenets of traditional Christian interpretation. In these chapters, an international group of scholars takes up major questions that arise from this alternative approach, for which the phrase the "*Paul within Judaism*" perspective seems most appropriate. While these scholars stand at the forefront of this new development, their views on particular details still represent considerable diversity. The conviction they share is that Paul should be interpreted *within* Judaism. The diverse expressions of their research have been variously described in recent years collectively as the "Radical New Perspective," "Beyond the New Perspective," and "Post-New Perspective."[1] Yet these monikers do not fully communicate the major emphases of this research paradigm, since it is not primarily a new development either *within* the New Perspective paradigm or in reaction *against* it, as important as interaction with the New Perspective has been and continues to be. Instead, this work represents a radically different approach to conceptualizing both Judaism and Paul. The challenge these scholars have undertaken is to interpret Paul within his most probable first-century context, Judaism, before putting him into conversation with their own contexts or any of the discourses that have formed around the interpretation of Paul over subsequent centuries. Thus our subtitle: "Restoring the First-century Context to the Apostle."

As a result, there are many differences between this research paradigm and others undertaken to date, ranging from the questions posed and the hypotheses pursued to the sensibilities expressed about the conclusions reached, to name a few. For example, on a number of important issues, profound discontinuities arise between the Paul constructed in this new paradigm and the theological traditions constructed around Paul in the past. To highlight the paradigmatic feature around which their research converges, the contributors refer to this approach as a, or the, Paul within Judaism perspective.

How the Paul within Judaism Perspective Compares to Prevailing Perspectives

What distinguishes this focus from that of other perspectives on Paul? The Paul within Judaism perspective is, of course, informed by other relatively new approaches to Paul developed over the past forty years, and especially by the proponents of the New Perspective. Indeed, it is

---

1. Pamela Eisenbaum, one of the proponents of this approach, refers collectively to some of the scholars represented here as "the Radicals" to distinguish them from New Perspective scholars: "Paul, Polemics, and the Problem with Essentialism," *Biblical Interpretation* 13, no. 3 (2005): 224–38, esp. 232–33. Magnus Zetterholm traces the early lines of this development under the subheading "Beyond the New Perspective" in *Approaches to Paul: A Student's Guide to Recent Scholarship* (Minneapolis: Fortress Press, 2009), 127–63.

indebted to many insights of scholars associated with that perspective, from Krister Stendahl to E. P. Sanders to James D. G. Dunn and others, but also to the perspectives of those who adumbrated elements of it such as George Foot Moore, Hans Joachim Schoeps, W. D. Davies, and Pinchas Lapide, to name a few of the most influential. It also draws deeply from the scholars responsible for the so-called "Sonderweg" trajectory, which detects in Paul's letters the belief in a "special way" for non-Jews to be included in salvation through Christ, alongside the historical Sinai covenant with Israel. This view, pioneered by Lloyd Gaston, John G. Gager, and Stanley K. Stowers, is advocated by some, but not all of those represented herein. The Paul within Judaism perspective is also, naturally, indebted to many insights developed over the centuries within traditional perspectives on Paul, the New Testament, and the origins of Christianity, and further, to research related to the study of the Greek and Roman as well as Jewish worlds and worldviews.

As obvious as it may seem, the traditional and prevailing perspectives such as the New Perspective and, all the more, the traditionalistic-oriented reactions to it, do not indicate significant awareness of just how different Paul's and his audiences' probable concerns would have been from those projected onto him, and them, by later interpreters engaged in their own various theological controversies. Even when the distance is recognized on principle, in practice the controversies of Paul's time have often been described in terms analogous to later conflicts. As a result, Pauline discourse (or discourse about Paul's theology or "Paulinism") has been developed by church fathers such as Augustine and by others he would have labeled "heretics"; by Aquinas and the Scholastics, and by the Reformers alike; by modern existentialists and proponents of postmodernism; and by advocates of the New Perspective and their traditionalist opponents alike, in ways that render Paul and his theology useful for purposes of later debates, but are anachronistic, making little sense of the man and his first-century concerns. As important as these subsequent interpretive traditions are (so much so that any interpretation of Paul must engage them to be relevant), they represent *constructions* of Paul no less than do the proposals gathered together here under the rubric of Paul within Judaism. To limit the interpretation of Judaism or of Paul within the framework of those anachronistic discourses would unnecessarily constrain the possibilities of determining what Paul may have meant, and this would represent something other than the practice of historiography.

The contributors, of course, do not propose to be free from cultural conditioning or exposure to the discipline, or from the influence of contemporary sensibilities and previous interpretations. They are committed to the science of historiography more than they are beholden to making Paul fit either into what they wish for him to say, or what he has been understood to have said in the service of the various theological positions that have prevailed. When seeking to understand, even to give voice to a historical figure, one must be aware of the tensions that arise from one's own conditioning. One must go about research humbly, remaining open to new discoveries even if these may not sit well with the researcher's predispositions, presuppositions, or even the commitments of one's faith or non-faith. Knowing how to keep oneself and one's interests distinct from one's historical subject is an art, and a practice in humility. It includes the challenge to listen to criticism open-mindedly and to be open to admitting that one's views need to be adjusted—or even dismissed if mistaken.

The work undertaken in this volume questions the traditional and still prevailing approaches to Paul as a founder and chief proponent of a new and distinct religious movement, "Christianity." To date, even when scholars have admitted that to describe Paul's day using this term is anachronistic, they have often persisted nevertheless in using terminology that corresponds to the conviction that he was already a participant in a distinct religious reality, however it should be named. He is often enough described simply as a "Christian," as are his "churches"; he is a "missionary." And what he is engaged in must be characterized as a new religious movement because it is built upon the conviction that there is something fundamentally, essentially "wrong" with, and within, Judaism. Further, what is wrong with Judaism is generally analogized with what Paul is understood to have found wrong with "paganism," however that, too, is named. This Paul—often identified, even in historical-critical scholarship, as "*Saint* Paul"—is conceptualized as one who "formerly" practiced Judaism, when he was a Pharisee known as "Saul." In his new ("Christian") "mission," however, he was planting ("Christian") "churches" that were unaffiliated with, and even in open conflict with Jewish synagogues and with Judaism as a broadly described way of life. He opposed the value of Jewish identity as well as Torah-defined behavior when practiced by other followers of Jesus. This pattern is evident in the way that scholars most often approach the topic in terms of "Paul *and* Judaism," with Judaism forming the "background" or "context" for constructing Paul and his work following his change of convictions about the meaning of Jesus. Generally, where the interpretation of Paul is concerned, Christianity, however named, and Judaism, however described, represent binary alternatives, and thus two different "systems" to be compared and contrasted.

As several of the chapters in this volume make clear, the contributors' reasons for challenging the New Perspective construction of Paul are very different from the ones that might be expressed by a group of Pauline scholars upholding a traditional and generally Protestant construction of Paul. If one might say that the latter oppose the New Perspective for being *too new* for their traditional theological positions to embrace, the contributors to this volume oppose it for being *not new enough*. It is, in their view, still too beholden to traditional theological positions, including the questions asked, the courses pursued to answer them, and the consistency of their answers with the fundamental views attributed to Paul in various traditional Christian theologies, not least the way that Jewish identity and Judaism are portrayed. Put differently, some oppose the New Perspective because it undermines the traditional view that what Paul found wrong with Judaism was its works-righteousness and legalism. They argue that the traditional view offers an accurate critique of Judaism, and makes sense of Paul's oppositional rhetoric privileging, for example, ("Christian") grace and faith and (inner) spirituality in direct contrast to ("Jewish") ethnicity and works and (outward) rituals. On the other hand, the contributors to this volume in general share (and are in many ways products of) the New Perspective proposition that Judaism was characterized by "covenantal nomism," which recognizes the initial role of divine grace and of faith to initiate the relationship, but also perceives a consequent responsibility to behave according to the terms of the agreement into which the participants have entered.[2] They endorse, then, the New Perspective's rejection of the traditional Christian characterization of Judaism as "works-righteousness."

The contributors do not resonate, however, with several other central elements of the New Perspective. They do not agree with the precept that Paul found something wrong with and in Judaism itself, something essentially different from Paul's "Christianity" (however labeled). They reject the proposal that what Paul found wrong with Judaism was its commitment to ethnic identity (variously described as

---

2. This is of course a Christian and largely Protestant way of framing the case and prioritizing what is valued positively versus negatively, versus the way that Judaism would be explained if presented on its own terms.

"ethnocentrism," "badges of identity," "particularism," "nationalism," and so on).

Because the New Perspective starts from the same deep conviction found in traditional Christian interpretation—that Paul *had* to have found *something* wrong with Judaism in order to write what he is understood to have written—it has gone on to replace the traditionally supposed "wrongs" of works-righteousness and legalism, which have been presumed to give rise to the ineluctable sin of arrogance at least since Augustine, with the supposed sin of ethnic particularism, variously described and named. On the premises of the New Perspective, this "wrong" is assumed to be the necessary sin involved in celebrating and guarding the boundaries of Jewish identity and behavior, as if claiming to be set apart for God was inherently arrogant, mistaken, and evidence of bigotry. It is this essentially Jewish sin to which the New Perspective says Paul objected.

What is attributed to Judaism as "wrong" in that approach is predicated on a logical necessity that is not only historically questionable but also based upon a premise that represents a double standard. That is, it makes no sense of Paul's objection except if Paul is objecting to Jewishness per se. Why is that so? Because to be consistent, New Perspective proponents would have to admit that Paul found something inherently wrong with the essence of group identity itself. But how could that be maintained logically, since Paul was involved in creating a group that claimed to be set apart by and to a god in distinction from all other groups?[3] How could it be claimed that Paul was against ethnocentrism or badges of identity if Paul's gospel is proclaimed to the nations in order to create groups gathering together (*ekklēsiai*) that consist of people from Israel and

---

3. This logical problem arises even if, as the interpreters here claim the case to be, that group was understood to be a sub*group* within Judaism.

people from the other nations (*ethnē*) who are set apart by and to God by way of faith in/of Christ? But if Paul is only against group identity when *Jewish* measures of identity are valued positively, not to claims of group identity per se or when "*Christian*" measures of identity are valued positively, that only reinforces the traditional negative caricatures, mutatis mutandis, to which the New Perspective interpreters otherwise claim to object, and that they seem to believe that their approaches have overcome.

The New Perspective also perpetuates the traditional Christian binary juxtaposition of "faith" (meaning faith in God and Christ) versus "works" or actions, whether described as "good" works in more general terms or in terms of Jewish behavior more specifically. One of the ways in which this juxtaposition surfaces, with which many of this volume's contributors take issue, is the New Perspective's continued translation and interpretation of the Greek *pistis* as "faith," as in "belief" in a propositional claim. The contributors tend rather to understand *pistis* in terms of "faithfulness," as in "trust" and "loyalty" or "steadfastness." The latter understanding of *pistis* would by implication necessarily *include* matters of affiliation and obedience, that is, of *behavior*. As a consequence, these contributors hold that Paul's gospel, which insisted that non-Jews not undertake proselyte conversion, did not create a "Law-free" apostle.

The Paul within Judaism Perspective

It follows that in the view of these contributors, at least in significant aspects, the prevailing constructions of the apostle have not begun from the most probable historical hypotheses; they have not been approached from the most historiographically grounded sensibilities; they have not been developed around the most historically likely choices; thus they have not reached the most convincing conclusions for reading Paul in his first-century context. The contributors are committed to proposing, and seeking to answer, pre-Christian, and certainly pre-Augustinian/Protestant questions about Paul's concerns and those of his audiences and contemporaries, whether friend or foe. They nevertheless seek to construct a historical portrait of Paul from which to engage the questions of today, including those that arise from putting the historical Paul into dialogue with the other Pauls that have come after him.

What is the focus of the approaches explored in these chapters? Foremost, beyond the commitment to the quest to understand the historical Paul already noted, letting the theological chips fall where they may, if you will, the research is undertaken with the assumption that the writing and community building of the apostle Paul took place *within* late Second Temple Judaism, *within* which he remained a representative after his change of conviction about Jesus being the Messiah (Christ). This also means that the "assemblies" that he founded, and to which he wrote the letters that still provide the major basis for this research (including the letter to Rome, although a community that he did not found), were also developing their (sub)culture based upon their convictions about the meaning of Jesus for non-Jews as well as for Jews *within* Judaism. Of course, Judaism—that is, the Jewish way(s) of life—was also an expression of Greco-Roman culture that included a great deal of diversity, not least in the Diaspora where Paul was active. These scholars work from the presupposition that Judaism, as a multifaceted, dynamic cultural development, took place within other multifaceted dynamic cultures in the Hellenistic world, and thus that there is a lot more interaction and combining of cultural ideas and behavior than categorical distinctiveness or social separation, as scholars traditionally supposed. They want to avoid perpetuating the usual habits of scholarship that implicitly, when not explicitly, represent Paul as engaged in creating an entirely new and different culture, new communities, and even a new religion; moreover, that he was doing so specifically in conflict with Judaism.

Although these contributors came to these sensibilities and interpretive alternatives relatively independently of each other, and thus see the issues and state them in various and sometimes conflicting ways, they share an interest and concern, in contrast to the prevailing patterns in Pauline scholarship, to understand Paul as a representative of Judaism, and to reimagine what that would have meant for the communities that he founded and sought, by way of his letters, to shape. Although not all of the contributors would phrase the matter just this way, one might classify his endeavor, and that of the other apostles and representatives of Jesus as Messiah, as a new Jewish "sect" or "coalition" or "reform movement." He was shaping, and they were being shaped into subgroups of Judaism, that is, within a cultural way of life developed by and for Jews, even though many if not most of those who were joining these subgroups were and remained non-Jews. His concern to speak into the social tensions this created led to the writing of the letters we still seek to interpret today.

The participants are concerned with terminology and classification to be sure, and several essays address this matter directly. Nevertheless, this project is relatively new, and many of the concerns at this point, as the reader will witness, tend to turn around re-conceptualizing the way to think about Paul and his communities within Judaism and thus with proposing alternative paradigms and vocabulary rather than assuming agreement has already been reached. The process of crafting a new paradigm involves a lot of effort to avoid simply reconfiguring the familiar ways.

In short, the reader will find herein the formation of new hypotheses and experimentation with various methodological and terminological considerations in order to evaluate the proposition to read Paul *within* Judaism, instead of the way he has been read since the development of Paulinism within *Christianity*, when this initially Jewish movement changed into one that defined itself primarily *as different from* and *superior to* Judaism.

The Volume

The nucleus of this volume and the idea to develop it were inspired by a session entitled "Paul and Judaism" at the Society of Biblical Literature in 2010, where earlier versions of several of these essays were presented as papers, and several others were presented at subsequent annual sessions of that consultation. A few were developed for this volume to address specific issues that are important to research on Paul from any perspective, for example, to address the dynamic concerns arising from political- and gender-criticism.

The chapters focus on different research questions. As is well known, the answers most likely to be arrived at by research are in many ways a product of the kinds of questions asked, including how they are framed or loaded and contrasted, or not, with other alternatives. This process is in part tied to how the questions posed are presumably going to be answered, as well as to the methods employed in their pursuit.

In the interest of collegiality and productive debate within the field of Pauline studies, Terrence Donaldson has graciously accepted the invitation to offer a critical evaluation of the perspective(s) introduced in the contributors' essays. Aspects of Donaldson's interpretation of Paul fall within the framework of the New Perspective on Paul, and on occasion his premises appear different from those of the editors or some of the contributors. As might be expected, he is not entirely convinced by the arguments put forth in these essays. It will be interesting to see how reviewers and researchers who enter the discussion from various perspectives respond to the arguments set out, and his critique of them.

The Contributors

In the opening essay, Magnus Zetterholm introduces the state of the questions to be asked of research seeking to explore the interpretation of Paul as a first-century Jew and representative of Judaism. He explains the difference between beginning from traditional, normative Christian theological questions and then proceeding within and toward the goals they serve and seeking to do research according to the scientific standards of historiography, which may yield results that are quite different than supposed—even counter to one's initial expectations—which were likely based upon normative Christian constructions of Paul. The point is not to dismiss the interests of the former, but to clarify the need for cross-cultural engagement of Paul's historical voice, which is the task undertaken by the contributors herein.

Zetterholm traces the reception history of the anti-Jewish Paul constructed over the centuries from normative Christian theological perspectives. These have normally accentuated the distance between the Christianity (of the interpreters) and the Judaism (of the other) with which it has been unfavorably compared by way of the interpretation of Paul's voice. He also discusses the scholarly paradigms that have been advanced during the last two centuries. Then Zetterholm describes recent changes that have set the groundwork for this volume, the New Perspective, and several other approaches that have spun off from its basic insights. He also discusses some of the reasons that some scholars, such as those included in this volume, find the results to date inadequate to the task of constructing Paul within his own probable first-century context.

After setting out several themes that arise from reading Paul within Judaism that differentiate it from previous interpretive paradigms, Zetterholm explains that the idea of "Christianity" for Paul, and that it was conceived of as a "third race" made up of people who are neither Jews nor non-Jews, are anachronistic and almost certainly mistaken. Moreover, if one postulates that Paul still observed Torah, as do Zetterholm and several contributors, then the idea that Paul dismissed it as obsolete or antithetical to the goals of Christ-following Jews is illogical. Zetterholm explains that Paul was not against Torah observance for Jews, including himself; rather, he was adamantly against the observance of Torah by non-Jews who became followers of Jesus. Recognition of this distinction is central to the task at hand, but glossed over in most constructions of Paul to date. Paul shared this objection to Torah for non-Jews with some other Jews and Jewish groups; it was a way for Jews to protect Torah rather than an expression of resistance to its guidance. However, since this Jewish "faction" drew in many non-Jews, who would naturally be thereafter practicing the Jewish norms of communal life even if not under Torah technically as non-Jews, this led to various conflicting views about the standing and behavior to be expected of these non-Jews from within the movement and from those outside of it, to which Paul's letters attest.

When Paul's letters are approached attending to these kinds of dynamics, it becomes apparent that one cannot read straight through from Paul to later Christianity, even to later Paulinism, which were "gentile" phenomena that did not take place within Judaism. One must therefore engage in a cross-cultural endeavor that begins with the observation that Paul was writing his letters from within Judaism, not Christianity, even if that is not the way that his letters have been read since at least some point in the second century.

Anders Runesson examines the question of terminology for constructions of Paul as well as of Judaism. He focuses on two terms, "Christianity" and its cognates, and "church," although the implications of his methodological and related considerations for approaching historical information extend to many other terms and topics. Runesson recognizes that the way these titles have been used has served later Christian interests, yet observes that they are inadequate for the historical task of interpreting Paul's perspective in his first-century Greco-Roman Jewish context. In order to explain this, he traces how the process of cross-cultural reading works. Reading these texts involves the need to translate the seemingly new things encountered in terms already familiar to ourselves, and thus, it runs the risk of missing the meaning that these held for the other. Therefore, the historian must seek to de-familiarize as well as decolonize his or her own interpretive perspective as much as he or she is able to do so, even if that will never be completely possible to accomplish. Changing our vocabulary is one important element in this undertaking.

It is widely recognized that the first appearances of *christianos* postdate Paul and that he never refers to himself or anyone else by this term or its cognates. In addition to the effort to avoid the anachronistic use of this terminology when discussing Paul's views, Runesson discusses how, even if qualified when used, it nevertheless still significantly inhibits our ability to conceptualize Paul's worldview as something inherently different from the later development of Christianity as a "religion." Those whom we seek to understand asked different questions and expected different answers than did later Christians (and later Jews, too). Moreover, the term *Christian* has and still functions in a binary relationship with the terms Jew, Jewish, and Judaism, as well as Torah, which inhibits the ability to consider what it means to talk about Paul as a Jew or as Jewish or within Judaism or observing Torah apart from that contrastive way of conceptualizing the possibilities.

Then Runesson explains how the term *ekklēsia*, from which the translation "church" derived, has also come to represent something that is by definition distinguishable from "synagogue." Yet we know that this terminology was already used in the Septuagint before Paul's time, and it was still used interchangeably to refer to assemblies or gatherings of Greeks, Romans, and others, including those of Jews. Runesson shows how New Testament translators have developed a convention of referring only to Christ-following assemblies as "churches" and those of Jews who do not follow Christ as "synagogues." The cases of Galatians 1:22 and 1 Thessalonians 2:14 demonstrate that *ekklēsia* was a term that, if not also qualified as being specifically Christ-following, would naturally be understood to represent synagogue gatherings of Jews that were not assumed to be affiliated with Christ-followers: the *ekklēsia* were not yet what "church" came to represent. Thus it is anachronistic and unhelpful for understanding Paul in his own context to use the translation "church" when reading and discussing Paul and his Jewish "assemblies."

Karin Hedner Zetterholm discusses the important question of assumptions when engaging in historical investigation. She applies this concern to the topic of interpreting Torah observance in the first-century, and thus for discussing Paul in terms of Torah. Her essay provides important clarifications relevant to any discussion of Paul's relationship not only to Torah observance, but to Jewish identity and to Judaism more broadly: these terms refer not to static, but to dynamic concepts. Each is highly nuanced; so too must be later discussions of them. She questions the assumptions of many pronouncements of Paul's views on Torah and Judaism by exploring the spectrum of meaning during Paul's time, as well as later and during our own time. She both simplifies and complexifies the realities of these topics and the ways that they are discussed by way of investigating texts and through analogous contemporary examples.

The interpretation of Torah and the observance of halakah are governed by various moral considerations based upon the conviction that God is moral. Yet defining God's morality naturally involves interpretation, just as does defining how to observe Torah. Each of these are variously perceived and weighted by different Jews and Jewish groups, which includes different decisions made at different times and places and situations, and so on. There is a difference between making interpretive decisions about how to best observe Torah and making decisions to ignore Torah or specific halakah, and also between how one or one's group perceives the decisions of its own Jewish group and those made by other Jews and Jewish groups. In addition, there is the matter of failing to entirely, always, live up to the interpretive decisions to which a person or group otherwise fully subscribes, for which Torah also prescribes solutions.

Hedner Zetterholm develops the issues arising for defining these matters in a first-century context by way of discussing the idol food related instructions Paul issued in 1 Corinthians 8–10. She observes that the kind of rulings Paul makes therein—when addressing non-Jews attending Jewish assemblies in a Diaspora setting in a social environment that involved Greco-Roman cultic practices—are in many ways similar to the kinds of rabbinic debates and rulings on idolatry that arise in the Mishnah tractate *Abodah Zarah*. Emphasizing the difference between the intentions of the adherent and the perceptions of his or her intentions by others likely to witness the actions, she traces the reasoning within Paul's arguments alongside the arguments of various other Jews, including contemporary examples. Like the rabbis when discussing what constitutes idolatry for non-Jews, which includes evaluation of the specific social elements involved, she understands Paul to be developing halakic practices for Christ-following non-Jews in the non-Jewish social world of Corinth. Even though Paul's conclusions may in any given case be different from those of the later rabbis, like them he is not dismissing the role of Torah, but interpreting God's guidance, with the major difference being that the texts we have show Paul doing so to instruct non-Jews.

Mark Nanos undertakes to answer the question of how one should conceptualize Paul within Judaism on the topic of circumcision and thereby on the topics of Judaism and Torah observance more generally. He examines Paul's opposition to circumcision in conversation with an example from Josephus, who presents a story involving several Jewish advisors to King Izates. These Jews do not agree about whether or not this non-Jewish king of a non-Jewish people, who is interested in practicing Jewish customs and even in becoming a Jew, ought to become circumcised. Nanos observes that the views of these advisors were each predicated upon what each argued would be the more faithful course for Izates to take. Neither advisor conceded to the other the ideal of faithfulness, and each based their position upon the specific aspects of the case of Izates in question. They did not seek to apply these positions to all non-Jews, much less to any Jews. So too, Nanos proposes, Paul's arguments in his various letters to the Christ-following non-Jews that he addressed were based upon his assessment of what would represent the specific faithful course for them, rather than upon general principles that he would apply to all non-Jews per se or to any Jews. Similarly, those whom Paul opposes in Galatia—for seeking to influence these non-Jews to become proselytes by way of completing circumcision—would almost certainly have predicated their own positions upon what they believed to be the more faithful course. It follows that neither Paul nor his opponents likely would have yielded the ideal of faithfulness to the other.

When analyzing the positions taken by Jews and Jewish groups on circumcision and related topics, as in the case of Izates, scholars are usually able to distinguish cases involving the "conversion of non-Jews into Jews" from the "adoption of Jewish behavior by non-Jews," and to distinguish both from the "circumcision and behavior of Jews." Nanos proposes that if the same discipline were applied when conceptualizing Paul, many of the sharp distinctions between Paul's ostensible reasons for opposing circumcision and other "Jewish" behavior on the part of non-Jews would be interpreted very differently than they have been, both traditionally and in the New Perspective on Paul. In addition to the specific topic of faith and faithfulness as used by Josephus and Paul, Nanos draws attention to the contexts in which *ergon* and *ergōn* (possessive plural) arises with respect to faith(fulness), drawing out a new proposal for how to understand Paul's phrase, *ergōn nomou* (usually translated "works of law"). These moves open up a new way to frame the entire topic of "faith versus works." Nanos concludes that Paul's opposition to *ergōn nomou* was only to the rites involved in proselyte conversion (circumcision and related "acts/works") not to Jewish behavioral norms for Jews or even for non-Jews more broadly. Paul was not against good works or Jewish works or markers of identity—*for Jews*; he was against the imposition of conversion to Jewish ethnic identity (the works/rites of proselyte conversion) for these non-Jews since they were (according to the gospel) already members of God's family as non-Jews, through Jesus Christ. They were already practicing the good works within Judaism as non-Jews, although not the specific "works/rites" of circumcision that would render them Jews, thereby bearing witness to the arrival of the awaited age of the reconciling of the nations alongside Israel, according to Paul's understanding of what Nanos describes as Paul's "chronometrical" gospel proposition.

In conclusion, Nanos spells out several methodological guidelines as well as terminological and other discursive elements that should help interpreters to avoid conflating these matters when discussing Paul as well as other Jewish authors, not least the rabbis, going forward.

Caroline Johnson Hodge considers the question of identity, and specifically of the identity of the non-Jews within Paul's assemblies. She begins by noting that Paul regularly addresses his non-Jewish audiences (who are the target audiences for all of his instructions) as *ethnē* (members of the nations [other than Israel]), but also distinguishes them from non-Christ-following non-Jews who worship other gods. However, in one interesting case that Johnson Hodge explores, Paul refers to his audiences as no longer *ethnē*: "You know that when you were gentiles [*ethnē*], you were led astray, led to speechless idols" (1 Cor. 12:2). At the same time, Paul never calls them "Christians" or identifies them as Jews or Israelites. Articulating the elements of this identification conundrum and seeking to understand what is signified by the label *ethnē* for Paul—and what is not—is at the heart of this essay.

Johnson Hodge eschews the use of "gentiles" to translate *ethnē* for a variety of reasons and in concert with the preferences of several other contributors. The way that identity and ethnicity have typically been conceptualized is part of the problem that she seeks to nuance in order to understand how Paul is sorting out how to reconfigure their relationship to God and Israel as neither Jews nor *ethnē* in the ways commonly conceptualized within Judaism, or by Paul previously. They are a different kind of *ethnē*; they have multiple identities that are not entirely fixed, and the ambiguity this creates is an aspect of how Paul is working out a construction of their identity. His rhetoric is prescribing behavior for them that is tied to his theological understanding of how the story of Israel's redemption, and that of the nations, are playing out.

Following a discussion of the general issues, Johnson Hodge examines how the idea of the "holy seed" functions in Ezra and *Jubilees*, and how Paul uses a similar argument in Galatians 3 to support the inclusion of these non-Jews in Christ as that of being in the "seed of Abraham" without becoming Jews. With this analogy in hand, she examines how Paul draws from Jewish purity discourses to explain how, in 1 Corinthians 6, these non-Jews have become holy members of Christ's body, alongside Jews such as Paul.

Identifying these *ethnē* as in Christ is itself a Jewish way of understanding who they are, yet one that does not collapse the distinction between their continued identification as non-Jews/non-Israelites: "They are tucked into the seed of Abraham as gentiles and they remain gentiles, of a special sort, after they are made holy through baptism." This hybrid ethnic identity involves new ambiguities; Paul's letters provide evidence of the ways that he was trying to work these issues through from within Judaism.

Paula Fredriksen examines the question of worship, in particular, the worship of gods by those who are not Jews and how that contrasts with the worship of the God of Israel to which Paul brought non-Jews, and how this is predicated upon his understanding of the restoration of Israel having begun. She asks the reader to ponder what it meant for non-Jews, whose world and worldviews were populated with gods who were involved in every facet of personal, family, and civic life, to enter into worship within the Jewish worldview of Paul's Christ-following communities. The contrasts were startling, and Paul's insistence that they desist from common practices of cult to these gods, unlike what was expected of non-Jews who were guests in other Jewish groups in the Diaspora, created severe consequences. She asks why Paul would approach their responsibilities in this way.

The answers are several. Fredriksen sketches why referring to them as "pagans" rather than as "gentiles" is helpful: it keeps salient the combined ethnic and religious identity of their worldviews in terms of family, city, and empire; "ancient gods ran in their blood." Jews had for generations figured out how to negotiate their identity as Jews in Diaspora cities, which by definition involved living "*within* a pagan religious institution." They also understood, as the Scriptures too depicted the world of the Israelites, that while they worshipped their God as the highest of gods, each people had their gods to worship. Living among non-Jews thus required negotiating this complexity. There is some evidence of non-Jews "converting," but it was more common for non-Jews to express various levels of respect for the Jewish communities and their god while remaining "pagans." It is from this latter group that Paul likely found those interested in the message he proclaimed. But he insisted that even though they not become Jews, they must cease to participate in the worship of the gods of the non-Jews, which elicited a strong reaction from both Jews and non-Jews, for that was not the way these matters had been negotiated in the past. Why did Paul take this course?

Paul worked from the conviction that the apocalyptic expectations of a time when those from the nations would worship the God of Israel as their own God alongside of Israel had arrived. The present crises that the difference between this conviction of its arrival and of its ultimate consummation would be brief, and thus the stress created by this deviation from normal social arrangements would not last long, but it was necessary for the moment. It served as the "trip switch" by which God would eventually restore the nations as well as Israel, just as Scripture had foretold, which was now decoded by the followers of Jesus Christ.

These "pagans" had received the Spirit; they could no longer worship other gods. Having been "justified by faith," Fredriksen argues that these non-Jews were, according to Paul, under nine of the Ten Commandments: they were to adhere "steadfastly" to fulfilling all of the moral obligations but not to the Jewish ritual of Sabbath observance, since they had not become Jews but nevertheless had become "righteous ones." She thus suggests that we translate *dikaiosynē ek pisteōs* in such a way as to signify "right behavior according to the Law on account of steadfast attachment to the gospel."

Neil Elliott takes up the question of politics, of what it means to discuss Paul as a Diaspora Jew under Roman rule. He spells out a number of the political implications that follow from reading Paul within Judaism. He undertakes this task in conversation with a variety of contemporary approaches that seek to read Paul and his setting differently, but nevertheless perpetuate rather than challenge deeply held ways of conceptualizing Paul's theology and practice in sharp contrast to Judaism, which is still (mis)portrayed as inferior. Elliott examines the arguments representative of the New Perspective on Paul by focusing on a landmark essay by Jörg Frey, then evaluates similar issues in the social-scientific reading of Bruce J. Malina and John J. Pilch. These different scholars (sometimes) explicitly deny that Paul left Judaism; nevertheless, Elliott shows how their interpretive decisions continue to undermine such assertions. This naturally follows methodologically when Paul is approached primarily through the received Christianized readings of him rather than from the very different assumption that Paul's concerns probably arose within his first-century Jewish context. Elliott observes a disconnection between the logical implications of new insights and approaches to Paul and to Judaism and the weight of habitual commitments to traditional conclusions and discursive practices.

Taking seriously the Jewish context of Paul and his communities in the first century means wrestling with what it meant to live within the Roman Empire as Jews, or in the case of the non-Jews to whom Paul writes, what it meant for them to join a Jewish movement centered around messianic claims of a Judean crucified by Rome. By way of interacting with work by John M. G. Barclay, Elliott clarifies how Judaism can be defined very differently than it has been, and thus so, too, can Paul. What would it mean to take seriously that being Jewish is not per se something other than being Greek or being Roman? Can we understand overlapping and intersecting identities, including the complex negotiations required for living under the Roman Empire, as fully part of being Jewish?

Kathy Ehrensperger discusses the question(s) of gender, of what it means to seek to relocate Paul in relation to Judaism. She observes just how little research has been conducted to date on the question of Paul's position on gender-critical matters from within Judaism of his time, or as a representative thereof. Then the "rule" stated in 1 Corinthians 14:33-36, which has traditionally been understood to indicate that Paul sought to keep women from active roles in assemblies that ostensibly had begun on more egalitarian terms in contrast to Jewish practices, would instead more likely indicate that these non-Jews were unprepared by the constraints on women's participation that were practiced within their native non-Jewish contexts. They did not yet know how to negotiate the new opportunities for the participation of women now offered by these Jewish subgroups. After surveying some of the evidence for the participation of women in synagogue gatherings of the time, Ehrensperger demonstrates how Paul's guidance for conducting prayer and prophecy implies their active involvement in these activities, albeit with certain constraints to ensure orderliness in ways that apparently conformed to prevailing traditions. Thus, although Paul was a man of his time, a time when hierarchical arrangements based on gender cannot be denied, it was the less hierarchical norms operative within Jewish groups that created the new opportunities for participation, not the other way around. She points to several ways to consider how Paul's instructions might align with other contemporary Jewish groups' distinctions where the matter of reading and instruction of Scripture were concerned, versus activities such as prayer and prophecy.

Ehrensperger also discusses the more general issues of universalizing often attributed to Paul, in this case with emphasis on the problem of logically negating gender differences in service of the mantra of "one new man," paralleling the negation of Jewish identity in the supposed universalizing of everyone as "Christians," a scenario in which everyone is by definition universalized to the status of not-being-Jews. She follows this with a reading of Paul preserving particularity, the embodiment of ethnic as well as gender difference among the participants in these Jewish *ekklēsia* in Christ, similar to what the evidence suggests was the case among other Second Temple Jewish *ekklēsia* of God that did not share their convictions about the meaning of Jesus.

The Respondent

Terrence Donaldson offers a critical evaluation of the essays as an advocate of the New Perspective, indeed, as one who has advanced several research trajectories within it. Critically evaluating perspectives that are in some important ways different from one's own is not an easy task, and it takes a great deal of work to do it well. Donaldson is an expert at this, and the editors are very grateful that he has begun the response to the various positions put forward in this volume in such a constructive and helpful way.

Donaldson traces the questions that have driven his own research and the solutions he has offered, which is very helpful for understanding some of the main lines of the New Perspective as well as where some diversity arises among its proponents. Then he traces some of the main lines of the arguments of the contributors. On many important points, Donaldson affirms the sensibilities and arguments of the contributors, including the idea of reading Paul within Judaism and the need to find new terminology for explaining what was taking place in Paul's communities. When Donaldson turns to critical assessment of the contributions, he highlights two major points. These are worth brief presentation here.

First, Donaldson notes that many of the contributors explain Paul's understanding of the inclusion of non-Jews in terms of Jewish "restoration theology" expectations. He finds this reading attractive, but finally inadequate, because he understands Paul to believe that Israel's restoration will only *follow* the inclusion of the *ethnē,* rather than precede it (as is generally indicated in the texts from which restoration theology is predicated). Donaldson appeals to traditions expecting the pilgrimage of the nations to Jerusalem to buttress his point. His observation gives valuable precision to this part of the debate; readers may judge to what extent it should qualify the arguments of one or another contributor to this volume. Most of the contributors do not build their appeals around such *pilgrimage* traditions specifically, but mention these among the many different eschatological scenarios anticipated in Scripture, including the anticipation of judgment of those from the nations and general reconciliation of all humankind. They emphasize, however, that Paul, like some later rabbis, chose to focus on one of the expectations also adumbrated in Scripture; namely, that people from the nations would also experience reconciliation and this was in some way tied to Israel being restored.[4]

---

4. E.g., Acts 15:12-21 explicitly appeals to Amos 9:11-12 to explain the inclusion of the nations in terms of the restoration of Israel in order to clarify the conundrum of a divided response from

Moreover, unlike Donaldson, many of the contributors, either here or in previous publications, haveunderstood Paul to maintain that the restoration of Israel has indeed begun first, that he and other Israelites who believe Jesus to be the Messiah represent that initial positive response, and that this positive response is as important to Paul as the negative one of others, representing a divided response of Israel overall. In other words, they already argue for an approach to the topic that Donaldson proposes as an alternative to explore. In this view, the process of Israel's restoration as well as the reconciling of the nations has begun but not yet been completed, and the process of bringing it to its final stages is the purpose of Paul's mission to the nations.[5] It was seemingly unanticipated in the bits and pieces of restoration theology that are fairly easily identified in scriptural and other surviving literature, for which reason Paul calls his explanation in Romans 11—which is based upon an appeal to things already declared in Scripture—the revealing of a "mystery."

Another matter that arises under Donaldson's first criticism is the matter of Torah observance for non-Jews, to which he understands

Israel at this point, and moreover, to argue that these non-Jews should not become proselytes but become righteous non-Jews within Judaism worshipping alongside of Israelites; cf. Isa. 45:22; 49:6; Zech. 2:11. Paula Fredriksen addresses Paul's rearranging of the sequence of events that bring about the restoration of Israel and salvation of the nations as a result of: a) pressure brought on the expected scenario because of the apparent delay of the end, and b) the decline of Jews attracted to joining the Jesus movement ("Judaism, the Circumcision of Gentiles, and Apocalyptic Hope," *Journal of Theological Studies* 42, no. 2 [1991]: 558–64, here 532–64; on p. 564 she cites E. P. Sanders to observe: "Paul's letter [to Rome] revises biblical history and 'rearranges the eschatological sequence so that it accords with the facts.'").

5. E.g., Mark D. Nanos, *The Mystery of Romans: The Jewish Context of Paul's Letter* (Minneapolis: Fortress Press, 1996), 239–88; Nanos, "Romans 11 and Christian and Jewish Relations: Exegetical Options for Revisiting the Translation and Interpretation of this Central Text," *Criswell Theological Review* 9, no. 2 (2012): 3–21, and the detailed exegetical essays to which that essay refers. These explain the scenario differently than does Donaldson, and also offer translation alternatives like "lagging behind" and "losing pace" that better fit the metaphor (than do "defeat" and "rejection"), which revolves around a gap opening up among the Israelites (with some in the lead and others stumbling but not falling, but who will also eventually finish the course); it is into this gap that some non-Jews are entering, thus alongside and after some Israelites but before some others.

Paul to object, and this seems to him to undermine the idea of Paul envisioning what he was doing within Judaism. This objection begins from a different paradigmatic set of premises, premises that arise within traditional as well as New Perspective interpretations of Paul's arguments—but *not* from the interpretive premises from which several of the contributors who address this topic work. These contributors speak to this matter in their essays and in previously published work, arguing instead that Paul does *not* object to Torah observance or the practice of Judaism more generally, including for non-Jews, and that he even promotes the practice of Judaism and Torah-oriented thinking and behavior for all Christ-followers. What Paul objects to, on these readings, is Christ-following non-Jews *becoming Jews*, that is, completing the rite of ethnic conversion that is signified by circumcision in Paul's arguments. Therefore they are not technically "under Torah" as are Jews (*hypo nomon*, Rom. 6:14-15), but they are joining Jewish groups with Jews such as Paul who *are* under Torah (God's "Guidance" for Israel), and thus learning to live according to Torah-based norms in order to understand how to live faithful to the righteousness expected of all humanity ("under grace . . . slaves . . . of obedience unto righteousness" [*hypo charin . . . douloi . . . hypakoēs eis dikaiosynēn*, Rom. 6:16). Differentiating the identity transformation of non-Jews into Jews, to which Paul objects, from the behavioral guidelines operative within Jewish communities, which Paul upholds, as two very different things is important to many of the contributors represented here. This distinction has not generally been observed by the New Perspective interpreters any more than by traditionalists, leading to very different understandings of what it is to which Paul objects, and the reasons for him doing so. This distinction is an important one to consider to enable reading Paul "within" Judaism.

Donaldson's second major objection is to the various contributors who see the new identity of the non-Jews in Paul's communities as in certain ways representing an anomaly. That is, on the one hand they are being made children of Abraham apart from becoming Israelites through the convention of proselyte conversion; but on the other hand, they are not simply remaining so-called god-fearers, guests but not members of the people of God. Various contributors explain this matter in different ways, but Donaldson is not convinced that any of these adequately address the way that Paul argues for the inclusion of these non-Jews as the "seed of Abraham."

Paul's arguments are indeed complex here, as Donaldson admits regarding his own preferred approach to the issues, but his objection turns on maintaining a contrast between two mutually exclusive alternatives that, in the view of some of the contributors, are not in fact incompatible and that Paul seems to combine. These non-Jews represent the blessing of all the nations promised to Abraham (Gal. 3:8; cf. 3:1–4:7), which Donaldson suggests would be the logical course for Paul to have argued, but he does not see evidence that Paul did so. Some representatives of the Paul within Judaism paradigm might contend, however, that Paul did make that argument in Galatians 3 (by citation in v. 8) and, differently, in Romans 3–4. Paul also argued in the direction of the alternative to which Donaldson points, that the non-Jews were seed because of being in Christ, who is "the seed" of Abraham that was promised, thus making them children of Abraham (Gal. 3:16; again, cf. Gal. 3:1–4:7, 28). One can quibble with either aspect of Paul's argument, of course, but several contributors to the Paul within Judaism paradigm maintain that they both are part of his thought.

Donaldson's concluding reflections turn around the complexity of defining what it means to discuss "within Judaism" as well as "Paul." The insightful issues he raises do not seem to the editors to represent binary alternatives as much as various strands and emphases in Judaism or in Paul's thought. Building around Donaldson's concluding reflections, it is helpful to recognize that: 1) Judaism in Paul's day was both a conceptual and a social reality; therefore, 2) interpreters ought to investigate both the conceptual and the social aspects of Paul and his (and other Christ-following) communities, especially in relationship to Judaism so understood; 3) historians ought to be concerned with the perspectives of every one of those interested parties; and finally, 4) researchers should always be concerned to understand Paul in conversation with the historical developments then and thereafter, not least with the trajectory that has come to be known as Paulinism (or Pauline Christianity).

The editors are very grateful for Terry Donaldson's raising these particular issues and for his broader engagement of the research undertaken here. Hopefully the reader will recognize that the contributors find his critique welcome, demonstrating a shared interest to understand Paul on his own terms, and at the same time, to do so in conversation with the various Paul(s) that have made their appearance down through the years, especially the ones that prevail within our own time. They now invite you to join them in the relatively new way to read Paul: *within* Judaism.

1

———

Paul within Judaism: The State of the Questions

Magnus Zetterholm

Introduction

I may not be inclined to agree with the late Christopher Hitchens that religion poisons *everything*,[1] but in the case of Pauline studies it could, however, easily be argued that this research discipline has indeed been negatively affected by Christian normative theology.

The study of the New Testament in general is, and has always been, a predominantly Christian affair. *Christians* study the New Testament, often within theological departments of seminaries and universities. Indeed, many scholarly commentary series are for

1. Christopher Hitchens, *God is not Great: How Religion Poisons Everything* (London: Atlantic Books, 2008).

Christians: The New International Greek Testament Commentary specifically states in the foreword that "the supreme aim of this series is to serve those who are engaged in the ministry of the Word of God and thus to glorify God's name." Similarly, in the editorial preface to the Word Biblical Commentary, it is stated that the contributors all are "evangelical," understood "in its positive, historic sense of a commitment to Scripture as divine revelation, and to the true power of the Christian gospel."

Furthermore, it is not unusual to find that *methodological atheism*, a quite natural assumption in most scientific research,[2] is challenged from scholars advocating what must be understood as an alternative theory of science, where supernatural events are possible, and where gods and angels intervene in human affairs. For instance, in his, in many ways excellent treatment of the resurrection of Jesus, presented as a scholarly contribution, N. T. Wright states in the introduction that he will argue "that the best *historical* explanation is the one which inevitably raises all kinds of *theological* questions: the tomb was indeed empty, and Jesus was indeed seen alive, because he was truly raised from the dead."[3] Theological conviction drives a comment expressed as if it were merely a historical reflection. From a methodological point of view, the Christian ideological perspectives that continue to characterize much of the ostensibly historical work done in New Testament studies is problematic.

This close connection between New Testament studies in general and normative Christian theology is itself, of course, the result of historical developments. Biblical exegesis started as a way for people to understand and explain what they perceived as divine revelation,

---

2. See Peter L. Berger, *The Sacred Canopy: Elements of a Sociological Theory of Religion* (Garden City, NJ: Doubleday, 1969), 100.

3. N. T. Wright, *The Resurrection of the Son of God: Christian Origins and the Question of God: Volume 3* (Minneapolis: Fortress Press, 2003), 10.

or as the *Mekilta* puts it: "when they [the Israelites] all stood before mount Sinai to receive the Torah they interpreted the divine word as soon as they heard it."[4] Jewish biblical interpretation was eventually carried over into the Christian church with the same aim of interpreting the word of God, but it found new expressions, for instance in the famous Alexandrian and Antiochean schools of interpretation.[5] It is even possible to talk about a rudimentary "scientific" form of biblical exegesis in connection with the formation of the canon.[6]

It would, however, take to the Enlightenment before any real attempts to read the biblical text from other points of departure than theological ones. In terms of radicalism, it is hard to imagine any modern biblical scholar creating stronger reactions from the audience than, for instance, Herman Samuel Reimarus (1694–1768), David Friedrich Strauss (1808–74), or indeed, the representatives of the famous Tübingen School.[7] However, in spite of the ambition to deconstruct and criticize influences from normative theology, New Testament scholarship during the nineteenth century and onwards was ironically heavily influenced by one of the most influential master narratives within Western culture—the theological dichotomy between Judaism and Christianity. This theme has determined the outcome of several important subfields within New Testament Studies, such as the historical Jesus, the historical Paul, the rise of Christianity, and the separation between Judaism and Christianity. On scientific grounds, the impact on normative Christian theology

---

4. *Mek.* Bahodesh 9 (trans. Lauterbach).
5. See, e.g., Anthony C. Thiselton, *Hermeneutics: An Introduction* (Grand Rapids: Eerdmans, 2009), 104–14.
6. For an overview, see Einar Thomassen, "Some Notes on the Development of Christian Ideas about a Canon," in *Canon and Canonicity*, ed. Einar Thomassen (Copenhagen: Museum Tusculanum Press, 2010), 9–28.
7. Overviews in William Baird, *History of New Testament Research* (Minneapolis: Fortress Press, 1992), 1:170–74, 246–58, 269–78.

obviously should not guide historiography, including historical-critical treatments of the biblical and related literary and material remains. Christian theological interests require cross-cultural constraints.

Only during the last decades has the theological enterprise's determination of what is historical been profoundly challenged from new, avowedly scientifically based perspectives. The so-called Third Quest of the historical Jesus is one example where the opposition between Jesus and Judaism has been replaced by a historically more likely view where Jesus is placed *within* Judaism and understood as representing Judaism. The same is now happening with Paul, but in his case the resistance from normative theology seems stronger. It is not hard to understand why. The binary ideas that Christianity has superseded Judaism and that Christian grace has replaced Jewish legalism, for example, appear to be essential aspects of most Christian theologies. Nevertheless, as in the case with the Jesus, proponents of the so-called Radical Perspective on Paul—what we herein prefer to call Paul within Judaism perspectives—believe and share the assumption that the traditional perspectives on the relation between Judaism and Christianity are incorrect and need to be replaced by a historically more accurate view. It is Christian theology that must adjust, at least learn to read its own origins cross-culturally when demonstrated to be necessary on independent scientific grounds. I am quite confident that Christianity will survive a completely Jewish Paul, just as it evidently survived a completely Jewish Jesus. Religions tend to adapt.

In the following, I will try to explain why I believe the dichotomy between Paul and Judaism to be incorrect and why most New Testament scholarship has been influenced by it.[8] I will also try to

---

8. For a more thorough presentation, see Magnus Zetterholm, *Approaches to Paul: A Student's Guide to Recent Scholarship* (Minneapolis: Fortress Press, 2009).

show how the interpretation of Paul is completely dependent on the overarching perspective of the individual scholar. If we alter the perspective, the result changes dramatically. If our goal is to get Paul right, it is important to apply historiographical rigor, including self-awareness of our own interpretive interests, which we ought to be willing to subordinate to outcomes that we might not actually prefer. Theological interest in Paul's voice should be conducted with respect for the cross-cultural nature of the historical discipline required for his later interpreters.

The Development of an Anti-Jewish Paul

Anti-Jewishness as an Ideological Resource

Anti-Jewish propaganda started promptly within early Christianity. However, Paul's infamous statement in 1 Thessalonians 2:14-15 on the Jews, "who killed both the Lord Jesus and the prophets, and drove us out; they displease God and oppose everyone,"[9] is probably best seen as mirroring intra-Jewish disputes within a highly rhetorical context.[10]

But beginning in the early second century we find harshly critical statements from *non-Jewish* followers of Jesus that seem to indicate that some form of division based on ethnicity has taken place. On his way to martyrdom in Rome around 115, Ignatius, the bishop of Antioch, wrote several letters to communities of followers of Jesus whom he sought to convince of their Christian as opposed to Jewish communal identities, warning them to beware of continued influence from Judaism. In his Letter to the Magnesians (8:1), Ignatius exhorts the community "not [to] be deceived by strange

9. Biblical quotations are from the NRSV.
10. On "anti-Judaism" in the New Testament in general, see Terence L. Donaldson, *Jews and Anti-Judaism in the New Testament: Decision Points and Divergent Interpretations* (Waco, TX: Baylor University Press, 2010).

doctrines or antiquated myths, since they are worthless. For if we continue to live in accordance with Judaism, we admit that we have not received grace."[11] In 10:3, he states that it is "utterly absurd [atopon estin] to profess Jesus Christ and to practice Judaism." The negative, binary terms around which Ignatius worked his prescriptions likely betray how blurred the emerging communal boundaries remained over fifty years after Paul's letters were written.

Somewhat later, around 160, another bishop, Melito of Sardis, apparently invented the deicide, the idea that "the Jews" collectively were responsible for executing not only Jesus, but God himself (*Peri Pasha* 96):

He who hung the earth is hanging;
he who fixed the heavens has been fixed;
he who fastened the universe has been fastened to a tree;
the Sovereign has been insulted;
the God has been murdered;
the King of Israel has been put to death by an Israelite right hand.[12]

This Christian anti-Jewish propaganda developed into an extensive literary genre, the so-called *adversos Iudaeos* tradition.[13] I have argued, however, that the emergence of Christian anti-Judaism was not originally only theological, but the result of a particular historical situation.[14] During the first decades, non-Jewish adherents to the Jesus movement were probably seen as part of the Jewish community

11. Michael W. Holmes, *The Apostolic Fathers: Greek Texts and English Translations*, 3rd ed. (Grand Rapids: Baker Academic, 2007).
12. Melito of Sardis, *On Pascha and Fragment: Texts and Translations* (Oxford: Clarendon, 1979).
13. For a collection, see A. Lukyn Williams, *Adversus Judaeos: A Bird's-Eye View of Christian Apologiae until the Renaissance* (Cambridge: Cambridge University Press, 2012 [1935]).
14. Magnus Zetterholm, *The Formation of Christianity in Antioch: A Social-Scientific Approach to the Separation Between Judaism and Christianity* (London: Routledge, 2003).

and were in fact considered as Jews by outsiders. This has to do with the religio-political system in the Greco-Romans city-states. All inhabitants in a city were expected to express loyalty to the religion(s) of the city. Jews were exempt from this through locally issued decrees,[15] and seem to have found other ways of expressing loyalty to the city and to Rome that did not challenge Jewish sensitivities regarding "idolatry."[16]

Since all Jews within the early Jesus movement seem to have agreed that non-Jews should refrain from what from a Jewish perspective was considered "idolatry,"[17] this evidently left the non-Jewish adherents of the movement in a rather vulnerable situation, especially in Paul's communities, since he argued that although non-Jews should convert to Judaism they should nevertheless remain non-Jews.[18] The most reasonable strategy for such non-Jews would be to pretend to be Jews in relation to the civic authorities.

However, after the Jewish War in 70 CE, negative feelings toward Jews (no longer carefully distinguished from the Judean Jews who had revolted) permeated Roman society at several levels. In this situation, it is reasonable to assume that some non-Jews who were followers of Jesus developed another strategy—to separate from the Jewish Jesus movement. Such an enterprise involved several difficulties. On the one hand, Rome was quite suspicious of new so-called *collegia*, or voluntary associations, the normal form of

---

15. Mikael Tellbe, *Paul Between Synagogue and State: Christians, Jews, and Civic Authorities in 1 Thessalonians, Romans, and Philippians* (Stockholm: Almqvist & Wiksell, 2001), 37–59.

16. Philip A. Harland, *Associations, Synagogues, and Congregations: Claiming a Place in Ancient Mediterranean Society* (Minneapolis: Fortress Press, 2003), 215–28.

17. See, e.g., Acts 15:19-20; 1 Cor. 6:9, 10:14. There seems, however, to have coexisted several ideas on how this should be achieved; see Magnus Zetterholm, "'Will the Real Gentile-Christian Please Stand Up!': Torah and the Crisis of Identity Formation," in *The Making of Christianity: Conflicts, Contacts, and Constructions: Essays in Honor of Bengt Holmberg*, ed. Magnus Zetterholm and Samuel Byrskog (Winona Lake, IN: Eisenbrauns, 2012), 373–93.

18. 1 Cor. 7:17-24, but cf. Acts 15:1, 5. See also J. Brian Tucker, *'Remain in Your Calling': Paul and the Continuation of Social Identities in 1 Corinthians* (Eugene, OR: Pickwick, 2011).

organization for cults, burial societies, or social clubs. In the decades after the war it is hardly likely that a *collegium* involving Judaism would be approved. On the other hand, Romans admired ancient traditions, sustaining the advantage of practicing Judaism. The emerging non-Jewish part of the Jesus movement made the most of the circumstances by combining the ancient traditions of Judaism with a vigorous denial of Jews. In effect, early Christianity emerged as a form of Judaism stripped from Jews, and anti-Judaism became an important ideological resource for non-Jewish followers of Jesus in their effort to become a legally recognized religion.

Now, this would take some time. Only with the decree of 311, which legalized Christianity, did the church achieve these aims. However, by then, the church's own propaganda against Jews and Judaism, originally motivated by *political* circumstances, had created a *theological* problem. How would it be possible to explain the fact that Judaism still existed considering that the grace of God now had been transferred from the Jews to the new and "true Israel"?[19]

From Augustine to Luther

During Late Antiquity and the Middle Ages this theological problem would find several solutions partly depending on theological changes. While Paul's problem seems to have been how to include the nations in the final salvation or how the categories "Jew" and "non-Jew" would be rescued from their respective constraints, the interest changes to the salvation of the individual. An important part of this development was the so-called Pelagian controversy. The monk Pelagius, who appeared in Rome around 380, argued that humans had to be capable of doing what God expected from them since

19. A concept introduced in the second century CE by Justin; see Peter Richardson, *Israel in the Apostolic Church* (London: Cambridge University Press, 1969), 9–14.

they were equipped with free will; otherwise, they could not be held accountable by a just God. Pelagius also denied any form of original sin that had so corrupted the human soul that it was impossible for one to choose to do what God commanded. Against this, Augustine claimed the opposite: humans can in no way please God, even choose to want to please God, and are, precisely because of their corrupted nature, incapable of doing what God demands. Human salvation is in every way a result of God's grace. The problem of free will, the extent of God's grace, the conditions of human salvation, and predestination (a consequence of Augustine's argument) would dominate the theological debate for many centuries.

As for the Jews, Augustine developed a somewhat different approach than his predecessors. Using a verse from Psalm 59:11 ("Do not kill them, or my people may forget; make them totter by your power, and bring them down, O Lord, our shield"), Augustine argued that the Jews were still chosen by God, but dispersed over the world, where they now served as eternal witnesses to the truth of Christian claims; they should thus be left alone.[20] This "doctrine of Jewish witness" may have helped save Jewish lives but it also gave a new theological reason for despising Jews and Judaism.

During the Reformation, the already wide gap between Judaism and Christianity would widen further and find new theological bases upon which to build. While the church had adopted a modified form of Augustinianism, according to which God's grace and human efforts interacted in salvation, Martin Luther returned to Augustine's original doctrine of justification. Luther, however, developed several dialectical relations that would result in an even sharper contrast between Judaism and Christianity. While "gospel" and "law" interact in bringing a person to Christ, "faith" and "works" must be separated

20. Paula Fredriksen, *Augustine and the Jews: A Christian Defense of Jews and Judaism* (New Haven, CT: Yale University Press, 2010).

when it comes to justification. For Luther, "works" are always a consequence of "faith" and the opposite relationship, that is, to believe it possible to please God through good deeds represents the worst sin of all: self-righteousness.

Thus, the normal way for a Jewish person to express his or her relation to the God of Israel by faithfulness represented by Torah observance, can, from Luther's perspective, only lead to condemnation. Luther's view on Jews and Judaism is rather well covered in his pamphlet *On the Jews and Their Lies*.[21] Here he suggests, among other things, that synagogues and Jewish schools should be burnt, rabbis should be forbidden to teach, and that Jewish writings should be confiscated. By stressing that "the doctrine of justification by faith" not only constituted a theological *interpretation* of Paul, but the correct understanding of the *historical* Paul, Luther's interpretation of Paul became established as an indisputable historical fact.

The Formation of a Scholarly Paradigm

During the nineteenth century the idea of a distinction between Judaism and Christianity was theologically well established. This dichotomy would eventually develop a kind of scientific legitimacy, predominantly within German scholarship.[22] One of the most important members of the so-called Tübingen School, Ferdinand C. Baur, drew on Georg Wilhelm Friedrich Hegel's idealistic proposition that the "Absolute Spirit" manifested itself in history through a dialectical process in which it always encounters

---

21. Martin Luther, *Von den Jüden und iren Lügen* (Wittemberg: Hans Lufft, 1543).
22. On German scholarship on Jews and Judaism, see Anders Gerdmar, *Roots of Theological Anti-Semitism: German Biblical Interpretation and the Jews, from Herder and Semler to Kittel and Bultmann* (Leiden: Brill, 2009).

oppositions. Baur applied Hegel's theory to the early church history, and found two opposing forms of Christianity: Jewish and gentile.[23]

Furthermore, in 1880, Ferdinand Weber published a study that would function as the standard work for anyone who wanted to know something about ancient Judaism.[24] Weber, who originally wanted to become a missionary to the Jewish people, had actually consulted original rabbinic texts, but it is hard to avoid the impression that he was heavily influenced by the theological *zeitgeist* of the period. Weber found that the God of the Jews was distant and that Judaism was a legalistic religion in which pious Jews strove to earn their righteousness through observing obsolete commandments.

Weber's reconstruction of ancient Judaism was passed on to new generations of scholars. Thus, in Wilhelm Bousset's and Emil Schürer's presentations of ancient Judaism we basically find Weber's view reiterated.[25] Through their students, these and other scholars perpetuated the idea of the sharp contrast between Judaism and Christianity and the inferiority of Judaism into the twentieth century. In the middle of the twentieth century we find a scholarly paradigm fully compatible with the traditional negative Christian theological understanding of the nature of Judaism and its inferiority in relationship to Christianity. This development was of course fueled by general changes in society: during the nineteenth century, Christian anti-Semitism merged together with secular, scientifically legitimated anti-Semitism based on racial-biological ideas. In connection with nationalistic ambitions around the time of the

---

23. See, e.g., Ferdinand C. Baur, "Die Christuspartei in der korinthischen Gemeinde, der Gegensatz des petrinischen und paulinischen Christenthums in der ältesten Kirche, der Apostel Petrus in Rom," *Tübingen Zeitschrift für Theologie* 4 (1831): 61–206.

24. Ferdinand Weber, *System der altsynagogalen palästinischen Theologie aus Targum, Midrasch und Talmud* (Leipzig: Dörffling & Franke, 1880).

25. Wilhelm Bousset, *Die Religion des Judentums im neutestamentlichen Zeitalter* (Berlin: Reuther & Reichard, 1903); Emil Schürer, *Geschichte des jüdischen Volkes im Zeitalter Jesu Christi* (Leipzig: Hinrichs, 1866–90).

unification of the German states in the 1870s, European Jews became increasingly marginalized and were perceived as an alien body. The picture of Jews and Judaism transmitted throughout the centuries was now developed within ideological contexts that essentially opposed Jews and Judaism within Western culture.

Paradigm Shift

There can be no doubt that this synthesis of theology and scholarship on Paul's relation to Judaism creates a logical Paul. Assuming that ancient Judaism really was a legalistic religion, without any chance for individuals to experience grace, mercy, or love, it follows that any decent person, including Paul, would naturally fight against such an ideology, and thus, attribute a negative value to the Torah. There are, of course, quite a few texts that seem to support such an interpretation. According to the NRSV, Paul states that "no human being will be justified in his sight by deeds prescribed by the law, for through the law comes the knowledge of sin" (Rom. 3:20); that "Christ is the end of the law" (Rom. 10:4); that "all who rely on the works of the law are under a curse" (Gal. 3:10). Translated in these ways, Paul seems to oppose the Jewish way of life based on Torah.[26]

It is, of course, fully possible that the theological interpretation of Paul that has developed over the centuries represents an accurate reconstruction of the historical Paul's thought world. However, if the fundamental assumption in this reconstruction—the vile character of ancient Judaism—would turn out to be mistaken, what would then happen to the reconstructions of Paul that were based on this assumption? As a result of E. P. Sanders's publication of *Paul and*

---

26. Each of these translations represent choices that have been challenged in ways that suggest instead that Paul is not opposing or degrading the role of Torah for guiding life for Jews, but the necessity of circumcision for Christ-following non-Jews; see Nanos's contribution in this volume, "The Question of Conceptualization: Qualifying Paul's Position on Circumcision in Dialogue with Josephus's Advisors to King Izates."

Palestinian Judaism in 1977,[27] combined with the challenges mounted by Krister Stendahl in several essays,[28] Pauline scholars began to question many time-honored truths regarding Paul (and Jesus for that matter).

Sanders did what Weber had done, but not so many after him[29]—he reread the Jewish texts in order to see if he could find a religious pattern, common to all texts from 200 BCE to 200 CE. What he found he labeled "covenantal nomism," by which he meant that there exists a relationship between covenantal theology and the Torah. In contrast to the prevalent view of first-century Judaism, Sanders found that the pious Jew does not observe the Torah in order to earn his or her righteousness, *but to confirm his or her willingness to remain in a covenantal relationship with the God of Israel*. Also, the Torah evidently presumes that it will not be observed perfectly since it includes a system for atoning sin:

> God has chosen Israel and Israel has accepted the election. In his role as King, God gave Israel commandments which they are to obey as best they can. Obedience is rewarded and disobedience punished. In case of failure to obey, however, man has recourse to divinely ordained means of atonement, in all of which repentance is required. As long as he maintains his desire to stay in the covenant, he has a share in God's covenantal promises, including life in the world to come. The intention and effort to be obedient constitute the *condition for remaining in the covenant*, but they do not *earn* it.[30]

---

27. Edward P. Sanders, *Paul and Palestinian Judaism: A Comparison of Patterns of Religion* (Philadelphia: Fortress Press, 1977).
28. Collected in Krister Stendahl, *Paul Among Jews and Gentiles, and Other Essays* (Philadelphia: Fortress Press, 1976).
29. Similar ideas had indeed been expressed before without making any major impact; see, e.g., Claude G. Montefiore, *Judaism and St Paul: Two Essays* (London: Goshen, 1914); George F. Moore, "Christian Writers on Judaism," *Harvard Theological Review* 14 (1921): 197–254.
30. Sanders, *Palestinian Judaism*, 180.

Moreover, Sanders found, again in contrast to the standard view, that ancient Judaism comprised forgiveness, love, belief in a personal God who was active in the history of the Jewish people, and salvation within a covenantal context.

This revision of ancient Judaism changed the rules of the game quite significantly for New Testament scholars. It now seemed apparent that previous scholarship on Paul was based, not on an adequate description of ancient Judaism, but on a Christian caricature. In his own interpretation of Paul, Sanders reached the conclusion that Paul represents another type of religion than the one found in almost every Jewish text from the period, that is, his was not a system characterized by *covenantal nomism*. For Paul, *justification* meant "being saved by Christ," whereas in all other texts the word referred to someone who observed the Torah. However, according to Sanders, Paul found nothing wrong with the Torah; rather, God apparently had chosen to save the world through Christ and not through the Torah. In short: *the problem with Judaism is that it is not Christianity.*

From New to Radical Perspectives on Paul

Not entirely convinced by Sanders's reading of Paul, but accepting his critique of Protestant scholarship, James D. G. Dunn published a very influential article in 1983 that would give a name to a completely new scholarly approach—the so-called New Perspective on Paul.[31] Unlike Sanders, Dunn believed that Paul's "religion" very well could be characterized by covenantal nomism. Departing from Galatians 2:16 ("a person is justified not by the works of the law but through faith in Jesus Christ"), Dunn argues that previous scholarship

---

31. James D. G. Dunn, "The New Perspective on Paul," *Bulletin of the John Rylands Library* 65 (1983): 95–122.

(including Sanders) had read the text to mean that no one is justified *by the law*. Dunn, however, understands "the works of the law" to refer to Jewish identity markers. Of course Paul had nothing against the Torah as such—what he objected to, Dunn argues, was *Jewish particularism*, the idea that the Jewish covenant was for Jews only. The "works of the law," in Dunn's view, refers to such aspects that create a barrier between Jews and non-Jews: food regulations, circumcision, regulations concerning purity, and so on.

Dunn's attempt to harmonize Sanders's reconstruction of first-century Judaism with Pauline scholarship opened up for even more radical interpretations. Inspired by, for instance, Krister Stendahl, Lloyd Gaston, and John J. Gager, scholars began to play with the idea of placing Paul completely within Judaism. Gaston provided an important piece of the puzzle by suggesting that Paul exclusively addressed non-Jews and thus never discussed how Jews should relate to the Torah.[32] According to Gaston, Paul's negative statements on the Torah were motivated by his conviction that the Torah indeed will bring death to those outside a covenantal relation with the God of Israel.

During the 1990s, several studies were published that approached Paul from a different perspectives but that were not precisely the same as the views held by those associated with the New Perspective on Paul. In 1990, Peter Tomson examined the link between rabbinic halakah and Paul's way of arguing (*Paul and the Jewish Law*), Stanley Stowers published his *A Rereading of Romans* in 1994, and Mark Nanos published his *Mystery of Romans* in 1996, followed by a study on Galatians in 2001 (*The Irony of Galatians*).[33] More recent examples

---

32. Lloyd Gaston, *Paul and the Torah* (Vancouver: University of British Columbia Press, 1987).

33. Mark D. Nanos, *The Mystery of Romans: The Jewish Context of Paul's Letter* (Minneapolis: Fortress Press, 1996); Nanos, *The Irony of Galatians: Pauls' Letter in First Century Context* (Philadelphia: Fortress Press, 2001); Stanley K. Stowers, *A Rereading of Romans: Justice, Jews and*

of studies attempting to firmly place Paul within Judaism are William Campbell's study *Paul and the Creation of Christian Identity* (2006); Pamela Eisenbaum's monograph *Paul Was Not a Christian* (2009); Brian Tucker's two volumes on Paul in 1 Corinthians (2010 and 2011) (*You Belong to Christ* and *Remain in Your Calling*); David Rudolph's monograph on 1 Corinthians 9 in 2011 (*A Jew to the Jews*); and Kathy Ehrensperger's *Paul at the Crossroads of Cultures* (2013).[34]

These, and several other studies, constitute reliable alternatives and real challenges to the traditional perspectives, which all, in one way or another, assume a fundamental break between Paul and Judaism. Considering the history of the theological development within the Christian church and its influence on scholarship, or put differently, the amalgamation of normative theology and Pauline scholarship, the traditional perspective on Paul is less convincing. The search for the historical Paul cannot be limited to finding a Paul who makes theological sense for the present-day church, but one who makes sense in a first-century context, before Augustine and Luther entered the scene.

As historians we need to look for the historical truth about Paul regardless of the consequences for Christian theology. To me, the natural methodological starting point would be to assume a Paul firmly rooted within Judaism—"circumcised on the eighth day, a member of the people of Israel, of the tribe of Benjamin, a Hebrew born of Hebrews" (Phil. 3:5).

Gentiles (New Haven, CT: Yale University Press, 1994); Peter J. Tomson, *Paul and the Jewish Law: Halakha in the Letters of the Apostle to the Gentiles* (Assen: van Gorcum, 1990).

34. William S. Campbell, *Paul and the Creation of Christian Identity* (London: T & T Clark, 2006); Pamela Eisenbaum, *Paul Was Not a Christian: The Original Message of a Misunderstood Apostle* (New York: HarperOne, 2009); Tucker, *Remain in Your Calling*; David J. Rudolph, *A Jew to the Jews: Jewish Contours of Pauline Flexibility in 1 Corinthians 9:19-23* (Tübingen: Mohr Siebeck, 2011); J. Brian Tucker, *You Belong to Christ: Paul and the Formation of Social Identity in 1 Corinthians 1–4* (Eugene, OR: Pickwick, 2010); Kathy Ehrensperger, *Paul at the Crossroads of Cultures: Theologizing in the Space-Between* (London: Bloomsbury, 2013).

What Difference Does it Make?

I will wrap up this brief overview of the rise and fall of the anti-Jewish Paul by indicating some areas where a Paul within Judaism perspective on Paul makes a considerable difference for our historical reconstructions.

Christians as a Third Race?

Traditionally it has often been assumed that people within the early "church," regardless of ethnicity, merged together into a third entity.[35] Former Jews and former gentiles thus constituted a third race—"the Christians." A fundamental part of such a construction is the idea that Paul stood in opposition to Judaism. Becoming "Christian" thus involved a radical identity transformation meaning, for instance, that Jews ceased to define themselves within Judaism or in terms of Torah observance. "Christians" were all characterized by a common Christ-oriented theology and a common religious behavior. "Former" Jews ceased observing the Torah and stopped eating Jewish food and observing purity regulations. This, orthodox (in the true sense of the word) Christian movement was threatened by heretic individuals or groups who still, mistakenly, were attached to Judaism. These "Judaizing" Jews (Jewish-Christians) were responsible for the major conflicts within the Christian church. They were, however, defeated, and eventually the Pauline, law-free gospel won the day. In this way we find a neat continuity, if not from Jesus (who almost everybody recognizes as truly Jewish), but definitely from Paul, to the present Christian church. This perspective motivates the use of designations like "Christian," "Christianity,"

---

35. See, e.g., E. P. Sanders, *Paul, the Law, and the Jewish People* (Minneapolis: Fortress Press, 1983), 171–79; Heikki Räisänen, *The Rise of Christian Beliefs: The Thought World of Early Christians* (Minneapolis: Fortress Press, 2010), 259–64.

and "church," even though the evidence that the Jesus movement identified itself as "Christians" is late and limited.[36]

If we, however, assume a Paul *within* Judaism, even a Torah-observant Paul, how does this affect the historical reconstruction of the development of the early Jesus movement? The first thing we have to do is reflect upon the ostensible critiques of the Torah, which are a salient feature in several of Paul's letters, especially Galatians and Romans.

If the author of these letters was a Torah-observant Jew, still believing himself to be faithful to Judaism, his instructions regarding Torah observance cannot have been universal, that is, cannot have been directed to Jewish disciples of Jesus.[37] The fact that all Paul's authentic letters seem to be addressing non-Jews might give us a hermeneutical key. Is it possible that Paul only objected to non-Jews observing the Torah or to non-Jews becoming Jews and thus under Torah on the same terms as Jews? As I have argued elsewhere, it is quite evident that there were various Jewish ideas on the relation between non-Jews and the Torah. Some seem to have welcomed non-Jewish participation in Jewish affairs such as Torah observance. Others found such an idea loathsome. There is also ample evidence indicating that many non-Jews were attracted to Judaism and imitated a Jewish life style,[38] probably as a result of interaction with Jews who believed that also non-Jews would benefit from observing the Torah.[39]

---

36. Acts 11:26, 26:28; 1 Pet. 4:16.
37. Mark D. Nanos, "Paul and Judaism: Why Not Paul's Judaism?" in *Paul Unbound: Other Perspectives on the Apostle*, ed. Mark Douglas Given (Peabody, MA: Hendrickson, 2010), 117–60; Nanos, "Paul's Relationship to Torah in Light of His Strategy 'to Become Everything to Everyone' (1 Corinthians 9:19–23)," in *Paul and Judaism: Crosscurrents in Pauline Exegesis and the Study of Jewish-Christian Relations*, ed. Didier Pollefeyt and Reimund Bieringer (London: T & T Clark, 2012), 106–40.
38. See Michele Murray, *Playing a Jewish Game: Gentile Christian Judaizing in the First and Second Centuries CE* (Waterloo, Ont: Wilfred Laurier University Press, 2004), 11–27.

Since it is likely that most non-Jewish adherents to the Jesus movement were recruited from synagogues where Jews and non-Jews socialized, and where non-Jews had been encouraged to adopt some Jewish cultural traits, Paul thus encountered non-Jews who could be regarded as partly Torah observant. It is possible that this is the heart of the problem since there is evidence, admittedly from the third century, showing that not all Jews were positive to non-Jews involving themselves in Torah observance.[40] Paul may very well have been positive to non-Jews turning to the God of Israel through Jesus-the-Messiah, yet opposing non-Jewish involvement in the Torah. Such a scenario could very well explain Paul's critique of the Torah (as directed toward Torah-observing non-Jews) while leaving room for Torah-observing Jewish followers of Jesus, including Paul himself.

From such a perspective, the idea of a unified movement with a common religious behavior must be called into question. If a Jewish-behaving Paul advocated continued Torah observance for Jewish disciples of Jesus, while dissuading non-Jews from getting involved in Torah affairs, we must allow for a much more complex social situation, such as, for instance, non-Jews being expected to conform to Jewish food conventions (without becoming formally "under" Torah), since they were joining groups where Jewish dietary customs guided group behavior.

Furthermore, assuming a Jewish, Torah-observant Paul emphasizes the Jewish character of the movement, then the early Jesus movement is, in fact, best described as one Jewish faction, like the Pharisees or the Qumran community (which no one claims to represent something other than Judaism). What we now know as

39. Marc Hirshman, "Rabbinic Universalism in the Second and Third Centuries," *Harvard Theological Review* 93 (2000): 101–15.
40. *m. Avot* 3:14; *Sipre* to Deuteronomy § 345.

"Christianity" did not yet exist. The normal religious identity within this movement was a Jewish identity, and people within this movement believed that at least some non-Jews also would have a place in the world to come (as in some other contemporary forms of Judaism). I firmly believe that different ideas of the nature of the relationship between Israel and the nations were the dominant source of conflicts. Since all Jews within the movement continued to live like Jews, while recognizing Jesus as the Messiah, the conflicts reflected in Paul's letters were not about Jewish Torah observance for Jews.

The problem this young movement had to overcome was how to incorporate non-Jews, not only to find ways of socializing safely with non-Jews, but how to include non-Jews in the eschatological people of God.[41] Paul evidently believed that non-Jews should remain non-Jewish, and that they should not observe the Torah, which possibly meant that they should not base their relation to the God of Israel on the Torah, but on Jesus-the-Messiah. As is evident from Acts 15:1, 5, other groups or individuals believed that non-Jews had to become Jews in order to be saved:

> Then certain individuals came down from Judea and were teaching the brothers, "Unless you are circumcised according to the custom of Moses, you cannot be saved. . . . But some believers who belonged to the sect of the Pharisees stood up and said, "It is necessary for them to be circumcised and ordered to keep the law of Moses."

Some scholars believe that this was the position of the Matthean community.[42] I have argued elsewhere, that the *Didache* perhaps

41. Mark D. Nanos, "Paul and the Jewish Tradition: The Ideology of the Shema," in *Celebrating Paul. Festschrift in Honor of Jerome Murphy-O'Connor, O.P., and Joseph A. Fitzmyer, S.J.*, ed. Peter Spitaler (Washington, DC: Catholic Biblical Association of America, 2012), 62–80.

42. See, e.g., J. Andrew Overman, *Matthew's Gospel and Formative Judaism: The Social World of the Matthean Community* (Minneapolis: Fortress Press, 1990); Anthony J. Saldarini, *Matthew's Christian-Jewish Community* (Chicago: Chicago University Press, 1994); David C. Sim, *The*

envisions a middle position: non-Jews should remain non-Jews but observe as much as possible of the Torah. Be that as it may, what is evident is that from this perspective, the perspective of Paul within Judaism, we find a movement in the process of defining its eschatological relationship with the nations, for whom they were supposed to be a light. The early Jesus movement was divided and various voices coexisted. It is quite natural and most likely that the process of self-definition was complicated and led to harsh conflicts.

Strangely enough, from the perspective of this Paul, the emergence of the phenomenon we call "Christianity" has to be significantly reconsidered. The continuity between the religion of Paul and the Christian church is simply not as clear-cut as is often assumed. What eventually became the Christian church differs in several important ways from the religion of Paul. While Paul believed that he represented the perfection of *Judaism*, the church quite swiftly became a religious movement opposed to the practice of Judaism. Similarly, while Jewish identity was normal within the early Jesus movement the church found Jewish identity to be incompatible with being Christian, and Christianity soon became an anti-Jewish religion devoid of any Jews.

These few examples show that assuming Paul within Judaism dramatically changes the basic conditions for our historical reconstructions. It increases the complexity, and forces us to think in new, innovative ways. It leads to quite interesting new results in a discipline that has long been dominated by one fundamental perspective—the opposition between Paul and Judaism. From historical and methodological considerations, this radical perspective on Paul—Paul within Judaism—is in great need of further examination.

Gospel of Matthew and Christian Judaism: The History and Social Setting of the Matthean Community (Edinburgh: T & T Clark, 1998).

2

The Question of Terminology: The Architecture of Contemporary Discussions on Paul

Anders Runesson

Over the last decade or so, more and more scholars of the New Testament have pointed to the need to re-think the terminology we use in our analyses as well as in our teaching. Several terms have been asked to retire, as Paula Fredriksen has phrased it,[1] and leave room for new words and expressions that may help us to better grasp

---

1. Paula Fredriksen, "Mandatory Retirement: Ideas in the Study of Christian Origins whose Time has Come to Go," *Studies in Religion* 35 (2006): 231–46. The potential of flawed terminology to mislead scholars to draw anachronistic or otherwise erroneous conclusions was pointed out already by Morton Smith, "Terminological Booby Traps and Real Problems in Second Temple Judaeo-Christian Studies," in *Studies in the Cult of Yahweh*, ed. Shaye J. D. Cohen (New York: Brill, 1996), 1:95–103. See also discussion in Anders Runesson, "Particularistic Judaism and

what was going on in the first-century Mediterranean world, a time and culture very distant from our own. The terminological question is a key problem for historical studies generally, but it receives an additional level of urgency as we deal with texts that are religiously authoritative for people today. The politics of translation has, in this regard, received increased attention in recent studies, such as in Naomi Seidman's book *Faithful Renderings* from 2006.[2] Matt Jackson McCabe's edited volume from 2007, *Jewish-Christianity Reconsidered*, deals to a large extent with the problem of terminology, a particular form of translation, as we attempt to describe the phenomena usually, and in my view problematically, referred to as "Jewish-Christianity."[3]

I would like to contribute to this discussion as it relates to Paul by focusing on two terms used in English translations of the New Testament and in historical analysis of texts included in this collection of ancient documents: "Christians" (including "Christianity") and "church." These terms are, in turn, related to how we use other words, such as "Jews," "Judaism," and "synagogue." It will be argued

Universalistic Christianity? Some Critical Remarks on Terminology and Theology," *Journal of Greco-Roman Christianity and Judaism* 1 (2000): 120–44.

2. Naomi Seidman, *Faithful Renderings: Jewish-Christian Difference and the Politics of Translation* (Chicago: University of Chicago Press, 2006). Cf. the contributions to the discussion in Scott S. Elliott and Roland Boer, eds., *Ideology, Culture, and Translation* (Atlanta: Society of Biblical Literature, 2012).

3. Matt Jackson-McCabe, ed., *Jewish Christianity Reconsidered: Rethinking Ancient Texts and Groups* (Minneapolis: Fortress Press, 2007). In this volume, note especially the contributions by Jerry Sumney ("Paul and Christ-believing Jews Whom He Opposes") and John Marshall ("John's Jewish [Christian?] Apocalypse"). See also Neil Elliott, *The Arrogance of the Nations: Reading Romans in the Shadow of Empire* (Minneapolis: Fortress Press, 2008), 15–16; Anders Runesson, "Inventing Christian Identity: Paul, Ignatius, and Theodosius I," in *Exploring Early Christian Identity*, ed. Bengt Holmberg (Tübingen: Mohr Siebeck, 2008), 59–92, especially 62–74. Cf. the categorization of religious types in Anders Runesson, "Rethinking Early Jewish–Christian Relations: Matthean Community History as Pharisaic Intragroup Conflict," *Journal of Biblical Literature* 127, no. 1 (2008): 95–132, here 105. On the origins, history, and use of the term "Jewish Christian" and "Jewish Christianity," see the informative survey by Matti Myllykoski, "'Christian Jews' and 'Jewish Christians': The Jewish Origins of Christianity in English Literature from Elizabeth I to Toland's *Nazarenus*," in *The Rediscovery of Jewish Christianity: From Toland to Baur*, ed F. Stanley Jones (Atlanta: Society of Biblical Literature, 2012), 3–41.

that "Christians," "Christianity," and "church" are politically powerful terms that are inadequate, anachronistic, and misleading when we read Paul, serving contemporary needs in the formation of religious identities rather than helping us to describe Jewish and Greco-Roman society in the first century. A few words on the nature of terminology and possible pitfalls for translating historical phenomena are in order before we address the specific problems connected with these terms.

Translating History: Colonizing the Past or Liberating the Dead?

People engage in historical research for a variety of reasons, some of which may be compared to a traveler's wish to encounter and learn about things unknown. Historians and travelers have something further in common with all of humanity, though, which problematizes the notion that the discovery of anything truly unfamiliar is possible. Each time new cultures are encountered, including lost historical landscapes, that which was previously unknown is immediately, with instinctive assistance from the observer's previous experiences and socialization, accommodated within a preexistent worldview foreign to the phenomena observed. With discoveries, as with all types of experiences, an instant and unceasing process of "translation" ensues in our brains as soon as we encounter the novel, aiming at turning it into something familiar, something we can relate to and understand.

This is, in fact, an important psychological process, a condition making it possible for human beings to function at all, making sense of the world around us. But this spontaneous hermeneutical mechanism, while psychologically necessary, also means that it is impossible, strictly speaking, for anyone to experience anything as truly *new*, since "otherness" is instantly absorbed, embedded, and modified by the familiar, even as a "foreign object." *New* discoveries, *new* understanding, are therefore, and must inescapably be, the result of our *conscious efforts to disentangle what we have encountered from the familiar that we know.* New insights are thus dependent on our willingness to de-familiarize ourselves with the phenomena we seek to understand; on our refusal to let our familiar, already in-use mindset and concepts control and categorize that which we encounter.[4] While voluntary alienation and detachment may prove especially difficult as we deal with religiously authoritative texts, this is one of the basic mental processes that invite the use of method in the humanities and the social sciences more generally; method in itself is, however, not a guaranteed solution to the problem of our limited ability to move beyond ourselves, since its very own construction is also entangled in the mold of culturally determined contemporarities that surround us.[5]

Human perception is ego- and ethno-centric, and by implication therefore colonial in nature since we, as the center, "violently" structure and give form to the periphery, to that which is not us. We construct the "other" in our own image, or distort encountered phenomena using perceived weaknesses in our own culture as building blocks in a process of "othering." Such colonial practices are at constant work in historical-critical biblical scholarship as much

4. Cf. James D. G. Dunn's discussion of our "default setting" as we interpret the world around us and the biblical texts: *A New Perspective in Jesus: What the Quest for the Historical Jesus Missed* (Grand Rapids: Baker Academic, 2005), 80–82. Dunn writes, "A default setting, then, a computer's preset preferences, is a useful image of an established mindset, an unconscious bias or Tendenz, an instinctive reflex response. The point is that to alter the default setting, to change a habitual attitude or instinctive perspective, requires a conscious and sustained or repeated effort, otherwise without realizing it we revert to the default setting, to our unexamined predispositions" (82).

5. On method as part of that which needs to be disentangled, see chapter three, "The Theoretical Location of Postcolonial Studies," in Anna Runesson, *Exegesis in the Making: Postcolonialism and New Testament Studies* (Leiden: Brill, 2011), esp. 36–39. See also Todd Penner and Caroline Vander Stichele, "Re-Assembling Jesus: Re-Thinking the Ethics of Gospel Studies," and Hans Leander, "Mark and Matthew after Edward Said," both studies published in *Mark and Matthew*, eds. Eve-Marie Becker and Anders Runesson (Tübingen: Mohr Siebeck, 2013), 2:311–34 and 289–309, respectively.

as in other historical disciplines. We need to make ourselves aware of these hermeneutical mechanisms that often go unnoticed and resist them if we seek understanding of the historical, the radical otherness of which is otherwise neutralized. This is a lifelong process. We need to listen before we speak, and radical listening leads to de-familiarization, the beginnings of historical research; listening to voices that are not our own, in a language that is not our own, in a world with a center that is not us.

Reconstructing and translating history inevitably begins and ends with language.[6] When we de-familiarize ourselves with texts and other artifacts, we engage in a process of decolonizing the past, liberating the dead from the bondage of our contemporary political identities. History, the reconstruction of silenced voices and the worlds they inhabited, always involves, therefore, both methodological and ethical decisions. One of the fundamental choices the historian has to make in this regard concerns the terminology applied as the analytical task is carried out, since the words we use tend to control the way we think.[7]

Changing the Architecture of the Conversation

Language is in many ways comparable to architecture. Via external, visible structures that are experienced and shared by others, we enter into edifices that influence our impression of reality. In architecturally constructed space, perception is reconfigured, our vision "re-visioned," and whatever is focused upon within that space is seen and

6. A word is a social agreement primarily related to contemporary, *not* past, realities, since the "now" is the only space we can, by definition, inhabit. Reconstruction of historical processes involves, like any translation, two languages: the ancient and the modern. Just as the two should not be conflated in the analytical process if we seek that which is not us, the resulting translation is by definition always an approximation since meaning is developed in context.

7. On this challenge, cf. Smith, "Terminological Booby Traps," 95, who notes that there is a "prejudice in favor of any established terminology; from infancy we have been trained to believe that what we have been taught is right. Moreover, this belief is convenient."

understood from within the landscape that we have entered and that encloses us. There is room for a variety of interpretations within the space created by the external structures, largely depending on our experiences prior to entering the space. Nevertheless, the structures still establish the points of departure for any discussion and provide the boundaries within which conclusions may ultimately be drawn.[8]

Scholarly terms and concepts, all of which are carriers for specific views and ideas, function in much the same way. They construct the "space" within which we focus on specific issues and topics in our conversations. Terminological edifices are built slowly over time and are not easily torn down. Now-unsustainable scholarly ideas from previous eras influence current discourses, because many of us still occupy the space created by the terminological walls, arches, and ceilings they have left behind. We need, therefore, to reconsider and discuss not only the conclusions we draw, but also the "architecture" within which we formulate them.

Since the answer to any question already lies, to a certain degree, within the question asked—the question forms the "room" in which we attempt to find the answer—the conclusions we give birth to become the offspring of the language we use. Terminology is pregnant with meaning that often goes unnoticed in the analytical process, which it nevertheless controls from within. Rethinking the way we speak may therefore result in the discovery of new landscapes. The terms we shall discuss are a couple of word-pairs that are of fundamental importance for our field since they determine much of both how questions are asked and what conclusions are drawn. These terms are, as noted above, "Christian"/"Christianity" (and "Jews"/"Judaism") on the one hand, and "church" (and "synagogue") on the other, and we shall begin our discussion with the former.

---

8. Cf. Runesson, "Inventing Christian Identity," 62–63.

"Christians"/"Christianity"

When we talk about New Testament scholarship in general and Paul in particular, it has been the convention to say that one is studying (earliest) "Christianity" and/or (the early) "Christians." *Already at this point we have framed the shape and thus the likely outcome of the discussion,* having established a firm link between, on the one hand, the modern phenomenon of mainstream (non-Jewish) Christianity and, on the other, whatever was going on in New Testament times and in Paul's letters. Some scholars who feel the tension created by this language would modify such terminology and suggest that we speak of "Jewish-Christians" instead of just "Christians," but such a hermeneutical move does not get us out of the modern paradigm, since it does not address the problem at its root.[9]

We must ask ourselves whether the earliest followers of Jesus would have recognized themselves as belonging under the umbrella term "Christianity," the companion word of "Christians." As is well known, the term *christianismos* does not occur in the New Testament;[10] Paul offers no evidence that he had ever heard of "Christianity."[11] *Christianos* occurs only three times, of which two are found in Acts (11:26; 26:28) and one in 1 Peter (4:16), both texts postdating Paul.[12] Paul neither speaks of himself nor describes others

---

9. For discussion of the term "Jewish Christian" and its inherent problems, see the studies listed in n. 3 above.

10. As opposed to *Ioudaismos* (Gal. 1:13, 14).

11. The first occurrence of the term *christianismos* is found in the letters of Ignatius of Antioch, dated to the early second century, either during Trajan's or Hadrian's reign: *Magn.* 10:1-3; *Rom.* 3:3; *Phld.* 6:1. See William R. Schoedel, *Ignatius of Antioch: A Commentary on the Letters of Ignatius of Antioch* (Philadelphia: Fortress Press, 1985), 126. Cf. Alexei S. Khamin, "Ignatius of Antioch: Performing Authority in the Early church," PhD diss., Drew University, 2007: "His [Ignatius] vividly imagined execution is configured as a kind of gladiatorial combat that resonates with the themes of noble death, sacrifice, and divine ascent. Ignatius attempts to construct a new solid identity, *Christianismos*, in opposition to *Ioudaismos*. Yet, the 'Judaizers' invade Ignatius's world, render the borders blurred and obliterate the dichotomy *Christianismos/Ioudaismos*."

as *christianoi*.[13] This means that, if we prefer to use emic terminology as we discuss what went on around Paul and his contemporaries, "Christian" and "Christianity" are off the table; these terms do not represent how these people defined what they were involved in.

If, then, from an emic perspective, these terms cannot be used, our only remaining methodological option is an etic terminological perspective, if we still want to use "Christian" and "Christianity" when we discuss Paul and his letters. In order to decide for or against an etic approach, however, we need to reflect on the fact noted above, that (historical) translation always involves two languages, and that we therefore first of all must consider current uses of the word "Christianity" to see if it is suitable for our purposes, if it matches what we believe is a reasonable historical reconstruction of Paul. What is it that inhabits the term "Christianity" today that makes it behave in certain ways in our discourses? What effects does the term have when we speak—what does it do? Which opposites does it invoke? Once such discursive patterns of effects and opposites have been mapped, not before, we may ask whether what is "inside" the term today can be said to be transferrable to ancient discourses, and, more specifically, to Paul's letters.

Most people, Pauline scholars and others, would agree that the word "Christianity" in mainstream uses relates to people who belong to a specific "religion," which locates Jesus at the center of their beliefs and rituals. In addition, there is, presumably, broad agreement about the fact that "Judaism" and "Jewish" belong among the phenomena that may be referred to in order to define what Christianity is *not*.

12. Acts 11:26: "So it was that for an entire year they met with the *ekklēsia* and taught a great many people, and it was in Antioch that the disciples were first called '*christianous*.'"; 26:28: "Agrippa said to Paul, 'Are you so quickly persuading me to become a *christianon*?'"; 1 Pet. 4:16: "Yet if any of you suffers as a *christianos*, do not consider it a disgrace, but glorify God because you bear this name."
13. Cf. Pamela Eisenbaum, *Paul Was Not a Christian: The Original Message of a Misunderstood Apostle* (San Francisco: HarperOne, 2009).

Already with these two comments we have encountered major problems with regard to the suitability of "Christianity" as an etic descriptive term applied to first-century followers of Jesus.

First, the modern phenomenon of "religion," which the term "Christianity" carries within it, and brings to all discourses into which it is invited, did not exist as such in antiquity, as has been shown by Steve Mason and others.[14] If we use the term "Christianity" when we describe what is happening in Paul's letters, we thus illegitimately impose our modern discursive habits on the ancient world and make it behave as if it shared Western, twenty-first century concerns as they relate to the divine. We create the "other" in our own image and in this way force, in colonial manner, other related aspects of the texts to make modern, not ancient, sense.

Second, as noted, the application of this term to the Pauline correspondence also releases a chain reaction with regard to our understanding of other phenomena, which we—often instinctively—think of in order to define what "Christianity" is or is not. The key term in this regard is "Judaism." Thus, in addition to the anachronistic use of "religion," our contemporary habits impose on the ancients the modern idea (and the praxis that follows with the idea) of "Christianity" as not being "Judaism," and "Judaism" as not being "Christianity."[15] Paul becomes, in one way or the other, a

---

14. Steve Mason, "Jews, Judaeans, Judaizing, Judaism," *Journal for the Study of Judaism* (2007): 482–88. "Religion," as we understand the term today, cannot be abstracted from but was integral to at least six categories of life in antiquity: ethnos, (national) cult, philosophy, familial traditions/domestic worship, voluntary associations (*collegia/thiasoi*), and astrology and magic. See also Philip F. Esler, *Conflict and Identity in Romans: The Social Setting of Paul's Letters* (Minneapolis: Fortress Press, 2003), 73: "Religion as we understand it did not exist in the ancient world, and the religious dimensions of human experience had a very different status." For broader contemporary discussions of the term "religion," see, for example, Jonathan Z. Smith, "Religion, Religions, Religious," in *Critical Terms for Religious Studies*, ed. Mark C. Taylor (Chicago: University of Chicago Press, 1998), 269–84; Russell T. McCutcheon, "The Category 'Religion' in Recent Publications: A Critical Survey," *Numen* 42 (1995): 284–309; Sam Gill, "The Academic Study of Religion," *Journal of the American Academy of Religion* 62 (1994): 965–75.

"Christian," and it only remains to discuss and debate the interpretive details that apply within that general religious concept, to find out what kind of "Christian" he was.

It should be emphasized that this general "conclusion," dressed up as a point of departure, as a research question, is accomplished already before any form of analytical work has been undertaken. Our terminology is pregnant with the conclusion, which, in due time, is delivered without much surprise. But just as in the case of anachronistic assumptions about "religion" as the content of Paul's concerns, the colonized text refuses to cooperate fully, and tensions, *which the terms "Christianity" and "Christians" themselves have created,* are not resolved, leaving many scholars with an acute sense of uneasiness.

Let us take our discussion one more step and consider the following. If, for the sake of the argument, we assume—against the evidence—that Paul in fact knew of the term *christianos*, as the author of Acts and 1 Peter did in the late first century, would this mean that we should translate the Greek *christianos* with the English "Christian"? That is, can we assume continuity in our translation simply because the English word is derivative of the historical Greek term? Obviously, the first point mentioned above about how the modern idea "religion" inhabits the English terms "Christianity" and "Christian" would militate against such a translation—for it is still a translation even if the word is the same in both languages—since it would lure us to think about Paul in ways Paul never would, despite his hypothetical use of the Greek term. Let me illustrate this point with an example from 1 Corinthians 14:23:

---

15. As noted above in n. 11, the earliest attempt at distinguishing "Christianity" from "Judaism," as if these were two mutually exclusive entities, is found in the second-century letters of Ignatius of Antioch.

If, therefore, the whole *ekklēsia* comes together and all speak in tongues, and *idiots* (*idiōtai*) or unbelievers enter, will they not say that you are out of your mind?

The question is *why* it is so plain and obvious to us that the Greek *idiōtai* should *not* be translated with the English "idiots." The NRSV has "outsider" and KJV has "unlearned." The Swedish translation from 1981, to take an example from a minority language, has "uninitiated."[16] Of course, it is because we know that the physical *form* of a word, the letters that make up a word, do not guarantee a fixed *meaning* over time and in different cultures and social settings. That is, we know that a word is like a vessel that we—unconsciously—fill with nuances, attitudes, and mindsets belonging to the time and context in which we happen to live. Meaning is not dependent on the form of the "vessel" but on the sounds, feelings, and discursive habits that people pour into it as it is made to perform its duties in different cultures.[17] And this is, of course, the very reason in the first place why a first-century Jewish apocalyptically oriented individual like Jesus came to have billions of followers throughout history and around the globe today. The written words, or "vessels," used to convey the message seem to function as links that connect us with the past. This creates a sense of historical continuity between our time and the time of

16. The Swedish word is "oinvigda." (While *Bibel 2000*, the official Swedish translation of the Bible, funded by the state, was released in the year 2000, the translation of the New Testament from 1981 was kept intact when the new translation of the Hebrew Bible was added.) To give another example from a language spoken by more people than Swedish, the Swahili translation (United Bible Societies, Union Version, 1952) reads "watu wajinga," which may be translated into English as "ignorant persons." In modern Swahili, however, this expression may be perceived as pejorative, as some have pointed out, noting that "watu ambao hawaelewi" would be a better translation. I am grateful to Victor Limbana for discussion of this issue.

17. Cf. the now classic critique of the *Theologische Wörterbuch zum Neuen Testament* (TWNT = *Theological Dictionary of the New Testament* [TDNT]) by James Barr (*The Semantics of Biblical Language* [Oxford: Oxford University Press, 1961], warning against etymologizing, as well as the dangers of illegitimate totality transfer.

the first followers of Jesus whilst the message itself is translationally inculturated in societies across the globe. The words and, more specifically, certain key terms such as "Christian" take on a role as historical stabilizers in the process of identity construction in contemporary communities.

The problem is, however, that while these words are thought to transport the ancient message to our time, in reality we are the ones filling the "vessels" with meaning, so that the flow of meaning goes more often than not from us to the historical text rather than from the text to us. For those who approach the text from a faith perspective this may not seem to pose an overwhelming hermeneutical problem since, with regard to the reading of religiously authoritative texts, divine revelation can be thought of as situated neither in the text nor with its readers but in the interpretive space that is brought into being as a result of the exchange of meaning between reader and text.[18] Such processes of exchange should, however, cause the historian to worry, since his or her task is to fill these words with meaning that, in context, make ancient, not modern, sense. The significance of the choice of terminology used in historical analysis can, in this regard, not be overstated.

In such a situation, since it is often difficult to find "open" terminology that imposes a minimum of control on the analytical process, it is important that alternative terms are at least tested in order to allow for the possibility of new insights growing from

18. It should be noted, however, that since the Enlightenment, and as a result of the reformation in the sixteenth century that called for a "return to the sources" (*ad fontes*), historical readings of biblical texts have often come to be understood as religiously authoritative. Today, also in official church documents of the Catholic Church, historical understandings of theological issues are explicitly acknowledged as being of key importance, and, as a consequence, exegetical and historical-critical methods have been sanctioned by the church as tools with which theological truths and, by implication, divine revelation may be retrieved. See discussion in Anders Runesson, "Judging the Theological Tree by its Fruit: The Use of the Gospels of Mark and Matthew in Official Church Documents on Jewish-Christian Relations," in *Mark and Matthew*, 2:189–228.

reconstructions of different historical landscapes. If, then, the terms "Christian" and "Christianity" are deemed to lead us astray and invite anachronistic historical reconstructions and are, consequently, to be avoided, with what should we replace them?

The most natural point of departure for renewed terminological reflection around who Paul was and how he self-identified would be to speak not of "Paul the Christian" but of "Paul the Jew"; of Paul as someone who practiced "Judaism," not "Christianity."[19] I would further argue that, despite some recent studies which favor "Judaean" over "Jew,"[20] *Ioudaios* is best translated "Jew."[21] Contrary to what became mainstream Christianity in Late Antiquity, Judaism never rejected the ancient connection between a people, their land, laws, and god(s).[22] Although Christians have, through the ages, tried to redefine Judaism as a "religion," a negative mirror image of themselves, mainstream Jews never accepted this rewriting of their identity and have continued to understand their ethnos as intertwined with the Jewish law, the land, and the God of Israel.[23] On the one hand, the development of what came to be "Christianity,"

19. See, for example, the discussion in John Gager, "Paul, the Apostle of Judaism," in *Jesus, Judaism, and Christian Anti-Judaism*, eds. Paula Fredriksen and Adele Reinhartz (Louisville: Westminster John Knox, 2002), 56–76; Mark D. Nanos, *The Irony of Galatians: Paul's Letter in First-Century Context* (Minneapolis: Fortress Press, 2002), 7–8; Nanos, "Paul and Judaism: Why Not Paul's Judaism?" in *Paul Unbound: Other Perspectives on the Apostle*, ed. Mark Douglas Given (Peabody, MA: Hendrickson, 2010), 117–60; Elliott, *Arrogance of Nations*, 15–16. See also Paula Fredriksen, "Judaizing the Nations: The Ritual Demands of Paul's Gospel," *New Testament Studies* 56 (2010): 232–52.
20. So, for example, Esler, *Conflict and Identity*, 62–74; Mason, "Jews, Judaeans, Judaizing, Judaism," 457–512.
21. I have argued in favor of this translation at some length in "Inventing Christian Identity," 64–70. See also Daniel R. Schwartz, "'Judaean' or 'Jew'? How should we Translate *Ioudaios* in Josephus?" in *Jewish Identity in the Greco-Roman World = Jüdische Identität in der griechisch-römischen Welt*, eds. Jörg Frey, Daniel R. Schwartz, and Stephanie Gripentrog (Leiden: Brill, 2007), 3–27; Nanos, "Why Not Paul's Judaism?" 117–18, n. 2.
22. So also Mason, "Jews, Judaeans, Judaizing, Judaism," 480–88.
23. It is true, though, that some forms of Reform Judaism, originating in the nineteenth century, did redefine this relationship and began to self-identify more along the lines of what in Christian Europe were, at the time, mainstream understandings of "religion."

thought of as something apart from "Judaism," really began to take form only in the second century as far as the source material can tell us, and this creates a break in continuity between us and Paul, both with regard to the term and its content. On the other hand, the majority of the phenomena we call "Judaism," in all their diversity and developments, have kept the basic characteristic traits of their ethnos since before the time of Paul. These two considerations, based both on how the words under discussion were used in antiquity and how they are used today, establishes, in general terms, that speaking of Paul as a Jew practicing a form of Judaism is a more historically plausible point of departure for interpreting his letters than are the impressions that are communicated by the continued use of "Christian" and "Christianity."

This does not mean, of course, that we should understand "Jewish" in essentialist terms as ahistorically referring to specific characteristics completely untouched by time and culture. As Daniel Langton has pointed out, we need to distinguish "between essentialist, ahistorical characteristics of Jewishness and historically and culturally determined characteristics of what constitutes Jewishness."[24] The historical and culturally sensitive approach to the definitional—and terminological—problem means that the observer needs to focus on how "a society understands and represents Jews at any given time and place, in order to reconstruct the meaning of Jewishness in the subject's own cultural environment."[25] It is, in my view, more historically realistic, based on Jewish uses of "Jew" and "Judaism," to try to reach an understanding of *what kind* of Judaism Paul was concerned with and tried to outline in his letters, than to speak

---

24. Daniel R. Langton, *The Apostle Paul in the Jewish Imagination: A Study in Modern Jewish–Christian Relations* (Cambridge: Cambridge University Press, 2010), 12. Langton deals with the modern period, but his reflections regarding how to define "Jewishness" (pp. 9–12) are useful to consider also when we discuss the ancient period.
25. Ibid., 12.

of what he was doing using terms he never applied to himself or others.[26] In other words, if Paul did not feel he needed to specify the newness of what he was proclaiming using a term that would distinguish his movement from "Judaism," historians should take that as an indication that, at this time and in the culture in which he lived, Paul's mission was a mission of a specific form of Judaism, which included the incorporation of non-Jews qua non-Jews.[27]

In order to meet these two criteria, both a general belonging within the wider phenomena described as "Judaism" and an affiliation with a specific form of Judaism, Mark Nanos and I have suggested "Apostolic Judaism" as a descriptive term applicable to the early Jesus movement, including with respect to Paul and his communities.[28] As such, Apostolic Judaism may be added to the list of other Judaisms,

26. It is sufficiently clear in his letters, I believe, that Paul is proclaiming what a specific god, the God of Israel, has done in terms of his Messiah, Jesus, and how the meaning of this new situation applies to both Jews and non-Jews. The continuity between God and God's people is emphasized strongly in Romans 9–11. Further, the centrality of Jerusalem to Paul is shown in several passages (Rom. 15:18-19, 25-27, 31; 1 Cor. 16:3; Gal. 2:1-2). Regarding Torah, some scholars argue that, for Paul, the Jewish law was valid only for Jews, not for non-Jews joining the movement (cf. J. Brian Tucker, *You Belong to Christ: Paul and the Formation of Social Identity in 1 Corinthians 1–4* (Eugene, OR: Pickwick, 2010); Anders Runesson, "Paul's Rule in All the *Ekklēsiai* (1 Cor 7:17-24)," in *Introduction to Messianic Judaism: Its Ecclesial Context and Biblical Foundations*, eds. David Rudolph and Joel Willits (Grand Rapids: Zondervan, 2013), 214–23. Other scholars interpret Paul as rejecting the law as invalid also for Jews (for a history of interpretation, see Magnus Zetterholm, *Approaches to Paul: A Student's Guide to Recent Scholarship* [Minneapolis: Fortress Press, 2009]). But just as few would argue that Reform Jews are not Jewish because they have renegotiated, e.g., the connection between Judaism and the land, this is hardly enough reason for understanding Paul, in his context, as self-identifying as something other than a Jew, proclaiming a specific form of Judaism. For further discussion emphasizing that Paul and his addressees practiced Judaism, see Mark D. Nanos, "Paul and Judaism"; Nanos, "Paul and the Jewish Tradition: The Ideology of the Shema," in *Celebrating Paul. Festschrift in Honor of Jerome Murphy-O'Connor, O.P., and Joseph A. Fitzmyer, S.J.*, ed. Peter Spitaler (Washington, DC: Catholic Biblical Association of America, 2012), 62–80.

27. See, especially, Fredriksen, "Judaizing the Nations." This is also how Acts portrays Paul, both from an outsider (18:14-16) and insider (13:14-42; 21:17-26; 23:6; 26:4-7) perspective. For later versions of Jesus-centered forms of Judaism and how they influenced Rabbinic Judaism precisely because they were understood as forms of Judaism by Jews, see Karin Hedner Zetterholm, "Alternative Visions of Judaism and Their Impact on the Formation of Rabbinic Judaism," *Journal of the Jesus Movement in its Jewish Setting* 1, no. 1 (2014), www.jjmjs.org.

28. Cf. Runesson, "Inventing Christian Identity," 72–74.

such as Pharisaic Judaism, Essene Judaism, Sadducean Judaism, and later, Rabbinic Judaism. The term aims at encapsulating all forms of Judaism that include Jesus as a central figure in their symbolic universe, as a key for the interpretation of what it meant for them to adhere to Judaism.[29]

Regardless of whether a basic terminology that identifies Paul as a Jew practicing Judaism is unreservedly accepted or not by all scholars, even those scholars who hesitate about the value of a terminological change may still be interested in what might result in terms of historical conclusions from such a modification of basic perspectives. What would happen, for example, if we translated *christianoi* in Acts 11:26; 26:28 and 1 Peter 4:16 with "messianics," and understood the term in the same sociocultural manner as we do *Pharisaioi*? What would change, and what would remain the same—and why? Restructuring our shared terminological edifice will, undoubtedly, change the way we perceive of that which is inside the "building."

I would like to illustrate the point of this essay with one more example, namely the use of "church" as a translation of *ekklēsia*, since such translation goes hand in hand with the use of "Christian" and "Christianity" and to no small degree determines how we understand socio-institutional realities in the first century.

"Church"

As is well known, the term *ekklēsia* ("assembly"[30]) is used in both Jewish and Greco-Roman texts referring to certain institutional settings or gatherings of people. In the Septuagint (LXX), *ekklēsia* translates the Hebrew *qāhāl*, which the NRSV almost always translates

---

29. As Hedner Zetterholm, "Alternative Visions of Judaism," points out, some of the later texts describe variants of Jesus-centered Judaism that included non-Jews without requiring circumcision for males, but still insisted that all, even these non-Jews, kept the Jewish law.

30. Translated in German as "Volksversammlung."

as "assembly" or, in a few cases, mostly in Psalms, as "congregation."[31] In the first century, however, *ekklēsia* could also be used as a designation for what we would call synagogue institutions.[32] In Greco-Roman societies *ekklēsia* refers to public assemblies and the English translation is, again, usually "assembly." As we look at English translations of the New Testament and, more specifically, of Paul's

---

31. *Qāhāl* is translated in the LXX using both *ekklēsia* and *synagōgē*. While the LXX also uses *synagōgē* when translating the related term *'ēdâ*, it never uses *ekklēsia* for *'ēdâ*. NRSV usually translates LXX occurrences of *ekklēsia* with "assembly" (Jth.; 1 Macc.) but in Sirach both "assembly" and "congregation" are used (the latter six times). (Sir. 26:5 is a special case, referring to the "gathering of a mob" [NRSV].)

32. Such references could be either to public synagogues or, less often, to semi-public Jewish associations. For the latter, see, e.g., Philo, *Spec.* 1.324-325; *Deus* 111; *Virt.* 108 (text and commentary in Anders Runesson, Donald D. Binder, and Birger Olsson, eds., *The Ancient Synagogue From its Origins to 200 C.E.: A Source Book* (Leiden: Brill, 2008), nos. 201-203. As for public synagogue gatherings designated *ekklēsia*, see Josephus, who often uses this term (e.g., *A.J.* 16.62; 19.332; *B.J.* 1.550, 654; 4.159, 162, 255; 7.412; *Vita* 267-268). Sirach also applies the term frequently to the public assemblies of the land (e.g., 15:5; 21:17; 23:24; 31:11; 33:19; 38:32-33; 39:9-10; 44:15). Cf. also *L.A.B.* 11.8 (*ecclesia*; for text and commentary, see Runesson, et al, eds., *Ancient Synagogue*, no. 64); 1 Macc. 14:18; Jdt. 6:16; 14:6. On the definition of synagogue as a public institution, or assembly, with its origins in the Iron Age city gates, see Lee I. Levine, *The Ancient Synagogue: The First Thousand Years*, 2nd ed. (New Haven, CT: Yale University Press, 2005), 21-44; Donald D. Binder, *Into the Temple Courts: The Place of the Synagogues in the Second Temple Period* (Atlanta: Society of Biblical Literature, 1999), 204-26; Anders Runesson, *The Origins of the Synagogue: A Socio-Historical Study* (Stockholm: Almqvist & Wiksell, 2001), 237-400. (Already the Targum understood the institution gathered in the city gate to be the same type of institution as the public institution called "synagogue" in the author's own time; see *Tg. Neb.* Amos 5.12.) On the definition of the synagogue as a semi-public association, see Runesson, *Origins*, 169-235; Peter Richardson, *Building Jewish in the Roman East* (Waco, TX: Baylor University Press, 2004), 207-21. Since the terminology designating these two types of institution, the public and the semi-public, was not fixed at this time, both types were, interchangeably, called by the same names, all in all seventeen Greek terms (of which one was *ekklēsia*), five Hebrew terms, and three Latin terms (with some overlap; see the synagogue term index in *ASSB*, page 328). *ASSB* does not deal with all occurrences of *ekklēsia* as a synagogue term, and the aforementioned studies by Levine, Binder, and Runesson are also lacking in this regard. For full discussion of the use of this term in Greco-Roman and Jewish texts and inscriptions, including the New Testament, see Ralph Korner, "Before 'Church': Political, Ethno-Religious and Theological Implications of the Collective Designation of Pauline Christ-Followers as *Ekklēsiai*," PhD diss., McMaster University, 2014. For a specific treatment of Josephus's use of *ekklēsia* as a synagogue term, see Andrew Krause, "Rhetoric, Spatiality, and First-Century Synagogues: The Description and Narrative Use of Jewish Institutions in the Works of Flavius Josephus" PhD diss., McMaster University, to be defended in 2015. The classic entry by K. L. Schmidt, "ἐκκλησία," in *Theological Dictionary of the New Testament* 3:501-36, needs to be revised in light of more recent research.

letters, things change drastically. Suddenly, we find "church" introduced as the English equivalent of *ekklēsia*. Why this *new* word, "church," we may ask, to label the assemblies of Jesus' followers, when Paul, in his context, did not choose a *new* term for his addressees gatherings but used one that was already in use by other Jews as well as by Greeks and Romans?

Answering that question, we need to redirect the spotlight for a moment to the term *synagōgē*, a word that in the NRSV is most often, but not consistently, translated as "synagogue." NRSV uses "synagogue" only as long as *synagōgē* refers to institutions that scholars think of as *not* being run by Jesus-followers. It is only as long as modern translators perceive of the institution in question to belong to the "other," with the "other" identified as Jewish, that we find the translation "synagogue." Paul never uses the word *synagōgē*, but since *ekklēsia* as a term was applied also to Jewish synagogue institutions at this time, it is instructive to compare how translators work with *synagōgē* in relation to *ekklēsia*.

Reading Paul against the background of James and Matthew reveals how the terms *ekklēsia* and *synagōgē* are used in English translations of the New Testament, in particular the NRSV, to create the impression of two distinct and oppositional institutional contexts: "church" and "synagogue." This institutional separation is constructed on the basis of another anachronistic dividing line between "Christians" and "Jews," as if these were two distinct "religious" groups already at this time, as discussed above. The NRSV's hermeneutic of separation can be brought to light through a rather straightforward process of comparison. *Ekklēsia* occurs 114 times in the New Testament. The NRSV translates all but five of these with "church"; the five exceptions are found in Acts and Hebrews. In Acts, as the context makes clear, *ekklēsia* may refer to either Greco-

Roman assemblies or to Israelite gatherings in the Hebrew Bible.[33] In Hebrews, we find a reference to a public assembly in Psalm 22 as well as to a future assembly of the saved in the heavenly Jerusalem.[34]

Now, in terms of translation from one language and culture to another language and culture, the crucial question is this: When Paul uses *ekklēsia*, and this is done forty-four times in the undisputed letters,[35] should we assume that people thought of this institution in the same way as we do today when we hear the word "church"? If so, this would justify translating *ekklēsia* as "church." However, while such a correlation between followers of Jesus in the first-century Mediterranean world and English-speaking Christians in the twenty-first century is implied by the NRSV, this interpretive decision is historically questionable for several reasons.

The *Oxford English Dictionary* defines "church" as a "building for public Christian worship, esp. of the denomination recognized by the State (cf. chapel, oratory); public Christian worship." Other meanings listed include a (Christian) "community or organization," the "body of all Christians," a "particular organized Christian society," a "congregation of Christians locally organized into a society for religious worship," and so on.[36] These definitions match the most common uses of the word "church" today. When we hear "church," we associate the term with a *non-Jewish Christian religious* institution. But this was not what Paul and his contemporaries heard when

---

33. Acts 7:38; 19:32, 39. KJV has "church" in 7:38, but not in 19:32, 39, indicating continuity between the assembly of Israel in the Desert, led by Moses, and the institutions of the New Testament in which Christ-followers gathered.

34. Heb. 2:12; 12:23. KJV has "church" in both of these passages; the former emphasizes "Christian" continuity with the Psalms, the latter with the future assembly of the saved.

35. The term occurs in all of the undisputed letters (Romans, 1 Corinthians, 2 Corinthians, Galatians, Philippians, 1 Thessalonians, and Philemon). In the disputed letters *ekklēsia* occurs eighteen times (in Ephesians, Colossians, 2 Thessalonians, and 1 Timothy). *Ekklēsia* is found most frequently in 1 Corinthians, where it occurs twenty-two times.

36. Lesley Brown, ed., *The New Shorter Oxford English Dictionary on Historical Principles* (Oxford: Clarendon, 1993), 1:399. Other, specialized uses of "church" in, for instance, the social sciences, have their own problems and need not detain us here.

ekklēsia was used. For them, *ekklēsia* could be a referent to a democratic-like Greek or Roman institution, a Jewish public institution, or a Jewish voluntary association.[37] These institutions were thus either civic (Greco-Roman or Jewish) or non-civic (Jewish associations); none of them were exclusively "religious" organizations.[38]

We may be reasonably sure that when Paul used the term *ekklēsia*, he did so with a Jewish understanding of the term in mind, thus, to a degree, setting it apart from Greco-Roman uses. This does not mean that the term did not resonate on the political register that was associated with Greco-Roman institutional settings. The point that is important to emphasize here, though, is that using the word *ekklēsia* in the first century triggered an understanding of the phenomenon for Paul and the members of his assemblies that was intertwined with a Jewish (institutional) identity, which, in turn, was expressed within a larger pattern of Greco-Roman institutional culture. In light of this ancient terminological and sociopolitical context it becomes quite clear that the English translation "church" is inappropriate and misleading, since it conjures up not only a (modern) religious non-civic, non-political setting, but more importantly, imposes on the ancients a separate non-Jewish institutional identity for those who claimed Jesus to be the Messiah.

Since *ekklēsia* was used for different types of institutions, even within a Jewish setting, it is reasonable to assume that people sometimes had to specify the exact reference of the word, especially if a Jew was in conversation with non-Jews in the Diaspora with its diverse cultural and political milieus. This is probably the reason why Paul at two occasions seems to add what would otherwise—had

---

37. See n. 32 above.
38. As noted above when discussing the terms "Christianity" and "Judaism," "religion" as the phenomenon is defined today did not exist in antiquity. See the literature referred to in n. 14.

ekklēsia been obviously referring to a "Christian" institutional setting (a "church")—be redundant information. In 1 Thessalonians and Galatians, respectively, Paul writes as follows:

> For you, brothers and sisters, became imitators of the *ekklēsiōn* [i.e., assemblies/synagogues] of God *in Christ Jesus* that are in Judaea, for you suffered the same things from your own compatriots as they did from the Judeans[39] (1 Thess. 2:14).

> I was still unknown by sight to the *ekklēsiais* [assemblies/synagogues] of Judea *that are in Christ* (Gal. 1:22).

In other words, since *ekklēsia* in Jewish settings was used to designate synagogue institutions beyond those run by Christ-believers, Paul specifies for his non-Jewish addressees that what he is referring to are the assemblies, or synagogues, of those who, like the addressees, were "in Christ." Far from denoting non-Jewish institutions, Paul's use of *ekklēsia* indicates that as the "apostle to the nations" he is inviting non-Jews to participate in specific Jewish institutional settings, where they may share with Jews the experience of living with the risen Messiah, of living "in Christ."

Such an approach in terms of institutional belonging matches well what Paul has to say in theological terms about the place of non-Jewish followers of Jesus in relation to Jews.[40] They have been invited to join (a specific group of) Jews, not to replace them or their institutions, as if living "in Christ" for non-Jews necessitated a life in isolation from synagogues. The NRSV, however, overwrites this first-century institutional and theological approach and imposes, in colonial manner, its own twentieth-century theological worldview that not only builds on, but also—to the degree that the translation

---

39. On the translation of *Ioudaioi* as "Judean" in this verse, see Runesson, "Inventing Christian Identity," 70 n. 32.
40. Cf. Rom. 11:17-18; 1 Cor. 7:17-24; Gal. 3:28.

is used in normative Christian settings—proclaims the separation between "Jews" and "Christians."

Looking beyond Paul, I have argued elsewhere that *ekklēsia* in Matthew (16:18; 18:17) should not be translated "church," as NRSV has it,[41] but rather "synagogue" or "assembly"; what we see in Matthew is the birth of a Jewish messianic association synagogue rather than a "Christian church."[42] In James 2:2 and 5:14 we find additional comparative material for both *synagōgē* and *ekklēsia*. In these passages the theo-historical bias of the NRSV comes into sharp focus. Since the scholars behind the NRSV have agreed on the hermeneutical principle not to translate as "synagogue" any historical institution that is run by followers of Jesus, we read in James 2:2: "if a person with gold rings and in fine clothes comes into your *assembly*." "Assembly" is chosen here despite the fact that the Greek *synagōgē* is used and NRSV always, without exception, translates this word as "synagogue" elsewhere in the New Testament. This interpretive strategy then allows the NRSV to translate the *ekklēsia* of James 5:14 with "church": "Are any among you sick? They should call for the elders of the *church* and have them pray over them." This translation effectively avoids the terminological overlap of and connection between the institutions of followers of Jesus and other Jews.

---

41. Not only does NRSV translate *ekklēsia* in these verses with "church," it also adds the word "church" to two passages, Matt. 18:15, 21, where the word *ekklēsia* does not occur in the Greek text. In these passages "church" replaces the Greek *adelphos* ("brother") in a move to use gender-inclusive language. Such a move is in and of itself to be commended on both historical and hermeneutical grounds, since the gender-inclusive English mirrors the reality behind the Greek (i.e., the rules listed were meant for both men and women). However, the use of "church" conceals another aspect of the reality behind the text, namely the Jewish character of the Matthean *ekklēsia*, and should therefore have been avoided.

42. See, e.g., Anders Runesson, "Behind the Gospel of Matthew: Radical Pharisees in Post-War Galilee?" *Currents in Theology and Mission* 37, no. 6 (2010): 460–71, here 462–64. For the relationship between Jewish institutions, see the chart in Runesson, "Re-Thinking Early Jewish–Christian Relations: Matthean Community History as Pharisaic Intragroup Conflict," *Journal of Biblical Literature* 127, no. 1 (2008): 95–132, here 116.

The politics of separation between "Jews" and "Christians" to which the NRSV gives expression is neither provoked by the sources, where synagogue terms overlap between those who followed Jesus and those who did not, nor always mirrored in other translations. While the modern Greek version of the New Testament from 1989 replaces *synagōgē* with *"synaxis"* in James 2:2,[43] and thus also avoids the Jewishness of the word "synagogue," and Luther's German translation, which has "Versammlung," does the same,[44] the Swedish translation from 1981 has "synagogue" ("synagoga"),[45] and so has the Swahili translation of 1952 ("sinagogi").[46] The United Bible Societies' Ivrit translation from 1976 translates *"bet haknesseth,"* that is, "synagogue," in James 2:2. Interestingly, the Ivrit translation of *ekklēsia* in James 5:14 is *"hakehila,"* which in modern Hebrew refers to a Jewish assembly or congregation, and not *knesiah*, which means "church."[47] Thus, of the translations mentioned, only the Swedish (1981), the Swahili (1952), and the Ivrit (1976) choose terminology that explicitly suggests to their readers that James was probably addressing Jewish assemblies of followers of Jesus.[48]

Is it not clear, in light of the above, that we need a new way of speaking about institutional phenomena that we encounter in

43. The Greek Bible Society (the ancient text with today's Greek translation). *Synaxis*, which is the same word in English, refers to "a meeting for worship, esp. for the Eucharist" (Brown, *Oxford English Dictionary*, ad loc.).

44. *Die Bibel, oder die ganze Heilige Schrift des Alten und Neuen Testaments nach der Übersetzung Martin Luthers* (Württembergische Bibelanstalt Stuttgart, 1970). However, *ekklēsia* in James 5:14 is translated *Gemeinde* ("community" or "congregation"), not *Kirche* ("church")

45. Bibel 2000. *Ekklēsia* in James 5:14 is translated *församling* ("community," "congregation").

46. Biblia (Union Version; United Bible Societies, 1952). The translation of *ekklēsia* in James 5:14 is, however, *kanisa*, "church."

47. Reuben Alcalay, *The Complete Hebrew-English Dictionary*, 3 vols. (Tel Aviv: Massada, 1990), ad loc.

48. Among English translations, it may be interesting to note, especially considering its translation method, that *The Bible in Basic English* (BBE), produced under the leadership of Hebrew Bible scholar Samuel H. Hooke in cooperation with Cambridge University Press and the Orthological Institute, presents us with an exception, as it translates *synagōgē* as "synagogue" in James 2:2.

our investigations of Jesus' followers and other Jews if we seek to avoid losing historical probability in our translations? Just as Acts 26:11 states that Paul persecuted people who believed Jesus was the Messiah *within* synagogues, for first-century writers like Paul *ekklēsia* did not refer to synagogue-external bodies of people, but either to synagogues, public or semi-public, or to messianic assemblies regardless of whether they gathered in the same institutional space as other Jews or in their own association synagogues.[49] If we translate *ekklēsia* with "church," however, we infer that Pauline *ekklēsiai* were unique and incompatible with any other ancient institution, Jewish or Greco-Roman, since our contemporary discursive habits prohibit alternative historical interpretations; in the twenty-first century, a "church" cannot, by definition, exist within a "synagogue."

Conclusion: On Carrying One's Own Hermeneutical Burden

The use of the terms "Christian"/"Christianity" and "church" in Pauline scholarship misleads us to create the past in our own image and hinders historical investigations from reaching beyond that which is "us." We need to decolonize the past, and liberate the dead from the yoke of a hermeneutical burden that is ours to carry, not theirs. In the end, as we listen to and de-familiarize ourselves with the culture of the New Testament, our sense of being in a place that is

---

49. For Pauline Christ-believers as subgroups within synagogues also consisting of Jews who did not belong to the Jesus movement, see Mark D. Nanos, *The Mystery of Romans: The Jewish Context of Paul's Letter* (Minneapolis: Fortress Press, 1996); Nanos, "To the Churches within the Synagogues of Rome," in *Reading Paul's Letter to the Romans*, ed. Jerry L. Sumney (Atlanta: Society of Biblical Literature, 2012), 11–28; Nanos, *Irony of Galatians*. As for the Gospels, the meting out of punishment in synagogues is also an irrefutable indication that Jesus' followers interacted with other Jews in shared synagogue settings. Only Matthew's Gospel includes additional evidence suggesting the creation of a separate association synagogue (an *ekklēsia*) run by messianic Jews, most likely former Pharisees, who made their own rules and administered punishment for disobedience; see Matt. 18:15-18. For discussion of Matthew in this regard, see Runesson, "Rethinking Early Jewish–Christian Relations."

not our own is a twenty-first century, not a first-century, problem to solve.

In order to do so, we need to challenge, as I have suggested here, the ideology of distinct identities, religions, and institutions, which surface as the NRSV uses the terms "church" and "synagogue," as well as when we speak of "Christians" and "Jews" in the New Testament. This challenge applies to the translation of the entire New Testament, but is especially problematic as we read Paul. Simply by listening to weekly readings from translations of the Bible, generations of churchgoers and Sunday school children internalize modern religious identity politics, as if these belonged in the first century. Then, if a historically informed preacher would happen to describe a different and more historically attuned scenario when he or she explains the text, a scenario in which we find overlapping identities and institutions, such a scenario is immediately understood by the congregation as in tension with, or even contradicted by, the Bible itself!

Since English is the research language for the majority of scholars in the world today, such an ideology of separation and incompatible identities, which originates with translations rather than with the ancient texts themselves, is easily incorporated in academic articles and monographs. Unconsciously, the language we use when we ask our questions, a language that has been shaped by the way we learned to speak as we grew up, almost forces us to "discover" a "Christian" Paul. But seeking to give voice to people and worlds that have been silenced by time and politics, the historian's task is to go beyond—not to reinforce—contemporary religious identities, be they Christian or Jewish. The terminology used by the sources themselves invites us to understand Paul as practicing and proclaiming a minority form of Judaism that existed in the first century. Such an invitation is, however, not the end of the research project; it is its very beginning.

3

———

The Question of Assumptions: Torah Observance in the First Century

Karin Hedner Zetterholm

Much of the debate about whether Paul was a representative of first-century Judaism has centered on the question of his relationship to Jewish "law," that is, Torah. Although a majority of proponents of the traditional view presume that following his "conversion" Paul no longer attributed an intrinsic value to Jewish identity and no longer considered Torah to be binding, adherents of the Paul within Judaism perspective generally maintain that Paul remained a Torah observant Jew throughout his life.[1] Both these positions run the risk of assuming

---

1. For a survey of the different positions see Magnus Zetterholm, *Approaches to Paul: A Student's Guide to Paul* (Minneapolis: Fortress Press, 2009), 69–90 (the Traditional View), 127–163 (the Radical New Perspective).

that Torah observance is a rather static and unproblematic phenomenon, and, moreover, that our knowledge of halakah in the first century permits us to determine whether or not Paul was Torah observant, and, if so, to what degree.

However, in order to understand Paul's relation to Jewish law, we need to free ourselves from the common (scholarly) notion of Torah observance as a simple clear-cut phenomenon and approach the issue in a more nuanced way. To gain a better understanding of what observance of Torah in reality entails, I believe a discussion of some general assumptions and conditions related to Torah observance, as well as examples from contemporary Judaism, will be helpful. We will then be in a better position to explore what it meant to be a Torah observant Jew in the first century, and the implications this has for understanding Paul's relation to both Jewish identity and behavioral standards as they relate to Torah.

What Does It Mean to be Torah Observant?

Let me begin by stating the obvious: Torah observance means different things to different groups and people, and, accordingly, different people define a violation of Torah observance differently. This is self-evident, but nevertheless often not taken sufficiently into account when discussing Paul's relation to the Torah. Scholars frequently talk about "breaking Jewish law" as if it were something absolute like running a red light, but Jewish law is generally not as clear-cut, and the assessment of whether a given act is a violation of halakah depends on the perspective of the group and individual making the claim.

For instance, when an Israeli friend of mine, who defines himself as "liberal Orthodox," has dinner in our home, which has a non-kosher kitchen, and eats on our non-kosher plates, this would be considered a violation of halakah from a strict Orthodox point of view. But my friend would not agree that he is breaking Jewish law by eating in our home. He would argue that Jewish law allows for a certain degree of interaction with non-Jews, and that observing Jewish law also involves not offending his non-Jewish hosts by not eating in their home, or making them go to extra trouble by requiring them to buy paper plates. He assumes, naturally, that we would not serve food forbidden by Jewish law.

Another friend, who belongs to the Conservative movement, once invited us to his home for Shabbat dinner, and when the evening was over he picked up the phone and called a taxi for us. This would be considered a violation of Jewish law according to Orthodox standards, but according to our host's interpretation of halakah it was not. In his view, he was not "breaking the law," but interpreting it, or rather, applying the interpretation of the denomination to which he belongs.

Since Jewish law is the result of an ongoing collective interpretation and extension of injunctions and principles laid out in the Hebrew Bible, disagreements over their correct understanding are bound to develop. Many biblical commandments, such as abstaining from work on the Sabbath (Exod. 20:8-11; 31:13-17; 35:1-3), are rather general in nature. They lack the detailed prescriptions necessary to put them into practice, necessitating the elaboration of more precise definitions and instructions. In the case of Sabbath observance, the rabbis had to decide which specific activities are implied by the word "work" (*m. Shabb.* 7:2). The Qumran literature and the New Testament provide ample evidence that there was no consensus on this issue or in other areas of Jewish law in the first century.[2] The Qumran community disagreed with the Pharisees

2. Adela Yarbro Collins, *Mark: A Commentary* (Minneapolis: Fortress Press, 2007), 200–205; E. P. Sanders, "The Life of Jesus," in *Christianity and Rabbinic Judaism: A Parallel History of Their Origins and Early Development*, ed. Hershel Shanks (Washington, DC: Biblical Archaeology Society, 1992), 41–83, esp. 70–73. It is evident from the New Testament, for instance, that the

on which activities were prohibited on the Sabbath, and the common people cannot be assumed to have adhered strictly to either of these halakic systems. Many centuries later, the Karaites would develop their own Sabbath halakah in opposition to rabbinic Judaism. It is evident from rabbinic literature that the halakic decisions arrived at eventually were preceded by long-standing debates and disagreements.

Although contemporary Jews who are committed to observing Jewish law all agree that the Mishnah's interpretation is binding, disagreements still abound as technology develops and new issues not specifically addressed by the Bible or Mishnah arise. One such issue is the use of electricity on the Sabbath, generally prohibited by Orthodox Jews, but permitted by many belonging to the Conservative movement. Numerous additional examples can be found in the area of medical ethics.[3]

In other cases, changed circumstances and evolving moral sensitivities have led to new understandings of biblical decrees and prohibitions. For instance, the rabbis found a literal understanding of "an eye for an eye" (Exod. 21:23-25; Lev. 24:17-21; Deut. 19:18-21) and the decree to execute a rebellious son (Deut. 21:18-21) irreconcilable with their understanding of moral behavior. They thus reinterpreted "an eye for an eye" to mean monetary compensation,[4] and rendered nonfunctional the law of the rebellious son by

---

Pharisaic custom of washing one's hands before a meal was not shared by everyone (Mark 7:2; Matt. 15:2).

3. See Elliot N. Dorff, "A Methodology for Jewish Medical Ethics," in *Contemporary Jewish Ethics and Morality: A Reader*, eds. Elliot N. Dorff and Louis E. Newman (New York: Oxford University Press, 1995), 161–76; David H. Ellenson, "How to Draw Guidance from a Heritage: Jewish Approaches to Mortal Choices," in *Contemporary Jewish Ethics and Morality*, 129–39; Louis E. Newman, "Woodchppers and Respirators: The Problem of Interpretation in Contemporary Jewish Ethics," in *Contemporary Jewish Ethics and Morality*, 140–60.

4. *Mek.* R. Ishmael Nezikin 8 (trans. Lauterbach 3:62-69); *m. B. Qam.* 2:6, 8:1-3; *b. B. Qam.* 83b-84a.

introducing so many impossible prerequisites that it could never be applied in practice.[5]

One of the reasons the rabbis found these decrees problematic is that they saw them as a violation of major moral and theological principles of the Torah, such as the call to "love your neighbor as yourself" (Lev. 19:18), "justice, justice shall you pursue" (Deut. 16:20), and characterizations of God as good, compassionate, gracious, and forgiving: "God is good to all, and his mercies extend to all his creatures," (Ps. 145:9), and "a God compassionate and gracious, slow to anger, and abounding in steadfast love and faithfulness, extending kindness to the thousandth generation, forgiving iniquity, transgression, and sin" (Exod. 34:6-7). Moreover, retaliation and the execution of rebellious sons seemed to conflict with the very goal and purpose of Jewish law, which for the rabbis was to create an ideal world and a moral society.[6]

Thus, Jewish law is more than just detailed prescriptions or prohibitions concerning specific situations. The detailed laws are based on the Torah's ethical principles and the Jews' perception of God, and these two parts of Jewish law—its body and soul, as it were—are intimately connected so that the specific laws translate moral values into concrete modes of behavior.[7] The foundation of

---

5. *b. Sanh.* 71a.

6. Elliot N. Dorff, *For the Love of God and People: A Philosophy of Jewish Law* (Philadelphia: Jewish Publication Society, 2007), 222–26.

7. For the intimate relationship between general principles and specific laws, see Haim N. Bialik, *Halachah and Aggadah*, trans. Leon Simon (London: Education Dept. of the Zionist Federation of Great Britain and Ireland, 1944) who compares them to two sides of the same coin, or to ice and water. He writes, "*Halacha* [i.e. specific laws] wears a frown, *Aggada* [i.e. lore, general principles] a smile. The one is pedantic, severe, unbending—all justice; the other is accommodating, lenient, pliable—all mercy . . . The one is concerned with the shell, with the body, with actions; the other with the kernel, with the soul, with intentions" (9). See also Abraham J. Heschel, *God in Search of Man: A Philosophy of Judaism* (New York: Farrar, Straus & Giroux, 1989), 336–37. Heschel writes, "Agada deals with man's ineffable relations to God, to other men, and to the world. Halacha deals with details, with each commandment separately; agada with the whole of life, with the totality of religious life. Halacha deals with the law; agada with the meaning of the law" (336).

Jewish law is the belief in a moral God; thus, the law is interpreted and shaped by moral considerations.[8]

If a specific law is understood to violate the moral principles of the Torah, it may be necessary in certain circumstances to suspend that particular law in order to preserve and safeguard the Torah. The rabbis had a term for this, namely "to act for the Lord" (based on a midrashic understanding of Ps. 119:126), by which they meant that in certain situations, acting in the interest of God may require dissolving a particular law. A variation of the same theme appears in the Babylonian Talmud in a statement attributed to Resh Lakish: "At times, abolition of the Torah is its foundation" (*b. Menah.* 99b).[9]

The idea that suspension of the Torah in the sense of a particular law may serve to preserve the Torah in the sense of Jewish law as a whole draws attention to the potential confusion caused by the fact that the word *Torah* has several different meanings. Although it can be used in the sense of particular laws, the word *torah* signifies a broader and more nuanced concept that in Hebrew refers to "instruction," "teaching," or "guidance." The legal portions of the Torah include many different kinds of laws, ranging from ethical norms to laws about purity as well as customs connected to Jewish identity.

Again, an example from contemporary Judaism can serve to illustrate the different senses of the word Torah: A Reform Jew would readily acknowledge that he "breaks the law" in the sense of not observing halakah, since he does not consider traditional Jewish law to be binding, but the person would not say that he "breaks the Torah." On the contrary, he would claim that the Torah's ethical principles, on which Reform Judaism has traditionally focused, is the most important part of divine revelation (Torah). Accordingly he

8. Dorff, *Love of God*, 211–43.
9. Eliezer Berkovits, *Not in Heaven: The Nature and Function of Halakhah* (New York: Ktav, 1983), 64–70.

would claim that his version of Judaism and his interpretation of what it means to be a Jew is more true to the divine intention behind the Torah than an Orthodox Jew's preoccupation with the details of halakah.

Jewish law is simply a much more complex and flexible system than it may at first appear. Its development is shaped by its internal parts—moral principles, theology, history, eschatology—as well as what is happening in the environment in which it functions.[10] Specific laws take form in a dialectical process between traditional Jewish texts (the Bible and its rabbinic interpretation), on the one hand, and non-textual factors such as social reality, including developments in science and technology, on the other. Among the textual factors, consideration is given both to general principles and explicit commandments or prohibitions. Because different halakic authorities put different emphasis on different factors, giving priority to some over others, their rulings in specific cases will differ, although they are all committed to Jewish law and consider halakah to be binding.

A recent debate on same-sex relations within the Conservative movement and subsequent rulings about what is halakically permissible may illustrate these dynamics. For some Conservative rabbis, the medical discovery that sexual orientation is inborn and that attempts to change it do not work (non-textual factor) meant that the traditional view that homosexual acts constituted a deliberate rebellion against Jewish law could no longer be upheld. As a result, retaining the tradition's ban on any form of homosexual relations was seen as violating the Torah's command not to oppress others and as undermining the view of God as moral and compassionate; it subverted the Torah's numerous calls to care for other people.

10. Dorff, *Love of God*, 225.

Motivated by the psychological harm that the traditional stance imposed on homosexuals and their families, these rabbis wrote a responsum abrogating the rabbinic extensions of the biblical ban (Lev. 18:22; 20:13), permitting lesbians to engage in sex, and gay men to engage in forms of sexual expression with the exception of anal sex.[11] Opponents of this ruling argued that contemporary moral considerations based on non-legal portions of the Torah could not outweigh an explicit biblical prohibition and its interpretation by generations of halakic authorities. They accordingly issued a ruling upholding the traditional ban on homosexual relations.[12] The two positions taken on this issue reflect different emphases on the multiple factors involved in the process of establishing specific laws, one giving priority to an explicit prohibition and the other to the general principles behind individual laws. Both were formulated by rabbis who are fully committed to observing Torah. In this particular case, however, they disagree over how God's instructions and intentions should be translated into specific rules, that is, how Jewish law is best safeguarded.[13] Thus, not only do different denominations issue different halakic rulings, halakic authorities within the same movement may at times also produce different rulings.

Halakic authorities also differ over the role and significance attributed to non-textual factors in the shaping of laws. Although there are numerous exceptions, Orthodox rabbis in general are more

11. Elliot N. Dorff, Daniel S. Nevins, and Avraham I. Reisner, "Homosexuality, Human Dignity, & Halakhah: A Combined Responsum for the Committee on Jewish Law and Standards," 2006, at http://www.rabbinicalassembly.org/sites/default/files/public/halakhah/teshuvot/20052010/dorff_nevins_reisner_dignity.pdf. In a responsum that is also a general essay on the different approaches to law, Gordon Tucker discusses the interrelationship between law (halakah) and narrative (aggadah) in the decision-making process of the Conservative movement; Tucker, "Halakhic and Metahalakhic Arguments Concerning Judaism and Homosexuality," 2006, at http://www.rabbinicalassembly.org/sites/default/files/public/halakhah/teshuvot/20052010/tucker_homosexuality.pdf.
12. Joel Roth, "Homosexuality Revisited," 2006, at http://www.rabbinicalassembly.org/sites/default/files/public/halakhah/teshuvot/20052010/roth_revisited.pdf.
13. For a summary of the debate see Dorff, *Love of God*, 232–43.

text-centered and less inclined to let modern moral sensibilities and social reality influence their halakic decisions. In the case of same-sex relations, for example, this leads to a conservative position, but this is not necessarily the case in other areas. In the absence of explicit prohibitions, text-centeredness may result in a stance that is more progressive than that of the denominations, which attribute a greater significance to moral considerations, as is evident from halakic rulings within Orthodox Judaism on matters of medical ethics.[14]

Just as a specific law may be in tension with a moral or theological principle, individual laws may sometimes conflict with one another too, requiring that priority be given to one law over another. To be a Torah observant Jew requires a constant balancing act, giving priority to some laws over others in a given situation. The details of this balancing act are negotiated individually, although the different denominations each set a general standard. A person involved in such a balancing act, who sets aside one law in order to give priority to another law or general principle in a given situation, is naturally not violating Jewish law or denying his or her commitment to it: he or she is interpreting and applying it. Living in a non-Jewish or non-observant environment makes such balancing acts even more complex. Denominations and individuals negotiate these situations in different ways, which means that Orthodox Jews might claim that some halakic rulings issued by Conservative rabbis are outside the bounds of halakah—that they are breaking the law, in other words—but this is an assessment based on a set of Orthodox priorities that cannot simply be adopted uncritically by an outside observer or scholar.

---

14. See, for instance, the position taken on cloning: Elliot N. Dorff, *Matters of Life and Death: A Jewish Approach to Modern Medical Ethics* (Philadelphia: Jewish Publication Society, 1998), 313–24.

The point of all this is to illustrate that establishing and applying halakah are processes that are both complex and multifaceted, in which multiple factors are taken into account, including contemporary social reality. A common commitment to Jewish law can nevertheless lead to very different rulings. Accordingly, deciding whether or not a given act constitutes "breaking the law" is not that simple. The assessment depends upon the group to which an individual belongs, upon the personal interpretation of the details of halakah of the individual or group in question, as well as on the particular situation. What is for one group or individual a violation of halakah is for another a legitimate interpretation that is necessary in order to preserve Jewish law!

Although the scope of Jewish law was much more limited in the first century than it came to be in subsequent rabbinic tradition, there is no reason to think that the halakic system worked in an inherently different way. Examples from rabbinic literature show that the rabbis were involved in a dialectical process of narrowing some laws and expanding others, which is similar to the process in which contemporary rabbis still engage.[15] Thus, just as in our time, two ancient Jews committed to Jewish law may have had very different views about how to translate the goal and mission of Jewish law into practical regulations, and like modern observant Jews in the Diaspora, they would have had to constantly balance their commitment to Jewish law against the customs and reality of everyday life in their non-Jewish environment.

Naturally, a person committed to Jewish law may at times nevertheless fail to observe a particular commandment or violate a prohibition without any good reason, but does that mean this person is by definition not Torah observant? When I mentioned this

---

15. Dorff, *Love of God*, 222–32.

article on Paul and Torah observance and the common claim that Paul "broke the law" to a Jewish friend of mine, he said simply, "Oh, like most Jews, then." He is right, of course, if one focuses on the observance of every single commandment over the course of a lifetime. However, someone who occasionally fails to fulfill a particular commandment or violates a prohibition may nevertheless be Torah observant in the sense that he or she is committed to Jewish law and has the intention of keeping it. At the same time, repentance and restitution are included in the Torah and should accordingly be taken into account when defining what constitutes "Torah observance."

Pauline scholars tend to miss this point, applying a rigid and legalistic understanding of what it means to observe Jewish law. If perfect Torah observance is expected from Jews (which involves a host of interpretive assumptions), then anyone who fails to meet those expectations would be considered to "break the law." Jewish tradition, however, explicitly recognizes the fact that nobody will keep all the details of the law at all times! This important element seems to be generally overlooked when Christians discuss this topic. So too is the fact that Jewish tradition appeals to God's forgiveness and grace to solve this conundrum. When a religious Jew puts on his prayer shawl, with the fringes symbolizing the 613 commandments, he prays, "May it be before you . . . as if I had fulfilled the commandment of the tzitzit in all its details, implications, and intentions, as well as the six hundred thirteen commandments that are dependent upon it."[16] He knows that he has not managed to do this, but he asks God to account it to him *as if* he had.

"Obeying the whole Law" is a phrase that admittedly appears both in Paul's letters and in rabbinic literature. In Galatians 5:3, Paul writes

16. *The Complete Artscroll Siddur.* Translation and Commentary by Nosson Scherman (Brooklyn: Mesorah, 1988), 2.

to the gentile adherents to the Jesus movement: "Once again I testify to every man who lets himself be circumcised that he is obliged to obey the entire law." Pauline scholars have generally understood this to indicate that Paul is calling for obligation to observe every single commandment. But the warning arises in the context of him seeking to dissuade Jesus-oriented gentiles from undertaking a transformation of identity if they have not been properly advised of the consequences: following circumcision a non-Jew becomes a Jew; thereafter, he must be *committed* to keeping the entire part of the Torah that the Jews are commanded to observe.

In rabbinic sources, the phrase refers to the entirety of the rabbinic body of law, namely the Written and the Oral Torah.[17] In these instances it is perhaps more readily apparent that the commitment enjoined to "observe the entire Torah" is not focused on the observance of every single commandment, but on the scope, or body of laws to which the rabbinic tradition is committed. For instance, in *b. 'Abod. Zar.* 2b, God boasts that Israel has "kept the entire Torah," which is repeated three times. Unless we assume that God is lying, this statement must be understood to refer to a general commitment to the law by the people of Israel rather than the fulfillment of every single commandment by every single Israelite.[18]

---

17. For instance, *m. Qidd.* 4:14: "Abraham, our father, observed the entire Torah." *Lev. Rab.* 2:10 and *b. Yoma* make very similar statements. The claim in *b. Yoma* 28b that Abraham "observed the entire Torah" is clearly apologetic and is explicitly said to mean that Abraham observed both the Written and the Oral Torah (from the plural form "toratai" in the quoted verse, Gen. 26:5). Cf. *Gen. Rab.* 49:2, 64:4, and 95:3, according to which Abraham knew rabbinic law.

18. Cf. James 2:10, "For whoever keeps the whole law but fails in one point has become accountable for all of it." Here the emphasis is on the importance of keeping every single commandment, but the phrase "keep the whole law" obviously does not mean that, but rather seems to refer to a commitment to the Torah.

Torah Observance in the First Century

In addition to the general factors pertaining to Torah observance outlined above, a discussion of Paul's relation to the Torah is further complicated by the fact that we know very little about halakic observance in the first century. The various groups with their different halakic systems—Pharisees, Sadducees, and the Qumran community—aside, there were also the common people who likely did not belong to any particular group at all. Thus, we cannot assume that a commonly accepted established halakah existed, and there does not seem to have been a uniform practice even within each of the halakic systems. For instance, the two famous first-century sages, Hillel and Shammai and their respective disciple circles, both seem to have been associated with the Pharisaic movement, but rabbinic sources record numerous legal disputes between them.[19] Even the rabbinic movement in its initial stages was not in a position to establish a commonly accepted halakah;[20] hence, rabbinic literature abounds with the different opinions of rabbis.

For all the reasons enumerated above, and because we do not know what first-century halakah looked like, except that it was diverse, we cannot easily determine which acts constituted a violation of it. For instance, is Paul's permission in 1 Corinthians 10:25 to eat food purchased at the market in Corinth and to eat whatever is served when invited to dine with "an unbeliever" (10:27) really evidence that he no longer considered Jewish law binding, as scholars commonly claim,[21] or is it better understood as an *expression of* first-century

---

19. *m. Ber.* 8:1-8, for instance, lists their different opinions concerning blessings in connection with meals. They are also said to have had different attitudes toward non-Jews, with Hillel being more welcoming and open to Gentiles than Shammai (*b. Shabb.* 31a).
20. Catherine Hezser, "Social Fragmentation, Plurality of Opinion, and Nonobservance of Halakhah: Rabbis and Community in Late Roman Palestine," *Jewish Studies Quarterly* 1 (1993): 234–51.

Jewish Diaspora halakah for Jesus-oriented gentiles, as others more recently have suggested?

I will briefly discuss 1 Corinthians 8–10 below, a passage generally considered crucial for understanding Paul's relation to Jewish law, elaborating the arguments of Peter Tomson and Magnus Zetterholm that Paul's reasoning in 1 Corinthians 8–10 makes sense as a halakic argument and that this passage is better understood as an example of first-century Jewish halakah for Jesus-oriented gentiles than a violation of Jewish law.[22] I hope to illustrate that a less rigid view of Jewish law and the process of establishing halakah may yield insights of interest to scholars of the New Testament. Taking into account the Diaspora situation of Jesus-oriented gentiles that required balancing the commitment to Israel's God with their commitments and daily life in a society permeated with the cult of Greco-Roman gods, Paul's arguments make sense *within* the framework of Jewish law, and when compared to later rabbinic debates and legislation on idolatry as laid out in tractate *Avodah Zarah* of the Mishnah, the similarities are striking.

The main issue in 1 Corinthians 8–10 is how to relate to food, which in a "pagan" society may previously have been sacrificed to Greco-Roman gods, in which case it would forbidden to Jews and gentile Jesus-believers because of its connection with idolatry. Although Paul did not consider gentile Jesus-adherents to be bound by all the laws that applied to Jews, involvement in idolatry was to be

---

21. E.g. Jerome Murphy-O'Connor, "Freedom or the Ghetto (1 Cor VIII:1–13, X:23–XI:1)," *Révue Biblique* 85 (1978): 541–74, reprinted in J. Murphy-O'Connor, *Keys to First Corinthians: Revisiting the Major Issues* (Oxford: Oxford University Press, 2009); Charles K. Barret, "Things Sacrificed to Idols," in *Essays on Paul* (London: SPCK, 1982), 40–59.

22. Peter J. Tomson, *Paul and the Jewish Law: Halakha in the Letters of the Apostle to the Gentiles* (Assen: van Gorcum, 1990), 187–220; Magnus Zetterholm, "Purity and Anger: Gentiles and Idolatry in Antioch," *Interdisciplinary Journal of Research on Religion* 1 (2005): 3–24, esp. 10–16. I am making no pretense at an exhaustive treatment of this much-discussed passage and will only quote a limited number of scholars in order to make my point.

avoided at all costs since idolatrous acts could be seen as undermining the belief in Israel's God as the only God.[23] Thus, in this particular case, the problem for these gentile adherents to the Jesus movement was essentially the same as that which faced Jews living in a non-Jewish environment; namely, how to live in a pagan society and not get involved in idolatry. This question must have been even more urgent for Jesus-believing gentiles (former "pagans") who were used to participating fully in the public life of Greco-Roman cities, and who likely had relatives and friends still devoted to the Greco-Roman gods with whom continued interaction was both necessary and desirable.[24]

Food bought at the market in Corinth or offered in the home of a pagan friend may have been involved in sacrifices to Greco-Roman gods, and the question is how the gentiles of the Jesus community should relate to such food whose origin and history are not known. What should they do in this uncertain situation: inquire about the provenance of the food, or refrain from eating altogether? Paul responds that they can eat whatever is sold in the market without raising any questions for "the earth and its fullness are the Lord's" (1 Cor. 10:26), a statement often understood by scholars to mean that Paul permits consumption of food sacrificed to pagan gods, and hence as evidence that he no longer attributed significance to Jewish law.[25]

---

23. Cf. Acts 15:20, where James declares that gentile Jesus-followers must abstain "from things polluted by idols and from fornication and from whatever has been strangled and from blood," and *Didache* 6:3: "For if you can bear the entire yoke of the Lord, you will be perfect; but if you cannot, do as much as you can. And concerning food, bear what you can. But especially abstain from food sacrificed to idols; for this is a ministry to dead gods."
24. On the social situation of gentiles who had joined the Jesus community and had to adjust to refraining from "idolatry," see Zetterholm, "Purity and Anger," 11–13.
25. E.g., John C. Brunt, "Rejected, Ignored, or Misunderstood? The Fate of Paul's Approach to the Problem of Food Offered to Idols in Early Christianity," *New Testament Studies* 31 (1985): 113–24.

However, in view of the fact that Paul in the immediate context (10:1-22) urges the community to keep away from idolatry and specifically to refrain from participation in cultic meals in a temple context (1 Cor. 8:4-13), it appears unlikely that his permission to buy food in the market means that he is abolishing the prohibition against eating food sacrificed to idols, especially given the overwhelming agreement on the prohibition of idol food within the early church.[26]

In chapter 8, Paul seems to be responding to a specific question raised by some Jesus-oriented gentiles who appear to question the prohibition of food offered to idols: "Hence, as to the eating of food offered to idols, we know that 'no idol in the world really exists;' and that 'there is no God but one'" (1 Cor. 8:4). These Jesus-oriented gentiles appear to argue along the following lines: We have learned (from Paul and in concert with other Jews) that there is only one God. Accordingly, the Greco-Roman deities are mere idols with no power. Knowing this, it really doesn't matter if we were to eat food offered to them, does it? (And it would make our lives so much easier!) To this, Paul replies that they are right in theory, but since everyone within the Jesus community is not yet convinced that these gods have no real power it *does* matter:

> It is not everyone, however, who has this knowledge. Since some have until now been so accustomed to idols, they still think of the food they eat as food offered to an idol; and their intention (*syneidēsis*), being weak, is defiled . . . But take care that this liberty of yours does not somehow become a stumbling block to the weak. For if others see you, who possess knowledge, eating in the temple of an idol, might they not, since their intention is weak, be encouraged to the point of eating

---

26. Tomson, *Paul and the Jewish Law*, 177–86. Clement of Alexandria and Tertullian understood Paul's ruling in 1 Corinthians 10:25 to mean that everything bought in the market could be eaten *except* idol food, while Chrysostom, Ambrosiaster, Novatian, and Augustine understood it to mean that in Paul's view food of unspecified provenance is permitted without questioning, but if specified by others as consecrated food, it is prohibited. Notably, none took it to mean that Paul permitted the consumption of idol food.

food sacrificed to idols? So by your knowledge those weak believers for whom Christ died are destroyed. (1 Cor. 8:7-11)

The Greek word *syneidēsis* is crucial here. Although usually translated as "conscience," the Greek term can mean both "intention," "consciousness," and "conscience." Tomson persuasively argues that "intention" or "consciousness" better renders the meaning of *syneidēsis* as used by Paul. The reason it is commonly translated as "conscience" may be due to the fact that the Latin equivalent, *conscientia*, acquired a predominantly moral meaning, shifting the focus from the intention toward idolatry of "the weak" to the conscience of the Jesus-believer generally. Notably, the Greek-speaking Chrysostom understood Paul's words to mean "intention."[27]

When Paul is talking about the intention or consciousness of the weak here, he is presumably referring to former pagans who have recently joined the Jesus community but still attribute reality to pagan deities.[28] These people have turned to the God of Israel but not having completely abandoned their past, they are not convinced that the gods they used to worship are mere powerless idols. For such a person, whose intention is not wholly directed toward Israel's God, the eating of food sacrificed to Greco-Roman gods will be an act of idolatry and hence lead to destruction. Therefore, consideration for those Jesus adherents in whose minds pagan deities still have some reality and power, takes precedence over the theological principle

27. Tomson, *Paul and the Jewish Law*, 195–96, 210–16. Tomson (p. 210) points out that the moral interpretation given to the passage by Augustine, who knew no Greek, is likely to have influenced later readings.

28. Mark D. Nanos, "The Polytheist Identity of the 'Weak,' and Paul's Strategy to 'Gain' Them: A New Reading of 1 Corinthians 8:1—11:1," in *Paul: Jew, Greek, and Roman*, ed. Stanley E. Porter (Leiden: Brill, 2008), 179–210, however, argues that "the weak" are pagans for whom Paul believes that Jesus also died and whom he hopes will one day turn to him. Considering the fact that there was likely various levels of commitment among the former pagans who had recently joined the Jesus community, the distinction between some of them and those who remained committed to Greco-Roman gods was probably less clear than we tend to think.

that the God of Israel is the only God and all other gods merely idols with no power.[29]

Paul's argument here bears resemblance to the rabbinic idea of *mar'it 'ain*,[30] the principle according to which one must refrain from acts that are permitted but inappropriate because they may lead a less knowledgeable Jew to draw false conclusions and cause him or her to do something that is not permitted. An example from a modern context may illustrate this: Eating a vegetarian cheeseburger is obviously no problem from the point of view of Jewish law, but a religious Jew should nevertheless avoid doing so in public because another Jew who sees him and does not realize that the hamburger is vegetarian may think that cheeseburgers are permitted and thus violate halakah by eating a cheeseburger made of meat.

The significance attached to certain acts by other people is a concern in early rabbinic literature also. Thus, one should not bow down toward a pagan temple in order to collect a coin from the ground or drink from a fountain because it looks as if one is bowing before an idol. Instead, one must turn one's back to the temple in order to bow down, but if one is not seen, one can do it the normal way (*t. 'Abod. Zar.* 6:4-6). While the pagan temple itself has no special meaning to the Jew and his intention is not toward idolatry, the act is nevertheless forbidden because of the significance that other people may attribute to it.[31] Thus, in theory these gentile Jesus adherents are

---

29. Tomson, *Paul and the Jewish Law*, 193–98. Jews would agree, of course, that there is no reality in idols, but the argument seems to spring from the situation of the gentile Jesus adherents who may have thought that this logic might allow them to continue to participate in the pagan temple cult. Jews who were accustomed to live according to Jewish law presumably had no such needs.

30. E.g. *y. Demai* 6:2.

31. Tomson, *Paul and the Jewish Law*, 162–63. Likewise, it is ruled that in certain exceptional circumstances a Jew may visit Roman theaters and stadiums, although they were considered places of idolatry and bloodshed, but if he "draws attention," it is forbidden (*t. 'Abod. Zar.* 2:5-7). Similarly, a Jew may not lease a bath house to a gentile, "since it is referred to by his [the Jew's] name," because the gentile may heat it up on the Sabbath and thus people might believe that the Jewish owner is profaning the Sabbath (*m. 'Avod. Zar.* 1:9).

correct to suppose that it does not matter if they eat food sacrificed to Greco-Roman gods, since these gods have no real existence, but in practice they are nevertheless prohibited from eating such food because of the harmful impact this might have on other people.[32] In fact, the argument that since there is no reality to idols it does not matter if one eats food sacrificed to them seems entirely theoretical and has no bearing on halakah.

How then, is this prohibition to be reconciled with Paul's permission to eat food sold in the market or that offered in the home of a pagan friend?

> Eat whatever is sold in the meat market without raising any question on the ground of intention [toward idolatry] for "the earth and its fullness are the Lord's." If an unbeliever invites you to a meal and you are disposed to go, eat whatever is set before you without raising any question on the ground of intention [toward idolatry]. But if someone says to you, "This is sanctified food," then do not eat it, out of consideration for the one who informed you, and for the sake of intention—I mean the other's intention, not your own (1 Cor. 10:25-28).[33]

Food offered in the temple of an idol (8:10) is known to be sacrificed to idols and hence forbidden, whereas food bought at the market or served in the home of a pagan friend are of unspecified nature. Unless explicitly announced to be consecrated to idols, Paul does not consider such food of unspecified origin to be idol food. One need not assume that food sold in the market was sacrificed to idols, and perhaps, as Tomson suggests, food sold at the market to non-worshippers of Greco-Roman religion, such as members of the Jesus community, might even have been desacralized by the vendor, or

---

32. Nanos, "Polytheist Identity" 189–202, argues that Paul is concerned not only with the harmful impact on fellow members of the Jesus community but also with the effect it might have on pagans. Like the rabbis, Paul was anxious to avoid any behavior that could be seen by idolaters and create the impression that worship of Israel's god had simply been added to the pantheon.
33. My translation is informed by the Greek and Tomson's interpretation.

simply quietly considered desecrated. Alternatively, like some later rabbis, he considered the act of selling to disconnect objects from a cultic context (*m. 'Abod. Zar.* 4:4-5).[34] It is also possible that Paul reasons along the same lines as the rabbis did later, attributing significance to the cultic context: eating in the temple of an idol is clearly a cultic act, while food from the market lacks an immediate cultic context.[35]

The food served in the home of a pagan friend may likewise be eaten without any questions asked, unless at such a meal, someone announces, "This is sanctified food." Then the food is no longer unspecified, and by his choice of words—"sanctified" (*hierothytos*) rather than "offered to idols" (*eidōlothytos*) that a Jew or a Jesus-oriented gentile would have used—the person shows his commitment to these gods. In such a case, the food represents idolatry and is hence forbidden, according to Paul. This is somewhat similar to rabbinic reasoning when doing business with gentiles. Goods of specified intention, which by quality or condition are evidently intended for idolatry, are forbidden, but if unspecified, they are permitted and one may sell them "without anxiety," and there is no need to inquire about their purpose. As long as idolatrous intentions are not explicitly stated, they do not represent idolatry, but if the pagan specified his intention to use the goods for idolatrous purposes, it is forbidden even to sell water and salt to him (*t. 'Abod. Zar.* 1:21).[36]

---

34. Tomson, *Paul and the Jewish Law*, 218–19. Nanos, "Polytheist Identity," 202, points out that Paul's instruction implies that the market has available for purchase non-idol-related food; otherwise, everything there would be known to be idol food and thus by definition prohibited. A statement attributed to R. Akiva in *m. 'Abod. Zar.* 2:3, "Meat brought to a place of idol worship is permitted [to benefit from]; that which is taken out is forbidden since it is like the sacrifices of the dead," might indicate that slaughtered meat was not *a priori* regarded as being consecrated to idols and hence such non-consecrated meat may possibly have been for sale at the market.

35. Zetterholm, "Purity and Anger," 15.

36. Tomson, *Paul and the Jewish Law*, 203–20.

As in the previous example, Paul seems to be saying that it is a person's religious orientation (intention toward God or toward "idols") that determines whether or not the food should be considered an idol offering, which determines whether the Jesus-believing gentile can eat it or not. The power of idolatry, according to this way of reasoning, is not in the food, but in the attitude and intention of those who are devoted to Greco-Roman gods. Thus, upholding the prohibition on food sacrificed to idols, Paul appears to be engaged in defining the circumstances in which food in a pagan society should be considered "idol food," restricting the category to situations involving people with an intentional attachment to Greco-Roman cultic activities. Only in such cases should the food be regarded as being consecrated to idols and hence forbidden.[37]

Far from declaring Jewish law null and void, Paul is engaged either in *establishing* a halakah concerning idol food for Jesus-oriented gentiles, or *teaching them an existing* local Corinthian Jewish halakah. In light of the rabbinic parallels, it is not unconceivable that he draws from a local Jewish halakah concerning food bought at the market in Corinth. Either way, he is taking into account the particular situation and dilemma of the Jesus-oriented gentiles when writing his responsum to the specific question they have raised.

As indicated above, intention or attitude as a decisive halakic factor in defining idolatry is present in rabbinic sources also, and was a way of handling everyday life in a pagan society where public spaces were filled with images of Greco-Roman gods and emperors, places associated with gods, and items offered to gods. Coexistence with gentiles was accepted as a fact of life; the problem was determining the precise moments and dealings with them or their possessions

---

37. Bruce N. Fisk, "Eating Meat Offered to Idols: Corinthian Behavior and Pauline Response in 1 Corinthians 8–10 (A Response to Gordon Fee)," *Trinity Journal* 10 (1989): 49–70, esp. 60; Tomson, *Paul and the Jewish Law*; Zetterholm, "Purity and Anger," 13–15.

that implied association with idolatry. In the end the rabbis settled for a definition of pagan religiosity that consisted exclusively of cultic activity, including speech. For instance, while it was strictly forbidden to do anything that might assist a pagan to carry out an act of idol worship, benefit may be derived from business with idols assumed not to have been worshiped, or which have been abandoned, slightly disfigured, or in one opinion, sold by a pagan (m. 'Abod. Zar. 4:4-6). This focus on the ritual aspects of Greco-Roman religion rendered everything not directly associated with the cult permissible and made it possible for Jews to live and function in Diaspora cities and even participate in public life to a certain extent. Accordingly, many of the debates in tractate Avodah Zarah of the Mishnah focus on defining which acts or behavior by pagans should be considered part of their cult.[38]

Clearly, the rabbis did not perceive the power of idolatry as being in food, things, or actions themselves, but in the way the pagans treated them. A distinction was made between the human relationship to gentiles, which was to be promoted (within certain limits) "for the sake of peace" (t. 'Abod. Zar. 1:3), and their idolatrous cult, which was to be avoided.[39]

Rabbinic literature provides an example of a similar doubtful case of idolatry where the intention of the pagan worshipper is decisive regarding objects found next to what the Mishnah calls Markolis, a representation of the Roman deity Mercurius, the patron of travelers and merchants (m. 'Abod. Zar. 4:1-2). Passersby would throw stones or deposit food in front of the statue to express their devotion. The underlying question of this mishnah is how one can know if objects

---

38. Tomson, Paul and the Jewish Law, 158–63; Seth Schwartz, "Gamaliel in Aphrodite's Bath: Palestinian Judaism and Urban Culture in the Third and Fourth Centuries," in The Talmud Yerushalmi and Graeco-Roman Culture, ed. Peter Schäfer (Tübingen: Mohr Siebeck, 1998), 203–17, esp. 206–11.

39. Tomson, Paul and the Jewish Law, 163.

found in its vicinity are intended for the idol or not. If they are, the Jew may not derive benefit from them, but if not, the stones could be used and the food could be sold to a gentile. The Mishnah states that if two stones are found next to the deity, they can be assumed to be there by accident and may accordingly be used by Jews, but three in a row seem to signify intention, and thus, may not. Thus, the intention and significance given to the objects by the pagan determines whether or not the objects are considered associated with idolatry.[40]

Another example of intention as a decisive factor in rabbinic halakah is the famous story about Rabban Gamliel, who saw no problem in visiting a bathhouse featuring a statue of Aphrodite, referring to the rule: "Only what they [the pagans] treat as a deity is prohibited, but what they do not treat as a deity is permitted" (*m. 'Abod. Zar.* 3:4). Rabban Gamliel argues that since the pagans do not treat the statue of Aphrodite in the bathhouse as a god, it can be regarded as mere decoration.[41] By narrowing down the definition of idolatry to include cultic activity only, the rabbis rendered acceptable the non-cultic but still religious aspects of pagan society, making it possible for them to live and function in an environment permeated with idolatry.[42]

The rabbinic parallels are instructive because they illustrate that Paul's reasoning fits nicely into the Jewish context of halakah as it developed among the rabbis, including how to deal with the challenge to avoid idolatry in a society permeated with the cult of Greco-Roman gods. Far from "breaking the law," Paul seems to be engaged in the process of applying it, defining which acts in which

---

40. Ibid., 208–10.
41. Ibid., 159–60, 213–14; Schwartz, "Gamaliel in Aphrodite's Bath," 213–17.
42. Rabbinic legislation at times strikes one as rather lenient. For instance, R. Yohanan is reported to have permitted to the Jews of Bostra a spring whose waters were used in the local cult of Aphrodite (*y. Sheviit* 8:11/38b-c), Schwartz, "Gamaliel in Aphrodite's Bath," 216.

circumstances constitute idolatry and which do not, in a manner quite similar to the rabbinic debates in tractate *Avodah Zarah* of the Mishnah.

In establishing a rule of law for Jesus-oriented gentiles, Paul was engaged in the balancing act involved when establishing halakah, taking into consideration the biblical prohibition on idolatry and its prevalent interpretations, as well as the social situation of Jesus-oriented gentiles in a pagan society, including their need to interact with worshippers of Greco-Roman gods, the specific conditions of the community in Corinth, including the various degrees of commitment among its gentile members. Ruling that intention is the crucial factor that determines whether or not food in a given situation should be considered consecrated to idols, he may well represent a halakic trend within first-century Judaism that was later picked up and developed by the rabbis.

On a final note, one may add that Jewish law is flexible; interpretations and rulings differ among different groups and within the same group, and change over time. Rabbinic sources are much more lenient concerning relations with gentiles than for instance the Qumran texts or *Jubilees,* which call for a clear separation in relation to gentiles:

> Separate yourself from the gentiles, and do not eat with them, and do not perform deeds like theirs. And do not become associates of theirs, because their deeds are defiled, and all of their ways are contaminated, and despicable, and abominable. They slaughter their sacrifices to the dead and to the demons they bow down; and they eat in tombs. And all their deeds are worthless and vain. (*Jub.* 22:16-17)

If any *Jubilees* sympathizers still existed in the time of the Mishnah, they would likely have regarded the rabbis' more lenient rulings as constituting a violation of Jewish law. Indeed, had the rabbis not been the ones to define Jewish law as we know it, a comparison with the strict biblical prohibition of idolatry might have led scholars as well to decide that the rabbis were "breaking the law."

We have no means of knowing whether other Jews regarded Paul as lenient or strict, but in light of the complex nature of Torah observance in general and rabbinic legislation on idolatry in particular, nothing in his reasoning seems to indicate that he had abandoned Jewish law. Taking social reality into account when establishing a rule of law is not a compromise of Jewish law—it is an intrinsic part of the halakic process. As I hope to have illustrated using examples from the decision-making processes within contemporary Judaism, different halakic authorities negotiate the balancing act between the various factors involved in the process differently, but to varying degrees they all take into account social reality along with precedents within Jewish law together with theological and ethical general principles.

4

The Question of Conceptualization: Qualifying Paul's Position on Circumcision in Dialogue with Josephus's Advisors to King Izates

Mark D. Nanos

Jews practicing Judaism in the first century observed the rite of circumcision,[1] so it may seem natural enough to conclude that Paul's arguments depreciating,[2] when not opposing, circumcision

---

1. A version of this essay was presented at the "Re-Reading Paul as a Second-Temple Jewish Author," Nangeroni Meeting of the Enoch Seminar, Rome, June 23-27, 2014.
2. In one of the few comments that could suggest some Jews might not have practiced circumcision, the Jewish allegorist Philo objects to those who might propose that the literal practice can be annulled because circumcision signifies excising passions and destroys impious opinions (*Migration* 89–91); his objection serves to prove the rule. Knowledge of this Jewish practice among non-Jews is widely attested; e.g., from the first and early second cent. ce:

undermine the very idea that Paul should be interpreted as a representative of Judaism.[3] But Paul's position is much more nuanced than the readings on which the interpretive tradition's conclusions depend; so too is the practice of the rite within Judaism. I will argue that when Paul's statements on circumcision are qualified contextually and examined alongside similarly qualified statements made by other Jews, they reveal a Jew who opposed the circumcision of a particular group of non-Jews for very specific reasons, reasons that logically imply that he did not in any way trivialize or oppose the continued covenantal value of circumcision for Jews who expressed faith in (or better yet, faithfulness to) Jesus Christ, including himself. Another way to put this is that Paul opposed Christ-following non-Jews becoming Jews (i.e., "converting" to Jewish ethnic identity), but he did not oppose, and instead promoted, them practicing Judaism, (i.e., "converting" into a Jewish way of living), alongside of Jews who did so, such as himself.

When Jews discuss circumcision, unless specifically stating otherwise, they are referring to Jewish parents dedicating their eight-day-old infant sons to a rite of passage that appealed to a covenant initiated by God. In that covenant, Abraham and his descendants through Isaac and Jacob/Israel (the Israelites) were commanded to faithfully practice this rite forever (Gen. 17:9-14; Lev. 12:3).[4] Jewish texts almost always address the circumcision of Jews; they rarely

---

Horace, *Sat.* 1.9.68-70; Petronius, *Sat.* 102.14; Josephus, *Ag. Ap.* 2.137; Epictetus, *Discourses.* 2.9.19-21; Juvenal, *Sat.* 14.96-106 (for non-Jews as part of a progression of taking up Jewish practices); Tacitus, *Hist.* 5.5.1-2 (for non-Jews who become Jews); Suetonius, *Domitian* 12.2; see Shaye J. D. Cohen, *The Beginnings of Jewishness: Boundaries, Varieties, Uncertainties*, Hellenistic Culture and Society 31 (Berkeley: University of California Press, 1999), 29–49. See also Neil Elliott's chapter in this volume, "The Question of Politics: Paul as a Diaspora Jew under Roman Rule."

3. E.g., Rom. 2:25-29; 1 Cor. 7:19; Gal. 5:2, 6; 6:15; Phil. 3:2-8.

4. David A. Bernat, *Sign of the Covenant: Circumcision in the Priestly Tradition*, Ancient Israel and Its Literature 3 (Atlanta: Society of Biblical Literature, 2009); Matthew Theissen, *Contesting Conversion: Genealogy, Circumcision, and Identity in Ancient Judaism and Christianity* (New York: Oxford University Press, 2011).

discuss the circumcision of *non-Jews*, and when they do, these cases are explicitly signaled (e.g., those who are a part of extended Jewish households such as slaves, those who live in the land of Israel, and those seeking to become Jews). When it comes to conceptualizing and drawing conclusions about Paul's arguments regarding circumcision, however, the (otherwise) exceptional case of whether certain non-Jews should undertake this rite is the explicit topic at issue, not the circumcision of Jewish infant sons. In spite of this contextual qualification, Paul's arguments continue to be read as if he was expounding a universal rule applicable to Jews as well as to non-Jews, Christ-followers or not, as if he opposed circumcision for everyone.

Notwithstanding the fact that there were other peoples who practiced circumcision according to different customs, Paul employs the term *circumcision*, like other Jews in general, to signify the identity of males marked as Jews or Israelites according to the guidelines of Torah, who are thereby distinguished from all other peoples. Paul sometimes uses the term "circumcision" and "circumcised" as metonyms for "Jew," and "foreskinned" as a metonym for "non-Jew" (e.g., Rom. 3:29—4:12; 15:8-9; Gal. 2:7-12). The way that Paul uses the metonym "the circumcision" in these texts suggests that he has in mind Jews by birth as well as any males who have had their foreskin cut off in order to become Jews (i.e., proselytes), and, by logical extension, any (physically uncircumcised) women belonging to the households of these circumcised men.

Interpreters recognize that when Paul addresses the topic of circumcision, he has in view a procedure only performed on males, even though his metonymical usage applies to Jews as a group differentiated from non-Jews, and thus implicitly includes females in spite of their not being physically circumcised (or, alternatively, foreskinned).[5] However, a comparable implicit qualification is not applied to defining whose circumcision Paul specifically opposes, and why. Yet in every case available to us, Paul's arguments to resist being circumcised have nothing to do with opposing Jewish parents committing their eight-day-old sons to this rite, or of non-Jews committing their infant sons to circumcision either, just as they are not about women (the circumcision of whom interpreters assume was not the concern of Paul or those with whom he argued). Rather, his arguments are specifically directed to and about whether *adult, male, non-Jews* should undertake circumcision. Moreover, and just as importantly, Paul's opposition is further qualified: he opposes the circumcision of specific adult male non-Jews who are *already followers of Christ.*[6] That being the case, then it follows that Paul's position on circumcision is misrepresented if it is stated, without proper qualification, that *Paul opposed circumcision.*

If we want to make comparisons between Paul and other Jewish interpreters, we must seek to find and qualify any comparative material from other Jews and Jewish groups on *circumcision of non-Jews.* In addition, we must attend to any additional qualifications of those non-Jews with respect to *time, location,* and *situation* in terms that recognize that we are comparing these views to Paul's teaching about non-Jews who have become identified in a particularly Jewish way, that is, as believers in the gospel's messianic claims about the meaning of Jesus for themselves as non-Jews (cf. Rom. 1:1-6; 1 Cor. 15:1-28; Gal. 1:1-3; 3:6-9, 14; Phil. 2:4-13). The message in which they have believed involves the propositional claim that the end of the ages has begun within the midst of the present age, initiating the reconciliation of the *kosmos.* I will refer to this claim throughout this

---

5. Circumcised/foreskinned is also used by Paul and other Jews in an obviously non-literal sense to refer to the state of the heart (Lev. 26:41; Deut. 10:16; 30:6; Jer. 4:4; *Jub.* 1:22-24; Rom. 2:29); see Bernat, *Sign of the Covenant,* 97–114, 129.

6. Christ = Jesus as Christ/Messiah, throughout.

essay as "chronometrical," to indicate that Paul's position on what is appropriate within Judaism for Christ-followers is specifically related to his conviction that the awaited age has dawned already within the present age, thus requiring some adjustments to prevailing halakah; it is not the result of a difference of opinion about the values of Judaism per se (such as "works" or "boundary marking behavior").

The gospel's chronometrical claim creates the basis for Paul's resistance to circumcision of Christ-following non-Jews. He believes that now they must represent those from the other nations turning to the One God of Israel and the world, and thus, that they must not become Israelites, as would have been the case before this change of aeons had begun, and instead remain representatives of the other nations. If they were to change their identity to Israelite or Jew at this point, the gospel's propositional claim that the future utopian period prophesied in Jewish Scriptures had arrived[7]—albeit, surprisingly, within the midst of the present "evil age"—would not be made manifest. But Paul believes this reality *is* manifest in how their subgroup gatherings (*ekklēsia*) of Israelites and non-Israelites live and worship together without discrimination even though retaining ethnic, gender, and other significant differences (cf. Rom. 3:29—4:25; 15:4-13; Gal. 1:4; 3:1—4:7; Acts 15). We will discuss this matter more below, because it significantly shapes the concerns of Paul's letters, creating the often confusing and even adversarial circumstances from which the Christ-following non-Jews he seeks to console and challenge are seeking relief.

Close consideration of some examples from other Jewish writers of Paul's period regarding circumcision, when similarly qualified, show that other representatives of "Judaism" also have been conceptualized

---

7. Such as the arrival of the day when the wolf will lie down and eat with the lamb; Isa. 65:25. See Terence L. Donaldson, *Judaism and the Gentiles: Jewish Patterns of Universalism (to 135 CE)* (Waco, TX: Baylor University Press, 2007), esp. 499–505.

by interpreters in ways that universalize what the players instead delivered in very particularistic terms. In this essay, we will consider an example from a story related by Josephus that includes sharply different views about whether, following his commitment to practice a Jewish way of life, the King of Adiabene, a non-Jew, should be circumcised, which, in this case, is interpreted as a step that would make him a Jew, and, moreover, could be understood by his subjects to mean that they must likewise become Jews.

Josephus's Narrative about the Circumcision of the Non-Jew Izates, King of Adiabene

The portrayal of King Izates sketched by Josephus is related in a story he purports to have taken place within Diaspora Judaism. It takes place during Paul's time and describes different Jewish teachers' views on the topic of non-Jews *behaving like* Jews (or "jewishly," practicing Judaism) versus also *becoming* Jews (*Ant.* 20.17-48; the story continues to 20.96). Josephus portrays two Jewish advisors, Ananias and Eleazar (a third is introduced in 20.35, although he remains unnamed and his views unclear), who strongly disagree about whether, for Izates, the prince and later king of a Parthian client territory, faithfulness required that he also become circumcised, thereby "definitively" (or "certainly" or "firmly," *bebaiōs*) becoming "a Jew," or whether faithfulness for him was best expressed by continuing to be a non-Jew who worshiped God and practiced pious adherence to a Jewish way of life while remaining foreskinned (20.38-48).[8]

8. Josephus does not indicate that these Jews are in any formal sense missionaries advocating non-Jews behave in Jewish ways or become Jews; they may well be engaged in business or travel and simply responding to interest expressed in their religious identity and practices. At the same time, Josephus is aware of many Jews in Babylon and in the major cities of Parthia, and of their collection, treasury, and transportation of the tax for the Jerusalem Temple, so it is possible that

Josephus characterizes the change that the non-Jew Izates makes to living like a Jew or practicing Judaism—short of undertaking circumcision, which is at issue—variously as a choice to live according to Jewish *ethos* ("custom" or "habit"), *nomos* ("law," "convention," or "principle"), or *patrios* ("ancestral [tradition]"). There is a clear demarcation in this story between a (male) non-Jew *becoming* a Jew via circumcision and *behaving like* a Jew, that is, behaving jewishly while remaining a non-Jew. One of the curious elements of this story is that besides the Jewish advisors to Izates and his mother Helena (and their entourages), Josephus makes no mention of Jewish communities or of their involvement in them, if present.[9] The case for their practice of Jewishness/Judaism while remaining non-Jews is described in very individualistic and familial terms for the time period, yet at the same time it expresses the importance of the implications of their actions for the people of the kingdom under their reign, which is the political context that influences the different positions advocated or taken by the few Jews and non-Jews around which the narrative turns.[10]

Josephus places the story within a Diaspora setting during Paul's period (20.15-17), even though Josephus published the account roughly fifty years later.[11] Moreover, Josephus discusses the specific

some exposure to Jewish communities is understood by him to precede the interest shown in Judaism by these non-Jews (*Ant.* 18.310-313, 314-379).

9. This case contrasts with Cohen's observation that "from the Jewish perspective, without social conversion—that is, without the integration of a gentile into Jewish society—there is no conversion at all; the gentile remains a gentile" (Cohen, *Beginnings of Jewishness*, 168). Moreover, the views expressed by Ananias and Eleazar, according to Josephus, provides evidence that some Jews did consider proselytes to be Jews, in addition to the many examples of non-Jews regarding that to be the case (cf. 160-62).

10. The subsequent interest in, e.g., travel to, patronage of, and burial in Judea—some of Izates's sons even joined the Revolt against Rome—is not to be overlooked, of course, so there is a salient geographical implication (i.e., Judeanness). However, it remains curious that no Jewish communities or participation in Jewish communal gatherings in Adiabene are mentioned, in addition to fact that none of the nobles or subjects of the kingdom beyond the royal family and entourage (although initially winning their respect [20.49]) are described as joining them either to observe Judaism or to become Jews.

matter of non-Jews (male and female) being taught conflicting interpretations regarding how best to express piety toward God by Josephus's various Jewish teachers, who articulate their positions by way of terminology very similar to Paul's.

Ananias, a Jewish merchant who has influenced several women of the royal family in Charax Spasini, where the prince was sent for safekeeping until his time to reign in Adiabene arrived, is presented as having "persuaded" or "urged" (*synanepeisen*) Izates, like these women, "to worship God [the Deity] according to the Jewish ancestral traditions [*ōs Ioudaiois patrion*]" (20.34-35). At the same time, Izates's mother is presented as taking up Jewish ways of living under the direction of a Jew (who remains unnamed) in Adiabene, where Izates's father ruled (20.34-35). Upon returning to become king in Adiabene, Izates learned of his mother's joy in taking up a Jewish way of life ("rejoicing in the Jew's customs [*tois Ioudaiōn ethesin*]," 20.38; referred to also as "their laws" or "conventions" (*nomous*) in 20.35). Izates thus resolved to go beyond merely adopting the customs, being now "zealous to also change [or "cross over" or "convert," *metathesthai*] into it himself" (20.38).

Izates is not depicted merely as deciding to begin to behave in Jewish ways but as reasoning that he would not be "definitively" [or "certainly" or "genuinely" or "firmly," *bebaiōs*] a Jew [*Ioudaios*] if he

---

11. Why Josephus developed the story in the way that he did and related it at the end of this volume are beyond the scope of this essay (cf. Daniel R. Schwartz, *Reading the First Century: On Reading Josephus and Studying Jewish History of the First Century* [WUNT 300; Tübingen: Mohr Siebeck, 2013].). Interestingly, there is corroborating historical evidence of some of the figures and features of the story; see Tessa Rajak, "The Parthians in Josephus," in *Das Partherreich und seine Zeugnisse: Beiträge des internationalen Colloquiums, Eutin (27. - 30 Juni 1996)*, ed. J. Wiesehöfer (Stuttgart: Franz Steiner, 1998), 309–24. For rabbinic material related to these figures, see Lawrence H. Schiffman, "The Conversion of the Royal House of Abiabene [*sp*] in Josephus and Rabbinic Sources," in *Josephus, Judaism, and Christianity*, ed. Louis H. Feldman and Gohei Hata (Detroit: Wayne State University Press, 1987), 293–312; Louis H. Feldman, *Jew and Gentile in the Ancient World: Attitudes and Interactions from Alexander to Justinian* (Princeton, NJ: Princeton University Press, 1993), 328–31.

has not been circumcised, which he was ready to do" (20.38; emphasis added). This deduction is made before the arrival of the other Jew, Eleazar, at Izates's court, who will advocate for that position (20.43, which we will discuss below), so it remains unclear how Izates reached this conclusion already in the narrative. The distinction between Izates having adopted Jewish customs until this point and what he now wants to do suggests that he understood his mother to be a Jewess, not simply a non-Jew who practiced Jewish customs such as he had been doing, although Josephus does not spell this out.[12] This matter remains unclear since circumcision did not apply to females.[13] Immediately, his mother strongly objects to the idea of his being circumcised, fearing that his subjects would reason that he "desired them to learn obedience to ways [or "customs," *ethōn*] that are strange and foreign for them," for they would not, she predicts, "endure being ruled by a Jew" (or "Judean," 20.39). Ananias, who accompanied Izates when he returned to Adiabene, agreed with the objection and threatened to leave the kingdom, fearing for his own welfare if the king would undertake to become a Jew through circumcision. Here the geo-politico-ethnic distinction "Judean," which is signified by the same word translated as "Jew," *Ioudaios*, may well be the better choice of translation, although it is not overall, since the rest of the narrative makes clear that Izates is the king of another people in another land, even though he and his mother (and others) adopt Jewish ways of life and even give aid to the people of Judea.[14]

---

12. Cf. Donaldson, *Judaism and the Gentiles*, 334–35.
13. Cf. Shaye J. D. Cohen, *Why Aren't Jewish Women Circumcised? Gender and Covenant in Judaism* (Berkeley: University of California Press, 2005). Perhaps circumcision was raised by the unnamed teacher of Helena in Adiabene, or perhaps if Helena was indeed regarded to have become a Jew under his direction then Izates inferred that for him this would involve the rite of circumcision.
14. Cf. Cohen, *Beginnings*, 79. See Daniel R. Schwartz, "'Judaean' or 'Jew'? How Should We Translate *Ioudaios* in Josephus?," in *Jewish Identity in the Greco-Roman World = Jüdische Identität*

Notably, in 20.41 (cf. 46-48), Ananias says he fears punishment because he would be held responsible for teaching the king of this people what they would object to as "improper deeds [or "works" or "rites," *erga*]" for their king or themselves. Moreover, Ananias finishes his sentence by instructing the king "to worship [*sebein*; literally, "honor," "respect," or "fear"] God without circumcision; even though he by all means did resolve to be zealous for the ancestral traditions [*patria*] of the Jews, this is superior [*kyriōteron*; literally, lordlier] to being circumcised" (20.41).[15] Ananias then argues that God "will have forgiveness" toward Izates for "not performing the act" (or "work" or "rite," *ergon*) of circumcision because of the constraints of his situation as king of a people who are not Jews (in this case Josephus uses the singular).

Ananias upheld *in his case—specifically for Izates as a king of a non-Jewish people—* that practicing the ideals of the group identified as

in der griechisch-römischen Welt, ed. Jörg Frey, Daniel R. Schwartz, and Stephanie Gripentrog (Leiden: Brill, 2007), 3–27; Mark D. Nanos, "Paul and Judaism: Why Not Paul's Judaism?" in *Paul Unbound: Other Perspectives on the Apostle*, ed. Mark D. Given (Peabody, MA: Hendrickson, 2010), 117 n. 2, for additional discussion and bibliography that leads me to usually prefer "Jew" over "Judean" to translate *Ioudaios* for discussing Paul.

15. Daniel R. Schwartz, "God, Gentiles, and Jewish Law: On Acts 15 and Josephus's Adiabene Narrative," in *Geschichte—Tradition—Reflection: Festschrift für Martin Hengel zum 70. Geburtstag*, ed. Hubert Cancik, Hermann Lichtenberger, and Peter Schäfer (Tübingen: Mohr Siebeck, 1996), 263–82, argues that Izates merely *decided* to follow Jewish customs rather than that he actually began to practice them, that *touton* refers back to the decision itself, so that what Izates had done is begun to fear the god of the Jews (267–72). But *touton* refers back not simply to Izates's decision/resolve per se, but to his specific decision/resolve "*to be zealous for the ancestral traditions.*" That suggests that Izates was already observing *all* of them *except* circumcision, which he wanted to rectify by being circumcised too: "he decided [or: resolved] *to be zealous for all* of the ancestral traditions of the Jews; to be this [*tout{on}*: i.e., decided/ resolved *to be zealous for . . .*] is superior of one to being circumcised" (20.41; emphasis added). That Ananias is reacting to the new development, Izates's decision to be circumcised, in the statement in 20.41, also undermines Schwartz's case that Ananias and Helena are objecting to any kind of practice of Jewish customs as dangerous, for Ananias has been "urging" (Schwartz's interpretation) Jewish customs on members of the royal house until the topic of circumcision now arises. Again, that it has suddenly arisen implies that the teacher of Helena, new to the storyline, has brought up this matter of becoming a Jew versus merely acting like a Jew (in a less than complete way, i.e., apart from circumcision).

circumcised is a more appropriate way to honor the God of the Jews (to practice Judaism) than being circumcised (becoming a Jew) would be.[16] Ananias does not fear reprisals from Izates's subjects for advocating that Izates live jewishly in terms of *nomos*, *ethos*, and *patria*, and he in fact teaches Izates to faithfully continue to do so, but Ananias insists that Izates *not* do so in terms of one particular Jewish *ergon* that would make him a Jew—circumcision![17] These arguments persuaded Izates to forgo circumcision—or at least to put it off for a while (20.42). That is, he decided to remain a non-Jew but to behave *jewishly*, or, perhaps to maintain this distinction from being Jewish in the sense of becoming a Jew, perhaps we should say that Izates

---

16. Cf. Donaldson, *Paul and the Gentiles*, 68–69, similarly argues that Ananias opposes proselyte conversion (becoming a Jew), although he does not distinguish between becoming a Jew and practicing Judaism as a non-Jew in the way I am proposing was at work here.

17. Gary Gilbert, "The Making of a Jew: 'God-Fearer' or Convert in the Story of Izates," *Union Seminary Quarterly Review* 44, no. 3–4 (1991): 299–313, argues that Izates was already regarded as a Jew before he was circumcised. Gilbert's argument that there were men born to Jews who were not circumcised yet regarded as Jews does not equally apply to men born to non-Jews who are not circumcised being regarded as Jews, and he presents no evidence under that qualification, which he also does not raise. Gilbert could have pointed to Paul's language in Romans 2:25-29, according to the prevailing interpretations, which conclude that Paul is calling foreskinned non-Jews true Jews if their hearts are circumcised. But I disagree with that interpretation for Paul too (see Mark D. Nanos, "Paul's Non-Jews Do Not Become 'Jews,' But Do They Become 'Jewish'?" *Journal of the Jesus Movement in its Jewish Setting* 1, no. 1 [2014]: 26–53, www.jjmjs.org). Paul argues that (male) non-Jews who are not circumcised implicitly endorse God's judgment of Jews who are but who do not live up to the set-apart lifestyle that being circumcised marks them to pursue, that circumcision of the flesh of such Jews is undermined if not accompanied by circumcision of their heart. That is not the same thing as attributing circumcision or Jewish ethnic identity to non-Jews; it only shows that they can be equals or even superior to ethnic Jews in terms of God's acceptance of them, although remaining non-Jews. Similarly, mutatis mutandis, one might speak of a non-Catholic showing up Catholics by behaving according to a Catholic ideal that some Catholics may fail to uphold—but that is not the same thing as maintaining that this non-Catholic is actually thereby a Catholic entitled to the sacraments. For Paul, at least, being a male Jew must include being circumcised, a point of ethnic identification that remains salient in all his extant correspondence to non-circumcised male *ethnē*, whom he seeks to persuade to remain non-Jews by not undertaking circumcision, and yet to practice Judaism wholeheartedly. Paul, at least, keeps ethnic identity of male Jews and religious identity of the practice of Judaism separate, as does Josephus here, at least with respect to the male Izates; as noted already, that distinction appears to have been ambiguous in the case of women, Helena being the case in point.

decided to continue to be and behave "Jewish*ish*." We will return to discuss this terminological matter more below.

Josephus then presents the arrival of a new figure on the scene in 20.43, Eleazar, who is introduced with the caveat that Izates had not yet given up his desire to become circumcised: thus Eleazar "urged him [Izates] to accomplish 'the work' [or "the rite," *ton ergon*]." Eleazar is a Jew from Galilee, and likely a Pharisee; at least Josephus identifies him in a way that he elsewhere characterizes as Pharisaism: "being extremely precise [*akribēs*] about the ancestral traditions [*ta patria*]."[18] Thereafter, the reader is made aware of two conflicting Jewish interpretations of what is faithful (appropriate/legitimate/ justified) for the non-Jew king Izates with respect to the practice of Judaism where circumcision arises for himself (and by implication, for his kingdom). Once more in this narrative Josephus refers to circumcision with the word *ergon*, commonly translated "work," preceded by the article, thus "*the* act" (or "deed" or "work"), in this context perhaps best translated as "the rite"[19] involved in a male's *becoming a Jew*! Eleazar challenges the teaching of Ananias that Izates ought *to remain a non-Jew who behaves jewishly, who adopts a Jewish way of life, who faithfully practices Judaism.*[20]

Finding Izates reading the Torah [*nomos*] of Moses, Eleazar confronts him for failure to comply with its prescriptions: "In your ignorance, O king, you are guilty of the greatest injustice [or "unrighteousness," *adikōn*] against the Torah and thereby against God. For you ought not merely to read the Torah but also, and even more, to do what is commanded in it. How long will you

---

18. See *Ant.* 17.41; *War* 1.110; 2.162; *Life* 191; cf. Acts 26:5.

19. For the Loeb volume, Feldman translates *ergon* as "rite" three times, in 20.42-43, 46, referring to circumcision. In view of the very specific ethno-religious re-identification at issue for undertaking this "act," rite seems warranted.

20. See Nanos, "Paul's Non-Jews Do Not Become 'Jews,' But Do They Become 'Jewish'?" for additional examples from Josephus.

continue to be uncircumcised? If you have not read the rule [or "law" or "principle," *nomos*] concerning this matter, read it now, so that you may know what an impiety [*asebeia*] it is that you commit" (20.44-45; Loeb with a few changes). Although Torah does not actually instruct non-Israelites to undertake circumcision (except, e.g., slaves of Israelites), Eleazar defines a faithful response to reading Torah for this non-Jew seeking instruction therein to involve *completing the action* of the rule that Torah commands for Abraham's descendants, and Israelites in particular—not simply the willingness to do so if one was free of constraints, such as the exception raised by Ananias depends upon. Hearing this logic, Izates calls for the physician in order to be circumcised and "complete what was commanded [*to prostaxthen etelei*]," thereby accomplishing "the act" or "rite" (*tou ergon*) around which the controversy turns.[21]

We must leave off the story here and turn to summarizing some of the details especially relevant for comparing various Jewish views on the circumcision of non-Jews raised by Josephus's account to the arguments of Paul against the circumcision of (Christ-following) non-Jews.

Josephus uses the word *ergon* in the singular and *erga* in the plural to refer specifically to the rite of circumcision involved in a non-Jew becoming a Jew, without it signifying additional ritual or other elements of Torah-defined behavior observed by Jews, or even by non-Jews, such as in diets and days. Josephus defines this *ergon* in the context of what *nomos* commands, specifically for males who wish to observe the Torah completely by becoming Jews through the action of circumcision, an action that completes an ethnic identity

---

21. Interestingly, the Priestly tradition in the Tanakh enjoining the rite of circumcision does not describe who carries out the act, just as it does not elaborate many of the other elements of the processes involved, although these will be delineated in later Jewish traditions, especially in the rabbinic literature. Bernat, *Sign of the Covenant*, 125, 129–31; Cohen, *Beginnings*, 198–238, discusses the later rabbinic conversion ceremony.

transformation, although Josephus does not employ the phrase *erga nomou*, a topic to which we will return. Although the word *ergon* simply means "work" as in "action," "deed," or "labor," in this case Josephus uses it to denote the "act" involving the "rite" of circumcision by which a (male) non-Jew becomes a Jew.[22] Moreover, Josephus later (20.48) summarizes Izates's piety (in context, by having completed this act/rite) in the face of the temptation to avoid doing so to protect his interests as an act of *"faith(fulness) alone [monō pepisteukosin]"!*[23] Because of his complete trust in God, Izates succeeded, against opposition both from his own people and from foreign invaders, which Izates (and through him, Josephus) attributes to "God's providence [*pronoian*]" (20.91 [75-91]). Izates's trust is defined by Josephus according to Eleazar's interpretation of proper faith(fulness) as involving this act/rite in spite of the political risks involved, versus Ananias's interpretation according to which proper faith(fulness) called for *avoidance* of this act/rite due to the unique contingencies of Izates's present situation.

22. The physician is not identified as a Jew, and likely was not, and there is no indication that a Jewish *mohel* or anyone else capable of performing the ritual of *brit milah* was available in Adiabene. Apparently, a non-Jew undergoing this act with the intent to become a Jew was deemed by Josephus's characters to be equivalent to undertaking the ethno-religious rite that it signifies in Torah.

23. I use "faith(fulness)" throughout to both respect and challenge the way that *pistis* is generally translated and interpreted for Paul as if it represented "belief" in contrast to action or deeds or works or effort, and for translating Josephus's story, to highlight the comparison being drawn within Judaism. I am convinced that faithfulness in the sense of "trust," "loyalty," inclusive of the commitment to take the actions concomitant with what one believes, expresses better what Paul sought to communicate by way of *pistis* and its cognates, just as it does for Josephus and other Jewish writers in general, including the LXX when translating *'emuna*. See now my effort to demonstrate this throughout Romans in the annotations presented in Mark D. Nanos, "The Letter of Paul to the Romans," in *The Jewish Annotated New Testament: New Revised Standard Version Bible Translation*, ed. Amy-Jill Levine and Marc Zvi Brettler (New York: Oxford University Press, 2011), 253–86; see also Caroline Johnson Hodge, *If Sons, Then Heirs: A Study of Kinship and Ethnicity in the Letters of Paul* (New York: Oxford University Press, 2007), esp. 79–91; Neil Elliott, *The Arrogance of Nations: Reading Romans in the Shadow of Empire*, Paul in Critical Contexts (Minneapolis: Fortress Press, 2008), 44–47; Kathy Ehrensperger, *Paul at the Crossroads of Cultures: Theologizing in the Space Between* (London: Bloomsbury, 2013), 160–74.

In spite of Josephus's upholding the ideal of Izates's decision to become a Jew by circumcision as the faithful course supported by God, Josephus depicts both Jewish teachers articulating what actions would best express faith(fulness) for Izates. Eleazar holds that *faithfulness* would only be demonstrated on Izates's part by his *completing the act or rite of circumcision* to become a Jew, in concert with all the rest of the acts involved in observing a Jewish way of life as prescribed in Torah. Ananias bases his argument that Izates will be forgiven by God for not being circumcised on the premise that Izates's *faithfulness* would be best exemplified by the king of a non-Jewish people *observing a Jewish way of life* as prescribed in Torah *apart from circumcision*, apart from becoming a Jew, and thus, apart from becoming under Torah on the same terms as a Jew (a distinction that the people of his kingdom are represented as grasping, along with the implications for themselves as subjects).

As noted, Izates (and his mother) are already practicing a Jewish way of life consisting of many Jewish customs (or laws or rules); nevertheless, Izates is not a Jew in the way that faith(fulness) to undertake the work or act or rite of circumcision would make him. Moreover, taking this particular Jewish action or rite (*ergon*) to be circumcised (or, in the case of the plural *erga*, we might paraphrase: the actions or rites related to this transformation ultimately signified by the act or rite of circumcision) is expected to lead to rebellion against him, although no fear is expressed concerning resistance to his zealous pursuit of a Jewish way of life *while remaining a non-Jew*.

That Izates's (and Helena's) Jewish behavior is otherwise not portrayed as objectionable raises the prospect that Josephus understood that such behavior in honor of another people's god was acceptable within this pantheistic culture, whereas converting to that god in full (at least in the case of the Jewish deity) represented a rejection of all other gods and concomitant cultural standards. In other words, according to this narrative, a non-Jew can practice Judaism (faith[fulness] to God according to a Jewish way of life) without becoming a Jew (by way of the *ergon* of circumcision), but a non-Jew who practices Judaism (faith[fulness] to God according to a Jewish way of life) inclusive of the *ergon* of circumcision experiences an ethnic identity transformation from non-Jew into Jew.[24]

Thus the issue around the *ergon* of circumcision in this story about non-Jews is solely about the rite that transforms a non-Jew's identity into that of a Jew; it is not about the value of the rite for Jews, for example, whether a Jew such as Ananias should circumcise his own son, if he had one. Moreover, this raises interesting comparisons with Paul's insistence that faith(fulness) for Christ-following non-Jews requires abstaining from becoming Jews through circumcision, while at the same time insisting that they turn away from cult associated with familial and civic gods, which would be expected to apply to themselves in most Jewish groups, it appears, only if they had become Jews. Such unorthodox behavior creates for them an anomalous identity leading to sociopolitical marginalization, both from Jews, who do not share their chronometrical gospel claim to be neither guests nor proselytes but full members alongside of Jews, and, for different reasons, from their non-Jewish families and neighbors. If even those who become proselytes may be regarded with suspicion as atheists and traitors, then likely all the more threatening would be those who remained non-Jews, if they simultaneously claimed the right to abstain from honoring their fellow non-Jewish people's gods and lords (cf. Josephus, *War* 2.463; Tacitus, *Hist.* 5.5.1-2).[25]

---

24. Not all Jews agreed that non-Jews could become Jews even by completing circumcision (see Theissen, *Contesting Conversion*); however, those Jews who held that non-Jews could become Jews/Israelites, even those who differentiated between proselytes and Jews/Israelites, maintained the requirement of (adult male) circumcision (see Cohen, *Beginnings*).

Caveat: A Few Discursive Suggestions for Those Seeking to Evaluate Paul and His View of Circumcision in Terms of Judaism

Changing the discourse about Paul by adding a contextual tag to virtually every statement made about his standing on Jewish matters, such as the circumcision of non-Jews, is a good place to begin for those who are attempting to conceptualize Paul within Judaism, and a discipline that ought to be considered by those who oppose the enterprise as well.[26] In the shortest sense, this could consist of no more than adding the phrase ". . . *for Christ-following non-Jews*" to statements made about them in particular in order to avoid universalizing the matter under discussion. Occasionally this will need to be revised to define some other group identity, depending upon the referents of Paul's argument, such as, "*for non-Christ-following Jews*," and so on. Moreover, while hardly making for elegant or punchy writing, it would also be useful to signal regularly that we are talking about a social context within subgroups of the Jewish communities, and thus to state that this is Paul's view on a topic by adding: "*for Christ-following non-Jews who are participating in Jewish communal life*"; this phrase could be shortened to "*for Christ-following non-Jews who practice Judaism*." To qualify it more specifically, and, again, sacrifice brevity, the phrase could be completed, ". . . *who practice Judaism according to the teachings of Paul*," or, in short form, ". . . *who practice Paul's Judaism*" or, in terms of Paul's role within the broader coalition, ". . . *who practice Apostolic Judaism*."[27] Furthermore,

---

25. Cf. Paula Fredriksen's essay in this volume, "The Question of Worship: Gods, Pagans, and the Redemption of Israel." I have traced this sociopolitical dynamic in depth for the Galatian addressees in *The Irony of Galatians: Paul's Letter in First-Century Context* (Minneapolis: Fortress Press, 2002).

26. Nanos, "Paul and Judaism," 117–60.

27. "Apostolic Judaism" is one possible way that Anders Runesson and I have proposed to express the idea that Paul is a representative of a larger movement or coalition within Judaism that

it is important to continually articulate that Paul's position on these matters is predicated upon the chronometrical claim of the gospel that the end of the ages, which many who practice Judaism await, has arrived, and that *this* is the reason for the policy changes toward these non-Jews; hence, for example, to write, *"for Christ-following non-Jews who practice Judaism according to the chronometrical claim of the gospel proclaimed by Paul and the other apostolic leaders of this Judaism."*[28]

Practicing this discipline of specificity for Paul's statements, and mutatis mutandis, for evaluating anyone else's statement to which we seek to compare or contrast Paul, will reveal the questionable bases for many of the features upon which the ubiquitous portrayals of Paul as an apostate or an anomalous figure in terms of Judaism depend. It can at least help those willing to consider conceptualizing Paul within Judaism to avoid inadvertently reinscribing the paradigmatic portrait of a Paul who by definition must find fault with and distance himself from Judaism (whether ostensibly for wrong ideas or motives, works-righteousness, ethnocentrism, and so on, as traditional and New Perspective on Paul interpreters have done and continue to do).[29]

With these basic parameters for conceptualizing and discussing both Paul and Judaism on the topic of circumcision now set out, we are prepared at least to consider the option of reading Paul within Judaism.

---

believes Jesus is the Messiah, a Jewish subgroup whose leaders are known as "apostles," even if there may be tensions or conflicts, even factions developing among these subgroups.

28. For an approach to Paul as representative rather than rival of the Jerusalem apostolic leadership as usually portrayed, see Mark D. Nanos, "Intruding 'Spies' and 'Pseudo-brethren': The Jewish Intra-Group Politics of Paul's Jerusalem Meeting (Gal 2:1-10)," in *Paul and His Opponents*, ed. Stanley E. Porter (Boston: Brill, 2005), 59–97.

29. See Appendix.

Portraying Paul's View of Circumcision (of Christ-Following Non-Jews) within the Context of Jewish Views Related in Josephus's Narrative

Certainly of interest for comparisons to Paul's views on circumcision is Josephus's use of *erga* and *ergon* to signify the rite of male proselyte conversion by the specific action of circumcision. Although Izates's advisors do not use the word *pistis* in direct contrast to *ergon*, as discussed, both make their case based upon whether the action or rite best represents faithfulness for him. Ananias argues for maintaining a distinction between faithfulness for the non-Jew Izates, which is properly expressed by turning to God and practicing Jewish ways of life (*nomoi, ethoi, patria*), and becoming a Jew by way of the *ergon* of circumcision, which would in his view be inappropriate and express unfaithfulness in this case. In contrast, Eleazar argues that to properly express faithfulness Izates must also become a Jew through the *ergon* of circumcision, which is a special action (or work or deed or rite) having to do with identification as a Jew that is distinguishable from undertaking to practice Jewish ways of life while remaining a non-Jew. Importantly, Josephus explicitly connects *pisteuō* (the act of faith[fulness]) with the decision to undertake circumcision later in the story (20.48), when he attributes God's preservation of Izates to his *decision to be circumcised* as the "fruit of piety [*eusebeias*]" toward God by "*faith(fulness)/trust alone* [*monō pepisteukosin*]."

While the contrast between both of these advisors and Paul regarding what signifies faith(fulness) alone for non-Jews is striking, the significant similarities should not be overlooked. Josephus does not attribute God's protection of Izates to his having undertaken the "rite(s)" of circumcision per se, but rather to the *trust in God* that completing this "rite" (or these "rites") signifies, regardless of the potential threat to his welfare that the act (or "acts") is (or are) likely to provoke. This reasoning parallels Paul's argument about Abraham's becoming circumcised as a "sign" of his faithfulness (based upon Gen. 17:11); yet Abraham for Paul illustrates why faith(fulness) for Christ-following non-Jews is shown by their *not* becoming circumcised (Rom. 3:27—4:25; Gal. 3:1—4:7; passim). Paul insists that these non-Jews represent the children promised to Abraham from the other nations before he was circumcised, and thus that they must remain non-Jews, that is, must not become members of Israel.[30]

Josephus expresses approval of Eleazar's approach, wherein *faith(fulness) alone* involves circumcision as the decisive action for the non-Jew Izates, even though it came at the risk of rebellion by his people. In contrast, Paul argues for *faith(fulness) alone* exclusive of circumcision as the decisive action for the Christ-following non-Jews he addressed, even though it came at the price of marginalization. This resulted from the chronometrical gospel based claim to be entitled to full membership within the larger Jewish communities as more than mere guests who adopted certain Jewish behavioral norms; so, for example, they were no longer going to participate in family and civic cult when returning home from Jewish gatherings, unlike what would normally be expected of those who were merely guests. However, it is unlikely that most Jews or non-Jews would accept that such non-Jews were in a position to claim exemption from normal non-Jewish cult observance on the same terms to which Jews could appeal.[31] Paul reminds them that he also suffered marginality on their behalf in order to proclaim this "truth of the gospel." For each position, although upholding the opposite opinion about whether circumcision was appropriate for the non-Jews in view, *faith(fulness)* is expressed in certain ways deemed appropriate/justified/legitimate,

---

30. Cf. Johnson Hodge, *If Sons, Then Heirs*, 93–107.
31. Josephus, *Ant.* 12.138-153; 14.185-267; 16.27-65, 160-178; 19.278-291, 299-316; *War* 2.195-203; Nanos, *Irony of Galatians*, 257–71.

and not in others, depending upon *the interpreter's perspective* about what represents the most faithful course for the person or group in view.

I submit that Paul also means by faith(fulness) apart from circumcision not simply believing in contrast to taking action, especially not in contrast to acts of righteousness, for it is precisely to such behavior that the gospel calls them to be enslaved (cf. Rom. 6; 13; Gal. 5). Paul was not seeking to bifurcate faith and action/deeds by advocating that faith(fulness) for Christ-following non-Jews meant not becoming circumcised, any more than Josephus's Ananias or Eleazar were making such a bifurcation when they alternatively urged the non-Jew Izates to avoid or undertake circumcision as the appropriate course of faith(fulness). The work (or "deed" or "act" or "rite," singular or plural) in view in all of these articulations of faith(fulness) specifically revolves around whether faith(fulness) requires identity transformation into becoming Jews/Israelites or not; it does not revolve around whether Jewish customs such as the observation of Torah-based diets and days are to be undertaken (they are assumed to be already begun by these non-Jews). The contrast Paul draws, just as does Josephus's characters, is in terms of what best represents faithfulness for the players in view with respect to circumcision. Apart from the actions involved in the process of ethnic conversion, the contrast is not being drawn between faith and works in general (as one would expect according to the terms of a traditional Protestant reading), or between faith and so-called boundary marking behavior per se (as one would expect according to the prevailing understanding of the New Perspective).

At issue for Paul is specifically the choice of remaining foreskinned—a metonym for non-Jews that defines them in terms of not having undertaken this rite according to Jewish terms and, thus, as representatives of the nations other than Israel—over the alternative on offer to become Jews, that is, circumcised, which is required to become members of Israel. In contrast to Eleazar's argument, which turns around what is appropriate now for one who is a king of non-Judeans, Paul argues that such an identity transformation is not appropriate for them following the resurrection of Jesus. Why? Because Paul's understanding of what is appropriate now is based on a chronometrical interpretation of the Shema (that the God of Israel is the only God of all the nations "now"). Paul applies the logic of the Shema ("Hear, O Israel, the Lord is our God, the Lord is one [or: the Lord alone]") explicitly in Romans 3:29—4:25 to make the chronometrical gospel case that non-Jews must remain non-Jews with the arrival of the awaited age.[32] He proceeds from the premise that God is already and still unquestionably the God of the Jews, from which he argues that when the "foreskinned" now turn to God through faithfulness to Christ, God thus becomes also the God of the foreskinned, so they must remain representatives from the other nations and not become circumcised, that is, not become Jews/Israelites. According to the gospel's propositional claims for them as non-Jews, Paul requires that they must remain representatives of the other nations who now belong to the God who does right, and thus as those who are committed to doing right. They thereby demonstrate the arrival of the awaited day when all of the nations would submit to the reign of God alongside of Israel, when the One God of Israel will be hailed as the only God by representatives of all of the nations.[33] The argument requires the logical corollary deduction

32. See Mark D. Nanos, "Paul and the Jewish Tradition: The Ideology of the *Shema*," in *Celebrating Paul. Festschrift in Honor of Jerome Murphy-O'Connor, O.P., and Joseph A. Fitzmyer, S.J.*, Catholic Biblical Quarterly Monograph Series 48, ed. Peter Spitaler (Washington, DC: Catholic Biblical Association of America, 2012), 62–80; Nanos, *The Mystery of Romans: The Jewish Context of Paul's Letter* (Minneapolis: Fortress Press, 1996), 179–92.

33. In the Middle Ages, Rashi (on Deut. 6:4) similarly speaks of the futuristic element of the rest of the nations also turning to the One God implicit in Israel's present confession of the Shema: "The Lord who is our God now, but not (yet) the God of the (other) nations, is destined to be

that the circumcised who turn to Christ must remain Jews, hence, remaining under the covenant of Torah made with the nation of Israelites.

In Paul's arguments, faith(fulness) to God is expressed by Christ-following non-Jews when they choose to turn from the worship of the gods of their nations and concomitant behavior to the very ideals of righteousness incumbent upon Israelites as articulated in Israel's Torah (apart from becoming members of Israel through circumcision), even though these non-Jews are not "under" Torah technically, since they do not become Israelites. Why? Because these are the ideals of righteousness for all of humanity, although culturally constructed for Israel as the people of God in a special covenant relationship by which God can enlighten all of humankind.[34]

The reasoning of both Ananias and Eleazar is based on similar values even though they come to opposite conclusions regarding whether Izates should not or should undertake the *ergon* of circumcision. Eleazar clearly appeals to *faithfulness* in the sense of loyalty to the commandment that Izates is reading in the Torah/ Pentateuch. Josephus advocates for this interpretation by the way he refers to Izates's faithfulness to be circumcised in response to Eleazar. And, as discussed, in 20.48 Josephus explains that this accounts for God's faithfulness to preserve Izates when he is later attacked, characterizing this *faith(fulness) as trust in God alone.* Ananias's

---

the One Lord, as it is said, 'For then will I give to the peoples a pure language, that they may all call upon the name of the Lord, to serve Him with one consent' (Zeph 3:9). And (likewise) it is said, 'And the Lord shall be king over all the earth; on that day shall the Lord be One and His name One'" (Zech 14:9)" (trans. from Norman Lamm, *The Shema: Spirituality and Law in Judaism as Exemplified in the Shema, the Most Important Passage in the Torah* [Philadelphia: Jewish Publication Society, 2000], 31).

34. E.g., Paul's argument in 1 Corinthians 8–10 that Christ-following non-Jews must not eat food known to be idol food, provides a useful example of how he approaches them as not under Torah technically and yet beholden to the norms of Torah, including to teaching from the example of Israel; see Mark D. Nanos, "The Polytheist Identity of the 'Weak,' and Paul's Strategy to 'Gain' Them: A New Reading of 1 Corinthians 8:1–11:1," in *Paul: Jew, Greek, and Roman,* ed. Stanley E. Porter, Pauline Studies 5 (Boston: Brill, 2008), 179–210.

argument also does not revolve around bifurcating faith(fulness) from action (or deeds or works). They are two sides of the same coin, yet faith(fulness) for Izates would be compromised, according to his mother and Ananias, if he were to undertake the particular *ergon* of circumcision. Alternatively, according to Eleazar, faithfulness to Torah would be compromised if Izates were not to undertake the *ergon*. Neither one's case involves a denial of the role of faith(fulness), although each advisor might well represent the rival teacher's contrary advice (about circumcision, in this case) to fail precisely to uphold faith(fulness), just as do Paul's arguments against the implied contrary advice of his rivals (e.g., especially about these Christ-following non-Jews undertaking circumcision).

Yet we must account for the fact that Ananias explicitly appeals to *expedience* rather than to principle to dissuade Izates from becoming a Jew by being circumcised. He argues that because Izates is the king of a people who are not Jews, he should be wary lest his subjects reject this identity transformation for him because of its implications for themselves. The implicit premise of Ananias's argument, however, remains an appeal to *faithfulness*. Ananias reasons, as mentioned above, that as a king of a people who are not Jews he ought "to worship God without circumcision; even though he by all means *did resolve to be zealous* for the ancestral traditions of the Jews, to be this is lordlier of one [in your position] than being circumcised" (20.41; emphasis added). In other words, practicing the values of the group identified as circumcised is a more *faithful* way (more proper, more appropriate, more justified) to honor the God of the Jews *for Izates as a king* than being circumcised (becoming a Jew) would be *in his case*. If we translate *kyriōteron* as "lordlier" or "kinglier" rather than "superior," we preserve the possible pun that Josephus (via Ananias) may be making by this choice of adverb: for Izates as "lord" or "king" of a people who are not Jews, the commandment of circumcision is not appropriate. According to Ananias, however, Izates is justified by his faithfulness (alone!) as a non-Jew who is a ruler who seeks to worship the God of the Jews, which involves behaving faithfully according to Jewish customs, but doing so apart from becoming circumcised (i.e., a Jew), which would (inappropriately) imply that the people over which he reigns become circumcised (i.e., Jews) too. What Ananias would teach other non-Jews seeking to be "completely" faithful by becoming Jews through circumcision remains unknown, but, since his objection to Izates doing so is circumstantial, one could infer that given a different set of circumstances, he might agree with Eleazar that the "act" is warranted.

Paul's argument does not appeal to *expedience* in a way similar to Ananias's. Yet many of Paul's interpreters attribute that motive to Paul, suggesting, for example, that adding circumcision to believing the gospel would have inhibited the growth of this movement, both because it required a painful step many men would not undertake, and because such an action was seen as mutilation, thus violating Greco-Roman sensibilities as well as resulting in social limitations thereafter, not least exclusion from educational and related opportunities of *paideia*. It simply would not do for the elite or anyone with elite aspirations. Paul, however, never makes such a case when he insists that the non-Jews who have turned to God through Christ must not become circumcised. Quite to the contrary, he insists that those in Galatia resist any temptation to become circumcised, even though it appears to them that circumcision would actually be the more expedient course, and Paul's rhetorical approach to them suggests that it represents a step that they "want" to take (4:21; passim). In response, Paul appeals to principle, not expedience. He defines the principle as faith(fulness) according to what is appropriate for them as non-Jews, which can be different in specific ways from what faith(fulness) might consist of for those who are Jews.

Paul argues that what is faithful for those from the rest of the nations promised to Abraham and what is faithful for his descendant line are not the same where the *erga nomou* are concerned, that is, the works (or deeds, acts, rites) of the convention or law of circumcision. For Abraham and his ethno-historical descendant line, circumcision is a sign of faithfulness, but not for those from the rest of the nations promised to Abraham.

Paul argues that faithfulness is different for Jew and non-Jew because of the coming of Jesus Christ. The principle to which Paul appeals to make that case is both theological and eschatological. As we have seen, he appeals to the Shema and the chronometrical claim of the gospel that the time when the nations will worship God alongside of Israel has arrived. In other words, the Creator God has reached out to turn those from the nations from their national gods to the one God, the God of Israel, as the only God of all the nations too (see esp. Rom. 3:29-31). For them to undertake to become Jews, members of Israel, would empty that claim of meaning, for in the present age there was already a way for non-Jews to be reconciled to God, by becoming members of the Jewish people through proselyte conversion. Thus, Paul says, circumcision can no longer be undertaken by these Christ-believers, because then the meaning of Christ for the nations as the announcement of the awaited day would be undermined. Nothing would have changed. Those from the nations would have to join Israel to become members of the people of God, which would subvert the gospel's chronometrical claim that they represent the children from the rest of the nations promised to Abraham as a blessing (the argument throughout Rom. 3-4 and Gal. 3-5).

An additional point to be made here concerns the interpretive tradition's discourse about the other against whom Paul polemicizes, for example in Galatians. Interpreters ought to consider the likelihood that, if given a voice, those whom Paul opposes by appealing to faith(fulness) apart from circumcision would argue that *their* position is based upon faith(fulness) as well, albeit expressed through a different choice or set of choices (such as circumcision), rather than surrender the value of faith(fulness) to Paul. They might polemically dismiss Paul's position as representing *un*faith(fulness) in similar binary terms. In other words, appeal to the role of *faith(fulness)* ought to be postulated not only for Paul's position, but also as *likely central to the teaching of those whose positions his arguments oppose.*[35] There is little reason to suppose other Jewish groups would not uphold the value of faith(fulness), even if maintaining that it is manifest in different actions than Paul associates with faith(fulness) for *Christ-following non-Jews* in view of *the chronometrical claims of the gospel.* Both Paul and his adversaries, if representing Judaism, would maintain that *their interpretation of Torah is the more faithful one on the matter at hand!*[36]

Distinguishing Four Categories When Comparing Paul to Other Second Temple Authors

As a result of our qualification of the issues that arise in Josephus's narrative and Paul's comments about circumcision, there are (at least) four distinct categories that should be carefully considered when we seek to conceptualize and communicate Paul's positions on circumcision and Torah observance, or to compare Paul's positions to those held within Judaism by other Jews and Jewish groups.

---

35. See Nanos, *The Irony of Galatians*, 203–83.

36. The implications of this insight for how mistaken and anachronistic is the traditional contrast of what is essential to Christianity (faith) versus Judaism (works) can be hardly overstated!

1) *Circumcision of non-Jews is a special topic; faithfulness is the implied motivation whether arguing for or against it.* Neither Josephus nor the secondary sources discussing this story suggest that Ananias's resistance to the circumcision of the non-Jew Izates implies that Ananias is therefore against circumcision per se, so that Ananias would not circumcise his own son, if he had one. Discussing the *circumcision of non-Jews* by Jews or Jewish groups, including by way of terminology such as *ergon* ("work" or "act," "deed," or "rite") or *erga* (plural) should *not* be logically conflated with their probable implied view of *circumcision for Jews*. When Jews have their infants sons circumcised on the eighth day it is not a matter of debate (generally, assuming health and opportunity, for Jews who value the practice of Torah, anyway), for it expresses the parents' faithfulness to observe Torah commandments to which they are already beholden as Jews.

Similar consideration ought to be given to Paul's arguments about circumcision, which in the letters available to us are always directed to and about the question of circumcision for non-Jews, and more specifically, for non-Jews who have already become followers of Christ. When he makes general statements about the role of circumcision, such as "circumcision is nothing and foreskin is nothing, but keeping the commandments of God" (1 Cor. 7:19), many have understood him to devalue the role of circumcision for everyone, Jew as well as non-Jew. But that involves an interpretive move that *privileges foreskinned identity by definition*, for there can be for men (other than eunuchs) no such thing as neither circumcised skin nor foreskin; both states constitute "something" that defines the men as Jews or not in the context of Paul's rhetorical concerns. The statement also ignores the female half of the population, which does not have the physical feature characterized here in this binary formulation of humanity. Moreover, it fails to account for Paul's point in v. 19 that what ultimately matters is "observing the commandments of God."[37] For Jews, that involves the covenant of circumcision; however, and more importantly, according to Paul (and contrary to Eleazar), this commandment does not extend to members of the rest of the nations with whom Abraham is to be blessed. For non-Jews, it is not a commandment (nor is it generally recognized to be a commandment, ostensibly *pace* Eleazar), unless the non-Jews in question are slaves of Abraham's family and descendants, or seeking to become Jews/Israelites.

Paul is thus playing with the conceptual idea that the status value associated with circumcised or foreskinned identity "within Judaism" during the present age, is no longer to guide the hierarchical valuation of status within the Judaism of the subgroup gatherings (*ekklēsiai*) of the followers of Christ. They had different ethnic identities when they turned to Christ, and Paul's teaching requires that this will remain the case. However, the usual status discrimination associated with such differences—which within Judaism naturally (according to basic dynamics of social identification) favored circumcised identity while foreskinned identity was naturally (according to the same basic dynamics) favored in the larger Greco-Roman world from which the non-Jews Paul addressed had come[38]—should no longer obtain among themselves, for they were now "one" in Christ (Gal. 3:27-29).

The traditional conclusion that Paul sees circumcision as a matter of indifference for everyone, if not also as harmful and obsolete, a conclusion often expressed by representatives of the New Perspective on Paul as well (as discussed below), fails to keep in focus the specific

37. Cf. J. Brian Tucker, *"Remain in Your Calling": Paul and the Continuation of Social Identities in 1 Corinthians* (Eugene, OR: Pickwick, 2011).
38. Cf. Michael A. Hogg and Dominic Abrams, *Social Identifications: A Social Psychology of Intergroup Relations and Group Processes* (London: Routledge, 1988).

rhetorical situation for these kinds of statements.[39] When it is recognized that Paul writes to non-Jews who are suffering a crisis of identity within the Jewish context of the groups into which they have come, wherein Jewish identity is privileged by definition, then it follows that he must explain why they cannot become Jews. As we have seen, he does this by way of appeal to the Shema and their chronometrical role as representing the faithful from the nations in the present age, according to the norms of the age to come that has dawned in Christ. At the same time, he must convince them to be confident that these identity claims are justified and legitimate before God, that is, that they represent faithful interpretations of Scripture in the face of resistance by those who do not share their groups' chronometrical convictions about Christ and the arrival of the awaited age. He also seeks to ensure that these Christ-believing non-Jews learn to live graciously, according to the kindness of God that they themselves celebrate having received (the point of Rom. 9–11, and, arguably, Gal. 6:16), rather than indulge resentment toward others who do not accept them "as they are," or begin to judge them and behave indifferently or even destructively.[40]

Statements that seem to negate the value of circumcision function very differently when seen in this comparative, socio-rhetorical light. They are designed to benefit non-Jews suffering marginality arising from their membership as non-Jews in newly created *Jewish* subgroups. Precisely because the gospel prevents them from overcoming their marginal identities within Jewish communities via the prevailing solution for defining who are the members of the

---

39. Nina Livesey, *Circumcision as a Malleable Symbol*, Wissenschaftliche Untersuchungen zum Neuen Testament 2.295 (Tübingen: Mohr Siebeck, 2010), 123–54, offers a brief overview of the ways that Paul's view of circumcision has been interpreted over the centuries.

40. Cf. Mark D. Nanos, "Romans 11 and Christian and Jewish Relations: Exegetical Options for Revisiting the Translation and Interpretation of this Central Text," *Criswell Theological Review* 9, no. 2 (2012): 3–21.

righteous ones within the present age, which includes those who undertake proselyte conversion as members alongside of natural born Jews, Paul must play down the obvious advantages of identity for Jews and at the same time explain why they must not return to their former behavior as non-Jews, both of which are precluded by the gospel to which they have responded. They must now learn to live in their identity "in Christ," or better, "in Messiah," that is, within Judaism as non-Jews representing the awaited restoration of humankind to the one God through the Savior.

Paul's pronouncements do not represent universal or absolute dismissals of circumcision for Jews, including Christ-following Jews, such as Paul himself, any more than Ananias's argument against circumcision for Izates suggests that he was against Jews having their sons circumcised according to Torah, or even against it for non-Jews who want to become Jews (except for Izates!).

2) *The practice of Jewish behavior by non-Jews is not the same topic as whether or not non-Jews should undertake circumcision (proselyte conversion).* This categorical distinction has been largely overlooked in Pauline scholarship because *the identity transformation involved in becoming a Jew* that is at issue when discussing the *circumcision of non-Jews* has been conflated with discussing *non-Jews behaving according to the prescriptions of Judaism* (i.e., Torah, customs and ancestral traditions). Thus one finds discussions of Galatians as expressing Paul's opposition to Law or Torah, when what he explicitly argues against is circumcision for Christ-following non-Jews; these are otherwise instructed, for example, that "faith(fulness) works through love" (5:6), and to live according to Torah = love (5:14), rather than in competition for the right to be identified as circumcised (the context for the choice to which Paul calls them in this chapter and the letter overall). The circumcision of non-Jews is a very different

matter than the pursuit of *righteousness* by non-Jews in more general terms, for example, when non-Jews associate with Jews and Jewish communities as guests (as god-fearers or righteous gentiles), or in the case of Paul's addressees, when these non-Jews claim to be full members of the people of God apart from becoming Jews (as Christ-following non-Jews).

As we saw in the Izates narrative, Josephus describes a way of living according to the customs of the Jews, which a non-Jew can also practice, but he differentiates that from the ethnic transformation whereby a male non-Jew becomes a Jew through circumcision. The case deals specifically with the difference between two options: 1) the cultural practice of Judaism by non-Jews (what we might call "converts" to the practices of Jews developed in honor of their God, sometimes referred to as "god-fearers"); and 2) the decision of non-Jews to become Jews by way of (males) undertaking circumcision (i.e., what we might call ethnic "converts," "proselytes"), who would thereafter practice Judaism as Jews (former non-Jews). This story reveals that the figures in Josephus's narrative recognize a difference between adopting (some or many of) an ethnic group's cultural practices and becoming a member of that ethnic group, which Josephus describes as the difference between deciding "to honor God [the Deity] according to Jewish ancestral tradition" while remaining a non-Jew or deciding "to be completely a Jew" (*Ant.* 20.34 compared to 20.38). I submit that Paul was dealing with the same kind of distinction for these non-Jews in his arguments about faith(fulness) versus undertaking *erga nomou* (more below).

The particular identity discussed in the Josephus story and in Paul's letters can usefully be called "Judaism," the way of life based on Jewish traditions, and the ethnic identity "Jews" is signified by the word *Ioudaioi* in this context. *Judaism* denotes the beliefs and behavior that is "Jewish," that expresses "Jewishness," which are descriptions that can be applied to the behavior of non-Jews who live in the same ways that Jews live.[41] In other words, these are descriptive labels that are not limited in application to people who are identified as ethnic "Jews," whether because someone was born to parents identified ethnically as Jews (which continues to apply even to those who no longer behave "jewishly" according to the opinions of other Jews or even of themselves), and independent of whether one was born in or lived in Judea. This ethnic identity can extend (according to some Jews) also to a person who has undertaken the processes involved in becoming members of the people named "Jews," such as is attributed to completing the act or rite of circumcision by the Jews in this story (and thus, Josephus), which is, at least later, referred to as proselyte conversion, and by Paul as "Judaizing" (Gal. 2:14).[42]

With this distinction in mind, we can recognize that a non-Jew can practice Judaism and a Jew can choose not to; a non-Jew can behave in a more Jewish way or more jewishly than a Jew, thereby expressing more Jewishness, but the distinction between being a Jew or a non-Jew—at least for males—remains salient. Adopting Jewish behavior neither makes the non-Jew into a Jew, nor does the lack of such behavior make the Jew into a non-Jew. We might say, there is a difference between being Jewish and being Jew*ish*, or perhaps better to make the point that one is referring to something that can apply to non-Jews, being Jewish*ish*. It might be helpful to use lowercase when applying these adjectives and adverbs to non-Jews: thus, "jew*ish*," "jewish*ish*," and "jewishly," so that the reader will not suppose that these non-Jews are being described as if they had also become "Jews," as if members of "the *Jewish* people," but only as non-Jews who

41. Cf. Paula Fredriksen, "Judaizing the Nations: The Ritual Demands of Paul's Gospel," *New Testament Studies* 56 (2010): 232–52.
42. Mark D. Nanos, "What Was at Stake in Peter's 'Eating with Gentiles' at Antioch?," in *The Galatians Debate: Contemporary Issues in Rhetorical and Historical Interpretation*, ed, Mark D. Nanos (Peabody, MA: Hendrickson, 2002), 306–12.

behave like Jews might be expected to behave, at least in some ways and at some times.

Attending to these conceptual and descriptive dynamics when discussing Paul's texts makes it possible to begin to speak of the jewishness of Paul's non-Jews. They represent non-Jews practicing Judaism and behaving jewishly within Paul's Jewish subgroups.[43] Paul highlights the importance of their continued identity as non-Jews who have chosen to follow the Jewish person Jesus and gather with those Jews who proclaim him to be the Messiah of Israel and Savior of the rest of the nations too. All of this is explicitly based upon the worldview of Israel's Scriptures and Jewish traditions and norms developed within the context of life under Rome, which are elements of the Jewish perspective into which Paul enculturates those he brings to faithfulness to Jesus as Christ.[44] This categorical differentiation is traditionally missed when discussing Paul; I believe that this is in large part a result of the way that *erga nomou* has been defined in his arguments.

Paul used the phrase *erga nomou* in Romans and Galatians in contrast to *pistis*, which has been understood traditionally to signify a contrast between behavior and belief. But it seems to me that it was specifically designed to discuss what *faithfulness* involved *for non-Jews who have turned already to God through Jesus Christ:* specifically, that *they must not also become Jews.* It signified only the *work* (or deed or act or rite) *of circumcision*, inclusive of any other works (or deeds or acts or rites) involved in the process of identity conversion to becoming a Jew. But it did *not* signify the behavioral works (or deeds or acts or rites) involved in a Jew *or non-Jew* behaving jewishly per se, such as observing Sabbaths and other designated Jewish holidays, or dietary

---

43. Cf. Nanos, "Paul's Non-Jews Do Not Become 'Jews,' But Do They Become 'Jewish'?"
44. Cf. Ehrensperger, *Paul at the Crossroads of Cultures*; Neil Elliott, "The Question of Politics: Paul as a Diaspora Jew under Roman Rule" in this volume).

commandments, and so on. A non-Jew on the path to becoming a Jew would be enculturated into Jewish communal life consisting of such observances, just as were the non-Jews to whom Paul wrote, but Paul's phrase was not inclusive of these matters: it only referred to the rite(s) involved in becoming Jews.

The traditional definitions of the phrase *erga nomou*, as well as those of the New Perspective, conflate Paul's opposition to these non-Jews undertaking circumcision with opposition to Torah observance. That remains the case when New Perspective scholars such as James Dunn stipulate that Paul has in view specifically those observations that function as identifiers of Jewishness.[45] I maintain that Paul only meant to signify *the identity transformation rites*, which he signaled synonymously by the metonym *"circumcision."* The tension is not between faith and good works or Jewish behavioral norms as traditionally posed in Pauline theology when discussing his opposition to *erga nomou*; Paul's opposition is only to the rites involved in Christ-following non-Jews becoming Jews.

This is not the forum to demonstrate this proposition in detail, but I submit that Paul's arguments about faith(fulness) versus *erga nomou* will become more transparent by translating the latter phrase not as "works of law," but with the paraphrase *"rites of (the) convention (of circumcision)."*[46] At issue in each case is whether undertaking that identity transformation represents *"faith(fulness)" for Christ-following non-Jews* in particular, hence the contrast with *pistis* for them. Paul's position on this matter is in direct contrast to the position that

45. James D. G. Dunn, "Yet Once More – 'The Works of the Law,' A Response," in *The New Perspective on Paul: Collected Essays*, ed. James D. G. Dunn (Tübingen: Mohr Siebeck, 2007), 207–20.

46. If Paul was discussing the topic of *erga nomou* for Jews (e.g., in Gal. 2:16, in order to make a point about why it should not be observed by Christ-following non-Jews), the paraphrase would be the "rites of (the) convention (of circumcision for eight-day-old sons)." If clearly applied to non-Jews, then the "rites of (the) convention (of proselyte conversion)" might be more helpful.

Josephus portrayed Eleazar as advocating, with Josephus's approval. Advocating the need for proselyte conversion was a normative position for Jews who believed that in the present age God worked in and through Israel (at least for those who maintained that non-Jews could become Jews/members of Israel, a view that not all Jews shared), whatever else they might have believed about what would be appropriate for non-Jews who turned to worship the one God when the age to come arrived. It was likely the position Paul advocated before his encounter with Christ, but that now he so vehemently opposed because of the chronometrical gospel claims (Gal. 5:11).[47]

3) *Circumcision of non-Jews and Torah observance for Jews (which includes circumcision of their eight-day-old sons) are categorically different.* Discussing *the circumcision of non-Jews* (just like discussing *the observance of Torah by non-Jews*) is *not* of the same category as discussing the *observance of Torah for those who are Jews already* (i.e., under Torah), which would include discussing those who have already become Jews following the completion of *erga nomou*, the works (or acts or deeds or rites) involved in completion of ethnic conversion, signified by circumcision, making them Jews (proselytes). Naturally, those who have begun the course leading to this transformation but have not yet completed it (i.e., proselyte candidates) would logically begin the process of learning to observe Jewish life, but that remains different from the binding obligation to Torah that follows completion of the rite(s) (to which Paul appeals in Gal. 5:2-5). Those completing that rite are no longer non-Jews; they are thereafter Jews (according to Paul's terms, and Josephus's in

47. Cf. Donaldson, *Paul and the Gentiles*, 277–84, who also argues that Paul's perspectives on this were likely similar to Eleazar's before his views changed about Jesus, appealing to Gal. 5:11. Since Eleazar (and Josephus) may have been, like Paul, a Pharisee, might this suggest that some subgroups of Pharisees were more disposed (even zealously so?: cf. 1:13-16) to the inclusion of non-Jews through their transformation into Jews than were some other Pharisaic as well as other Jewish sects (to which, perhaps, Ananias was beholden?), as long as this entailed completion of the appropriate rites, especially circumcision of males?

this narrative, although not according to all Jews). Thus, discussions of obligations for them would be different than discussions of obligations for non-Jews.

The traditional decision to approach Paul's arguments with the working assumption that his audiences knew him to regard Torah observance as a matter of indifference, obsolete for Jews such as himself as well as for the non-Jews he addressed, has profoundly shaped the interpretations and discourse that prevail today. However, there is evidence throughout Paul's letters that he held that Jews who were followers of Jesus, such as himself, were still members of Israel and thus were beholden to be faithful to the covenant; that is, they were to observe Torah as a matter of covenant fidelity, which would include circumcising their sons and observing Jewish diets and days. Approaching his texts from the perspective that his audiences knew him to observe Torah because he remained a Jew profoundly alters the way that an interpreter conceptualizes the possibilities for understanding Paul's messages, not least what he is trying to communicate to non-Jews about how to live righteously apart from them becoming Jews. That topic is much too involved to discuss here, and I have done so at length elsewhere,[48] but the point to raise here is that it has not been sufficiently recognized in Pauline interpretive history in part because of the failure to attend to just these kinds of categorical distinctions, which were obvious to Paul and his addressees, although not to their later interpreters.

4) *Discussions of circumcision or the observance of Judaism/Torah, whether by non-Jews or by Jews, should be qualified with respect to context.*

48. See, e.g., Mark D. Nanos, "The Myth of the 'Law-Free' Paul Standing Between Christians and Jews," *Studies in Christian-Jewish Relations* 4 (2009): 1–21, at http://ejournals.bc.edu/ojs/index.php/scjr/article/view/1511; Nanos, "Paul's Relationship to Torah in Light of His Strategy 'to Become Everything to Everyone' (1 Corinthians 9:19-23)," in *Paul and Judaism: Crosscurrents in Pauline Exegesis and the Study of Jewish-Christian Relations*, ed. Didier Pollefeyt and Reimund Bieringer (London: T & T Clark, 2012), 106–40. A complete listing is available at http://www.marknanos.com/projects.html.

When we evaluate and discuss these topics we must attend to the probable *contingencies* that might be at issue in each case, as well as the *underlying premises* on which the arguments depend, dynamics that were discussed above for the arguments of Ananias and Eleazar as well as for Paul.

It is important to qualify Ananias's argument in terms of his concern for *place*, for what is appropriate *here*, in Adiabene, as well as *person*, for what is appropriate for Izates as king of a people who are not Jews. Likewise, we must consider how Paul qualifies his positions in terms of *place* (each letter's contingencies) and *person* (each letter's addressees are non-Jews who are followers of Jesus), the latter of which has been a central topic of this study.

When discussing Jewish groups, these contextual qualifications also extend to considering the element of *timing*, of what is deemed by any party to be appropriate *now*, in this case *at this time,* versus what might be otherwise deemed appropriate at *another time.* This would naturally include consideration of any apocalyptic and other eschatological convictions, of what might be acknowledged as possibly appropriate *then.* This consideration is widely recognized to be central to understanding Paul's position, but its importance is obscured when discussions proceed as if the differences of opinion between him and his rivals revolve around essentials such as "faith" or "works." Rather, these qualities should be discussed in terms of what each group considers to be the appropriate way to act faithfully (or: to express faith) "now" in view of their convictions about whether (or: to what degree) the end of the ages has begun. The figures in Josephus's narrative do not presume that there has been a change of aeons, which is an element that should be considered when comparing their views to those of Paul. I have referred to Paul's qualification as the chronometrical gospel claim that the end of the ages has dawned with the resurrection of Christ (though within the midst of the present age, and thus awaiting additional elements to arrive in full).

There may be similar or different elements involved in the opinions expressed by any Jews or Jewish groups about various temporal or other relative concerns. The views expressed should be expected to be different for different groups of people and even individuals at different times and in different circumstances. They would almost certainly be different from the views that would be presented if each was asked to discuss what applies to all people in all circumstances at all times.

Conclusion

Interpreters of Josephus's narrative have naturally recognized the particularity of the situation and the solutions prescribed. They have not conflated the advice given on circumcision and the practice of Judaism to a non-Jew who is king of a non-Jewish people with the views that either Eleazar or Ananias—or Josephus—would uphold for Jews, or even for other non-Jews.[49] Is it not time, by now, that similar consideration be given to Paul's arguments about topics such as *pistis*, *erga*, circumcision, and the practice of Judaism, all the more?

---

49. As a case in point, on p. 22, note a, in the Loeb volume of Josephus, *Ant.* 20, ed. and trans. Louis Feldman (Cambridge, MA: Harvard University Press, 1956–81), a possible rabbinic parallel (!) is provided, wherein Rabbi Joshua argues in *Yebamot* 46a that circumcision was not required for a convert, just baptism. In addition, a logical reason for this teaching by a Jew and within Judaism is offered: the policy of exception for circumstances where life would be endangered.

Appendix: A Categorical Error in the New Perspective on Paul that Perpetuates the Traditional Conceptualization of Paul Outside of Judaism

I have emphasized that Paul's letters offer relatively unique evidence from which to work when discussing Jewish views on the circumcision of non-Jews, because most other Jewish literature to which Paul is compared *is addressed to fellow Jews or is about Jews*; moreover, that literature does not involve discussions of what is appropriate for non-Jews on the part of Jews who believe that the end of the ages has already begun. As simple as this insight may be, the implications for evaluating Paul with respect to, if not also within, first-century Judaism continue to be inhibited by the failure to recognize this dynamic, or to follow through with the implications for research and discussions of Paul *and* Judaism.

New Perspective interpreters of Paul, like traditionalists, often read what Paul writes regarding the practices of Judaism such as circumcision as if they represent *universal* statements equally applicable to everyone, to Christ-following Jews and non-Jews, even to non-Christ-following Jews and non-Jews. A brief review of the work of E. P. Sanders, a very influential interpreter involved in redrawing the portrayal of Judaism and of comparing and contrasting Paul to it, will demonstrate the importance of what material is selected, and just how influential the way that material is qualified remains to the comparative conclusions drawn regarding Paul and Judaism, and specifically with regard to circumcision.

Sanders is widely recognized as one of the most informed and talented interpreters of Judaism and of Paul, thus making his construction of both highly relevant to this discussion. As is well known, his work, along with that of Krister Stendahl and several others, inspired the development of the so-called New Perspective on

Paul. Few Pauline scholars can claim to know more about either the topics of Paul or Judaism. Nevertheless, when Sanders discusses Paul's soteriology, comparing "how *one* [or: "a man"] gains righteousness" in Paul's religious system to that of so-called Palestinian Judaism, he finds Paul's view to be very different from that of the rabbis.[50] However, that should surprise no one! Framing the comparison in *universal* terms of gaining righteousness, as if the subject for the rabbis (and Paul) was the same for *everyone*, is neither the topic of the rabbis' discussions, nor of Paul's. They both conceptualized the issue of gaining righteousness and related issues in terms of two different groups: Jews and non-Jews. And their conceptualizations were different for each group. Thus the topic of gaining righteousness must be approached with attention to the ethno-religious distinctions implicit (or explicit) in these texts. Only in this way can we make sense of the views of either Paul or the rabbis, whether to compare or to contrast the results.[51]

As Sanders knows well, the rabbis are almost always discussing how *Jews* are to behave righteously (exceptions are signaled), whereas Paul is usually if not always discussing how *non-Jews* are to behave righteously, or, alternatively, how non-Jews *must not become* Jews. That distinction between *getting in* (covenantal identity as the people

50. E. P. Sanders, *Paul and Palestinian Judaism: A Comparison of Patterns of Religion* (Philadelphia: Fortress Press, 1977), 12 (emphasis added); "when a man" on 75.
51. This same criticism applies to those now seeking to undermine the New Perspective by supposedly substantiating works-righteousness in Jewish texts. For example, in D. A. Carson, Peter Thomas O'Brien, and Mark A. Seifrid, eds., *Justification and Variegated Nomism*, vol. 2: *The Paradoxes of Paul* (Tübingen: Mohr Siebeck, 2004), contributors regularly single out comments in various Jewish texts across the centuries as if written to a universal audience (i.e., non-Jews) when they call for proper works in order to be declared righteous at the final judgment. However, these texts address Jews who are already in the covenant, not non-Jews about how to enter the covenant, so they do not support these interpreters' claims that many Jews required works (for non-Jews) to be saved in supposed contrast to Paul. To use their Christian categories, these texts were written to those already regarded to be saved (i.e., Jews) to instruct them to remain faithful to the end, a message that is similarly evident throughout Paul's letters to those (non-Jews) whom he regards to be already "saved" according to the gospel, yet Paul instructs them to "work out your own salvation in fear and trembling" (Phil. 2:12).

of God) and *staying in* (good standing in that covenantal relationship) is at the center of Sanders's and the subsequent New Perspective on Paul's projects, as advanced, for example, by James Dunn and N. T. Wright. But the insight is undermined by the conflation of prescriptions for Jew and non-Jew as if all ethnic distinction had been erased, and thus, logically, as if the covenant with Israel was no longer in effect as a basis for identifying Israelites as the historic people of God in distinction from all other peoples, including the non-Jews who have joined them in the family of God apart from becoming Israelites. Only in the case of discussing the *entrance* of non-Jews (non-Israelites) into the people of God (which God by grace confined by covenant to Jews/Israelites) as fellow inheritors of the promises made to Abraham, Isaac, and Jacob/Israel, should we expect to find soteriology arising in the terms that this category usually bespeaks when discussing Paul.[52]

This point is in fact a central feature of Sanders's own arguments elsewhere regarding the difference between *getting in* and *staying in*. What faithfulness to God means for Jews and for non-Jews is very different, and this must be highlighted continually or risk being conflated into universal principles that misrepresent the positions under discussion. Paul's instructions are specifically about what is appropriate *for non-Jews* who turn to God through Jesus Christ. They do not address what is appropriate (e.g., with respect to circumcision) *for Jews* who are convinced that Jesus is the Christ. Thus, for discussing Paul's views on non-Jews, the issue should be restated something like this: *How does one not born a Jew, and thus not within the covenant, get into covenant standing among the righteous ones* (i.e., as non-

---

52. When Sanders does look specifically at rabbinic texts regarding the question of the inclusion of *non-Jews* as righteous ones both in this age and in the age to come, he clarifies that unlike the literature addressing the members of the covenant from which he develops the notion of covenantal nomism, "the Gentiles are dealt with only sporadically, however, and different Rabbis had different opinions about their destiny" (*Paul and Palestinian Judaism*, 207).

Jews alongside Jews, also known as Israelites, children of Abraham, people of God), to which Paul's answer is, by faith in (or faithfulness to) Christ; and, *thereafter, how does that non-Jew stay in good standing therein?* For Jews, however, if put in comparable terms, the matter would instead be: *How does one born and raised as a Jew, that is, already within the covenant, stay in/retain covenant blessings among the righteous ones* (or *regain* them when suffering discipline for failure to uphold the obligations of Torah to which one was already covenantally beholden)?

There is another qualification that must be highlighted here. In any group understood to represent Judaism, and thus for Paul and his groups if he and they are going to be compared therewith, categorical differences would be expected to arise with respect to halakic decisions for his groups, based upon the gospel's chronometrical claim (that the awaited change of aeons has begun within the midst of the present age), and for other Jews and groups, regarding how Jews are to remain faithful, since the latter do not share that chronometrical conviction. This chronometrical factor—whether or not the age to come has begun within the present age—is signaled by keeping in view a distinction already mentioned: the centrality of these non-Jews' identification specifically as *Christ-followers.*

Surprisingly, as important as the identity of these non-Jews being in Christ is to the entire enterprise of Pauline interpretation, the profound implications of Paul's opposition to their circumcision precisely because they are *already* followers of Christ has not been highlighted when comparative evaluations of Paul and other Jews have been drawn either by those representing the New Perspective, or by those representing the traditional approaches to Paul. This oversight is likely, at least in part, attributable to the continued use of the label "Christians," which obscures the fact that Paul's audience belong to a special group within Judaism consisting of Jews and non-Jews, rather than constituting an entirely new people, what came to be called by the church fathers a "third race."[53] Our approach ought to at least allow us to consider the likelihood that Paul and his adversaries may well agree about what is theoretically appropriate after the arrival of the awaited age on any number of matters, not least with respect to how to incorporate non-Jews into the people of God, yet disagree entirely about what is appropriate *now*, unless they share the view that the awaited age has begun. In other words, the conflicts may not be about the essence of the matter at issue (e.g., whether non-Jews should be initiated into the people of God, and if so, how), but whether the timing for the policy advanced by this Jewish subgroup, of incorporating members from the other nations as the children also promised to Abraham apart from them becoming members of Israel, is warranted "now."

We can see clearly how the problem of universalizing the portrayal of Paul, and finding thereby that it does not parallel Judaism, influences Sanders when he turns to discussing Paul on circumcision. He writes, "In the surviving literature he [Paul] treats circumcision both as rejection of Christ and as indifferent (Gal. 5:1-4; 6:15; 1 Cor. 7:19)."[54] Such an observation is an important one among many that convince Sanders that Paul is doing something other than Judaism. But the rabbis with whom Sanders compares Paul are, unless specifically stating otherwise, addressing and discussing what applies to *Jews*, while Paul, unless specifically stating otherwise, is addressing and discussing what applies to *non-Jews*—who are also *Christ-*

---

53. The use of "gentile" is also problematic, suggesting a category other than the binary of Jew/non-Jew; as Caroline Johnson Hodges makes plain, Paul was himself struggling with how to re-identify these non-Jews. See "The Question of Identity: Gentiles as Gentiles—but also Not—in Pauline Communities" in this volume.
54. E. P. Sanders, *Jewish Law from Jesus to the Mishnah: Five Studies* (London: SCM, 1990), 283.

followers—about *the circumcision of themselves*. Paul is not discussing whether Jews should circumcise their infant sons (or even a male Jew later in life whose parents did not have him circumcised as a child). Paul only argues that circumcision must not be undertaken by adult (male) non-Jews who have already gained standing as righteous ones through turning to God in Christ. Why? Because, as argued above, if they now would seek to "*get in*" by becoming proselytes, they *would be logically denying* that they have already *gained* that standing in accordance with the gospel's chronometrical claim that God has already reconciled them through the faithfulness of Jesus Christ, to whom they have already faithfully turned from the gods of their native nations (Gal. 3:1-5; 4:8-19; 5:2-12, passim). If they are *already* incorporated into the family of God, how can they seek to be incorporated without denying that it is already the case?

Once again, the chronometrical element cannot be overlooked. Paul may well have held that non-Jews should be circumcised and even been actively engaged in circumcising them previously (implied in Gal. 5:11),[55] but he believes that this is no longer appropriate in view of the gospel now bringing salvation to the nations too. So it is not circumcision that Paul opposes per se as a rejection of Christ, contra Sanders, but only the circumcision of Christ-following non-Jews, since they represent the propositional claim of the gospel that the end of the ages has arrived with the resurrection of Christ. It is the presence of these non-Jews, turning from idols to the one God, that bears witness to the truth of the gospel's propositional claims. Therefore this Jewish subgroup gathering must exemplify the ideal of the end of the ages in the midst of the present age by retaining difference between Jew and non-Jew, but at the same time they must

---

55. Cf. Terence L. Donaldson, *Paul and the Gentiles: Remapping the Apostle's Convictional World* (Minneapolis: Fortress Press, 1997), 277–84.

not express the discrimination that usually entails in terms of defining who had standing as the people of God.

Paul sought to explain this dynamic principle by way of relating the incident at Antioch. Table fellowship among Christ-followers must exemplify the claims of the gospel for equality of Jew and non-Jew according to the ideals of the age to come in the midst of the present age, where difference generally creates discrimination (Gal. 2:11-15).[56] Even though the eating follows Jewish guidelines, since it is a Jewish subgroup, it must not do so in a way that suggests that the non-Jews are not equal members apart from becoming Jews, for example, by arranging the seating or serving portions based on ethno-religious hierarchical distinctions, instead of exemplifying age-to-come standards. Rather, the utopian ideals of shalom in the messianic age should prevail, such as the harmonious dwelling together of animals in ways that would create chaos in the present age (Isa. 11; 65:17-25). For the present, as Woody Allen purportedly quipped (although underplaying the likely result!): "The lion and the calf [sic] shall lie down together, but the calf [sic] won't get much sleep." It is not hard to imagine that the larger Jewish communities would have responded negatively to the chronometrical claims Paul's gospel makes to receive these non-Jews as full members of the family of Abraham, as more than guests and yet not candidates for becoming Jews. Likewise, their non-Jewish families and friends would have found incomprehensible and scandalous such claims as the basis to disregard family and civic cult, apart from them becoming Jews.

As mentioned earlier, Paul's rhetorical strategy in Romans 3:29-31, which asserts that God is the God of the foreskinned *also* when they turn *faithfully* to the one God from idols, only makes sense if it is assumed that God is, of course, the God of the Jews, of the

---

56. Nanos, "What Was at Stake," 282–318.

circumcised, and that the latter must remain Jews. Moreover, this proposition can only stand if it "upholds" rather than nullifies the teaching of Torah, and specifically salient here, *the commandment of circumcision for Israelites/Jews*! Paul's argument from the Shema revolves around the conviction that the awaited time of restoration of the nations as well as of Israel to God has begun, so that one need no longer be a member of the nation Israel to be reconciled to the one and only God of all creation. Paul argues from the circumcision of Jews to the uncircumcision of non-Jews: logically, for Jews in Christ, who are *already circumcised*, Paul's arguments against undertaking circumcision do not apply, and do not imply that they should not circumcise their infant sons.

In short, it is a category error of significance to universalize Paul's position against the circumcision of Christ-following non-Jews without distinguishing that special topic from the issue of the circumcision of sons born to Jews, Christ-followers or not, and then to compare that conclusion to other Jewish groups' positions on the circumcision of Jews. The way that Sanders (mis)framed the matter continues to inhibit research among those at the forefront of the New Perspective. For Sanders's statement(s) (and those of others identified with that perspective) to be viable for comparison with the statements of other Jews and Jewish groups, one must minimally alter his observation to read: "In the surviving literature he [Paul] treats circumcision *of non-Jews who have already turned from their gods to Israel's God through Jesus Christ.* . . ."

The qualification of Paul's view on circumcision revolves around Paul's adamant objection to circumcision of *Christ-following non-Jews* specifically. Paul's argument (in the texts that Sanders cites, i.e., 1 Cor. 7:19[57] and Gal. 5:3) logically requires that *Paul uphold the circumcision of Christ-following Jews*, and concomitantly, *the complete observation of Torah by Jews*, since circumcision is a marker of covenant identity under the Mosaic covenant that requires continued fidelity for Jews. In other words, when the specificity required to qualify Paul's argument is articulated, which includes how the questions asked of his texts are framed, it undermines some of the conclusions that the universalizing proposition supposedly supported, such as that Paul regarded circumcision "as indifferent." Instead, its continued importance is logically inferred for Jews, including Christ-following Jews, such as himself.

57. Cf. William S. Campbell, "'As Having and as Not Having': Paul, Circumcision, and Indifferent Things in 1 Corinthians 7:17-32a," in *Unity and Diversity in Christ: Interpreting Paul in Context: Collected Essays*, ed. William S. Campbell (Eugene, OR: Cascade Books, 2013), 106–26.

5

The Question of Identity: Gentiles as Gentiles—but also Not—in Pauline Communities

Caroline Johnson Hodge

I have long puzzled over how to understand the gentiles in Paul, both from his perspective and their own perspective.[1] I operate under the assumption that he is writing primarily to them and his goal is to articulate and manage just how they are connected to Israel through Christ. In the process, as I have discussed elsewhere, both he and they undergo various transformations in identity, changes that, I maintain, never separate him from Judaism and that affiliate gentiles with Israel but not as full members.[2] They are not Jews and, in my view, they

1. I would like to thank Paula Fredriksen for her helpful comments on a draft of this essay.

are not Christians; and they are not really gentiles any longer either. Paul does call them a number of things including beloved, holy ones, faithful ones, brothers and sisters, and a new creation. But what is it they have become? Who are these gentiles-in-Christ? This chapter explores this question.

Many scholars use the term "Christian" for these gentile believers, even though there is fairly widespread agreement that it is anachronistic. There are good reasons not to use it: Paul does not use it himself and it inevitably imports into our interpretation, despite our good intentions, later understandings of Christianity. Using "Christian" encourages us to see the letters as the founding documents of a new religion, and masks some of the ambiguities that are crucial to Paul's arguments. Furthermore, the term "Christian" makes it harder to see how Paul's nuanced treatment of gentiles-in-Christ draws upon Jewish ways of talking about gentiles.

In what follows I will trace a number of ways that Paul draws upon Jewish conceptions of gentiles, especially where they approach the boundaries of Jewish identity. Jewish discourses of descent and purity are Paul's resources for constructing an identity for these gentiles-in-Christ that resists classification. These gentiles occupy an in-between space, hovering around the borders of identities that they are not quite. Along with Cavan Concannon, who has recently worked on ethnicity in 1 Corinthians, I see Paul's definitions of gentiles as shifting with his rhetoric. Concannon argues that "Paul's imagining of the Corinthians remains in a state of continual flux, often emerging out of the space between the ethnic labels Judean and Greek."[3] In previous work I have tried to understand gentile believers as embodying multiple identities, negotiating among them as the

---

2. Caroline Johnson Hodge, *If Sons, Then Heirs: A Study of Kinship and Ethnicity in the Letters of Paul* (New York: Oxford University Press, 2007); Johnson Hodge, "Apostle to the Gentiles: Constructions of Paul's Identity," *Biblical Interpretation* 13, no. 3 (2005): 270–88.

situation required.[4] Here I will complicate this notion and argue that multiple identities might be partially occupied in such a way that resists any fixed identification with one or the other.[5] And in Paul's interpretation, this ambiguity is necessary in the larger narrative of Israel's redemption. Indeed, this investigation of Jewish ways of categorizing gentiles ultimately questions the idea of "identity" and "ethnicity" as we typically understand them.

To explore these issues, I will first discuss the term "gentiles" and how Paul uses it in a double-sided way. I will then compare the holy seed ideology in Ezra and *Jubilees* to Paul, to show how Paul appropriates this language in Galatians 3, but uses it for inclusion instead of exclusion. I will then turn to 1 Corinthians 6 to discuss how biblical purity language informs his crafting of gentiles as the holy members of Christ's body. I conclude by reflecting critically on my initial query—who are the gentiles?

Two Kinds of Gentiles

The ambiguities that attend the identity of gentile believers in Paul's discourse are already signaled by the term "gentiles" itself. As a Jewish term for all non-Jews, *ethnē* flattens any ethnic specificity and

---

3. Cavan W. Concannon, *"When You Were Gentiles": Specters of Ethnicity in Roman Corinth and Paul's Corinthian Correspondence* (New Haven, CT: Yale University Press, 2014), 80. I am grateful to Concannon for sharing his manuscript with me prior to publication.

4. Johnson Hodge, *If Sons*, 117–35. I have also used the term "hybridity" to describe gentile identity (*If Sons*, 150), following Sze-kar Wan's helpful suggestion in "Does Diaspora Identity Imply Some Sort of Universality? An Asian-American Reading of Galatians," in *Interpreting Beyond Borders*, ed. Fernando F. Segovia (Sheffield: Sheffield Academic Press, 2000), 107–31.

5. I am thinking here more in terms of ambiguity than simply going back and forth among different identities. Homi K. Bhabha has been helpful to me in finding the language to talk about this inbetweenness. I draw on some of his phraseology in *Location of Culture* (London: Routledge, 1994), where he is talking about artist Renée Green's depiction of a stairwell: "The stairwell as liminal space, in-between the designations of identity, becomes the process of symbolic interaction, the connective tissue that constructs the difference between upper and lower, black and white. The hither and thither of the stairwell, the temporal movement and passage that it allows, prevents identities at either end of it from settling into primordial polarities" (5).

multiplicity. "Gentiles" expresses a Jewish mapping of the world; it lumps a bunch of different peoples into one category based on their lack of loyalty to the God of Israel.[6] And in Paul's usage, this term has a doubleness to it in that there are two kinds of gentiles. First, there are the audiences of his letters, whom he addresses explicitly as gentiles in a number of places (Rom. 1:5-6, 13; 11:13; 15:6). Second, there are all the other gentiles who are not in Christ, the sort of gentiles that believers used to be. This second category is familiar from other Jewish literature, which sometimes casts these gentile others as idolaters who lack self-control, resulting in all sorts of sexual sins.[7] Paul himself details their plight in Romans 1:18-32.

In Paul's rhetoric, these gentile outsiders serve as a foil for the members of the *ekklesia*. "You know that when you were gentiles," Paul reminds the Corinthians, "you were led astray, led to speechless idols" (1 Cor. 12:2). Or he admonishes this same community, exclaiming that the sexual immorality he has heard reported about them is "of a kind not even existing among the gentiles!" (1 Cor. 5:1). Finally, Paul exhorts the Thessalonians, "For this is the will of God, your sanctification: that you abstain from *porneia*; that each one of you know how to control your body in holiness and honor, not with lustful passion, like the gentiles who do not know God" (1 Thess. 4:3). Although believers are no longer those kinds of gentiles, Paul reminds them of their origins in this group, as if to warn them they could revert back if they are not careful.

---

6. Johnson Hodge, *If Sons*, 49–58. For more detailed studies of the term "gentiles," see Terence L. Donaldson, *Paul and the Gentiles: Remapping the Apostle's Convictional World* (Minneapolis: Fortress Press, 1997); James M. Scott, *Paul and the Nations: The Old Testament and Jewish Background of Paul's Mission to the Nations with Special Reference to the Destination of Galatians* (Tübingen: Mohr Siebeck, 1995). Also see Shaye J. D. Cohen, *The Beginnings of Jewishness* (Berkeley: University of California Press, 1999).

7. For discussion of this category, see Paula Fredriksen, "Judaism, the Circumcision of the Gentiles, and Apocalyptic Hope: Another Look at Galatians 1 and 2," *Journal of Theological Studies* 42 (1991): 544; Donaldson, *Paul and the Gentiles*, 52–54.

So the gentiles-in-Christ occupy a kind of liminal space between being *those* kinds of gentiles and now *these* kinds of gentiles. Furthermore, Paul expects many changes from these gentiles, including that they reject idolatry and sexual immorality and practice self-mastery "in holiness and honor." Elsewhere Paul describes this as the life of the spirit, which they receive at baptism, so that, Paul says, "the just requirement of the Law might be fulfilled in us" (Rom. 8:4). But he is adamant that they not keep the Jewish Law, especially with respect to circumcision for male gentiles. Indeed, gentiles-in-Christ are not quite gentiles and not quite Jews.[8]

This ambiguous status of gentiles who are somehow attached to Israel is not unknown in Jewish literature; in fact, it seems to be the norm. I am thinking here not of proselytes, who, according to many texts, adopt Torah observance (including circumcision for males) and are perceived as members of Israel.[9] Instead I have in mind a category of non-Jews more akin to the gentiles addressed by Paul: those who honor the God of Israel and who participate in some Jewish practices, but who remain gentiles.[10] There are a variety of ways that these gentile sympathizers were perceived by Jews in the Second Temple period and, as Terence Donaldson writes, it is difficult to find a clear set of categories for these groups of non-Jews affiliated with Jewish communities.[11] In a wide range of materials, we find references to gentiles adopting Jewish practices such as Sabbath observance, making offerings at the temple, attending synagogue

---

8. Paula Fredriksen discusses this ambiguity as well. See her "Judaizing the Nations: The Ritual Demands of Paul's Gospel," *New Testament Studies* 56 (2010): 243–44.

9. Donaldson, *Judaism and the Gentiles*, 479, 483–92; Fredriksen, "Judaism," 546 and passim and "Judaizing the Nations," 239–40, 242.

10. Sometimes these are referred to as "god-fearers." Fredriksen, "Judaism," 541 and passim; Pamela Eisenbaum, *Paul Was Not A Christian: The Original Message of A Misunderstood Apostle* (New York: HarperOne, 2009), 99–115.

11. Donaldson, *Judaism and the Gentiles*, 479. Donaldson divides the evidence for gentiles affiliated with Jews into four categories: general sympathization, conversion, ethical monotheism, and eschatological salvation.

meetings, and so on.[12] But there seems to have been little interest in defining these gentiles as a group or thinking about the religious status of these gentiles.[13]

A number of sources recognize a sliding scale of gentile participation in Judaism, with different degrees of involvement. Josephus tells of Metilius, who, to save his life, promises "to Judaize, even until circumcision" (*War* 2.454).[14] Still other evidence, including inscriptions, show gentiles who honor the God of Israel and still participate in their own cults.[15] As Paula Fredriksen points out, this may be implied by the Aphrodisias inscription which lists fifty "god-fearers" (*theosebeis*), a term that can refer to gentiles who worship the God of Israel.[16] Nine of these are also public officials (*bouleutai*), which means that they would have participated in the civic cult as a part of their official duties.[17] Indeed, in the ancient context this loyalty to multiple gods is not at all remarkable. Julia Severa offers another example: she was both a priestess in a local cult and a donor to a synagogue in Phrygia.[18] In a few cases, ancient sources

---

12. Ibid., 471. See also Cohen, *Beginnings*.

13. Donaldson, *Judaism and the Gentiles*, 479–80.

14. "To Judaize" (*Ioudaizein*), which means "to act like a Jew," is a verb that tends to be used by Jews about non-Jews. For a more detailed discussion, see Cohen, *Beginnings*, 175–97. See also Fredriksen, "Judaizing the Nations," 240 n. 16, where she corrects Cohen's characterization of "God-venerators" as not worshipping other gods. Mark D. Nanos argues (against Dunn and Cohen) that "judaize" can refer to not only a change in behavior, but also a transformation of identity (so that judaize can mean "to become a Jew"); "What Was at Stake in Peter's 'Eating with Gentiles' at Antioch?" in *The Galatians Debate*, ed. Mark D. Nanos (Peabody, MA: Hendrickson, 2002), 305–12. These discussions illustrate precisely the complexities and ambiguities that I attempt to highlight here.

15. Donaldson, *Judaism and the Gentiles*, 473.

16. Fredriksen, "Judaism," 542. But note the cautions of Ross Shepard Kraemer, who comments that the meaning of *theosebeis* in this inscription is not clear: *Unreliable Witnesses: Religion, Gender and History in the Greco-Roman Mediterranean* (New York: Oxford University Press, 2011), 224.

17. And as Paula Fredriksen points out, if Angelos Chaniotis is correct in his argument that the inscription is later than traditionally thought, these public officials could be Christians as well! See Angelos Chaniotis, "The Jews of Aphrodias: New Evidence and Old Problems," *Scripta Classica Israelica* 21 (2002): 209–42, and Fredriksen, "Judaizing the Nations," 238 n. 14.

explicitly recognize the mixedness of these gentiles. Josephus, for example, refers to "Judaizers" (gentiles who adopt Jewish practices) as "mixed" (*memigmenon*; *War* 2.463).[19] Thus Paul's portrayal of gentiles-in-Christ fits into a larger trend among Jewish writers, who tend to view the status of sympathetic gentiles as in-between.

To take a closer look at gentiles in Paul, I will trace two lines of argument in which he draws upon Jewish ethno-racial discourses: one uses the logic of lineage and another uses the logic of purity. In Galatians 3, Paul argues that baptized gentiles have become the descendants, or seed, of Abraham. In 1 Corinthians 6, Paul draws boundaries around the gentiles with purity language, asserting that they have become pure, like priestly bodies or like the temple itself. Both of these stem from his conception of baptism, which is a ritual of initiation and kinship-making that endows these gentiles with the spirit or *pneuma* of Christ (Gal. 4:6). It is this ritual that transforms them from being *those* gentiles into being *these* gentiles.

Seed of Abraham

As a number of scholars have noted, Ezra draws upon the biblical prescriptions for priests as a holy lineage to be protected and kept pure, and applies these to laypeople.[20] Just as priests have been set

18. Donaldson, *Judaism and the Gentiles*, 463–64. See also Fredriksen, "Judaizing the Nations," 237–40 (including notes), for more examples.
19. Johnson Hodge, *If Sons*, 56–57. See also Donaldson, *Judaism and the Gentiles*, 473; Mark D. Nanos, "Paul's Non-Jews Do Not Become 'Jews,' But Do They Become 'Jewish'?" *Journal of the Jesus Movement in its Jewish Setting* 1, no. 1 (2014), www.jjmjs.org.
20. Jonathan Klawans, *Impurity and Sin in Ancient Judaism* (New York: Oxford University Press, 2000), 43–46; Michael L. Satlow, *Jewish Marriage in Antiquity* (Princeton, NJ: Princeton University Press, 2001), 133–47; Christine Hayes, *Gentile Impurities and Jewish Identities: Intermarriage and Conversion from the Bible to the Talmud* (New York: Oxford University Press, 2002), 68–91. See the critique of Klawans and Hayes by Saul M. Olyan, "Purity Ideology in Ezra-Nehemiah as a Tool to Reconstitute the Community," *Journal for the Study of Judaism* 35 (2004): 1–16. See also the recent volume on Jewish views of intermarriage: Christian Frevel, ed., *Mixed Marriages: Intermarriage and Group Identity in the Second Temple Period* (New York: T & T Clark, 2011).

apart by God, so has all of Israel. This strategy emerges out of a postexilic context and the author's concern for restoring and defining Israel as God's people. Ezra expresses this idea through an attack on exogamy for at least all male Israelites, as he exclaims over the Israelite men who have married outsiders: "They have taken their daughters as wives for themselves and for their sons, so that the holy seed has become intermingled with the peoples of the land; and it is the officers and prefects who have taken the lead in this sacrilege" (Ezra 9:2).[21] Ezra's zealous call for endogamy serves to circumscribe and protect Israel as a people through generations, a holy seed, pure and set apart from others. Ezra's defense of endogamy is an ethno-racial discourse that casts mixed marriage as an unholy mixing, a profaning of God's people.

Jubilees follows and amplifies this line of reasoning, arguing, with some creative interpretation of Genesis, that a universal ban on intermarriage is found in the Pentateuch, that it constitutes a sexual sin, and that it generates moral impurity and thus defiles the seed of Israel.[22] *Jubilees* claims that Israel is "holy unto the Lord" (30:8) and that "it is unclean and abominable to Israel" when daughters of the gentiles are taken in marriage (30:13).[23]

Furthermore, *Jubilees* uses the holy seed idea to distinguish between gentiles and Jews. Although gentiles number among Abraham's seed:

> . . . in Isaac should his name and seed be called . . . from the sons of Isaac one should become a holy seed, and should not be reckoned among the Gentiles. For he should become the portion of the Most High, and all his seed had fallen into the possession of God, that it should be unto the

21. Translation from Hayes, *Gentile Impurities*, 28.

22. Ibid., 75.

23. Translation from *The Book of Jubilees or Little Genesis*, translated by R. H. Charles (London: Adam and Charles Black, 1902), 180 (30:8) and 181 (30:13); available online through Open Library at http://openlibrary.org/books/OL23282255M/The_book_of_Jubilees. See Hayes, *Gentile Impurities*, 73–81, for a discussion of *Jubilees* on intermarriage.

Lord a people for (His) possession above all nations and that it should become a kingdom of priests and a holy nation." (*Jub.* 16:17-19a)[24]

Jubilees cobbles together a number of biblical passages to construct the argument that although gentiles are included in the larger pool of Abraham's descendants, they are not part of the holy seed that belongs to God. We see Ezra's application of the sanctity of the priesthood to this holy lineage, which *Jubilees* calls a "kingdom of priests" (echoing Exod. 19:6). We also hear echoes of a number of patriarchal succession passages from Genesis, which identify the chosen heir in the succeeding generation, the one who will transmit the promises and blessings to descendants (Gen. 12:3; 18:18; 28:4). Specifically in Genesis 21:12, in response to Sarah's worry over which of Abraham's sons will be his heir, God explains to Abraham, ". . . for your seed will be said to be in Isaac."

These arguments issuing from Ezra and *Jubilees* and others, which Christine Hayes calls "genealogical impurity," are intended, in Hayes's view, to draw a firm and permanent boundary around Israel.[25] Appeals to origins and lineages, which are allegedly fixed components, secure Israel's identity. Whereas many Second Temple texts express a more lenient attitude toward gentiles, accommodating their interaction with Israel in a number of ways, the rhetoric in Ezra and *Jubilees* shows little tolerance for mixing or close interaction.

Paul also uses the concept of the "seed" to argue about gentiles, even echoing some of the same passages as *Jubilees*, but the rhetorical intent is quite different. Paul, too, capitalizes on Genesis passages that associate "gentiles" (*ethnē*) with Abraham.[26] For his purposes, though,

---

24. Translation from Charles, *Book of Jubilees*, 115–16.
25. Hayes, *Gentile Impurities*, 32–33. Although as I have argued, even as many texts claim a kind of fixedness to kinship ties, many also see kinship and genealogy as mutable and open for negotiation (Johnson Hodge, *If Sons*, 19–42).
26. All of the Genesis passages discussed here in reference to Paul are from the LXX.

these passages support his argument that gentiles are actually included in the blessed lineage from the beginning. He maintains this inclusive argument even as he later applies an exclusive one of God privileging certain lineages over others.

As I have discussed at length elsewhere, baptism in Paul is a ritual of adoption, creating a kinship relationship between gentiles and Abraham (Gal. 3; Rom. 4).[27] To support his case, in Galatians 3:6-9 Paul refers back to a founding moment in Israel's history, when God called Abraham, recognized him as faithful, and conferred upon him blessings and promises. Indeed, one of these promises, foretold by Scripture to Abraham long ago, is that, "All the gentiles (*ethnē*) will be blessed in you" (Gal. 3:8; Gen. 12:3; 18:18).

This phrase, "All the gentiles will be blessed in you," is likely a conflation of two passages from Genesis, both of which recount this moment of Abraham's call and God's blessings upon him, Genesis 12:3 and 18:18.[28] These moments of call and blessing are replicated elsewhere in Genesis, both for Abraham (again) and also for Isaac (Gen. 26:4) and Jacob (Gen. 28:14). Genesis 22:18 helps us understand what Paul might mean by the gentiles being blessed "in" Abraham, "And in your seed shall all the *ethnē* of the earth be blessed." The gentiles are blessed in Abraham's seed. These blessings rely on a logic of descent in which future generations are thought to be contained in the seed of the founding ancestor, a logic reflected in the use of the same term, *sperma*, for seed and for descendants.[29] Paul's own creative interpretation of Scripture allows him to claim that these *ethnē* mentioned in Genesis are those gentiles who have been baptized into Christ. We should not be surprised at their inclusion

27. Johnson Hodge, *If Sons*, 67–116.
28. Gen. 12:3: "And I will bless those who bless you and curse those that curse you and in you all the tribes of the earth shall be blessed." Gen. 18:18: "But Abraham shall become a great and populous nation and all the *ethnē* of the earth will be blessed in him."
29. Johnson Hodge, *If Sons*, 97–100.

in God's plan; they were present in Abraham's body at the time of the blessing. They, too, upon receiving the spirit at baptism, are the descendants (*sperma*) of Abraham, as Paul declares in Galatians 3:29.[30]

Part of what Paul is doing in these passages is reworking kinship. His larger task is to explain how it is that gentiles have been included in Israel's story of redemption. To do this, he relies on the language of descent and peoplehood, the same language Jews have always applied to their relationship with God. But it is not just kinship of the flesh, Paul argues, generated by human procreation, but kinship defined and arranged by God. The calling of Abraham passages serve as Paul's scriptural warrant to show that relationship to God is defined not just through physical descent, but also through faithfulness and the promises made by God to Abraham.

This is the argument at work in Romans 9, where Paul refers to the same Genesis passage as the *Jubilees* passage above, the blessing of Isaac. Here Paul argues that God is managing the lines of descent and that "not all of Abraham's children (*tekna*) are his descendants or seed (*sperma*), but" (and here he quotes Gen. 21:12), "'your seed will be said to be in Isaac'" (Rom. 9:7). It is not just flesh, Paul goes on to explain, but the promise that determines who the descendants are. God is in charge of lineages.

Jubilees uses this Isaac blessing in Genesis to exclude gentiles; they may have been a part of Abraham's seed, but they do not make the cut into the holy lineage of Isaac and Jacob after him. Paul uses the same passage, also to make a point about exclusivity and selection of one over the other, but it serves his larger argument that faithful gentiles are included in God's promises. So Paul takes a different turn with the seed ideology, choosing to open it up wide enough for gentiles

---

30. Paul makes a similar argument in Romans 4, where he concludes that Abraham is the father of the "uncircumcised" and the "circumcised" (vv. 11-12).

to come in, harkening back to a time before the Law was established to show the universal reach of the God of Israel.

What does it mean for the status of gentiles that they are in the original seed of Abraham? This seed argument does not emphasize a pure and holy origin, either for Jews or gentiles, but an inclusive mixture, planned by God.[31] Yet Paul does not envision a blending of the different components of this mixture; gentiles remain gentiles and Jews remain Jews, even among those who share their "in-Christness." In fact, his whole point is that it is precisely their inclusion in Abraham's seed, before the Law was given, that guarantees gentiles the benefits of the promises of God *as gentiles*, without being circumcised and keeping the Law in other ways. Their Abrahamic lineage, ironically, preserves their separation from Israel.

Holy Bodies

Paul does not develop a concept of a holy seed, but he does develop the idea of holy bodies for gentile believers. In 1 Corinthians 6, Paul offers a "before and after" assessment of the Corinthians, in a similar passage as those mentioned earlier, comparing them to their previous lives as gentiles who do not know God. Some of you used to be sexually immoral, idolaters, adulterers (and so on), Paul tells the Corinthians, "But you were washed, you were sanctified, you were justified in the name of the Lord Jesus Christ and in the Spirit of our God" (6:9b-11).[32] Here Paul seems to refer to their baptism with the

31. Discussing 1 Corinthians, Tat-Siong Benny Liew makes a similar observation, "What one finds in Paul is not a nostalgia to recover a lost authenticity and/or purity; instead, it is one that incorporates Gentiles through a new racial/ethnic and religious construction," in Liew, *What is Asian American Biblical Hermeneutics?: Reading the New Testament* (Honolulu: University of Hawaii Press, 2008), 106.

32. First Corinthians 6:9b (which I paraphrase here) is complicated to translate and I will not address the issues involved here. See Dale B. Martin, "*Arsenokoitēs* and *Malakos*: Meanings and Consequences," in his collection of essays, *Sex and the Single Savior: Gender and Sexuality in Biblical Interpretation* (Louisville: Westminster John Knox, 2007), 37–50. See also Bernadette

term "washed," implying that he understands it as a purifying rite that brings the gentiles into a right relationship with God. In this passage and in others that similarly mark the baptized gentiles as now holy, Paul uses, as Paula Fredriksen argues, the language of the biblical prescriptions that monitor access to the temple cult.[33] These gentiles have been separated out, dedicated, prepared for God. As Fredriksen explains, the language of the temple cult provides "the chief terms by which Paul conceptualizes the incorporation of his pagans-in-Christ into Israel's redemption."[34] This is most explicit when Paul asserts that the gentiles are temples themselves (1 Cor. 6:19; 3:16-17). This architectural metaphor suggests bodies that are protected, sanctified, and bounded from other types of space; yet they are also inhabited by God's *pneuma* (6:19; 3:16) and are therefore holy (3:17). Baptism has thus sanctified the gentiles so they can be a dwelling place for God.[35]

One result of this new status is that these holy bodies must be protected. In language that echoes Levitical prescriptions for the bodies of priests, Paul argues that these gentiles, too, must abstain

J. Brooten, *Love Between Women: Early Christian Responses to Female Homoeroticism* (Chicago: University of Chicago Press, 1996), 260.

33. Fredriksen, "Judaizing the Nations," 247. Other passages with this language include: 1 Cor. 1:2 ("to those who are sanctified [*hegiasmenois*] in Christ Jesus"); Rom. 6:19: ("For just as you once presented your members as slaves to impurity [*akatharsia*] and to greater and greater iniquity, so now present your members as slaves to righteousness for sanctification [*hagiasmon*]"); Rom. 15:16 ("Paul a minister of Christ Jesus to the gentiles in the priestly service of the gospel of God, so that the offering of the gentiles may be acceptable, sanctified by [*hegiasmene*] the holy spirit"); 1 Thess. 4:7 ("For God did not call us to impurity but in holiness [*hagiasmō*]"); 1 Thess. 5:3 ("May the God of peace sanctify [*hagiasai*] you entirely"); 2 Cor. 7:1 ("let us cleanse ourselves in body and spirit, making our holiness [*hagiosunēn*] perfect"); 2 Cor. 12:21 ("I fear that when I come again, my God may humble me before you, and that I may have to mourn over many who previously sinned and have not repented of the impurity [*akatharsia*], sexual immorality, and licentiousness that they have practiced").
34. Fredriksen, "Judaizing the Nations," 250. See also Jorunn Økland, *Women in Their Place: Paul and the Corinthian Discourse of Gender and Sanctuary Space* (New York: T & T Clark, 2004), 133–34, and sources cited there.
35. If, as J. Z. Smith argues, rituals create sacred space in the ancient world, so we might see baptism as a ritual that has created sacred space of these gentile bodies: they were washed, sanctified and justified (1 Cor. 6:11). See Økland's discussion of Smith in *Women in Their Place*, 145–49.

from *porneia*. Leviticus instructs that because priests are "holy to their God" (Lev. 21:6), they are not to "marry a woman who is a prostitute (*pornē*) and defiled" (21:7, 14). Furthermore, a priest must marry "a virgin from his own kin, so as not to profane his offspring (seed, *sperma*) among his people" (21:15). Priestly lineages have been set apart, sanctified by God, and this holy status requires maintenance.

Paul describes the Corinthian bodies in similar terms. As priestly bodies are "holy to the Lord," Corinthian bodies "belong to the Lord" and not to *porneia* (1 Cor. 6:13, 19-20).[36] As a priestly body is responsible for his seed or descendants, and must keep his lineage holy, so Corinthians are "members of Christ" (6:15) and must protect this holy body. As priests are not to marry prostitutes, so Corinthian bodies are not to engage in *porneia*, such as uniting with a prostitute (*pornē*).[37] You can hear the horror in Paul's voice as he poses the rhetorical question: "Should I take the members of Christ and make them members of a prostitute? Never!" (1 Cor. 6:15).[38]

As I discussed earlier, Ezra democratizes the notion of priestly holiness by applying it to all Israel, creating the idea of holy seed. Paul does the same thing here, but applies it specifically to baptized gentiles to create holy bodies. Ezra's argument serves his larger interest in defining Israel in the postexilic context. Paul, too, attempts to define and circumscribe the community of believers, the body of Christ, with the purity of priests.

Once again, as with the image of the seed in Galatians, Paul's description of this new creation produces a mixed identity. These

36. See also Rom. 15:16.
37. Although note that being married to a non-believer is not polluting, but sanctifying (1 Cor. 7:12-16). See Caroline Johnson Hodge, "Married to an Unbeliever: Households, Hierarchies and Holiness in 1 Corinthians 7:12-16," *Harvard Theological Review* 103, no. 1 (2010): 1–25.
38. Christine Hayes argues that Paul is creating a new kind of impurity here, a combination of ritual impurity and moral impurity in Jewish tradition. In the case of these gentiles, moral behavior creates a contagious impurity. Hayes calls this innovation "carnal impurity." See *Gentile Impurities*, 92–98.

gentile bodies are now also Christ's Jewish body. Paul elaborates on this notion of the *ekklesia* in Corinth constituting the body of Christ in the well-known passage from 1 Corinthians, in which Paul compares the members of the community to body parts such as hands, ears, and feet (12:12-26). Filled with Christ's *pneuma* at baptism, these gentile bodies have undergone a material transformation that makes them into the Jewish body of Israel's messiah. Benny Liew comments on this multiethnic mixture, "Paul is engineering here nothing less than an inter-racial/ethnic bodily substitution . . . The Corinthian body . . . is, in other words, built on and through a racial/ethnic 'other'. . ."[39] Gentile believers inhabit racially mixed bodies that need protection. Instead of becoming "one flesh" with a prostitute, Paul exhorts, become "one spirit" with the Lord (1 Cor. 6:17). This pneumatic unity with the Lord in a gentile body results in a holy, mixed identity.

Gentiles as a Part of Israel's Story

Each of these two lines of argument, seed of Abraham and purity discourse, serves a different rhetorical purpose. In Galatians, Paul contests the notion that gentiles-in-Christ should keep the Law and uses the seed of Abraham argument to support his view. Because they were "in" Abraham when the promises were made, and before the Law was given, gentiles-in-Christ are still recipients of those promises, despite the fact that the men among them are not circumcised. In 1 Corinthians, Paul responds to competing ideas about how to live this new life in Christ. Throughout the letter he tries to control gentile bodies, urging harmony, cooperation, and

---

39. Liew, *Asian American Biblical Hermeneutics*, 106.

self-control.[40] These different persuasive aims are responsible at least in part for the ways Paul portrays gentile identity in each.

Nevertheless, I notice some intriguing similarities between the two. They both apply biblical ethno-racial discourses—descent and purity—to gentiles-in-Christ. They show that, like Israel, these gentiles are included in God's people from the beginning, and are separated from other gentiles upon their receipt of the sanctifying spirit in baptism. Inherent in both of these arguments is mixture: gentiles are lodged in the seed of Abraham so they count as his descendants, but as gentile descendants. And the Corinthian bodies are themselves body parts of Christ, the Jewish messiah. They are inhabited by his *pneuma*. Both images hold together these contradictions without attempting to resolve them. In striking contrast to ethnic discourses of Ezra or *Jubilees*, the sort of mixture embodied by gentiles-in-Christ is, according to Paul, holy.

Furthermore, this mixed status of gentiles is non-negotiable for Paul. He adamantly argues against the position that they should keep the Law in the way Jews do (specifically, circumcision for men), as others seem to have taught (Gal. 1:6; 5:2-12). For in Paul's view, God's larger plan requires gentiles to worship the God of Israel *as gentiles*, not as proselytes or something else. Paul allies himself here with the Jewish eschatological expectation that God will establish his kingdom for Israel and for favored nations. As the apostle to the gentiles, he sees himself in the tradition of the prophets who call gentiles to Jerusalem on the Day of the Lord, when "all the nations shall stream to [the Lord's house]" (Isa. 2:2).[41] As Paula Fredriksen has

40. On these themes see Margaret M. Mitchell, *Paul and the Rhetoric of Reconciliation: An Exegetical Investigation of the Language and Composition of 1 Corinthians* (Louisville: Westminster John Knox Press, 1991); Laura S. Nasrallah, *An Ecstasy of Folly: Prophecy and Authority in Early Christianity* (Cambridge: Harvard University Press, 2003), 78–79; Johnson Hodge, "Married to an Unbeliever."

41. When Paul describes his own calling from God in Gal. 1:15-16, his language echoes closely the calls to the prophets Isaiah and Jeremiah (see Isa. 49:1-6 and Jer. 1:5).

argued, this eschatological pilgrimage tradition—both in Paul and in earlier Jewish literature—envisions gentiles turning to God as non-Jews, not as proselytes.[42]

Mark Nanos agrees, and sees the concept of the Shema as crucial for understanding Paul on this point.[43] If "the Lord is One," as the Shema states, then he is Lord of all, not just Israel. Paul lays out this logic in Romans 3:29-31, and, as Nanos argues, it underlies Paul's understanding of God's plans for the future. Because God is the one God of all, when Christ returns to establish God's kingdom, it is necessary for Israel and gentiles to worship God not as one people, but as separate peoples—now worshipping together, as expected in the awaited age. Paul is clear in Romans 9–11, where he lays out this larger plan, that Jews and gentiles remain separate.[44] As Paul explains, once the "full number of gentiles has come in," then "all of Israel will be saved" (Rom. 11:25-26).[45] Thus for Paul there is a lot at stake in the specific, ambiguous position of gentiles-in-Christ.[46]

Rethinking the Question

If my analysis has shown that Paul's portrayal of gentiles as mixed or ambiguous makes some sense in a Jewish context of eschatological

---

42. Fredriksen, "Judaism," 547; see also Eisenbaum, *Paul Was Not A Christian*, 96–98.

43. The Shema is a Jewish prayer, "Hear, O Israel, the Lord is our God, the Lord is One." See Mark D. Nanos, *The Mystery of Romans: The Jewish Context of Paul's Letter* (Minneapolis: Fortress Press, 1996), 179–201; Nanos, "Paul and the Jewish Tradition: The Ideology of the Shema," in *Celebrating Paul. Festschrift in Honor of Jerome Murphy-O'Connor, O.P., and Joseph A. Fitzmyer, S.J.*, Catholic Biblical Quarterly Monograph Series 48, ed. Peter Spitaler (Washington, DC: Catholic Biblical Association of America, 2012), 62–80.

44. Johnson Hodge, *If Sons*, 137–48. Krister Stendahl calls this arrangement God's "traffic plan" in *Final Account: Paul's Letter to the Romans* (Minneapolis: Fortress Press, 1995), 7.

45. See the recent survey of this phrase by James M. Scott, "'And Then All Israel Will Be Saved' (Rom 11:26)," in *Restoration: Old Testament, Jewish, and Christian Perspectives*, Supplements to the Journal for the Study of Judaism 72, ed. James M. Scott (Leiden: Brill, 2001), 491–92.

46. In keeping with this general idea, Brent Nongbri argues in his dissertation that the addressees of Paul's letters are gentiles who have been made holy by *pneuma* in baptism so they are prepared to worship at the temple along with Israel: "Paul Without Religion: The Creation of a Category and the Search for an Apostle Beyond the New Perspective," PhD diss., Yale University, 2008.

expectation, it simultaneously raises some important cautions about concepts of identity. My initial question—who are the gentiles?—itself assumes that there is an answer, that they have an identity that can be discovered through an analysis of the text.[47] I suggest two problems with this assumption. One is that it betrays an understanding of identity that is perhaps overly simplistic, in which people change wholesale from one to the other. Rogers Brubaker critiques this view especially when applied to groups of people, like ethnic groups. He objects to a common, yet naïve, assumption among scholars that groups operate ". . . as if they were internally homogeneous, externally bounded groups, even unitary collective actors with common purposes."[48] Evidence from anthropology, from cognitive science, from ancient texts, including those discussed here, suggest a much more complex dynamic at work.[49]

A second, closely related problem is that such an assumption confuses the strategies of the speaker with a description of reality.[50] The letters, after all, give us access to *Paul's construction* of who the gentiles are. As feminist scholarship has long argued, his rhetoric is prescriptive, not descriptive, and his goal is to coax the gentiles to think and behave in certain ways.[51] How the gentiles understand

---

47. For this critique I draw upon Rogers Brubaker, *Ethnicity Without Groups* (Cambridge, MA: Harvard University Press, 2004), 37 and passim, and Stanley K. Stowers, "The Concept of 'Community' and the History of Early Christianity," *Method and Theory in the Study of Religion* 23 (2011): 238–56.

48. Brubaker, *Ethnicity Without Groups*, 8, see also 37.

49. This complexity includes people identifying with multiple groups, assuming partial identities, and holding different interpretations of who they are. See Brubaker, *Ethnicity Without Groups*, esp. 64–87; Stanley K. Stowers, "Kinds of Myth, Meals, and Power: Paul and the Corinthians," in *Redescribing Paul and the Corinthians*, eds. Ron Cameron and Merrill Miller (Atlanta: Society of Biblical Literature, 2011), 105–49. For compatible views on the activities of forming and defining groups with ethnic and racial language, see Denise Kimber Buell, *Why This New Race: Ethnic Reasoning in Early Christianity* (New York: Columbia University Press, 2005).

50. Brubaker, *Ethnicity Without Groups*, 9. Scholarship on Paul has been vulnerable to this slippage, where Paul's persuasive rhetoric has been taken as neutral, reliable information about his audience and context.

themselves and their relationships to Paul and to each other may have had little to do with Paul's categories.

Instead, Brubaker argues that ethnic identity should be viewed as a process, a perspective on the world, rather than a thing that exists independent of human arguments. Thus it is important to rethink the question: instead of asking who the gentiles are, it is more fruitful to ask what sort of work ethno-racial rhetoric—or any sort of claim about identity—does. Brubaker offers different language to signal this perspective: instead of using "identity," he proposes "identification" and "categorization," both of which derive from verb forms and remind us that comments about identity are acts of identity-creation themselves.[52] There are myriad social formations in the ancient world that generate categories around which people might form alliances: households, patrons and clients, associations, neighborhoods, groups of artisans, religious cults, markets, and so on.[53] Thinking of identity as a practice based on identifying and categorizing allows us to account for this wide variety. In the ancient world, ethno-racial language is often deployed in practices of identity-creation, a discourse Denise Buell names "ethnic reasoning."[54] Buell and others have shown the great flexibility of ethnic language to argue for human difference and sameness among authors in Paul's time. The language of peoplehood is useful for "group-making projects."[55]

51. Here I name just a few monographs in a vast bibliography: Elisabeth Schüssler Fiorenza, *In Memory of Her: A Feminist Theological Reconstruction of Christian Origins* (New York: Crossroad, 1983); Elizabeth Castelli, *Imitating Paul: A Discourse of Power* (Louisville: Westminster John Knox, 1991); Margaret Y. MacDonald, *Early Christian Women and Pagan Tradition: The Power of the Hysterical Woman* (Cambridge: Cambridge University Press, 1996); Ross Shepard Kraemer and Mary Rose D'Angelo, eds., *Women and Christian Origins* (New York: Oxford University Press, 1999).

52. Brubaker suggests three clusters of words that might replace "identity": 1) identification and categorization, 2) self-understanding and social location, 3) commonality, connectedness and groupness (*Ethnicity Without Groups*, 41–48).

53. Stanley K. Stowers, "Concept of Community," 249–50.

54. Buell, *Why This New Race.*

55. Brubaker's phrase from *Ethnicity Without Groups*, 13–14.

This shift in our question helps us with Paul's treatment of gentiles-in-Christ, as one final example from Paul's text illustrates. In Galatians 3:28, Paul suggests a radical unity among the different groups who belong to Christ, including Jews and Greeks, "for you are all one in Christ." In his own group-making project, Paul urges them to coalesce around the category of being "in Christ," which both Jews and gentiles would have understood as a Jewish position. But, as I have argued above, he does so while insisting that gentiles remain gentiles. Paul is not asking for an ethnic transformation from non-Jew to Jew. Instead, he argues that gentiles adopt Jewish attributes but remain gentiles.

Think about the differences of being "in-Christ" for gentiles and Jews. Jews do not cross ethnic boundaries by virtue of their commitment to Christ; they do not change their God, their ancestry, or their ancestral customs. Gentiles do.[56] Thus, of the various people identified as descendants—gentiles in Christ (Gal. 3:8, 29) Jews (Rom. 4:12), Paul (2 Cor. 12:2), Jesus (Gal. 3:16)—gentiles are the ones for whom this implies a hybrid ethnic identity. To be in Christ, gentiles give up their gods and religious practices, profess loyalty to the God of Israel, accept Israel's messiah, Scriptures, and ancestry. All of these are Jewish ethnic markers, yet the gentiles do not become Jews. They are tucked into the seed of Abraham as gentiles and they remain gentiles, of a special sort, after they are made holy through baptism. This complex and mixed status for gentiles-in-Christ is crucial to Paul's argument: their separateness is necessary for God's plan for Israel, as Paul sees it.

It is striking that with all of Paul's talk of transformation and being made new (e.g., in 2 Cor. 5:17 and Gal. 6:15), he does not clearly define what gentiles have become. Scholars have long supplied

---

56. For more discussion of this argument, see Johnson Hodge, *If Sons*, 125–35.

"Christian" to fill this void. But this misses the whole point. An exploration of how Paul portrays gentiles helps us see these letters not as founding documents of new religion, but as efforts by a faithful Jew to play his part in the larger narrative of the redemption of Israel.

6

_____

The Question of Worship: Gods, Pagans, and the Redemption of Israel

Paula Fredriksen

Paul's convictions about the impending dawn of God's kingdom place him securely within the world of late Second Temple Jewish apocalyptic hope. But Paul's biblical tradition was Greek, not Aramaic or Hebrew. His audience—unlike that of Jesus and of the earliest disciples—was pagan, not Jewish.[1] And he stretched his time-driven gospel over the spatial frame provided by antiquity's map of the cosmos. Paul's universe, in brief, was much larger—ethnically,

---

1. "Pagan," a fourth-century Christian neologism, is an anachronistic word choice to translate *ethnē*. I use it nonetheless to communicate the connectedness of ethnicity with divinity: non-Jews, like Jews, were born into obligations to their gods. The translation "gentile" confusingly effaces that connection. The discussion later in this writing will further clarify this point.

geographically, celestially, theologically—and much more populated than was that of the earliest movement, and of Jesus himself. Jesus of Nazareth seems to have battled chiefly low, local, illness-inducing demons.[2] Paul (like the risen Christ) combatted cosmic forces: *daimonia* (by which Paul meant pagan gods), *stoicheia, archontes, exousiai, theoi,* and *kurioi,* "the god of this *aion.*"[3]

The situation on earth was as it was in heaven: these gods also thickly inhabited the ancient city, structuring human time, space, and social relations. Dedicated festivals, celebrating seasons and days sacred to divine patrons celestial and imperial, punctuated the civic year. The venues of these celebrations—the theatre, the circus, the stadium, the amphitheater—held altars to and images of these gods. Household calendars and domestic space replicated in miniature these civic structures, where celebrations of the family—marriages, the *pater*'s *genius,* a child's passage to adulthood—also invoked and honored presiding deities.[4] The gods were everywhere, not only in the public and private buildings of ancient municipalities, but also on insignia of office, on military standards, in solemn oaths and contracts, in vernacular benedictions and exclamations, and

2. After facing off with Satan in the wilderness, Jesus chiefly confronts demons or unclean spirits that cause mental or physical illness (e.g., Mark 1:23-27, 32, 34, 39; 3:11-12, 22; 5:2-16, cf. 6:7, 13; 7:13-29; 9:17-29, 38).

3. *Archontes, exousiai, dunameis,* 1 Cor. 2:8, 15:24; *daimonia,* 1 Cor. 10:21, cf. Ps. 95:5 LXX; *stoicheia,* Gal. 4:8-9; *theos* of this world, 2 Cor. 4:4; *theoi* and *kurioi,* 1 Cor. 8:5. See further James D. G. Dunn, *The Theology of Paul the Apostle* (Grand Rapids: Eerdmans, 1998), 33-38, 104-10, on Paul's references to gods and to heavenly powers; Paula Fredriksen, *Sin: The Early History of an Idea* (Princeton, NJ: Princeton University Press, 2012), 50-57, on cosmic architecture and its impact on Paul's theology, his rhetoric, and his ideas about redemption. Further on the genealogy of these lower divinities, see Dale Martin, "When Did Angels Become Demons?" *Journal of Biblical Literature* 129, no. 4 (2010): 657-77.

4. Caroline Johnson Hodge, "'Married to an Unbeliever': Households, Hierarchies and Holiness in 1 Corinthians 7:12-16," *Harvard Theological Review* 103 (2010): 1-25, explores the complications that domestic cult would cause for believing wives married to unbelieving husbands. Further, on worshiping the divine *genius* of the household, see Michael Peppard, *The Son of God in the Roman World* (New York: Oxford University Press, 2011), 39, 43, 63-66, 113-15.

throughout the curricula of the educated. It was impossible to live in a Greco-Roman city without living with its gods.[5]

This god-congested environment, civic and cosmic, was the matrix of Paul's mission. As Paul worked with pagan communities, he also worked with—or, rather, against—their gods. Accordingly, both he and his *ekklēsiai* had to deal with divine anger, because Paul insisted that being "in Christ" required that these people withhold cult to their gods. But *why* would Paul demand this? What does this pagan ritual reorientation have to do with Paul's summons to "justification by faith"? And finally, what do these gods and their humans have to do with the salvation of "all Israel" (Rom. 11:26)?

Much in every way.

Gods and Their Humans in the Ancient City

We are so used to knowing that "gentiles," in order to join this new messianic movement, had to foreswear the worship of "pagan" gods, that we easily fail to see what an odd idea this was, both in the context of the ancient city and in the context of Diaspora Jewish communities.

Our very vocabulary undermines our efforts to see its oddness clearly. Modern English uses two words, *gentiles* and *pagans,* where the Greek on which both rest has only one, *ta ethnē,* "the nations." And the two different English words have different connotations. *Gentile* refers to ethnicity: the person is not a Jew. *Pagan* refers to religion: the person is neither a Jew nor a Christian. But this

---

5. My description draws particularly upon Tertullian's fulminations in *de spectaculis* and in *de idololatria*. Palestinian rabbis were no less aware of the gods and their civic throw-weight: *m. Avodah Zarah* 1:3 names the Kalends (a winter festival eight days after the solstice), the Saturnalia (eight days before the winter solstice), and the *kratasis* (days celebrating imperial accession to office) as well as imperial birth days and death days as "the festivals of the gentiles;" see esp. Fritz Graf, "Roman Festivals in Syria Palestina," *The Talmud Yerushalmi and Graeco-Roman Culture,* ed. Peter Shäfer (Tübingen: Mohr Siebeck, 2002), 435–51.

distinction between ethnicity and religion conjured by *gentile/pagan* is not native to ancient Mediterranean cultures, where gods and humans formed family groups. Connections between heaven and earth were configured precisely along ethnic lines. From the micro-level of one's family to the macro-level of one's city, ancient gods ran in the blood.[6] What we think of as "religion" ancient people accordingly constructed as an inheritance: *mos maiorum, fides patrum, ta patria ēthē, paradoseis tōn patrikōn* (this last from Paul, Gal. 1:14). "Religion" as a category separable and separate from one's "family"—household to empire—did not exist.

Finally, *gentile* versus *pagan* masks the degree to which not only households but also cities were family-based religious institutions.[7] The ties of "blood" relations bound the citizens of a city together both with each other and also with their gods. Sometimes these bonds were configured as royal descent, whereby the offspring of a primordial divine/human coupling conferred semi-divine status on a much later ruler.[8] But whole populations might descend from a god, and such lineages could be put to practical political use: Hellenistic and Roman diplomats, negotiating treaties between cities, would establish shared kinship, traced through lines of descent back to a god, or to his or her offspring. This ancient bond of shared "blood"

---

6. Peppard, *Son of God*, 60–67, explores the ways that the emperor Augustus, in positioning himself as *pater familias* of empire, constructed a family relationship between himself and others in the Roman world, thereby spreading abroad the worship of his *genius*. In this way, the empire itself became a family-based religious institution.

7. On family cult, see Jonathan Z. Smith, "Here, There, and Anywhere," in *Relating Religion: Essays in the Study of Religion* (Chicago: University of Chicago Press, 2004), 323–39; and the essays in *Household and Family Religion*, ed. John Bodel and Saul M. Olyan (Malden, MA: Blackwell, 2008). On the civic construction of blood ties, see especially Christopher P. Jones, *Kinship Diplomacy in the Ancient World* (Cambridge, MA: Harvard University Press, 1999).

8. In this way, Alexander the Great "descended" from Heracles, and the Julian house, via Aeneas, from Venus. On Octavian's status as "son of God," see Peppard, *Son of God*, 46–48. More metaphorically, Jews mobilized the same idea to describe the relationship between their god and rulers of the house of David, e.g., Ps. 2:7; 2 Sam. 7:12, 14. On Israel as God's son, e.g., Exod. 4:22; Jer. 31:9; Rom. 9:4.

stabilized current agreements. So concretely did ancient people construe these relationships that Hellenistic Jews, whose god did not leave behind children in the ways that Greek gods did, had to scramble to get into the system. They did so by mobilizing the progeny of the patriarchs: in this way, through the marriage of Heracles with a granddaughter of Abraham's, they established *syngeneia* ("kinship") between Sparta and Jerusalem.[9]

The strength of this family association of gods and citizens accounts for two interesting remarks made about first-century Alexandrian Jews. Apion, in the wake of the turmoil of 39 CE, complained, "If the Jews wish to be citizens of Alexandria, why don't they worship the Alexandrian gods?" Membership in the citizen body immediately implied this divine/human connection.[10] The author of Acts, on the other hand, noting the hometown of Apollos, describes him with intriguing incoherence as "a certain *Ioudaios* . . . an Alexandrian by *genos*" (Acts 18:24). *Genos* ("race"), like *ethnos* ("people"), and like the Latin *natio* by which it was sometimes translated, communicates a "birth"/"blood" connection. *Ioudaios* ("Jew" or "Judaean") and *Alexandreus* ("Alexandrian"), two different *genē*, are notionally mutually exclusive. This is so not only when "family" was construed biologically (how many different sets of biological parents does one have?), but also, given the peculiarities of the Jewish god, when "family" was construed theologically. (The

---

9. "After reading a certain document," announces a Spartan king to the Jewish high priest, "we have found that Jews and Lacedaemonians [Spartans] are of one *genos*, and share a connection with Abraham," 1 Macc. 12:21. This *suggeneia* also appears in 2 Macc. 5:9 and in Josephus, *Ant.* 12.226; for Heracles's union with Abraham's granddaughter, *Ant.* 1.24–41. Analysis of this tradition in Jones, *Kinship Diplomacy*, 72–80; Erich Gruen, "Jewish Perspectives on Greek Ethnicity," in *Ancient Perceptions of Greek Ethnicity*, ed. I. Malkin (Cambridge, MA: Harvard University Press, 2001), 347–73, at 361–64. Paul will also avail himself of this idea of Abraham as "the father of many nations," Rom. 4:11–18; Gal. 3:7–14; cf. Gen. 17:5; Stanley Stowers, *A Rereading of Romans* (New Haven, CT: Yale University Press, 1994), 227–50.

10. *Ag. Ap.* 2.65; cf. the similar complaints from cities in first-century Asia Minor, *Ant.* 12.126.

Jewish god demanded that his people worship him alone; Alexandrian gods were more accommodating.) Yet so strong is the "genetic" construal of citizenship in Luke's culture that he presents Apollos as both.[11]

Luke's odd statement nevertheless makes an important point: Jews fit, and fit well, into their Diaspora cities.[12] Classical authors groused about the Jews' *asebeia* (atheism, meaning refusal to worship the gods), their separateness, and their lack of sociability. But these authors repeat many of the same complaints about other ethnic groups as well: ancient ethnographers seem not to have much liked other *ethnē*.[13] Our inscriptional evidence and the vast production of Hellenistic Jewish literature tell a different story. Hellenistic Jews mastered the schools' curriculum, availing themselves of gymnasia educations (which means that as *ephēbes*, thus citizens-in-training, they were actively involved in honoring the city's gods). They served as soldiers and as generals in foreign armies, and as town councilors in their cities of residence. They funded pagan liturgies and, when manumitting slaves, dedicated inscriptions to their own god while invoking Greek gods as well.[14] Simply by living in a Diaspora city,

---

11. This passage in Acts is a vivid illustration of the ways in which ancient constructions of ethnicity are both fluid and fixed. Another possible interpretation of Luke's phrasing here would be that Apollos was an Alexandrian pagan convert to Judaism, but elsewhere, passim, Acts designates such people *prosēlytoi*.

12. The most recent review of Jewish Diaspora acculturation to Hellenism is René Bloch, *Moses und der Mythos* (Leiden: Brill, 2010); before him, Erich Gruen, *Diaspora: Jews Amidst Greeks and Romans* (Cambridge, MA: Harvard University Press, 2002), and John Barclay, *Jews in the Mediterranean Diaspora* (Edinburgh: T & T Cark, 1996). Inscriptional materials are gathered, organized, and analyzed in Margaret Williams, *Jews Among the Greeks and Romans: A Diasporan Sourcebook* (Baltimore: Johns Hopkins Press, 1998); Irina Levinskaya, *The Book of Acts in its Diaspora Setting* (Grand Rapids: Eerdmans, 1996); also Terence Donaldson, *Judaism and the Gentiles* (Waco, TX: Baylor University Press, 2007), 437–66.

13. Benjamin Isaac, *The Invention of Racism in Classical Antiquity* (Princeton, NJ: Princeton University Press, 2005), provides an exhaustive survey of this literature, broken down by ethnic targets (Goths, Scythians, Persians, Celts, and so on).

14. The first-century CE inscriptions listing the *ephēbes*' names in Cyrene (Jesus son of Antiphilos and Eleazar son of Eleazar) are dedicated to the gods of the gymnasium, Hermes and Heracles, as noted by Barclay, *Mediterranean Diaspora*, 235; on Jewish *ephēbes* and participation in civic

Jews lived *within* a pagan religious institution; and they evidently found ways to negotiate between their own god's demand for exclusive worship and the regular requirements of ancient Mediterranean friendship, loyalty, patronage/clientage, and citizenship wherever they lived.[15]

Jews met these gods not only in their cities, but also in their own Scriptures, where Israel's god is praised "among the gods" (e.g., Pss. 82:2; 97:7; 136:2; 2 Chron. 2:5; Exod. 15:11; cf. Exod. 12:12; Isa. 46:2; Jer. 46:25; Mic. 4:5). True, the Bible execrated the worship of these gods' images, but the image of a god is not the same thing as the god himself. Any human can destroy an idol; no human can destroy a god. An idol may be "nothing," but a god is definitely something. Jews found ways to subordinate these other beings to Israel's god, whether explaining their existence as errant angels (or angelic hybrids, Gen. 6:5) or as low-level powers, *daimonia* (Ps. 95:5 LXX), who ultimately depended on Israel's god for their own existence.[16] The Septuagint seemed to counsel showing these powers

---

life, further, 232–36; on the Moschos Ioudaios inscription in the temple of two local gods, Emil Schürer and Geza Vermes et al., *History of the Jewish People in the Age of Jesus Christ* (Edinburgh: T & T Clark, 1973–87), 3:65 (hereafter cited as *HJP*). Pothos son of Strabo opens the inscription recording the manumission of his slave Chrysa "in the prayer-house" by invoking "the most high god almighty, the blessed one," and closes on "Zeus, Gaia, and Helios." What is the ethnicity of this donor: Jewish or pagan? See Levinskaya, *Acts*, 111–16, with full text of the inscription on p. 239, and cf. Lee Levine, *The Ancient Synagogue* (New Haven, CT: Yale University Press, 2000), 113–23. Further on Jews as *ephēbes*, town councilors, and officers in pagan armies, see Williams, *Jews Among Greeks and* Romans, 107–31. On Jewish funding of pagan liturgies, *HJP* 3:25 (Niketas); on Herod's largesse to pagan activities, Josephus, *Ant.* 16.136-149; further discussion in Paula Fredriksen, "Judaizing the Nations: The Ritual Demands of Paul's Gospel," *New Testament Studies* 56 (2010): 232–52, at 236f. The complaints of the ethnographers notwithstanding, Diaspora Jews were hardly uninvolved with the gods.

15. A late second-century Roman law explicitly excused Jewish decurions from liturgies that "transgress their religion [*superstitionem eorum*]," *Digest* 50:2:3:3; see Amnon Linder, *The Jews in Roman Imperial Legislation* (Detroit, MI: Wayne State University Press, 1987), 103–106. No doubt there was a great degree of diversity: arrangements likely would have varied across different communities, and probably to a degree between individuals within a given community, or, to look at Philo's case, between individuals within a given Jewish family.

16. On the multiplicity of divinities ranged beneath the Jews' high god, see the literature cited in n. 3 above; see also Pieter van der Horst, "'Thou Shalt Not Revile the Gods': The LXX

some respect: "Do not revile *tous theous*, the gods" (Exod. 22:28 LXX). The Jewish philosopher Philo, commenting on this verse, likewise counseled respect for pagan rulers who are "of the same seed as the gods" (*Questions and Answers on Exodus* 2.6); while elsewhere, interpreting Genesis, he designated the heavenly bodies created by God as *theoi*, "gods" (*On the Creation* 7.27). Ancient Jewish monotheism, in brief, accommodated a vast number of other—in the Jewish view, lesser—deities.

Pagans living with Jews in turn encountered the Jewish god, and variously found ways to show respect to him. The most extreme way (and for that reason, probably the most rare) was by becoming an "ex-pagan," what moderns call "conversion." Given divinity's ethnic embeddedness in antiquity, the term, and the phenomenon, scarcely make sense.[17] To fully change gods was tantamount to changing ethnicity: a pagan's "becoming" a Jew in effect altered his own past, reconfigured his ancestry, and cut his ties to his own pantheon, family, and *patria*. For these reasons, some hostile pagan witnesses considered what we call "conversion" an act of cultural treason.[18]

Translation of Exodus 22.28 (27), its Background and Influence," *Studia Philonica* 5 (1993): 1–8; also Annette Y. Reed, *Fallen Angels and the History of Judaism and Christianity* (Cambridge: Cambridge University Press, 2005).

17. Twentieth-century scholars argued that Hellenistic Jews ran missions to convert pagans to Judaism: James Parkes, Bernhard Blumenkranz, and Marcel Simon all conjectured that the rivalry between Christian and Jewish missions accounted for the vituperation of Christian *adversus Iudaeos* rhetoric and theology. For a review and a refutation of this scholarly position, Paula Fredriksen, "What 'Parting of the Ways?'" in *The Ways That Never Parted*, ed. Adam Becker and Annette Y. Reed (Tübingen: Mohr Siebeck 2003), 35–63, at 48–56; on the confusions with using the term "conversion" given the correspondence of ethnicity and divinity in antiquity, see Paula Fredriksen, "Mandatory Retirement: Ideas in the Study of Christian Origins Whose Time Has Come to Go," *Studies in Religion/Sciences Religieuses* 35 (2006): 231–46.

18. Juvenal complains about the consequences of a pagan's keeping the Sabbath: eventually, his sons "worship nothing but the clouds and the divinity of heaven, see no difference between eating swine's flesh . . . and that of a man; and in time they take to circumcision," after which point they "flout the laws of Rome, and learn and practice and revere the Jewish law, and all that Moses handed down . . ." *Sat.* 15.96–106, analyzed in Menachem Stern, *Greek and Latin Authors on Jews and Judaism* (Jerusalem: Magnes, 1980), 2:94–107; also Tacitus's complaints

Roman analogues existed: both adoption and marriage ritually created a bond of (legal but fictive) kinship, obligating the adoptee, or the wife, to new deities, rituals, and ancestors.[19] "Becoming" a Jew did occur; and since Judaism was known to be ancestral and ancient—two essential criteria of respectable cult—most pagans, disapproval notwithstanding, by and large tolerated such transitions.

More conventionally, however, pagans could simply "visit with" Jews, and thus with their god. Before 66 CE, they traveled to the temple in Jerusalem, where the largest courtyard was reserved for them.[20] And in their own cities, they could and did appear in their neighbors' "ethnic reading house": pagans frequented Diaspora assemblies.[21] Though the term is currently contested, I will designate these pagan drop-ins as "god-fearers." Free to observe as much or as little of Jewish custom as they chose—free, indeed, to continue worshiping their own gods—pagan god-fearers ranged across a broad spectrum of affiliation, from occasional, perhaps casual contact to major benefaction and patronage, to the assumption of some Jewish ancestral practices.[22] The point, for the present purpose, is to note

about a convert's disloyalty to the gods, the *patria*, and the family, *History* 5.5, 2; cf. Celsus's remark in *Cels.* 5.41. On the variety of ancient Jewish views on the circumcision of pagans and "conversion," see most recently Matthew Thiessen, *Contesting Conversion: Genealogy, Circumcision, and Identity in Ancient Judaism and Christianity* (Oxford: Oxford University Press, 2011).

19. "It is becoming for a wife to worship and to know only those gods whom her husband esteems," Plutarch, *Mor.* 140D. On the protocols of Roman adoption, and the ways that the new son becomes involved with his adopted pantheon, see Peppard, *Son of God*, 50–60.

20. On the layout of Herod's temple, and the ways that it could accommodate a vast number of visitors, see E. P. Sanders, *Judaism: Practice and Belief, 63 BCE–66 CE* (Philadelphia: Trinity Press International, 1992), 55–76. The wall demarcating the largest outer court ran for nine-tenths of a mile.

21. The phrase is Frances Young's, *Biblical Exegesis and the Formation of Christian Culture* (Cambridge: Cambridge University Press, 1997), 13. On the wide dispersion of synagogues and their archaeological remains, see Levine, *Ancient Synagogue*; also Gruen, *Diaspora*, 105–32. On the range of pagan affiliations, Fredriksen, "Judaizing the Nations," 238–39 and nn; on pagan benefactors, Levine, *Ancient Synagogue*, 111, 121, 479–83.

22. Terms translated as "god-fearer" (*theosebes* et sim.) might sometimes simply mean "pious" and thus have nothing to do with the specific type of cross-ethnic activity that I focus on here; see Judith Lieu, "The Race of the God-fearers," *Journal of Theological Studies* 46 (1995): 483–501;

that such arrangements were ad hoc, voluntary, and inclusive: pagans were present within synagogue communities qua pagans.

Such flexible arrangements for voluntary Judaizing were evidently comfortable for everybody, Jews and pagans alike. Indeed, it made eminent political sense for Diaspora Jews to encourage the interest and to solicit the patronage of sympathetic outsiders, who represented the vastly greater cultural (therefore religious) majority in their cities of residence. So long-lived and stable was this urban "synagogue habit" that for centuries after Paul's lifetime, gentiles, whether pagan or Christian, continued to show up. Hostile Christian witnesses, like their pagan predecessors, complained in their turn, now criticizing Jews for *not* putting pressure on interested pagans to convert. Bishops made the same point differently: bitterly denouncing the Christian presence in synagogues, they nowhere complain that Jews tried to convert these Christians to Judaism.[23]

In the first century, this shifting synagogue population of interested outsiders would have provided Paul with the bulk of his target audience: active pagans[24] who were nonetheless interested to

more recently Ross Kraemer, "Giving up the Godfearers," *Journal of Ancient Judaism* 1 no. 1 (forthcoming 2014). I thank Professor Kraemer for sharing with me a pre-publication version of her article, which includes a valuable review especially of the epigraphical evidence. Kraemer seems concerned to refute "god-fearing" as a "sweeping, static" and "technical category," a term with "precise technical meaning," which is not its current usage. As Levinskaya observed in 1996, pagan god-fearing was "a wide and loose category," *not* a technical designation for a clearly demarcated or defined group, *Book of Acts*, 79. See also Fredriksen, "Judaizing," 237–40 and nn.

23. On the continuing presence of non-Jews both pagan and Christian in Jewish assemblies, Paula Fredriksen and Oded Irshai, "Christian Anti-Judaism: Polemics and Policies, from the Second to the Seventh Centuries," *Cambridge History of Judaism*, ed. Steven T. Katz (Cambridge: Cambridge University Press, 2006), 4:977–1034, at 985–98. Commodian scolds Jews for not trying to convert the pagan sympathizer (*medius Iudeaus*), *Instructiones* 1.37, 1-10. Chrysostom's bitter complaints about his own congregations' Judaizing—coupled with no complaints about Jewish proselytizing—appear throughout his infamous sermons of 387, *Discourses against Judaizing Christians*, in *Fathers of the Church* 68, trans. Paul W. Harkins (Washington, DC: Catholic University Press of America, 1999). The condemnations of episcopal councils preserve a record of Christian voluntary Judaizing: material collected and analyzed in Amnon Linder, *Jews in the Legal Sources of the Early Middle Ages* (Detroit, MI: Wayne State University Press, 1997).

some degree in the Jewish god, and who had some sort of familiarity, through listening, with the Bible.[25] "Son of David," "*christos*," "kingdom of God," the Law," "the commandments," "the prophets," "Jerusalem," "Abraham" and so on would already have meant *something* to them. And it is on account of this target audience that Paul would have encountered resistance, resentment, and opposition. From whom? If we can extrapolate from Paul's list of woes in 2 Corinthians 11, from everyone: Jews resident in these urban Diaspora communities (v. 24, and perhaps v. 26); Roman magistrates (v. 25); irate pagans (vv. 25f.); other Jewish apostles to pagans who disagreed with Paul's interpretation of the gospel (v. 26); and, last but not at all least, lower gods (whose media—wind, water, and weather—fight Paul every inch of his way, vv. 25-26).[26]

Idols in the Messianic Age

What was everyone, human and divine, so upset about? Paul (and others like him), in proclaiming the gospel, radically disrupted the long-lived and socially stable arrangements prevailing between synagogues, god-fearers, and the larger pagan community; and they disrupted relations within the pagan community itself, from those of

24. E.g., 1 Thess. 1:9 ("you turned to God from idols"); Gal. 4:8 (bondage to lower gods); 1 Cor. 11:10-11 (former idol-worshipers); Rom. 1:5-6 (Paul is called to preach the gospel among "all the *ethnē*, including you").

25. "James," commenting on this pagan population, notes, "From early generations Moses has had in every city those who proclaim him, for he is read every Sabbath in the synagogues," Acts 15:21; cf. Philo on the co-celebration by pagans and Jews of the translation of the LXX, *Life of Moses* 2.41-42; see too Donaldson, *Judaism and Gentiles,* 467-82. Against this view of synagogue-going pagans as Paul's mission field, E. P. Sanders, "Paul's Jewishness," in *Paul's Jewish Matrix,* ed. T. G. Casey and Justin Taylor (Rome: Gregorian & Biblical Press, 2011), 51–73, at 66–67.

26. Paul comments on the (usually hostile) activities of lower gods in 1 Cor. 2:8 (assuming that by *archontes* Paul means astral powers, not Roman officials); 2 Cor. 4:4 (the "god of this world" who has blinded unbelievers); Gal. 4:8-9 (*stoicheia*, cosmic lightweights, not "gods by nature"); 1 Cor. 8:10-11 (many gods and many lords); 1 Cor. 10:20-21 (*daimonia*); 1 Cor. 15:24-27 (Christ's cosmic resistance).

immediate family right up through the larger family of fellow citizens and the cities' gods. How so? Because a non-negotiable proviso of the gospel was that pagans had to cease honoring their native gods with sacrifices before cult statues (*idololatria*).[27] Such disrespect was bound to anger the gods, and gods, when slighted, acted out. Earthquake, flood, and famine; shipwreck, storm, disease: these were the normal repertoire of divine anger. "No rain, because of the Christians!"[28] By urging his pagans to cease their traditional worship and to honor only Israel's god—indeed, by insisting that they assume that public behavior associated universally and solely with Jews—Paul put at risk both the local Jewish community (the obvious source of such a message) and the larger host pagan city. Anxious pagans might target the synagogue; angry gods might target the city.[29]

But *why* should the gospel have occasioned such disruption? Was pagan culture not long used to varying degrees of synagogue affiliation? Yes. And no. It is on this point precisely that the radical novelty of the gospel message made itself socially felt. Yes, pagan culture—and Diaspora Jewish culture—were long familiar with "converts" and with god-fearers. But Paul's pagans fell into neither category. *Like* converts, his pagans made an exclusive commitment to the god of Israel; *unlike* converts, they did not assume Jewish ancestral practices (food ways, Sabbath, circumcision, and so on). *Like* god-fearers, Paul's people retained their native ethnicities; *unlike* god-

27. Paul says this early (1 Thess. 1:9), late (Rom. 1:18-32), and frequently in-between (1 Cor. 5:10-11; 6:9; 10:7, 14, 20; 2 Cor. 6:16; Gal. 4:8-10, here the gods themselves, *stoicheia*; 5:20; cf. Acts 15:3, 19). Women and slaves, however, were constrained by obligations to household cult, and Paul seems to acknowledge this; cf. Johnson Hodge, "Married to an Unbeliever."

28. Repeated by Augustine, *Civ.* 2.3; cf. Tertullian, *Apology* 40.2, 2.

29. On the dynamics of violence caused by these tensions, in the first generation of the movement and later, see Paula Fredriksen, "Paul, Practical Pluralism, and the Invention of Religious Persecution in Roman Antiquity," in *Understanding Religious Pluralism: Perspectives from Religious Studies and Theology*, ed. Peter C. Phan and Jonathan Ray (Eugene, OR: Wipf & Stock, 2014), 87–113.

fearers, they no longer worshiped their native gods. *Paul's pagans-in-Christ are neither converts nor god-fearers.* So who and what are they?

In the social (thus religious) context of the ancient city, such people were, precisely, nothing.[30] Neither "Jews" of a special sort (that is, *prosēlytoi*) nor "normal" pagans (that is, people who showed respect to their own gods), they occupied a social and religious no-man's land. *Eschatologically,* however, they represented a population long anticipated within centuries of Jewish restoration theology: they were pagans-saved-at-the-End.

We find this eschatological tradition articulated in (or interpreted into) Jewish texts that range from the canonical prophets through the writings of the late Second Temple period and after, including Paul's letters and the Synoptic Gospels. While some apocalyptic writers looked forward to the destruction of idolators together with their idols,[31] others anticipated the redemption of these pagans—and even of their gods—together with a restored Israel at the End; and some writers, such as Isaiah and Paul, inconsistently express both views.[32]

30. "The social distinctiveness of his converts was obvious to Paul. . . . they were isolated, without a recognizable social identity," Sanders, "Paul's Jewishness," 67, also n. 26. On the appeal of circumcision as a way to resolve the tensions inherent in this anomalous position, Mark D. Nanos, *The Irony of Galatians: Paul's Letter in First-Century Context* (Minneapolis: Fortress Press, 2002), 86–109, 203–321.

31. Foreign rulers will lick the dust at Israel's feet, Isa. 49:23; cf. Mic. 7:16; pagan cities are devastated, Isa. 54:3; Zeph. 2:1—3:8; *1 En.* 91:9; God destroys the nations and their idols, Mic. 5:9, 15; maledictions against the nations, bespeaking destruction or servitude, Sir. 36:1-10; Bar. 4:25, 31-35; *Sib. Or.* 3:417-440, 669, 761; *Pss. Sol.* 7:30; 1QM 12:10-13.

32. The nations will stream to Jerusalem and worship together with Israel (Isa. 2:2-4/Mic. 4); they will together eat on the Temple Mount the feast that God will prepare (Isa. 25:6); gentiles will accompany Jews at the Ingathering (Zech. 8:23), or will themselves carry the exiles back to Jerusalem (*Pss. Sol.* 7:31-41); gentiles will bury their idols and direct their sight to uprightness (*1 En.* 91:14); many nations will come from afar to the name of the Lord God, bearing gifts (Tob. 13:11); after the temple is rebuilt, all the nations will turn in fear to the Lord and bury their idols (14:5-6); God will restore Jerusalem so that "all who are on the earth" will know that he is the Lord God (Sir. 36:11-17); at the coming of the Great King, the nations will bend knee to God (*Sib. Or.* 3:616), will go to the temple, and renounce their idols (715-724), and from every land will bring incense and gifts to the temple (772). For discussion of these positive traditions of pagan eschatological inclusion, see especially James M. Scott, *Paul and the Nations* (Tübingen: Mohr Siebeck, 1995); Donaldson, *Judaism and Gentiles,* 499–513; in the context

According to this inclusive tradition, when the Lord of the Universe revealed himself in glory, pagans would destroy their idols and *turn* (*epistrephō*) to worship the god of Israel. "Turn (*epistraphatē*) to me!" (Isa. 45:22 LXX, addressed to "the nations"). "All the nations will turn (*epistrepsousin*) in fear of the Lord God . . . and will bury their idols" (Tob. 14:6). "You turned (*epistrepsate*) to God from idols, to worship the true and living god" (1 Thess. 1:9).

But "turning" is not "conversion", and these end-time pagans do not thereby "become" Jews.[33] Rather, they enter God's kingdom *as ethnē*, but they do not worship idols any more. In other words, this anticipated population represented a unique and a purely theoretical category, an apocalyptic trope and an apocalyptic hope. By severing the *ethnē* from their gods in this way, *Jewish apocalyptic thought likewise severed antiquity's normal and normative correspondence of ethnicity and cult.*

In the work of the first generation of the Jesus movement in the Diaspora, we find the unprecedented social expression of this apocalyptic trope in those pagans who committed themselves to the *ekklēsiai*. Their participation, and the *terms* of their participation (no more sacrifice to idols!) in turn gives us the measure of the apocalyptic commitments of the earliest apostles: the messiah had already come, and would shortly come again. It is this conviction alone that accounts for the apostles' rejection of the Diaspora synagogues' long-lived and socially stable practice of allowing pagans qua god-fearers to worship Israel's god while continuing in their native cults. Knowing what time it was on God's clock (Rom. 13:11),

---

of Paul's mission, Paula Fredriksen, "Judaism, the Circumcision of Gentiles, and Apocalyptic Hope," *Journal of Theological Studies* 42 (1991): 532–64, at 544–48.

33. On the confusions occasioned by *epistrephō* coming into Latin as *converto* (thus, at 1 Thess. 1:9: *conversi estis*), thence into English as "conversion," Fredriksen, "Mandatory Retirement," 232–35.

racing in the (for all they knew) brief wrinkle in time between Christ's resurrection and his second coming (1 Cor. 15), seeing in the pneumatic behavior of their new pagan members the confirmation of their own convictions, Jewish apostles chose to live as best they could with the social tensions mounting between the ekklēsia and its larger host communities of synagogue and city (cf. 2 Cor. 11:23-28). Such problems would be short-lived. Time was hastening to its end. God's kingdom would come soon.

But in the rapidly diminishing meanwhile, what were these people to do?

Pagan *Dikaiosynē* ("Righteousness")

Through baptism, the Spirit of God or of Christ infused the ekklēsia's pagans. Their new behavior, both toward the divine and toward the human, registered the Spirit's presence in them. First and foremost, and despite the press of all their other gods, these pagans committed to the worship of the one true god (e.g., 1 Thess. 1:9; 1 Cor. 8:5-6). The Spirit also enabled their charismatic acts: like Paul himself, his pagans could speak in tongues, prophesy, heal, teach, and discern between spirits (1 Cor. 12:4-13). The Spirit also "sanctified" or "separated" these pagans from the ones who did not know God (1 Thess. 4:4-5): thus, Paul addresses them as *hagioi*, "sanctified ones" (RSV: "saints;" 1 Cor. 1:2; Rom. 1:7). Like the temple in Jerusalem, they too are filled with God's Spirit (1 Cor. 3:16; 2 Cor. 6:16); like the sacrifices brought to the temple, they too are now "acceptable" (Rom. 15:16). [34] They now do the "works of the Spirit" rather than the "works of the flesh," those sins long identified in Jewish anti-

34. On Paul's adaptation of the categories of temple sacrifice (*hagios, katharos*) to his pagans-in-Christ, see Fredriksen, "Judaizing," 244–49; cf. Thiessen's remarks on Acts, *Conversion*, 124–37; Friedrich W. Horn, "Paulus und die Herodianische Tempel," *New Testament Studies* 53 (2007): 184–203, esp. 201–203.

pagan rhetoric as the moral consequences of idolatry: "fornication, uncleanness, licentiousness, idolatry, sorcery, enmity, strife, jealousy, anger, selfishness, dissention, divisions, envy, drunkenness, carousing" (Gal. 5:16-24; cf. Wis. 13–15). Now they, too, "fulfill the law" (Rom. 13:8-10; cf. Gal. 5:14-15; 1 Cor. 14:34). Pagans-in-Christ were now *dikaiōthentes ek pisteōs* (Rom. 5:1).

"Justified by faith," the usual English rendering of this phrase, disguises its resonance with a core teaching of the early movement, one on which the historical Jesus (and, for that matter, John the Baptizer) and Paul seem to converge: the Ten Commandments. These commandments were typically distinguished as the Two Tables of the Law, and widely coded in Greek by a two-word summary, *eusebeia* ("piety") and *dikaiosynē* ("justice"). "Piety" indicated the Law's First Table, concerning obligations to God; "Justice," the Law's Second Table, concerning obligations toward others. Thus:

Eusebeia: Piety toward God	*Dikaiosynē: Justice toward Others*
1. No other gods	6. No murder
2. No graven images (idols)	7. No adultery
3. No abuse of God's name	8. No theft
4. Keep the Sabbath	9. No lying
5. Honor parents[35]	10. No coveting[36]

---

35. See Philo, *Decalogue* 19, for a long meditation on why honoring parents falls on the Law's first table.

36. The Bible arranges these commandments variously: see Exod. 20:1-17 and Deut. 5:6-21. Sanders notes that "these two words were used very widely by Greek-speaking Jews to summarize their religion," *The Historical Figure of Jesus* (London: Penguin, 1993), 92. *Eusebeia* and *dikaiosynē* also appear in Philo's summary of the Law's two chief principles (*kephalaia*, *Spec.* 2.63.) David Flusser surveys the variety of twofold summaries of Torah (love of God and of neighbor; piety and justice) from *Jubilees* to Lactantius in "The Ten Commandments and the New Testament," in *The Ten Commandments in History and Tradition*, ed. Ben-Zion Segal (Jerusalem: Magnes, 1990), 219–46. Similarly, *b. Makkot* 23a runs the numbers down from 613 commandments to two (Isa. 56:1) to one (Hab. 2:4, the righteous man will live by his *emunah*,

Both the Baptizer and Jesus during their respective missions called fellow Jews to repentance in the face of God's coming kingdom. Within this Jewish context, repentance—*tshuvah* in later rabbinic idiom; "turn"—meant, precisely, *returning* to God's commandments as revealed in Torah. In his *Antiquities of the Jews*, Josephus describes John the Baptizer as exhorting his hearers to practice "*dikaiosynē* toward their fellows and *eusebeia* toward God"—in brief, the Ten Commandments (*Ant.* 18.116-119). So similarly Jesus: Asked about the greatest commandments, Mark's Jesus replies by citing Deuteronomy 6:4 ("Hear O Israel, the Lord our God, the Lord is one. And you shall love the Lord your God with all your heart, and with all your soul, and with all your might")—*eusebeia,* the First Table of the Law; and Leviticus 19:18 ("You shall love your neighbor as yourself")—*dikaiosynē,* the Second Table of the Law (Mark 12:29-31 and parr.). Elsewhere, his Jesus invokes the Ten Commandments directly: "You know the commandments: 'You shall not murder; you shall not commit adultery; you shall not steal; you shall not bear false witness; you shall not defraud; honor your father and your mother'" (Mark 10:19).[37]

"strength" or "steadfastness;" cf. Paul's *ek pisteōs zēsetai,* Gal. 3:11). On *emunah* not as "faith" but as "firmness, steadfastness, fidelity," *A Hebrew-English Lexicon of the Old Testament,* ed. Francis Brown, S. R. Driver, and Charles A. Briggs (Oxford: Clarendon, 1939), 53. We see this same tendency to streamline moral teachings in the philosophical epitomes of wider Greco-Roman culture (Epicurus's *Kyriai Doxai,* Epictetus's *Encheiridion*): Hans D. Betz, *Sermon on the Mount,* Hermeneia (Minneapolis: Fortress Press 1995), 76–79 with notes to the key literature.

37. Matthew's Jesus repeats and reinforces this message in his Sermon on the Mount (Matt. 5:21-22, against murder; vv. 27-30, against adultery; vv. 31-37 against lying/ "swearing falsely"). See Sanders's comments on this Matthean passage, *Historical Figure,* 210–12; also Flusser, "Ten Commandments," 234. Cf. Luke 11:42, another coded reference, where neglecting "judgment" (*tēn krisin*) indicates neglecting justice. Emphasis on the Ten Commandments in mid-first century Palestinian Judaism is perhaps reflected as well in tefillin from Qumran. The later tractate *y. Berakhot* i, 5, 3c comments that while the Ten Commandments used to be recited every day in the temple, they no longer are "on account of the *minim,*" who hold that no other commandments were given on Sinai. Ephraim Urbach, *The Sages* (Jerusalem: Magnes, 1975), 2:844 n. 75.

What about Paul? Paul's circumstances differed pointedly from those of the Baptizer and of Jesus. His "mission field" was the cities of the eastern empire. His hearers were not Jews but pagans. And these he called to repent not of "Jewish" sins (i.e., breaking the commandments), but of "pagan" sins (most especially idolatry and its perennial rhetorical companion, *porneia*).[38] Nonetheless—and despite Paul's insistence that pagans-in-Christ not "convert" and assume Jewish practices, thus Jewish law—these pagans' religious reformation went hand in hand with their social/ethical reformation; and their living according to Jewish law precisely indexed this reformation. Which Jewish law? What Jewish laws? Nine of the Ten Commandments.

The word *eusebeia* ("piety"), which signaled the First Table of the Law, appears nowhere in Paul. We can only speculate why not: perhaps because Sabbath observance featured in that list, and Paul had argued heatedly against his missionary competition, especially in Galatia, that pagans-in-Christ were "free" of Jewish ancestral practices; perhaps because these pagans' new piety had been brought about not through their own efforts (*ex ergōn*, "by works"), but rather by eschatological fiat by God through Christ (*chariti*, "by grace"). Their new orientation toward God, however, was ritually regulated precisely according to the Law's First Table: No other gods, and no idols.[39]

Unlike *eusebeia*, Paul frequently uses *dikaiosynē* and related *dik*-words—thirty-six times in Romans alone. He connects this word, "righteousness" or "justice," with *pistis*, which is often translated as "faith" or "belief." The two words taken together, "justification by

---

38. On the ways that their different mission fields affect their conceptualizations of sin, see Fredriksen, *Sin*, 6–51.
39. In other words, and despite his condemnation of the term (Gal. 2:14), Paul is himself demanding a high level of Judaizing of his pagans; Fredriksen, "Judaizing the Nations," 250–52.

faith," have served conceptually and polemically as a lodestar of Lutheran tradition, and of New Testament scholarship more broadly. In those contexts, it points a sharp contrast between "faith" and "Law."

But is this what Paul means? Here the connotations of our modern English words impede translation of our ancient Greek texts. Our word "faith," refracted through the prism of a long Christian cultural history that runs at least from Tertullian (*credo quia absurdum*) to Kierkegaard, has come to imply all sorts of psychological inner states concerning authenticity or sincerity of "belief." In antiquity, *pistis* and its Latin equivalent, *fides*, connoted, rather, "steadfastness," "conviction," and "loyalty."[40] For this reason, I would translate Romans 13:11 as "Salvation is nearer to us now than it was when we first became convinced" (cf. "than when we first believed," RSV). So too with "piety." Less about religious sentiment than about showing respect (a synonym for *eusebeia* was *phobos*),[41] *eusebeia* and its Latin equivalent, *pietas*, indexed a respectful attentiveness in the execution of inherited protocols of worship—what we call "religion," but what ancient authors, Paul included, thought of as a kind of family patrimony. And Paul's use of *dik-* words presents daunting challenges to English.[42]

Alerted to these problems, how can we translate Paul without anachronism, so that we can better catch his meaning? If we navigate by the Ten Commandments, we might find our way. Thus, when Paul's pagans adhered steadfastly (the cluster of ideas around *pistis/*

---

40. Hence Paul's use of "obedience" with "commitment" or "conviction" or "steadfastness" (cf. "faith"—not "the" faith, as RSV Rom. 1:5).

41. See *eusebeia* in *A Greek-English Lexicon of the Septuagint,* ed. Takamitsu Muraoka (Leuven: Peeters, 2009), 305.

42. E. P. Sanders gives a lengthy consideration of the defects of English for translating Paul's *dikasun,* et sim., in *Paul: A Very Short Introduction* (Oxford: Oxford University Press, 1991), 52–90, esp. 54–55. I will adopt his awkward neologism "righteoused" above, since it is preferable to "justified."

pisteō) to the good news (*euangelion*) that Paul brought (cf. RSV "believe in the gospel"), they ceased worshiping their own gods and committed themselves to the god of Israel through baptism into the death, resurrection, and impending return of his son. Made right by God toward God, they were likewise pneumatically enabled to make right toward each other by acting rightly toward each other—"not like the *ethnē* who do not know God" (1 Thess. 4:5; cf. Rom. 1:18-32). Their *pistis* in Christ (steadfast confidence that he had died, been raised, and was about to return) righteoused them (through the conferring of *pneuma*, "spirit") so that they could "fulfill the Law," meaning, quite specifically, the Law's Second Table, *dikaiosynē*. "Faith" and "Law" in this construction, far from contrasting with each other—much less opposing each other—actually mutually reinforce each other.

Thus in the same place where Paul reviews the sins of the flesh that Christ-following pagans have left behind (Rom. 13:13-14), and where he speaks urgently of the impending End (13:11-12), he also lists the commandments of the Second Table (13:8-10). "Righteoused" pagans, Spirit-filled, enact "righteousness" or practice "justice" toward others in community: no murder, theft, adultery, coveting (Rom. 13:9). Their loyalty to and confidence in the *euangelion* (*pistis*) enabled and resulted in this righteous behavior (*dikaiosynē*). In other words, "right behavior according to the Law on account of steadfast attachment to the gospel" is what Paul meant by *dikaiosynē ek pisteōs* (RSV: "justification by faith").

God, the *Ethnē*, and the Redemption of Israel

Christ was about to return, said Paul, to establish the kingdom of his father. Who enters this kingdom?

Since approximately the second century, in part basing their view on their reading of Romans 9–11, most Christians have answered "only Christians." This despite Paul's insistence, in this very passage of Romans, that "the fullness of the *ethnē*" and "all Israel" will be saved (11:25-26), and that God's promises are "irrevocable" (11:29; cf. 15:8). This deeply traditional, restrictive Christian reading rests on an interpretation of Paul's "all Israel" to mean only the *true* Israel, that is, the "new Israel" of Christian faith, a mixed community of Christian Jews and Christian gentiles, not the "old Israel" of fleshly lineage, Paul's "kinsmen by race" (*syngeneia*, Rom. 9:3); of fleshly Israel, only a remnant are saved (cf. Rom. 9:6; 11:5). Galatians' "peace upon the Israel of God" is read the same way: the "Israel of God" is clearly Israel *kata pneuma*, spiritual Israel, the church (Gal. 6:16).

Such a reading reduces the scope of Paul's vision to a narrowness exceeding even that of the least inclusive passages of the Dead Sea Scrolls, which restricted redemption to the sectarians' own community—some four thousand souls (*Ant.* 18.21).[43] If Paul's measure of "who's in" is limited to those members of the Jesus movement who, mid-first century, agree with him—"false brethren" (Gal. 2:4), "pseudo-apostles" (2 Cor. 11:13), "super-apostles" (2 Cor. 11:5), "those of the circumcision" (Gal. 2:12), "dogs, evil-workers and mutilators of the flesh" (Phil. 3:2), and all those other colleagues in the movement whom Paul anathematizes clearly being "out"—would Paul's envisioned saints, some fraction of this twenty-plus-year-old movement, reach even that number? The resurrection of the dead, the transformation of the living, of history and of the cosmos, of heaven and of earth, all culminating in the redemption of, say, some

---

43. Qumran's eschatology is no more consistent than is Isaiah's. Some texts speak of the final judgment, condemnation, or destruction of the nations (Heb. *goyim*), while others prophesy the inclusion of the nations in a redeemed Jerusalem. For discussion of the various texts, see Scott, *Paul and the Nations,* 119 and nn. 421–24.

three to four thousand people? It is possible, of course. But it is hard to imagine Paul's thinking so small, especially when we consider the traditions of Jewish restoration theology in which he stands.

We can trace these ideas more clearly if we consider, for a moment, the character of Israel's god. For Paul as for Paul's tradition, this god was first of all the god of Abraham, Isaac, and Jacob; the one who spoke with Moses and who gave the Law on Sinai; the god who chose David and blessed his house, and who promised to his line eternal sovereignty (Rom. 9:4-5). He was the god who brought his people back from captivity, and he was the god who would reassemble his people—even those who were lost in Egypt and Assyria—in the Final Days. Or, as Paul says in Romans, this god is the father to fleshly Israel, the glorious presence in Jerusalem's temple, the author of the covenants and giver of the Law (including those laws regarding temple sacrifice), the guarantor of Israel's promises of redemption (Rom. 9:4; cf. 11:28-29; 15:8). Israel's god, like most ancient gods—like Rome's gods or Alexandria's gods or Athens' gods—is clearly an ethnic god.[44]

And yet this god is also more, for the Bible begins not at Genesis 12, the calling of Abram, but at Genesis 1, "in the beginning," with the creation of the universe, of all life, of all humanity—*and* of the Sabbath (Gen. 1:1-2:3). "Is God the god of Jews only?" Paul asks rhetorically. "Is he not the god of *ethnē* also? Yes, of *ethnē* also, since God is one" (Rom. 3:29-30). Paul affirms his god's universality on the very Jewish principle proclaimed in the Shema ("Hear O Israel . . .").[45]

44. For this reason—his very ethnicity, pronounced so unambiguously in the LXX—the biblical god was seen by second-century gentile Christians such as Valentinus and Marcion as demonic and demiurgic, to be distinguished from the highest god, who was the father of Christ; Justin Martyr, for similar reasons, opined also that the god of the LXX was not the high god, the father of Christ, but rather the pre-incarnate Christ himself (a *heteros theos*, Trypho 56); Fredriksen, *Sin*, 53–92.
45. Further on the Shema, see Mark D. Nanos, "Paul and the Jewish Tradition: The Ideology of the Shema," in *Celebrating Paul. Festschrift in Honor of Jerome Murphy-O'Connor, O.P., and Joseph A.*

Two ancient scriptural episodes, much exploited in later restoration theology (including Paul's), inflected this Jewish god's universal significance in biblical accents: the repopulation of the earth after the flood by Noah's sons and their descendants (Gen. 10:1-32) and the promise to Abraham (Gen. 12:3; 18:18). Noah's sons, Japeth, Shem, and Ham, gave rise to all the rest of humanity, the seventy "nations" (the first occurrence in the LXX of *ethnē*, Gen. 10:32).[46] These *ethnē* later defined the universal scope of end-time redemption. "I am coming," God proclaims, "to gather all the nations and tongues" (*panta ta ethnē kai pas glōssas*, Isa. 66:18 LXX). Isaiah's great vision echoes Genesis' Table of Nations, which lists all the nations according to their "tongues" (Gen. 32:31). So similarly God's promise to Abram, that through him "all the nations" will be blessed (*panta ta ethnē*, Gen. 18:18): "all the nations" refer to the seventy of Genesis 32. So also Paul's prophesy of the *plērōma* of the nations in Romans 11:25: the nations' "full number" is seventy.[47] In other words, the ingathering of all Israel, all twelve tribes—*pas Israēl*, as Paul says (Rom. 11:26)—is linked immediately in Jewish restoration theology to the inclusion of all the nations as well.[48] God is the ultimate author of all these nations ("as many as you have made," Ps. 85:9), as, in a sense, Abraham is their father (Gen. 17:5; Rom. 4:16). But when these nations gather, they gather "with his [God's] people," Israel (Rom. 15:10; Deut. 32:43); and when they gather, they gather not

Fitzmyer, S.J., Catholic Biblical Quarterly Monograph Series 48, ed. Peter Spitaler (Washington, DC: Catholic Biblical Association of America, 2012), 62–80.

46. See especially Scott, *Paul and the Nations*, 5–6 n. 2, and his chart on 7.
47. Scott comments, "According to Deut. 32:8 mt, the number of the nations . . . was established according to the number of the sons of Israel. Hence, the numerical relationship in Rom 11:25-26 between the 'full number' of the nations and 'all Israel' is already traditional," *Paul and the Nations*, 135 n. 3.
48. "The ultimate goal of the Restoration is that Israel and the nations might worship together in Zion," Scott, *Paul and the Nations*, 73, cf. 133; so similarly Donaldson, "The inclusion of the Gentiles in the final consummation was an essential part of Israel's expectations and self-understanding," *Judaism and Gentiles*, 505, also 509.

just anywhere, but in Jerusalem, at the temple (Isa. 19:24; Ezek. 5:5; cf. Rom. 11:26).

God's universalism, in short, is a very Jewish universalism. And his particular universalism is reflected in the ways that Paul imagines ethnicity in the eschatological community, both the proleptic one of the present ekklēsia, before the Parousia, and the final community, once Christ returns. Within the current congregation, believers may be "one in Christ Jesus" (Gal. 3:28), but their social particularity continues: those "in Christ," Paul insists, remain and *should* remain Jew or gentile, circumcised or uncircumcised, just as they should maintain their social roles as male or female, slave or free.[49] The "oneness" of the current community is strictly *kata pneuma*.

In other words, Paul has no problem accommodating both difference and oneness, which abide together. He articulates this simultaneous difference-and-oneness as well through his (male-centered) vision of *huiothesia*, "sonship."[50] Paul's pagans, baptized into Christ's death and resurrection, have entered into a new brotherhood of the Spirit. They have become *adelphoi* by adoption, distinguished and distinct from Jews within the movement *kata sarka* (they were not circumcised; they were still *ethnē*), but united with them *kata pneuma*, through the spirit of Christ or of God. Paul's principled resistance to circumcising gentiles-in-Christ, in other words, precisely *preserves* the distinction *kata sarka* between Jews and the various other ethnic groups within the ekklēsia. And since Paul expects the Parousia in his own lifetime, he is utterly unconcerned with what coming generations are to do.[51] This missionary

---

49. 1 Cor. 7:17-24, on remaining in the state in which one was called; 11:2-16, on women's being veiled in the ekklēsia; 14:34-36 on female subordination, and silence in the ekklēsia; Philemon, on master-slave relations.

50. The gender-specificity of Paul's conceptualization on this point is explored in Caroline Johnson Hodge, *If Sons, Then Heirs: A Study of Kinship and Ethnicity in the Letters of Paul* (New York: Oxford University Press, 2007), esp. 19–42.

improvisation of spiritual "adoption" within the Diaspora Jesus movement, further, shows the strength of the broader Mediterranean construction of divine/human relations: If the nations, through an eschatological miracle, now worship Israel's god alone, then even though they remain ethnically distinct, they are spiritually joined to God's family. They too, through the Spirit, and like Israel, can call God "*Abba*, Father" (Gal. 4:6; Rom. 8:15).

What is true within the ekklēsia before Christ's second coming continues to be true at the End: once "the Deliverer [comes] from Zion," and the "full number of the nations comes in," *then* "all Israel" will be saved (Rom. 11:26). The Table of the Nations as linked to the restoration of all Israel, already long traditional by the time Paul uses it, defines his vision in Romans 11. Eschatological Israel will stand together with but distinct from the other nations, for they are the nation long ago set apart by God himself. So too in Paul's closing catena of scriptural citations in Romans 15: the *ethnē* glorify God for his mercy; the *ethnē* rejoice *with* God's people, that is, Israel; the *ethnē* praise God; the *ethnē* are ruled by the coming "root of Jesse," the messiah; the *ethnē* hope in him (15:9-12). The population of God's kingdom—for Paul as for the Jewish traditions that he draws on—recapitulates the biblical view of the quotidian: Israel and the nations.[52]

But what about those objects of God's wrath, both human and divine, against whom the apostle had also thundered? By the time that Paul reaches his paean of praise in Romans 11, the human sinners, whether pagans or Jews, seem excused: all humanity at the Parousia are saved. And the lower cosmic gods? In 1 Corinthians 15:25, Christ destroys them (*katarueitai*). But in Philippians 2:10-11, they seem to

---

51. 1 Cor. 7:14 is the only time that he specifically mentions children. Paul does not conceive a two-generation movement.

52. See Johnson Hodge, *If Sons*, 102, 137–53; cf. Thiessen, *Conversion*, 138–48.

submit ("all knees will bend"), joining in the universal confession "that Jesus Christ is Lord, to the glory of God the father." And in Romans 8, before concentrating on the redemption of humanity, Paul speaks of "all creation groaning" in bondage to decay and in travail while awaiting redemption at Christ's return (8:19-22), listing principalities, angels, and powers as part of this creation (8:38-39). Perhaps, then, when "the Deliverer will come from Zion" (11:26), these cosmic powers too, eschatologically rehabilitated, turn or return to God (cf. Ps. 97:7).

Conclusion

If we can judge from the rancorous confusions among Jewish Christ-followers in the Diaspora over the question of integrating pagans into the movement, Jesus of Nazareth had never given any instruction on the issue. Yet the movement, postresurrection, saw the integration of pagans as a natural extension of itself. Both of these data imply that Jesus himself had stood within the traditional paradigm of end-time restoration theology: redemption first to Israel—to *all* Israel, all twelve tribes—and then and as well, subsequently, to the nations.[53] Yet despite the resurrection's eschatological confirmation of Jesus' central prophecy—"the Kingdom of God is at hand!"—and despite the affirmation of the mission's success among pagans, the kingdom, inexplicably, continued not to come.

The kingdom's continuing delay, the pagans' continuing positive response, his own sense of his calling as divinely appointed *apostolos tois ethnesin*: all these combined to propel Paul's daring revision of the older eschatological scenario. The rearranged sequence of end-time events laid out in Romans 9–11 both aligns with the facts of the

---

53. The mission to pagans in the synoptic tradition is deferred to the period after the resurrection, implicitly in Mark 13:10, explicitly in Matt. 28:19 (the instructions of the risen Christ to his disciples) and in Acts 1:8, deferred until 11:20.

mid-century mission and accommodates this movement's apocalyptic *novum*: a messiah who would come not once, but twice. In that incandescent interim between the resurrection and the Parousia, Paul now knew, the *plērōma* of the nations would first heed the gospel, and only after that would God cease hardening Israel. The shocking new arrangement between gods and their humans wrought by the gospel confirmed Paul in his conviction that the kingdom truly was at hand. Indeed, this reform of pagan worship was, in his view, precisely the kingdom's trip switch.[54] By working to turn pagans from their gods to his god, Paul thus worked as well, beneath a canopy of biblical promises, for the ultimate redemption of his own people.

---

54. On Paul's rearrangement of these elements of the traditional eschatological scenario, Fredriksen, "Judaism, the Circumcision of Gentiles," 559–64; E. P. Sanders, *Paul, the Law, and the Jewish People* (Philadelphia: Fortress Press, 1983), 185.

7

———

The Question of Politics: Paul as a Diaspora Jew under Roman Rule

Neil Elliott

The measure of Paul's Jewish identity remains a matter of considerable controversy in current scholarship.[1] As Pamela Eisenbaum observes, the question has provoked anxiety among some scholars, and not surprisingly, since the study of Paul "continues to be the arena of discourse where Christians (and recently some Jews) work out their religious identity."[2] It is an indication of that anxiety that today, some thirty years since the announcement of a

1. In April 2009, I had the honor of engaging Alan F. Segal in public conversation about the implications of his pioneering work in ancient Judaism and, in particular, on the apostle Paul for Christian theology. The occasion was Professor Segal's visit to United Theological Seminary, one of the last such occasions before his untimely death. His wit, graciousness, and humility were as evident as his formidable intelligence. In gratitude I dedicate this essay to his memory.

New Perspective on Paul,[3] it remains profoundly difficult for many interpreters to escape the constraining categories of an older, "Christianizing" view of the apostle.[4] This may surprise us, given the increasing popularity of the New Perspective, which was premised on moving beyond those very constraints. One consequence is that significant *political* aspects of Paul's context (and of our own) continue to be minimized or marginalized in interpretation.

According to the older, Christianizing view, we must understand Paul fundamentally as someone whose thought and experience—however these may have been formed by his background in Judaism—had been decisively *reshaped* by his encounter with the risen Christ, which Paul described as a "revelation" or "apocalypse" of God's son to him (Gal. 1:11-16, *apokalypsis Iēsou Christou*). Thus, although most interpreters today acknowledge, in general terms, that various aspects of Paul's thinking derived from Jewish traditions, many hasten to qualify that acknowledgment by insisting that those aspects came to mean something very different to Paul, *something no longer compatible with Judaism*, after this "revelation" of Christ. That "event" is often described as an interruption, a "breaking in," implying that it defies explanation in terms of Paul's Jewish heritage alone.

Central to this Christianizing view are texts in Paul's letters in which he appears to look back on his own former conduct as a Jew with critical distance, regarding it as destructive "zeal" (Gal. 1:12-14),

---

2. Pamela Eisenbaum, "Paul, Polemics, and the Problem of Essentialism," *Biblical Interpretation* 13, no. 3 (2005): 224–38.

3. The phrase derives from James D. G. Dunn's landmark essay "The New Perspective on Paul," *Bulletin of the John Rylands Library* 65 (1983): 95–122.

4. On the concept of "Christianizing" interpretations of Paul or aspects of his historical context see H. Dixon Slingerland, *Claudian Policymaking and the Early Imperial Repression of Judaism at Rome* (Atlanta: Scholars, 1997), chap. 1; Richard A. Horsley, "Submerged Biblical Histories and Imperial Biblical Studies," in *The Postcolonial Bible*, ed. R. S. Sugirtharajah (Sheffield: Sheffield Academic Press, 1998), 152–73.

or describing his Jewish heritage now as nothing but "loss" (*zēmia*) or "rubbish" (a euphemism for the Greek *skybala*) compared with "the surpassing value of knowing Christ Jesus my lord" (Phil. 3:7-9). At the heart of centuries of Protestant exegesis and theology is the irreducible opposition between striving in futility for "righteousness" before God through "works of law"—phrases that in the past were usually taken as a virtual definition of Judaism—and receiving God's gracious offer of righteousness through Christ, which was taken as definitive of life in Christ. That opposition, too, is ostensibly drawn from Paul's letters (Rom. 3:21-25; 9:30—10:6; Gal. 2:15-21; 3:1-14; Phil. 3:2-9).[5]

That older view was imperiled, however, by criticisms, which were finally given exhaustive demonstration by E. P. Sanders, that Jews in Paul's day did *not* understand themselves to be securing God's approval through "works of law."[6] If Sanders was right, then interpreters seemed to be forced onto either of only two options. Either in the passages just named, Paul had been setting his gospel in unfair contrast with a caricature of Judaism that did not in fact exist, or else Paul's Protestant interpreters had misunderstood him regarding the nature of "works-righteousness." Sanders himself and Heikki Räisänen drew the first conclusion: Paul's letters were marked

5. The literature comparing the New Perspective with the assumptions of an "older" or "Lutheran" perspective is already vast. Documenting its daily expansion is the daunting task taken on by Mark M. Mattison when he launched "The Paul Page" in 1999. The "explosion of relevant online material" compelled him to seek out the corporate sponsorship of staff at Logos Bible Software, who now manage the site (http://www.thepaulpage.com/about). For an admirably coherent and accessible summary of the chief issues and schools of thought involved, see Magnus Zetterholm, *Approaches to Paul: A Student's Guide to Recent Scholarship* (Minneapolis: Fortress Press, 2009).

6. E. P. Sanders, *Paul and Palestinian Judaism: A Comparison of Patterns of Religion* (Philadelphia: Fortress Press, 1977). Sanders himself acknowledged his debt to predecessors who had made similar arguments, though in not so sustained a way, notably Claude G. Montefiore (*Judaism and St. Paul: Two Essays* [London: Goshen, 1914]) and G. F. Moore ("Christian Writers on Judaism," *Harvard Theological Review* 14 [1921]: 197-254).

by a certain logical incoherence that resulted from his enthusiasm as a convert to a new religious community.[7]

The latter conclusion is the core impulse behind much of the New Perspective, which is actually an umbrella category under which a range of interpretive proposals may be loosely and rather uneasily grouped together.[8] The most successful among these has been the proposal that by "works-righteousness" Paul meant, not the individual Jew's striving for God's approval, but the Jewish people's *collective* effort to preserve their ethnic distinctiveness among other peoples through the diligent maintenance of boundary-marking practices like circumcision, kosher diet, and the keeping of the Sabbath.[9] On this view, then, Paul's argument is not against a false Jewish understanding of how individuals may be saved, but against a supposed effort by antagonistic Jewish contemporaries to impose boundary-marking practices on Paul's largely non-Jewish congregations. That is, Paul's polemic against "works of law" springs from his desire to defend the law-free church of gentiles and Jews.

When put in these terms, we should recognize that much of the New Perspective is only as "new" as the nineteenth-century Tübingen school of F. C. Baur, with which it has much in common.[10] This approach nevertheless has gained in its appeal to

---

7. Sanders, *Paul and Palestinian Judaism*; Heikki Räisänen, *Paul and the Law* (Philadelphia: Fortress Press, 1983).

8. A third approach is to seek to refute or minimize the relevance of Sanders's arguments, an approach that often veers close to an exercise in special pleading: see Zetterholm, *Approaches to Paul*, chap. 6 ("In Defense of Protestantism"). Yet another approach implicitly refutes one aspect of Sanders's argument by postulating that the form of works-righteousness seen in *4 Ezra* or *2 Baruch*—later, post-70 texts that Sanders considered anomalous—were in fact representative of a much more prevalent form of Judaism in Paul's day, an argument Martinus de Boer has recently advanced ("Paul's Mythologizing Program in Romans 5–8," in *Apocalyptic Paul: Cosmos and Anthropos in Romans 5–8*, ed. Beverly Roberts Gaventa (Waco, TX: Baylor University Press, 2013). Unfortunately, this argument is not falsifiable.

9. This was the core insight and distinctive contribution of Dunn's essay "New Perspective"; it remains an important element in Dunn's magisterial discussion of *The Theology of Paul the Apostle* (Grand Rapids: Eerdmans, 1999).

many contemporary interpreters, in part, I suspect, because it has the apparent advantage of absolving Paul of having misunderstood Judaism. To the contrary, on this view, Paul appears as something of a champion of modern multiculturalism and as an opponent of ethnic chauvinism or ethnocentrism (which was exemplified by his Jewish opponents). It is not surprising that this approach has proven popular in the United States and the United Kingdom, that is, in ethnically diverse, democratic societies where more liberal interpreters see a happy integration of different peoples as a paramount value.

This interpretation (and cultural appropriation) of Paul comes at a cost, however, as a number of critics have pointed out. It routinely portrays as characteristically Jewish a collective insistence on ethnic distinctiveness, sometimes in negative terms formerly used to describe the boastful, arrogant, self-justifying Jewish *individual*. As Thomas Deidun put it years ago, New Perspective efforts to rehabilitate Paul as an opponent of Jewish ethnocentrism allow "practically all the old Lutheran demons" of Jewish caricature "to return unabashed to the Judaism which Sanders had by all accounts meticulously swept and put in order."[11] Similar criticisms have been raised by Mark D. Nanos and Daniel Boyarin, among others.[12]

Even when Christian interpreters today are careful to stipulate that they do *not* mean to pit Paul over against Judaism itself, but only to portray him as championing a "universal" strand of the Jewish

10. A point made by Scott Hafemann, "Paul and His Interpreters," in *Dictionary of Paul and His Letters*, ed. Gerald F. Hawthorne and Ralph P. Martin (Downers Grove, IL: InterVarsity, 1993), 666–79. See F. C. Baur, *Paul the Apostle of Jesus Christ*, 2 vols., trans. E. Zeller (London: Williams & Norgate, 1876).

11. Thomas Deidun, "James Dunn and John Ziesler on Romans in New Perspective," *Heythrop Journal* 33 (1992): 79–84.

12. Mark D. Nanos, *The Mystery of Romans: The Jewish Context of Paul's Letter* (Minneapolis: Fortress Press, 1996), 88–95; Nanos, "Paul and Judaism: Why Not Paul's Judaism?" in *Paul Unbound: Other Perspectives on the Apostle*, ed. Mark Douglas Given (Peabody, MA: Hendrickson, 2010), 117–60; Daniel Boyarin, *A Radical Jew: Paul and the Politics of Identity* (Berkeley: University of California Press, 1994), 209–24.

tradition over against a "narrowly ethnocentric" strand, the result is often to pose Paul as the *only* expression of the "universal" (that is, the "good") strand. The implication remains that any Jews who did *not* follow Paul into the "universalism" of Christianity were held back by the "bad" strand of Judaism, which is generally characterized by ethnic prejudice.[13]

The Constraining Power of Essentializing Categories

Pamela Eisenbaum deftly observes that there are two fundamental interpretive errors involved in much current interpretation of Paul, including aspects of the New Perspective. One is the "essentializing" of ancient Judaism; that is, the definition of Judaism, not in terms of the self-understanding expressed by actual Jews, but in predefined terms of its essential *otherness*, its inherent incompatibility with an (equally essentialized) understanding of Christianity.

> Put very simply, . . . Christianity is defined as devotion to Christ; Judaism is defined as devotion to Torah. . . . In the context of this discussion, essentialism exacerbates the problem of Christian-Jewish polemic in the study of Paul because Judaism and Christianity are assumed to be mutually exclusive as well as immutable categories of religious identity. Specifically, devotion to Christ necessitates repudiation of Torah, because devotion to Christ in terms of traditional

---

13. To take but one example of a wider phenomenon, Richard B. Hays takes pains to insist that he does *not* wish to oppose Paul to Judaism (*Echoes of Scripture in the Letters of Paul* [New Haven, CT: Yale University Press, 1989], 55, 59). But even as he repeatedly describes Paul as representing Judaism "rightly understood," over against "a narrowly ethnocentric form of Judaism," he fails to identify a single person or text *other than Paul* that might have represented the former. The inevitable impression is left that the "narrowly ethnocentric form" of Judaism is all that there was—other than Paul. This, to my eyes, is but another example of what Daniel Boyarin has criticized as the "allegorization of the Jew" in Christian scholarship (*A Radical Jew*, loc. cit.; see Neil Elliott, *The Arrogance of Nations: Reading Romans in the Shadow of Empire*, Paul in Critical Contexts [Minneapolis: Fortress Press, 2008], 128–32). A similar critique of N. T. Wright's description of Judaism "reconfigured," "redefined," and "perfected" in Paul's gospel (*Paul and the Faithfulness of God* [Minneapolis: Fortress Press, 2013], 415 and passim, following Richard B. Hays, 2005, 5f.) is a worthy task for a different venue.

Pauline theology implies a particular theology of grace that requires a negative valuation of Torah.[14]

The second error identified by Eisenbaum is bound up with the first in a vicious circular argument. Many interpreters understand Paul as being *ethnically* Jewish—feeling group affinity or loyalty for his people—but not *religiously* or *theologically* Jewish. That is, interpreters recognize that in his letters Paul occasionally identifies himself as a Jew, still in "solidarity" with other Jews, but insist that he "was so radically transformed by his experience of Christ that he moved outside the bounds of Judaism, or at least he moved so far to the margins that he ventured into something no longer recognizably Jewish." Eisenbaum describes advocates of this pattern of interpretation as "the *kata sarka* camp," understanding Paul as a Jew *only* ethnically, *only* "according to the flesh."[15]

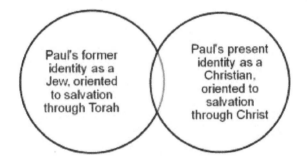

Fig. 1. The "*kata sarka*" interpretation of Paul's Judaism. The overlap between the two zones represents the vestigial aspects of Paul's merely "ethnic" identity, as a Jew "according to flesh," that continue even as Paul has come to think of himself primarily or essentially as a Christian.

14. Eisenbaum, "Paul, Polemics, and the Problem of Essentialism," 226. For an earlier critique of Christian stereotypes regarding Judaism contemporary with Paul, see Nanos, *Mystery of Romans,* Introduction and pp. 88–95.
15. Eisenbaum, "Paul, Polemics, and the Problem of Essentialism," 227–28.

Essentialism in the "Social-Science" Paul

So pervasive are the categories and habits of this "essentializing" thinking that one need not go far to find examples of its constraining power, even when scholars clearly and explicitly intend to avoid it.

One rather egregious example illustrates the problem. In their *Social-Science Commentary on the Letters of Paul,* Bruce J. Malina and John J. Pilch affirm repeatedly that "Paul was an Israelite" who "did not 'convert to Christianity' but rather continued to obey the God of Israel as he had previously done"; his work had an "exclusively Israelite nature."[16] These statements appear initially to range Malina and Pilch against the mainstream of Christian theological interpretation and on the side of some of the interpreters represented in the present volume. But Malina and Pilch go on to argue that our modern conception of Paul among "Jews and non-Jews (Gentiles)" is "completely inappropriate," and imply that under no circumstances should we think of Paul as a "Jew."

Malina and Pilch are concerned in part to "fix" the meaning of various ethnic labels in the "Mediterranean world." When Paul spoke of "Greeks," they contend, he didn't mean people from Greece, he meant "persons who were civilized," including civilized, Greek-speaking "Israelites." These, rather than "non-Israelites," were the targets of his mission as "apostle to the Gentiles" (another mistranslation, according to Malina and Pilch). They argue that "in ingroup contexts, any Israelite 'going to the other peoples' would be presumed to be going to *Israelites resident among* those other peoples."[17] The authors are aware, of course, that this claim flies in the face of the "received view," as they call it, but they insist the received view is wrong. Unfortunately, their case rests on a certain carelessness

16. Bruce J. Malina and John J. Pilch, *Social-Science Commentary on the Letters of Paul* (Minneapolis: Fortress Press, 2006), 10–13.
17. Ibid., 3–4, 7.

with categories,[18] and with a blunt essentialism that juxtaposes two oppositions from Paul's letters—*Hellēnoi* versus *Ioudaioi* (Rom. 1:16) and *Hellēnoi* versus *barbaroi* (Rom. 1:14)—and confuses them. That is, they at once assume that a term (like *Hellēnos*) always refers to just one thing, and that if two other terms are opposed to *Hellēnos,* those terms must be synonymous. "Greeks" (*Hellēnoi*), they consequently explain,

> referred to a status, to persons who were "civilized," indicated by the fact that they spoke Greek and adopted Hellenic values and habits in interpersonal relations. Similarly, the reference to "Jews" in poorly conceived English translations actually refers to "Judeans," people who followed the customs of one group of people living in that section of the Roman province of Syria called Palestine. The Hebrew term *yehudim* and the Greek *Ioudaioi* are simply erroneously translated in English [that is, as "Jews"]. . . . To "Greeks," including Israelite "Greeks," Judeans were barbarians.[19]

With this categorical infrastructure in place, Malina and Pilch are ready to interpret the whole Pauline corpus by distinguishing Paul and his fellow "Israelite Greeks," who are characterized as tolerant, even enthusiastic about the worship of other gods, from the "Judaizers" who plagued him. The latter were "Judeans" eager to impose a particularly narrow set of local Judean practices on Paul's

18. For example, Malina and Pilch tell their readers early on that "in the first-century Mediterranean there really were no 'Greeks' since there was no Greek nation nor any state called Greece" (ibid., 3), but proceed later to quote at length ancient authors talking about "Greeks" and "Greece" without explanation or correction. The heart of their argument, that Paul addressed Israelites rather than "Gentiles," is a single analogy, dressed up in social-science "ingroup" jargon: When Israelis speak of "'going to Americans' to sell U.S. tax-exempt Israeli bonds, they are presumed to be going to Jews resident in the U.S." (7). The analogy breaks down, of course, as soon as we imagine such an Israeli "apostle" speaking to American Jews (as Paul speaks to his congregations) and identifying them as "Americans" *rather than* as Jews. On Malina and Pilch's role in the wider discussion of ethnicity, see also Elliott, *Arrogance of Nations,* 47–52.

19. Malina and Pilch, *Social-Science Commentary,* 5. Note that the restriction of *Ioudaioi* to "that section of the Roman province of Syria called Palestine" is anachronistic, since the official Roman designation of the province Syria-Palestina followed the suppression of the Bar Kokhba rebellion in 135 CE. Its use here appears provocative.

"Israelite" communities. Chief among these peculiar practices was "infant genital mutilation," by which Malina and Pilch mean circumcision, which they assert appeared "rather late in Palestine (ca. 150 B.C.E.), and perhaps centuries later, if at all, among Yahweh worshipers far from the region of Judea."[20] To justify these remarkable claims, they invoke Shaye J. D. Cohen's careful study of Jewish identity, but show in doing so that they have misunderstood it. Cohen observed that in the Hasmonean period, after the persecution of Judaism by Antiochus Epiphanes, an "ethic of separation" between Jews and non-Jews emerged in which certain laws and rituals, paramount among them circumcision, gained "new prominence." The Hasmoneans also granted Judean citizenship to Idumaeans and Ituraeans, who were most likely "already circumcised" (though Cohen was careful to note that the event is often misrepresented as their "forcible conversion" to Judaism).[21] But Cohen never claimed, as Malina and Pilch imply, that the practice of circumcision was a second-century innovation, or that it was localized to the environs of Jerusalem. Those claims are Malina and Pilch's inventions. Unfortunately, they seem to be of a piece with their strained effort to attribute "modern Ashkenazi Jewishness" to the ninth-century Khazars, with whom "there was no lineal development from early Israel."[22] Contemporary Western Jews are thus deprived of any historical continuity with ancient Israel, at the same time Paul is held up as the personification of the ancient Israelite (and biblical) vision. It is hard to avoid the impression that the result is a form of Christian supersession dressed up as "social science."

20. Ibid., 13–15.
21. Shaye J. D. Cohen, *The Beginnings of Jewishness: Boundaries, Varieties, Uncertainties* (Berkeley: University of California Press, 1999), 130–39.
22. Malina and Pilch, *Social-Science Commentary*, 179–80.

Paul's Almost-Jewish Identity

Another example of an "essentialist" or "Christianized" interpretation of Paul is far more sophisticated. I turn to Jörg Frey's essay on "Paul's Jewish Identity," not because it is particularly egregious example of the pattern I am describing (it is not), but simply because Frey's clearly stated intention is to understand Paul *as a Jew*. Indeed, in his survey of recent scholarship, Frey celebrates the current dialogue between Christian and Jewish interpreters of Paul as "resulting in a mutual illumination of texts and perspectives" that he declares "the most promising progress in scholarship."[23] He decries as hopelessly one-sided and anachronistic the attempts by other scholars to deny that the apostle Paul was still a Jew; to the contrary, he insists (as we have seen Malina and Pilch do as well) that "Paul never abandoned 'Judaism' in order to join 'Christianity.'"[24] Frey also illustrates the various ways in which Paul professed solidarity with Israel, and relied upon concepts and themes (the importance of the law, the resurrection of the dead) that derived from Judaism.

Nevertheless, at several key points Frey continues to describe Paul's relationship to Judaism in essentializing ways that emphasize the distance of Paul and his "Christian" churches from Judaism, implying their fundamental incompatibility. The following review is not meant to be exhaustive, but simply to demonstrate that other scholars, including some represented in the present volume, have proposed alternative interpretations at a number of points that allow us to understand Paul's thought and experience within the categories of ancient Judaism, *understood in the political context of Roman rule,* apart from Christian assumptions. An examination of Frey's essay thus allows us to recognize the constraining power that older,

23. Jörg Frey, "Paul's Jewish Identity," in *Jewish Identity in the Greco-Roman World,* ed. Jörg Frey, Daniel R. Schwartz, and Stephanie Gripentrog (Leiden: Brill, 2007), 285–321, here 289.
24. Ibid., 291.

essentializing, or "Christianizing" assumptions continue to exert, even when interpreters are striving for a "new perspective."

Paul's Past Persecution of the Early Assemblies

Frey regards as thoroughly "Pharisaic" the "zeal by which [Paul] had persecuted the enemies of the law," prior to the "revelation" of Christ. "Paul's activity as a persecutor," he writes, "appears as part of an inner-Jewish struggle for the recognition of the Torah against its alleged opponents" in the early churches.[25] This appears to absolve Paul of any anti-Jewish animus by explaining his persecuting activity as a struggle *among Jews* over the observance of the law. But this is simply to project an essentialist dichotomy back *behind* Paul, into the early Jesus movement. That is, it portrays the Judean *ekklēsiai* as *already* moving away from, and hostile to, the law—presumably meaning, indifferent or hostile to the law's boundary function in excluding non-Jews. These early communities, by implication, provided a proto-Christian community into which Paul could later move.

However prevalent that assumption remains among Christian interpreters—Paula Fredriksen has described it as "an almost universal consensus"—it can hardly be judged historical, as Fredriksen has convincingly demonstrated.[26] One way Frey and other scholars portray the earliest proclamation of the messiah Jesus as being necessarily hostile to or opposed to the law is by reading Paul's aside in Galatians 3:13 as evidence that *before* the "revelation" of Christ, Paul straightforwardly regarded the crucified Jesus as "cursed" by law. This means the earliest believers in Jesus would necessarily have opposed the law in order to proclaim a crucified man as messiah,

---

25. Ibid.
26. Paula Fredriksen, *From Jesus to Christ: The Origins of the New Testament Images of Jesus* (New Haven, CT: Yale University Press, 1988), 142–56.

and that as a Jew, Paul would have shared that judgment until God's revelation decisively reversed it.[27] But as Fredriksen points out, this supposition is undermined by "an utter lack of evidence. . . . In no Jewish writing of this period, Paul included, do we find crucifixion itself taken to indicate a death cursed by God or by the Law."[28] To the contrary, archaeological evidence shows that crucified Jews were buried and memorialized honorably.[29] The notion that Paul (or any Jew) would have regarded a crucified Jew as "cursed" is historically improbable. As Fredriksen puts the question, "why, in brief, would Jews reject [another] Jew for a Roman reason?" Rhetorically, Paul's offhand reference in Galatians 3 to a text from Deuteronomy "gets Paul where he needs to go," in a "snarled" argument addressed to non-Jews—but to load this remark with the weight of explaining Paul's "conversion," as Frey and other Christian exegetes continue to do, imposes a burden the text cannot bear.[30]

Nor would the early Jesus assemblies have been opposing the law by including non-Jews alongside Jews in their community observances. In a variety of traditions, Jewish literature gives evidence of the expectation that at the last days, non-Jews would turn from idols to recognize the true God. That did not mean that they would stop being non-Jews, however, as Fredriksen observes that *"moral conversion is not halakic conversion.* These Gentiles would not, by abandoning their idols, have the legal and religious status of converts,

---

27. Frey, "Paul's Jewish Identity," 318–19. In Galatians 3:13, Paul declares, "Christ redeemed us from the curse of the law by becoming a curse for us—for it is written, 'Cursed is everyone who hangs on a tree'" (quoting Deut. 21:22-23).
28. Fredriksen, *From Jesus to Christ,* 147–48.
29. An excavated first-century tomb northeast of Jerusalem revealed the remains of a Jew, Yehohanan, who had been crucified but nevertheless given a proper family burial next to the remains of a relative named Simon, "the builder of the Temple" (V. Tzaferis, "Jewish Tombs at and near Giv'at ha-Mivtar," *Israel Exploration Journal* 20 [1970]: 18–32; J. Zias and E. Sekeles, "The Crucified Man from Giv'at ha-Mitvar: A Reappraisal," *Israel Exploration Journal* 35 [1985]: 22–27).
30. Fredriksen, *From Jesus to Christ,* 147.

that is, Jews. They would remain Gentiles and *as Gentiles* would they be saved." The very fact that Jews proclaiming Jesus as messiah could find non-Jews to accept their message showed that non-Jews were welcomed in synagogues; "and the original apostles so readily accepted these Gentiles because they saw in their response, as with their leader's resurrection, yet one more sign that the Kingdom approached—indeed, its effects were already manifest."[31] Neither the presence of non-Jews in synagogues (which could have happened, Fredriksen points out, *"in Paul's own synagogue"*) nor the close meal fellowship of Jews and non-Jews would have scandalized a good Pharisee, provided the meals did not involve non-kosher foods—and if they had, Fredriksen asks, how would Paul later have secured the acquiescence of those presumed monitors of Jewish observance, the Jerusalem apostles, for so long?[32]

Fredriksen concludes that the reason the Pharisee Paul persecuted the *ekklēsiai* had nothing to do with halakah. It had everything to do, she proposes, with the precarious political security of minority Jewish communities in Palestinian and Syrian cities. "The enthusiastic proclamation of a messiah executed very recently as a political insurrectionist—a *crucified messiah*—combined with a vision of the approaching End *preached also to Gentiles*—this was dangerous. If it got abroad, it could endanger the whole Jewish community."[33] In defense of what she admits is a "speculative" explanation, Fredriksen points out that her proposal has the merits of relying neither on anachronism nor the invention of otherwise unattested Jewish exegetical and halakic traditions (as "Christianizing" interpretations do); it simply "recognizes the politically precarious situation of urban Jewish communities in the Diaspora."[34] Alas, just the features that

31. Ibid., 150.
32. Ibid., 151–52.
33. Ibid., 153–54.

render Fredriksen's argument compelling also make it exceptional in contemporary interpretation, where the Jesus movement *even before Paul* is more usually—and more implausibly—characterized as entertaining attitudes and practices incompatible with the law.

The Christ-apocalypse as Distancing Event

Although he acknowledges that "some of the convictions [Paul] held as a Pharisee remained influential for his work as an apostle," including his dedication "to the careful study of the law," Frey declares that "especially the fact that he was called" by God to be an apostle of the risen Christ, "precisely when zealously acting in defense of the law . . . must have shaken his convictions fundamentally." This means especially that Paul's reflection as an apostle "on the relevance of circumcision and law"—by which Frey evidently means, their *irrelevance* to the new community gathered by Christ—"must have started quite early after his Damascus experience, when he began to preach the new message to the communities in Arabia or Syria and Cilicia," and "at the latest with the programmatic mission to pagan addressees."[35] Here, note again the equation of Paul's prior persecuting activity with a particular understanding of "defense of the law" as a matter of boundary observance.

Frey is certainly not alone among Christian interpreters in understanding the revelation of Christ to Paul ("his Damascus experience") as a radical *interruption* that caused a profound reversal in Paul's behavior, and in his attitude toward the law. But we should detect essentialist thinking in the assumption that the Christ-apocalypse was fundamentally incompatible with continued devotion

---

34. Ibid. I relied upon Fredriksen's argument in my own discussion of the politics of the "apocalypse" of Christ to Paul: *Liberating Paul: The Justice of God and the Politics of the Apostle* (Maryknoll, NY: Orbis Books, 1994), 144–49.

35. Frey, "Paul's Jewish Identity," 298.

to (the boundary-setting role of) the law. On these terms, Paul's dramatic break with his Jewish contemporaries seems inevitable, "built into" the encounter with Christ. But why? Frey offers no explanation of that inevitability; he simply asserts it. Given the frequency with which Christian discourse refers to Paul's "Damascus experience" in terms of divine revelation, perhaps Frey expects some at least of his readers to presume that the point does not need explanation. But this only renders dichotomous thinking even more impervious to criticism.

In contrast, Alan F. Segal understood Paul's visionary experience of Christ in the context of the apocalyptic-mystical tradition in early Judaism. Indeed, Segal demonstrated in *Paul the Convert* that Paul was our earliest and best (because first-person) witness to that tradition. In 2 Corinthians 12, Paul described an unnamed man's visionary journey into "the third heaven," a passage that is generally recognized to be an oblique reference to his own ecstatic experience. Segal argued that this experience was probably not an isolated event. Rather, here "Paul reveals modestly that he has had several ecstatic meetings with Christ over the previous fourteen years."[36] Participants in Jewish mysticism, "and perhaps apocalypticism as well, sought out visions and developed special practices to achieve them. Thus, we can assume that Paul had a number of ecstatic experiences in his life, [and] that his conversion may have been one such experience."[37] Hardly "incompatible" with Judaism in Paul's day, as language of a "rupture" or "irruption" implies, such an experience "parallels ecstatic ascents to the divine throne in other apocalyptic and merkabah mystical traditions." While those parallel sources are later than Paul, the close similarity of themes and terminology convinced Segal that Paul was

36. Alan F. Segal, *Paul the Convert: The Apostolate and Apostasy of Saul the Pharisee* (New Haven, CT: Yale University Press, 1990), 36.
37. Ibid., 37.

indeed an early participant in a wider stream of mystical-ecstatic experience that included those later sources as well. Indeed, "Paul alone demonstrates that such traditions existed as early as the first century."[38]

Most intriguing for my purpose here are Segal's tentative comments that "it is possible, if unlikely, that 2 Corinthians 12 records Paul's original conversion experience." More likely, "Paul is describing a revelation both similar and subsequent to his conversion." Segal argued that Paul "necessarily" had several ecstatic experiences, and "that his conversion may have been one such experience."[39] This suggests—though remarkably, Segal did not pursue the possibility—that the "apocalypse" of Christ may not have been the first such visionary ascent on Paul's part. That is, in a series of ecstatic experiences in which we may suppose, on the analogy of other visionary texts prior to and contemporary with Paul, that he perceived in heaven a divine figure at the right hand of the Ancient of Days (cf. Dan. 7:9-14), one such experience was the first in which that figure was perceptible to Paul *as the crucified Jesus.* Just here Segal provided us with a powerful explanation of the "apocalypse" of Christ *on fundamentally Jewish terms.*

For reasons I do not understand, Segal went on to conclude that "the meaning of these experiences" could only have been mediated to Paul "by the gentile Christian community in which he lived."[40] "We can ask," he wrote, "but we need not answer why a *Pharisee* would have a vision of *Christ.*"[41] Segal himself neither tried to answer the question nor even mentioned it again in the rest of his book.

---

38. Ibid.
39. Ibid., 26, 27.
40. Ibid., 37 and throughout the book. On just this point, Paula Fredriksen similarly draws back, referring the reader (in a footnote!) to the concept of cognitive dissonance (*From Jesus to Christ,* 134 n. 2).
41. Segal, *Paul the Convert,* 37 (emphasis added).

Rather, he turned away from the potential explanatory power of the very Jewish visionary tradition that he had so carefully described to seek a sociological explanation of Paul's "conversion" in which the ecstatic tradition played no further part. Perhaps Segal assumed that a *Jewish* vision of a crucified messiah in heaven was categorically incomprehensible. Indeed, he implied that such an intense ecstatic experience would have remained completely unintelligible to Paul until, years later, some friendly non-Jews explained it to him.[42] But that implication has no logical force behind it. I propose, to the contrary, that to suppose that such a vision could only be understood on "Christian" premises is to fall into the same essentialist thinking described by Eisenbaum.[43] But such dichotomous thinking is as unnecessary as it is unfruitful.

Instead, as I have argued elsewhere, we can in fact imagine what a Pharisee would have made of a vision of a crucified messiah, and we can do so *on Jewish terms*: based, that is, on the urgent ethical and political consequences that the apocalypses drew from visions of heaven. Following Fredriksen's argument, previously discussed, we may suppose that Paul's motives for persecuting the early *ekklēsiai* had to do with concern for the political vulnerability of Jewish communities:

> We must suppose that as a Jew, as an apocalyptist, and as a Pharisee, [Paul] assumed that God's triumph over the Romans was inevitable, however indeterminate that day might be. . . . If a Pharisee like Saul of Tarsus had looked upon Roman power with the eyes of the apocalyptists, he might well have concluded that God had given the sovereignty of the earth to Rome, "for a time." For that time, he might have concluded, resistance to Rome—however much he sympathized

---

42. Segal goes on to refer to "Paul's confusion over the nature of his ecstatic journey to heaven" (ibid., 39), but this "confusion" has to do with whether or not Paul was "in or out of the body." Segal himself shows this was a customary, almost ritualized element of visionary reports. It hardly means that Paul could not have made sense of what he "saw" in that vision.

43. See further my critical interaction with Segal's work in *Liberating Paul*, 141–43.

with its motives—was not only futile but impious. . . . So the messianists were not only wrong about what time it was; they were dangerously wrong . . .[44]

Further, strictly on terms of comparison with contemporary Jewish texts like *4 Maccabees* or the *Liber antiquitatum biblicarum,* we might suppose that Paul the Pharisee could have attributed to Jesus' death the atoning significance attributed to others executed by Rome.

> Paul would also have been taught by the apocalypses that the righteous martyred by Rome would "at the last day" be raised from the dead. We have only to suppose that this Pharisee experienced a vision of the martyr Jesus in heaven, a vision for which the Jewish apocalypses themselves provided the conceptual preparation.[45]

Once such a vision made clear to him that God had raised the martyred Jesus from the dead—again, a realization that would have been intelligible within the bounds of Jewish apocalyptic experience—the consequences would have followed a thoroughly Jewish apocalyptic logic: "The vision would have confirmed to [Paul] that what the apocalypses promised God *would* do *someday,* God had in fact begun to do *now.*"[46] The consequence would have been an abrupt about-face from persecuting the assemblies, but this turn would have been motivated and remains completely explicable within categories supplied by the Jewish apocalypses.

The last point is an important one and I do not wish it to be misconstrued. I am not arguing that the Jewish apocalyptic tradition in any way "proves" that Jesus was raised from the dead; only that the claim of Jesus' being raised is, from a historical point of view, as intelligible—no more, but certainly no less—than claims made in any number of Jewish texts regarding the resurrection of the righteous

44. Ibid.,169.
45. Ibid., 171.
46. Ibid., 172.

or the presence in heaven of human figures as agents of the divine purpose. In contrast to essentializing thinking, I suggest that there is nothing "essentially" Christian about a Pharisee experiencing a visionary ascent to heaven and seeing the resurrected Jesus there.

Israel's Rejection of the Messiah

Frey rightly affirms that Paul's vocation as apostle to the nations ("Gentiles," in Frey's usage) is "formed by several [scriptural] passages, chiefly from the book of Isaiah."[47] This is an important recognition, especially when compared with the implication, in the work of other interpreters (as different as Heikki Räisänen and Alan Segal), that Paul "backed into" the "Gentile" church and came to adopt a gospel that included them only gradually and unreflectively.[48] For Frey, however, this priority is explained by the "principle" that he finds in Romans 1:16, "first to the Jews, then to the Greeks." This "formula" refers, Frey declares, to "Israel's priority in salvation history (cf. Rom. 3:1)" and the "enduring primacy of Israel" in Paul's "missionary strategy." Frey explains this "principle" by reference to the narrative in Acts, where Paul is repeatedly presented preaching in synagogues to Jews and non-Jews alike:

> The account of Acts, even though it may be rather schematic, generally confirms the principle mentioned in Rom 1:16: According to Acts, Paul consistently preached among the Jews (cf. Acts 9:22; 13:15ff.; 14:1; 16:13; 17:1f., 10f.; 18:4; 19:4) and only turned toward the Gentiles when facing opposition from the Jews (Acts 13:46).[49]

For Frey, Paul's apostolate to the nations was decisively "shaped by the experience of the rejection of the Gospel by many of Paul's fellow Jews."[50] Indeed, Frey finds in Romans 10:20-21 Paul's attempt

---

47. Frey, "Paul's Jewish Identity," 300.
48. Segal, *Paul the Convert*, 58–61; 117; Heikki Räisänen, *Paul and the Law*, 258–61.
49. Frey, "Paul's Jewish Identity," 301.

"to demonstrate that the revelation to the Gentiles and the rejection of Christ by the majority of Israel are in accordance with the Scriptures."[51]

It is unfortunate that Frey has subordinated a few phrases in Romans to the narrative logic in Acts, with the result that the "primacy" of Israel in Paul's thought is thereby rendered a merely *chronological* priority: Paul preached to Jews "first," in place after place, and when they rejected his gospel, he "then" turned to non-Jews. This reads Israel's rejection of the (Pauline) gospel as a *fait accompli* in the past, a "theological fact" in the present (as Paul writes Romans). This understanding—all too common in Christianizing interpretation—fails to make sense (or in Frey's case, any mention at all) of Romans 11. Here we find Paul's clear and forceful admonition to non-Jews in the Roman *ekklēsiai* that he carries out his apostolic work among them "in order to make my own people jealous, and thus save some of them" (Rom. 11:13-14). That is, Paul declares that the nations are not "primary," *even in his work with them in the present:* rather, the salvation of "all Israel" is his paramount priority, as Romans 11:25-26 makes clear.

I have argued elsewhere that the "theological fact" that Frey attributes to Paul was in fact a premise of the non-Jewish readers he addressed in Rome, but a premise, we may observe, that Paul himself explicitly rejected. Romans 9–11 have been read, since Calvin, as a defense of the honor of God in the face of the apparent lapse of Israel's covenant; but as the rhetoric of these chapters in Romans itself makes clear, the supposition that God had in any way abandoned Israel or that God's covenantal word to Israel had failed was, for Paul, unthinkable. In Frey's discussion, it would seem, the "enduring primacy of Israel" has no necessary connection to actual Jews. It

50. Ibid.
51. Ibid., 300.

remains rather a wistful theological postulate, an expression of ethnic "solidarity" that certifies Paul's bona fides as a Jew, even after the "primacy of Israel" in any material sense has been tragically contradicted by history. Paul thus comes to stand, as in much recent Christian interpretation, as a noble survivor of a vanquished race, rather like the figure of the admirably stoic Native American in the US popular cultural imagination.

In contrast, the "enduring primacy of Israel" was the *horizon* of Paul's apostolate to the nations. I have argued at length elsewhere that Paul seeks, throughout this part of Romans, to disabuse some of his (non-Jewish) hearers in Rome of the very premise that Frey has attributed to Paul himself. The apostle

> distinguishes a *mistaken* apprehension of the present as the fulfillment of God's purposes—that is, reading present circumstances as if they exhaust God's mercy—from a *true* apprehension of the present as a period during which God's purposes are not yet fulfilled, but are still in suspense.[52]

The "present circumstances" that Frey, and almost all Christian interpreters, read as a Jewish failure to believe in the Christian gospel are more likely to be understood, I argue (following Wolfgang Wiefel), as the actual historical circumstances of Jews in Rome, and elsewhere, at the time Paul wrote this letter.[53] Yes, Paul concedes, *some* in Israel have "stumbled," but Paul does not narrate a Jewish rejection *of his gospel* (as the Christianizing interpretation requires), nor does he suggest that the "disobedience" of some (see Rom. 2 and 3) was tantamount to a failure *of Israel.* That was apparently a conclusion that was drawn in Rome, *by others,* but its basis had nothing to do with some imaginary Jewish plebiscite on the Pauline

---

52. Elliott, *Arrogance of Nations,* 113–14.
53. Ibid., 99–100; Wolfgang Wiefel, "The Jewish Community in Ancient Rome and the Origins of Roman Christianity," originally published in German in 1970; reprinted in Karl P. Donfried, ed., *The Romans Debate,* rev. ed. (Peabody, MA: Hendrickson, 1991), 85–101.

gospel (however often Christian interpreters have imagined it). The logic of "Israel's failure" aligns rather with elite Roman views of minority populations in Rome's streets. Paul insists that "the present circumstances of Israel *are God's doing*"; they are not the final consequence of Israel's failure, and they do *not* exhaust God's purposes.[54]

To repeat an important qualification: I am not examining elements in Frey's essay because it is in some way outlandish or exceptional today. Rather, I seek to point out a pattern of assumptions and premises that owe more to a received theological narrative of Christian origins than to historical consideration of Paul's letters in their Jewish context. I do not imagine that I have proved, in every part of this discussion, that Frey is wrong. It has been my goal to show that at point after point, an alternative interpretation of the data, *in terms of first-century Judaism* and without appeal to the language of "irruption" or divine revelation, is not only possible but readily available in the work of some contemporary scholars (including the contributors to this volume).

It is also worth notice that at several of these points, attention to the Jewish context has meant attention to the social and political situation of Jews *under Roman rule*. Jews were not only participants in an ethnic or religious identity, as a neat (and essentializing) opposition between "Jews" and "Christians" presumes. Jews were also the flesh-and-blood inhabitants of a world where conquest and the ideology of Roman supremacy were daily determinants of the possible.

Essentializing "the Political"

The last point will appear obvious to historians of Judaism. It often proves elusive, however, to proponents of what I am here calling

54. Elliott, *Arrogance of Nations*, 114–19.

a Christianizing interpretation of Paul. Considerable debate swirls today around whether, or to what extent, Paul was opposed to the Roman Empire (or "Roman imperialism"). The existence of that debate is a positive development, when we consider that thirty years ago many scholars presumed that the "politics of Paul" was simply coextensive with the exhortation to "be subject to the governing authorities" in Romans 13:1-7. I have been a participant in the more recent debate, but am less interested here in continuing it than in calling attention to some of the assumptions regarding what it means to be "Jewish" (and what it would have meant for Paul to be "Jewish") that continue to be decisive in it.[55]

At the end of his richly textured discussion of *Jews in the Mediterranean Diaspora*, John M. G. Barclay affirmed that Paul should be understood as a Diaspora Jew, but an "anomalous" one. Barclay's discussion thus provides another opportunity to explore how first-century Jewish identity in general, and Paul's Jewish identity in

55. The debate has become a field of study in its own right. A few representative works include my own *Liberating Paul* and *Arrogance of Nations* (op. cit.); Richard A. Horsley, ed., *Paul and Empire: Religion and Power in Roman Imperial Society* (Harrisburg, PA: Trinity Press International, 1997); Horsley, ed., *Paul and Politics: Ekklesia, Israel, Imperium, Interpretation* (Harrisburg, PA: Trinity Press International, 2000); Horsley, ed., *Paul and the Roman Imperial Order* (Harrisburg, PA: Trinity Press International, 2004); Davina C. Lopez, *Apostle to the Conquered* (Minneapolis: Fortress Press, 2008), and Christopher D. Stanley, ed., *The Colonized Apostle: Paul through Postcolonial Eyes*, both in Paul in Critical Contexts (Minneapolis: Fortress Press, 2011); and James R. Harrison, *Paul and the Imperial Authorities at Thessalonica and Rome*, Wissenschaftliche Untersuchungen zum Neuen Testament 273 (Tübingen: Mohr Siebeck, 2011). Surveys of the wider discussion in New Testament studies include Warren Carter, *The Roman Empire and the New Testament* (Nashville: Abingdon, 2006); Stephen D. Moore, *Empire and Apocalypse: Postcolonialism and the New Testament* (Sheffield: Sheffield Phoenix, 2006); and Stanley E. Porter and Cynthia Long Westfall, eds., *Empire in the New Testament*, New Testament Studies (Eugene, OR: Pickwick, 2011). Various dissenting views are available in Christopher Bryan, *Render to Caesar: Jesus, The Early Church, and the Roman Superpower* (New York: Oxford University Press, 2005); Bruno Blumenfeld, *The Political Paul: Justice, Democracy and Kingship in a Hellenistic Framework*, Journal for the Study of the New Testament Supplement Series 210 (Sheffield: Sheffield Academic Press, 2001); Scot McKnight and Joseph B. Modica, eds., *Jesus Is Lord, Caesar Is Not: Evaluating Empire in New Testament Studies* (Downers Grove, IL: InterVarsity, 2013); and John M. G. Barclay, *Pauline Churches and Diaspora Jews* (Tübingen: Mohr Siebeck, 2011), esp. chaps. 1, 18, and 19.

particular, might be understood. It bears particular attention because of Barclay's express interest in the social and political components of identity, informed by recent studies of Diaspora Judaism and by the experience of colonized persons in imperial contexts, ancient and contemporary.[56] Barclay wrote deliberately with an eye to the "contemporary social scene," paramount for which was "the need to foster respect and tolerance for minority ethnic groups, in the face of the complex problems created by modern social pluralism." The Jewish Diaspora was of interest on these terms because it "has proved throughout history a 'paradigm case' of minority endurance in an alien context."[57]

Despite the impressive erudition of this study, it is hard to escape the impression that Barclay's "paradigmatic" understanding of Judaism still involves an implicit attempt to describe the "essence" of Judaism. From the very first, he takes the words of Balaam's oracle in Numbers 23:9, about "a people who dwell alone, and will not be reckoned among the nations," as the defining characteristic of Judaism, "the sense of distinction which lies *at the heart* of the Jewish tradition."[58] His concern throughout the volume is with how Diaspora Jews, by definition a minority population, maintained their distinctiveness vis-à-vis "other ethnic groups."[59] Barclay is of course aware that identity is a complex matter, and thus he describes a complicated set of analytical tools to take separate measures of *accommodation, acculturation,* and *assimilation* of ethnic groups (in this case, Jews). Although these instruments are defined differently, however, they all end up in Barclay's discussion as measures of the

56. John M. G. Barclay, *Jews in the Mediterranean Diaspora: From Alexander to Trajan (323 BCE—117 CE* (Edinburgh: T & T Clark, 1996), 4–9, citing in particular Mary Smallwood's "valuable conspectus of political realities" in *The Jews Under Roman Rule from Pompey to Diocletian* (Leiden: Brill, 1976).
57. Ibid., 14.
58. Ibid., 1.
59. Ibid., 2–3.

extent to which Jews maintained their distinctive identity over against others—on the implicit assumption that being Jewish is primarily a matter of *not* being something else.[60]

Essentializing Judaism as "Other"

So, for example, Barclay relates *acculturation* to "the *linguistic, educational, and ideological* aspects of a given cultural matrix."[61] It follows that we should regard the likes of Philo or Josephus as thoroughly acculturated Jews because of their fluency in Greek language and even in the categories of Hellenistic philosophy and ethics. Barclay observes that when Josephus discusses Balaam's oracle (on Jewish distinctiveness), his "key terms, 'virtue' (*aretē*) and 'providence' (*pronoia*), are in fact derived not from his Scriptural but from his Hellenistic education." He goes on to ask, "What sort of acculturation did he and other Diaspora Jews undergo? In what respects, and to what degree, did they merge Jewish and non-Jewish cultural traditions, and how did they employ such cultural syntheses? If, despite this acculturation, Josephus and others maintained their Jewish distinction, how did they appropriate and re-employ the Hellenism they absorbed?"[62] But Barclay's language begs the question whether Josephus (or others like him) were conscious of "merging" fundamentally different cultural repertoires; that is, did Josephus *know* that "virtue" and "providence" were unbiblical, "un-Jewish" concepts, to be "merged" with Jewish ones? Or was talking as he did simply Josephus's way of being Jewish? Is the dichotomy "Jewish versus

---

60. In a subsequent work Barclay makes much the same equation: "'Judaism,' as the ethnic tradition of the Jewish/Judean people, is a tradition socially defined by *not* being 'opened' to non-Jews" (*Pauline Churches and Diaspora Jews*, 18).
61. Barclay, *Jews in the Mediterranean Diaspora*, 92.
62. Ibid., 3, discussing Josephus, *Ant.* 4.114.

Hellenistic" a lively component of Josephus's thought-world, or a flawed conceptual convenience of the modern scholar of antiquity?[63]

Assimilation, Barclay goes on, refers to "*social integration* (becoming 'similar' to one's neighbors): it concerns social contacts, social interaction, and social practices"; it is a measure of "the degree to which Diaspora Jews were integrated into, or socially aloof from, their social environments."[64] Appropriately, then, one end of the spectrum (low assimilation) means that "social life [is] confined to the Jewish community." So far, so good. But where one might then expect *high* assimilation to involve frequent social interaction with non-Jews, Barclay writes instead that it means the "abandonment of key Jewish social distinctives." That is, Jewish identity seems to *mean* non-assimilation: "as both Jews and non-Jews recognized, the Jewish tradition contained a number of taboos which impeded the assimilation of Jews."[65] Although Barclay recognizes that a Diaspora Jew like Philo could be, "in certain respects, Jewish to the core and Hellenized to the same core," his discussion of assimilation suggests that in social terms, this was simply a categorical impossibility. What should we make of the Jews of Alexandria who sought full citizenship alongside their non-Jewish neighbors: weren't *they* seeking to be Jewish *and* Alexandrian (or even Greek) to "the same core"? Barclay actually discusses a single Jew who petitioned for exemption from the poll tax, offering "a range of arguments . . . on the bases of parentage, education, and age." He even notes that the papyrus petition has been corrected by a scribe: Helenos, son of Tryphon (a good Greek name for a Jew!), identified himself as an "Alexandrian," but that

63. See Troels Engberg-Pedersen, ed., *Paul Beyond the Judaism/Hellenism Divide* (Louisville: Westminster John Knox, 2001). To be sure, Barclay seeks to avoid just such simplistic dichotomies: "undifferentiated comments about Jewish Hellenization are of little analytical use" (*Jews in the Mediterranean Diaspora,* 91). But the analytical categories Barclay sets up seem to fail him in execution.

64. Ibid., 92–93.

65. Ibid., 94.

word was "scored out by a scribe and replaced by the words 'a Jew from Alexandria.'" Barclay also recognizes that Jews in different social classes had widely different opportunities to make claims on Alexandrian citizenship; he recognizes that elite Greek citizens opposed the granting of privileges to Jews who did not (in their view) deserve them; he knows that the actions of particular emperors insulted lower-status Jews and demonstrated "the vulnerability of the Jewish community" to shifting political alliances.[66] But these are not aspects of Jewish self-identification; they are the actions of *non-Jews*, whose perceptions of Jewish identity were bound up with conceptions of class and legal status. Such nuance is missing from Barclay's own discussion of assimilation, which risks simply fusing Jewish identity with *amixia* in such a way that social interaction *means* the "abandonment of key Jewish social distinctives."

Accommodation means, for Barclay, "the *use to which acculturation is put,* in particular the degree to which Jewish and Hellenistic cultural traditions are merged, or alternatively, polarized." This spectrum he compares with the "variant uses of the colonizers' culture" among the colonized, "in some cases to modify or even obliterate their native cultural traditions, in others to equip them to resist the colonizers' cultural imperialism." Here at last we find a recognition of the power dynamics implicit in the colonial situation that shape the possibilities available to the colonized.[67] But there is no recognition of the extent to which colonized peoples may actively organize their own lives and identities in a *hybridizing* way that defies neat dichotomies—an important theme in postcolonial literature and one that Ronald Charles has identified as particularly absent from Barclay's analysis.[68]

66. Ibid., 50–51.
67. Ibid., 96.
68. See Homi K. Bhabha, *The Location of Culture* (London: Routledge, 1994). Ronald Charles discusses Barclay's understanding of Diaspora identity in light of Bhabha's work in *Paul and Diaspora Politics* (Minneapolis: Fortress Press, forthcoming), esp. chap. 3.

Thus, when Barclay presents a spectrum of "accommodation," the extreme points are "antagonism to Graeco-Roman culture" (that is, a *refusal* of accommodation) on the one side, and the "submersion of Jewish cultural uniqueness" on the other. But one might have expected accommodation to mean the *identification* of Jewish cultural uniqueness *with* the values of Hellenistic culture.

The latter possibility has been raised, albeit quite briefly, by Jacob Taubes in his discussion of Paul's Hellenistic environment. "There was an aura," Taubes writes, "a general Hellenistic aura, an apotheosis of *nomos*. One could sing it to a Gentile tune, this apotheosis . . . one could sing it in Roman, and one could sing it in a Jewish way."[69] Stanley K. Stowers has made a comparable suggestion regarding a pervasive Hellenistic ethos that valued self-mastery (*enkrateia*)—an ethos cultivated among the Roman (and Romanizing) elite in the provinces, and adapted by some Jews in terms of the cultural excellence of Jewish law.[70] These proposals suggest that if part of the Roman cultural project was, in Greg Woolf's elegant phrase, to promote ways for "becoming Roman, staying Greek,"[71] then the possibility of "accommodation" to which Barclay's analytical categories *should* point might best be described as "becoming Roman" or "becoming Greek, staying Jewish." To set Jewish identity always in opposition to Hellenistic or Roman identity, as if these were *essentially* incompatible, or as if Jewish identity was *essentially* a matter of being "not something else," would seem to be a categorical

---

69. Jacob Taubes, *The Political Theology of Paul*, ed. Aleida Assmann et al., trans. Dana Hollander (Stanford, CA: Stanford University Press, 2004), 23–24; see Elliott, *Arrogance of Nations*, 138–41 (on the piety of "works" in the Roman environment).

70. Stanley K. Stowers, *A Rereading of Romans: Justice, Jews, and Gentiles* (New Haven, CT: Yale University Press, 1994), esp. chap. 2.

71. Greg Woolf, "Becoming Roman, Staying Greek: Culture, Identity, and the Civilizing Process in Roman East," *Proceedings of the Cambridge Philological Society* 40 (1994): 116–43; Woolf, *Becoming Roman: The Origins of Provincial Civilization in Gaul* (Cambridge: Cambridge University Press, 1998).

error. (The fact that Diaspora Jews read their Scriptures in Greek, without, so far as we know, considering that language—for many of them, presumably, their first language—somehow a deficiency or fault, should tell us something about the artificiality of the dichotomy.) On the other hand, Barclay seems consistently to avoid an analysis in terms of political categories just where these might be most helpful.[72]

Paul the "Anomalous Jew"

The problem is exacerbated when Barclay turns at last to Paul, whom he labels an "anomalous Jew." He has already signaled that Paul's "Jewishness" was "doubted by his contemporaries," though he does not stop to explain what this means, or to offer any evidence.[73] (That Paul received synagogue discipline, 2 Cor. 11:24, is taken by other scholars as evidence that Paul continued to move in Jewish contexts; it hardly suggests that other Jews considered Paul to have ceased being Jewish, as Barclay himself seems at last to concede.)[74] What Barclay regards as "anomalous" in Paul is that although he continues to express both a profound connection and loyalty to his people and a tremendous "antagonism" to "Hellenistic culture," he also claims an unparalleled distance, or "freedom," from "Jewish

---

72. Though it takes us farther afield from Paul, Barclay's discussion of *4 Maccabees* highlights the inadequacy of dichotomous thinking. The writing extols obedience to the law (*nomos*) in categories known to us from Greek philosophy, yet Barclay argues that its author is not "really" Hellenistic: "his engagement with Hellenism has touched only the surface of his faith" (*Jews in the Mediterranean Diaspora*, 376). Barclay further observes that "the Gentile society which surrounds and threatens the Jewish heroes is noticeable by its absence. The martyrs are pitted against 'the tyrant' (and his human tools) but not against Gentiles or the Gentile world, and nothing is said to disparage non-Jews as such on moral or religious grounds." But this is remarkable only if one presumes that the opposition between Jewish and Hellenistic *ethnicity* and *culture* is the most adequate conception for understanding *4 Maccabees*, and Diaspora Judaism more generally.

73. Barclay, *Jews in the Mediterranean Diaspora*, 91.

74. "Such punishment represents the response of a synagogue to an erring member, *not quite* the expulsion and ostracism of one judged wholly apostate" (ibid., 393–94, emphasis added).

culture." Barclay cites several pieces of evidence for this distance. He considers Paul's claim, when addressing those outside the law, to have become "one without the law" (1 Cor. 9:19-23), to be the "most revealing comment on his mission strategy"; Paul's statement regarding foods in Romans 14:14, that "nothing is unclean of itself," is a "radical principle" that other Diaspora Jews would have considered "deeply corrosive to the Jewish way of life."[75] Barclay knows that these phrases can be read as expedient or "tactical" policies, but is intent on taking them as general descriptions of Paul's attitude to "Jewish culture" as such.[76] He draws the same conclusion from Paul's activity in founding and cultivating communities of non-Jews ("Gentiles") without obligation to the temple or to Torah. What makes Paul "anomalous" for Barclay is that he does not fit on a one-dimensional spectrum that opposes "Jewish" and "Hellenistic" identities: he did not, for example, resort to the sorts of allegorical methods that "Hellenizers" might have used to relativize the Torah's importance. To the contrary, "the main thrust of Pauline theology was inherently antipathetic" to any attempt "to find common cause with Hellenistic culture."[77]

Barclay describes Paul's theology broadly as "a sort of negative universalism" that "assaults all contemporary cultures—Jewish or Gentile" alike—with a "ferocious" antagonism. Paul thus appears to float free of any particular ethnic heritage precisely to the extent that his identity as a Jew has been interrupted by the appearance of Christ.[78] Remarkably, Barclay's chief basis for perceiving the apostle's

---

75. Ibid., 384–85.
76. Mark D. Nanos challenges that implication in "Paul's Relationship to Torah in Light of His Strategy 'to Become Everything to Everyone' (1 Corinthians 9:19-22)," in *Paul and Judaism: Crosscurrents in Pauline Exegesis and the Study of Jewish-Christian Relations*, eds. Reimund Bieringer and Didier Pollefeyt (London: T & T Clark, 2012), 106–40.
77. Barclay, *Jews in the Mediterranean Diaspora*, 391.
78. Paul's commitment to Jewish "ancestral traditions" was evident in his persecution of the churches, but "the direction of his life was fundamentally altered by his 'call' experience in or near Damascus . . ." That call required that he "questioned the authority of the 'ancestral

"antagonism" toward Jewish culture is Romans 1–3, which Barclay reads (along with many Christian exegetes) as involving an "indictment of Jews" and as intended "to demolish the religious and cultural claims of both Jews and Gentiles."[79] But that characterization of Paul's intention is problematic. Other scholars have emphasized, as a matter of methodological principle, that all Paul's letters be read as directed to predominantly non-Jewish audiences. Barclay is familiar with the principle.[80] The consequence drawn by others, however, is that Paul's statements about the significance of the Torah can be read only as describing the significance of the Torah *for non-Jews*.[81]

More specifically, reading Romans, and especially Romans 1–3, in accordance with the clear signals that it is directed to a *non-Jewish* audience—and an audience tempted to its own "cultural antagonism" against Jews!—has resulted in very different interpretations of Romans, particularly of chapters 1–3, and consequently of Paul's theology in general. I have argued elsewhere that read rhetorically, and without importing assumptions from the Christian dogmatic tradition, Romans 2 does not function as an "indictment" of Judaism.[82] Stanley K. Stowers has argued that a particular exemplar of the Jewish teacher, rather than Judaism as such, is Paul's target.[83]

customs' which he had once vigorously defended" (ibid., 384). As we have seen above in discussing Frey, an alternative narrative of these events is possible.

79. Ibid., 392.

80. Paul's letters "tell us what Paul said to his own converts but not, except by implication, how he spoke to non-Christian Jews or Gentiles" (ibid., 382).

81. See Lloyd Gaston, *Paul and the Torah* (Vancouver: University of British Columbia Press, 1987); John G. Gager, *The Origins of Anti-Semitism: Attitudes Toward Judaism in Pagan and Christian Antiquity* (New York: Oxford University Press, 1985); Neil Elliott, *The Rhetoric of Romans: Argumentative Constraint and Strategy and Paul's Dialogue with Judaism*, Journal for the Study of the New Testament Supplement Series 45 (Sheffield: Sheffield Academic Press, 1990); Stowers, *A Rereading of Romans*, esp. chap. 1.

82. Elliott, *The Rhetoric of Romans*, 127–57; Elliott, *The Arrogance of Nations*, 100–107.

83. Stanley K. Stowers, *The Diatribe in Paul's Letter to the Romans*, Society of Biblical Literature Dissertation Series 57 (Chico, CA: Scholars, 1981); Stowers, *A Rereading of Romans*.

Stowers further points out that the traditional reading of Romans, which works "to erase the gentile audience," does so as a "hermeneutical move that facilitates reading the letter as canonical scripture of the orthodox catholic church."[84] Barclay's reliance on a particular reading of Romans 1–3 is a case in point: it relies upon a *Christianizing* reading of Romans as an explosion of any claim to privilege other than Paul's boast "in Christ." The result is ultimately a *kata sarka* understanding, in which Paul's identification with Israel is primarily a matter of "the anguish Paul expresses over the unbelief of fellow Jews."[85] In Barclay's view, Paul's gospel may be in its fundamental theological conceptions a "development" out of Jewish tradition, and the apostle may be

> most at home among the particularistic and least accommodated segments of the Diaspora; yet in his utilization of these concepts, and in his social practice, he shatters the ethnic mould in which that ideology was formed. . . . By an extraordinary transference of ideology, Paul deracinates the most culturally conservative forms of Judaism in the Diaspora and uses them in the service of his largely Gentile communities.[86]

In other words, it seems, for Barclay Paul may be described as Jewish only to the extent that he is not Christian; but the call in Christ requires him to transcend his identity as a Jew.

Complicating Ethnicity Politically

As we saw in discussing Jörg Frey's essay on "Paul's Jewish Identity," here as well it must suffice simply to point to readily available alternative readings of Paul's "subversive" comments on Torah, without attempting to demonstrate their superiority. In different

84. Stowers, *A Rereading of Romans*, 33.
85. Ibid.
86. Barclay, *Jews in the Mediterranean Diaspora*, 395.

ways, a number of interpreters have argued that Paul's arguments regarding the Torah were motivated by "anxiety" *on the part of non-Jews* in the assemblies, rather than by some inherent aspect of Jewish identity. This anxiety fed the interest in Judaizing—that is, in the selective adoption of signal Jewish practices like circumcision—that Paul is at greatest pains to oppose.[87] Further, this "anxiety" has less to do with inherent aspects of stable ethnic identities, Jewish or "Gentile," than with the complex interaction of measures of status and privilege that were ascribed to different peoples in Paul's world. But these ascriptions were in part formed by the social and political realities of Roman Empire and the ideological representation of Roman power in terms of the superiority of the "Roman people" and of their divinely given destiny to rule the nations.

Against the essentialist notion that ethnicity is singular and invariant—that *Ioudaios* cannot be a *Hellēnos*—we must take seriously the existence of actual individuals, in Paul's world, who aspired to be both. The argument has often been made in fairly theoretical terms, as by the scholars just mentioned, but Lawrence L. Welborn has recently provided an intriguing example of the sort of active "Judaizing" that other scholars have posited. In the course of a very different argument, Welborn happens to discuss a Corinthian magistrate, one Gaius Julius Spartiaticus, whom Welborn identifies as "the sort of person" that the Gaius who was "host of all the assembly" in Corinth (Rom 16:23) "may have been."[88]

---

87. Gaston, *Paul and the Torah*, chap. 2, followed by Gager, *Origins.* Stowers similarly points to an interest on the part of non-Jews in the potential of the Torah as an instrument of "self-control" (*A Rereading of Romans*). Brigitte Kahl connects the interest in Judaizing among Galatian non-Jews with the Roman ideological presentation of Celtic peoples (= *Galatai*) as an inferior and conquered people (*Galatians Rediscovered: Reading through the Eyes of the Vanquished*, Paul in Critical Contexts [Minneapolis: Fortress Press, 2011]).

88. See L. L. Welborn, *An End to Enmity: Paul and the "Wrongdoer" of Second Corinthians*, BZNW 185 (Berlin: de Gruyter, 2011), 288–335; on the "spectacular" example of Spartiaticus in particular, 309–19.

Spartiaticus was the grandson of a Spartan officer in Octavian's navy at Actium. After the victory, Octavian rewarded this officer with property and tremendous wealth, some of which he used to insinuate himself into Herod's court in Jerusalem, in part because he shared a current belief in an ancient kinship between Spartans and Jews (see Josephus, *Ant.* 13.164). This officer, Eurycles, persuaded Herod that his own sons had conspired against him. Herod had his sons imprisoned and killed, and Eurycles returned to Sparta with even greater wealth. He was denounced in Augustus's court, however, by a Spartan aristocrat who "no doubt resented the fact that his ancient family still lacked Roman citizenship, while an upstart, who happened to choose the winning side at Actium, dominated Sparta."[89]

Eurycles died in exile. His son Laco, who strove to ingratiate himself with Tiberius's circle, similarly fell victim to court intrigues and was compelled to settle, with his son Spartiaticus, in Corinth around 33 CE. After Tiberius's death, however, Laco's fortunes were restored by Caligula, and Welborn speculates that "the [supposed] hereditary connection with Judaism may have played a role, since Caligula counted among his intimate friends the Jewish prince Herod Agrippa, grandson of Herod, the host of Eurycles."[90] Laco and Spartiaticus, father and son, both held citizenship in Corinth and "eventually attained the highest municipal offices." Spartiaticus appeared in inscriptions, around the time Paul was corresponding with the Corinthian congregations, as high priest of the house of Augustus "in perpetuity," the first Achaian to hold this, "the highest office in the province."[91]

Welborn's larger argument is that Gaius Julius Spartiaticus *might* have been the eminent "wrongdoer" of 2 Corinthians, who so vexed

89. Ibid., 315.
90. Ibid., 316.
91. Ibid., 311–12.

Paul with his contempt for the socially inferior apostle. My point here is simply to note that someone like Gaius—a *non-Jew* obsessed with establishing social connections through remote, or imagined, ethnic connections with Jews—existed on Paul's landscape. Here is Welborn's summation:

> Given the family history, it seems entirely plausible that Spartiaticus would have been attracted to Judaism as a God-fearer, that Spartiaticus would have formed a friendship with the respected ruler of the synagogue, Crispus, and that he would have responded with excitement to the message that the Messiah had appeared in the person of Jesus, and that, in all of this, Spartiaticus would not have sensed a conflict with his identity as an eminent Greek and Roman citizen, but would have viewed his interest in things Jewish as an act of filial piety to his great ancestor, Eurycles.[92]

So, then, if historian Greg Woolf can describe the cultural dynamics of "becoming Roman, staying Greek," and as our earlier considerations pointed us toward the possibility (against Barclay) of Jews seeking to "become Greek, remaining Jewish," we should now also consider the possibility of someone like Spartiaticus being Spartan, and seeking through a perceived link to Jewish ethnicity to enhance his prestige as a Roman.

For her part, in her extensive study of the identity of Galatians (*Galatai*) and Celts (*Keltai*), Brigitte Kahl points us to the possibility that some Celts/Galatians in Paul's assemblies might have sought, if not to "become Roman," at least to gain acceptance in Roman eyes by adapting aspects of Jewish identity (and thus obscuring their identity as defeated Celts). It quickly becomes obvious from such examples that a simple polarity between "Jewish" and "Hellenistic" ethnicities is inadequate to the data, and should not be allowed to limit our efforts to understand Paul and his context. A more adequate approach

---

92. Ibid., 316–17.

will ask about practices of affiliation and constructions of identity in a wider context where these realities were shaped, in part, by the constraining force of Roman political and economic power and the ideological force of what we may call Roman ethnic reasoning.

There is no self-evident reason why such "political" considerations should not inform our understanding of Paul and his apostolate. Indeed, at various points above, I have shown that coherent and, in my view, compelling arguments have been made by a number of scholars that allow us to understand Paul *as a Jew,* responding to realities occasioned by Roman power (and the ways in which people of various ethnicities in his assemblies responded to it).

Interpretive Choices

John Barclay has recently done interpreters a welcome service by surveying the current state of "political" interpretation of Paul, even if his goal is to question a number of its premises. The terminology is challenging; Barclay does not mean to propose that Paul's theology was "apolitical," but to challenge some of the maneuvers that have enabled what may be called the "Paul and Empire" circle of interpreters to describe Paul's gospel as posed directly in opposition to Roman imperial ideology.[93] He helpfully cautions against inferring what Paul "must have meant" or his readers "must have heard" from similarities between his expressions and the rhetoric of the imperial cult or imperial propaganda.[94] In Barclay's view, it is an error to give the Roman Empire "particular significance" in Paul's thought, by which he means seeing Rome as the direct, specific, and exclusive

93. John M. G. Barclay, "Why the Roman Empire Was Insignificant to Paul," originally presented at a special plenary session at the Society of Biblical Literature annual meeting in November 2007; *Pauline Churches and Diaspora Jews,* 363–87.

94. Barclay's particular target is N. T. Wright, whom he described (in the initial paper, though not in the published chapter) as the "most balanced" of the "Paul and Empire" interpreters. My own works are among those discussed peripherally in Barclay's argument, and I take many of his points as important cautions.

(though covert) target of one or another expression in Paul's letters. The point is well taken, and Barclay does well to ask greater precision of those of us who set Paul's letters in comparison with expressions of Roman claims in the course of our interpretation.[95] Surely it is appropriate, *in the course of historical description,* to "beware of distortions that may arise from situating Paul's theological politics within the categories and theoretical frameworks which shape our own (post)modern understanding of 'politics.'"[96]

But Barclay himself knows there is more to the sort of interpretation that he, for one, would like to do than simple historical description. Against the identification of "politics-as-state-power," a reductionist category that (to my knowledge) plays no significant part in contemporary political interpretations, he prefers to read Paul as opposing "anti-God powers wherever and however they manifest themselves on the human stage," a category that allows him to invoke modern realities from unregulated international finance to sex trafficking, from neocolonialism to domestic violence.[97] He acknowledges (in fact, insists) that the realities of the Roman Empire *were* given account in Paul's theology:

> The question is not whether Paul noticed the power of Rome—he clearly did to the extent of feeling its physical impact on his body; the question is what power he saw to be operative in such experiences. . . . If Rome is not specifically named from [Paul's] angle of vision, this does not mean that Paul's theology was apolitical, only that the political is for him enmeshed in an all-encompassing power-struggle which covers every domain of life, including but not limited to the religio-political domain we call "the Roman empire," and not neatly divisible into a battle between forces "for" and "against" Roman rule.[98]

95. To some extent, Barclay is also arguing against a straw man, as when he insists (with N. T. Wright) that Paul "is not opposed 'entirely to everything to do with the Roman empire'" or to the Roman Empire "as empire" (ibid., 370–71), or interested "in the Roman empire *as Roman*" (374)—positions that are rare, if they appear at all, in the secondary literature.

96. Ibid., 367.

97. Ibid., 387 and n. 74.

Phrased in such terms, it is hard to imagine any even among the "Paul and Empire" circle who would disagree. Who would insist that Paul's primary concern was a narrow focus on the structures and instruments of Roman state power? If anything, Barclay's wider "theo-political" reading shows the salutary effect of opening up the interpretive agenda to include the rich texture of imperial ideological and cultural expressions in Paul's day, rather than insisting (as some interpreters still do) that these are not proper topics for "Pauline theology."

This might be seen as simply a matter of Barclay's preference for theological language over overtly political categories. But there is a deeper point of contention here that requires clarification. One of Barclay's implied criticisms of the "Paul and Empire" circle is that they are motivated by other than purely historical concerns:

> For some it is attractive, even ideologically necessary, to interpret Paul's polemics as directed primarily (if not solely) against an imperial power, rather than against "Judaism"; at the very least, this offers a fresh frame for Pauline interpretation beyond both traditional and "new" perspectives, free of any possible hint of "supersessionism."[99]

Whether or not it is Barclay's intention, I see this as an unnecessary polarization of interpretive choices. Barclay does not mean, I presume, to hold open a space for a sort of interpretation that *would* be governed by Christian supersessionism (though in contrast to Barclay's use of scare quotes, I regard the dreary history of such interpretation as suggesting the risk is quite real). Nor do I take him to be arguing here for the opposite, an interpretation of Paul's polemics as directed *primarily* against Judaism, *not* an imperial power; though as we have seen, he does (quite problematically, from my view) describe Paul's experience of the Christ event as resulting in a

98. Ibid., 375–76.
99. Ibid., 367.

"ferocious" antagonism to "Jewish culture." It nevertheless seems clear that for Barclay, these are mutually exclusive alternatives between which the interpreter must choose. The risk in his eyes is that a "political" interpretation will dilute or diminish the distance between Paul and Judaism that he is at pains to emphasize. The point becomes clear in a footnote where Barclay explains his divergence from N. T. Wright:

> Where Wright places Paul in ideological continuity with the biblical/ Jewish tradition of monotheistic critique of paganism, I would place stronger emphasis on the new division of the cosmos created by the Christ-event (cf. Gal 1.4; 1 Cor. 1.18—2.16, which strongly reshapes and reapplies the biblical categories themselves.[100]

That is, in Barclay's eyes, Wright's openness to a political, empire-critical reading allows Paul to remain *too much* in continuity with the (biblical and) Jewish tradition, at just the point where Barclay seeks to pose the apostle *over against* his Jewish contemporaries precisely by virtue of a unique revelation in Christ.

In the earlier part of this essay, I sought to show that setting Paul squarely "within Judaism" means taking seriously the political situation faced by Jews under Roman rule; thus, questions about "Paul and Empire" belong within a wider discussion of Paul's place among other Diaspora Jews under Roman rule. Barclay's warnings about anachronism and imprecision in "political" interpretation should rightly direct us to closer attention precisely to the texture of ideological and cultural power relationships that conditioned the lives of Paul and other Jews. But this is not the direction Barclay himself appears to prefer. I also showed that it is possible to understand central elements in Paul's story—including his persecution of the Jesus assemblies, his vision of a crucified messiah in heaven, and the

---

100. Ibid., 384 n. 70.

resulting apostolic work among "the nations"—in terms that render these elements intelligible within Judaism and continuous with it. Against these proposals, Barclay appears to illustrate a clear alternative, in which the centrality of Paul's experience of Christ (and, at least by implication, the revelatory value of that experience) requires that Paul can be described as an "anomalous" Jew, at best. If it is appropriate to describe this as a "Christianizing" interpretation, it would seem that reading Paul *within Judaism* will require of Christian interpreters a certain relinquishment of theological presumptions; but that has always been the challenge that historical criticism has posed to the Christian tradition.

8

———

The Question(s) of Gender: Relocating Paul in Relation to Judaism

Kathy Ehrensperger

Paul and gender are an uneasy pair.[1] When Paul's Judaism is included in the combination it is considered often even more problematic. No doubt, Paul lived in a context of elite male domination at structural level, the level of perception, as well as in social practice. The views about women he explicitly formulates reflect to some extent this general perception, although his actual practice seems to indicate a different stance in that women are among those whom Paul explicitly

---

1. The field of gender-critical studies has extended in the last decade from a focus on the role of women in feminist and womanist studies and encompasses masculinity and queer studies. I have to confine my contribution here mainly to women in feminist perspective; thus, a limited and contextual perception of the issues involved is presented here.

considers to be playing a decisive and leading role in the work of the gospel. Concerning his role as a leading man in the movement, Paul clearly establishes his claim to authority in asymmetrical relationships; thus, he seems to cohere at a structural level with patterns of elite male leadership as prevalent in Mediterranean societies of the first century CE.[2] However, when the practice and perception of Paul's role (and that of other "workers" in Christ) are perceived in the context of the dominating political power and ideological discourse of the Roman Empire, a substantially different image emerges. Then the apostle is seen as a "feminized,"[3] vulnerable, beaten,[4] suffering apostle, a member of a conquered nation who in no way coheres with the image of the elitist ideal of masculinity in Greek and Roman perception.[5]

The tension between these images of Paul and the Pauline discourse with regard to the question of gender are mainly due to hermeneutical presuppositions in reading his letters, including the presupposed contexts within which they are rooted. Although gender-critical and feminist approaches to Paul present serious attempts to avoid replicating anti-Jewish patterns of interpretation, in-depth considerations of Paul's Judaism remain the exception.

Some earlier feminist approaches perceived Paul to have introduced hierarchical patterns of leadership and patriarchal or kyriarchal practices into a previously egalitarian movement, and in some instances attributed these to his Jewish tradition, but this is

---

2. Cf. Elisabeth Schüssler Fiorenza, *The Power of the Word: Scripture and the Rhetoric of Empire* (Minneapolis: Fortress Press, 2007), 69–109.

3. Davina C. Lopez, *Apostle to the Conquered: Reimagining Paul's Mission* (Minneapolis: Fortress Press, 2008).

4. Jennifer Glancy, "Boasting of Beatings (2 Corinthians 11:23-25)," *Journal of Biblical Literature* 123, no. 1 (2004): 99–135.

5. Cf., for example, Stephen Moore and John C. Anderson, *New Testament Masculinities* (Atlanta: Society of Biblical Literature, 2003), also Kathy Ehrensperger, *Paul and the Dynamics of Power: Communication and Interaction in the Early Christ-Movement* (London: T & T Clark, 2007).

a perception that is hardly found anymore explicitly formulated in recent gender-critical studies.[6] Nevertheless, although Paul's Jewishness may be admitted in general, and the risk of reintroducing anti-Judaism into the interpretation may be noted, little further analysis of the implications of such an acknowledgement is presented.[7] Notions of different kinds of Judaism, some with positive and some with negative implications for Paul's attitude to women, are still prevalent, with so-called "Hellenistic" Judaism considered to be the decisive context for Paul. It is maintained that he could have drawn on his Pharisaic tradition but he chose not to do so.[8] Paul is depicted as distancing himself from a "wrong," narrow kind of Judaism, that is, Pharisaism, and located in a good, more open, that is, "Hellenistic" Judaism.[9]

This perception resonates with New Perspective on Paul approaches, which consider an ethnocentric version of Judaism to be the problem that Paul overcomes in Christ.[10] In both cases, an

6. For an overview on recent gender-critical approaches to Paul, see Kathy Ehrensperger, "Paul and Feminism," in *The Oxford Handbook of Pauline Studies,* ed. Barry Matlock (Oxford: Oxford University Press, forthcoming).

7. Thus Melanie Johnson-DeBaufre and Laura Nasrallah state that "if we fail to see these complex negotiations of identity in the particular context of the Roman Empire, then Paul-the-Jew becomes a colonizer of the Gentiles (despite them being the dominant culture) and our interpretations replicate the anti-Judaism that has long characterized triumphalist Christianity" ("Beyond the Heroic Paul: Toward a Feminist and Decolonizing Approach to the Letters of Paul," in *The Colonized Apostle: Paul Through Postcolonial Eyes,* ed. Christopher S. Stanley [Minneapolis: Fortress Press, 2011], 161–74, here 170). Whilst it is highly significant to consider the sociopolitical and ideological contexts of Paul's theologizing and distinguish between the social locations of those in dominating power positions and dominated peoples, this article does not engage with the Jewishness of Paul and his letters per se.

8. See the discussion by Tal Ilan, *Silencing the Queen: The Literary History of Shelamzion and Other Jewish Women* (Tübingen: Mohr Siebeck, 2006), 109.

9. This distinction and characterisation of different kinds of Judaism is adopted uncritically and thus taken at face value. It is based on the assumption that "Hellenism" had liberating implications for Judaism, without questioning the concepts and hermeneutical presuppositions on which these are built. For a detailed critical discussion of the concept of Hellenism, see Kathy Ehrensperger, *Paul at the Crossroads of Cultures: Theologizing in the Space Between* (London: T & T Clark, 2013), 22–29.

10. E.g., James D. G. Dunn, *The New Perspective on Paul: Collected Essays* (Tübingen: Mohr Siebeck, 2005), 353.

evaluation of a "good" or "bad" Judaism is the basis for acknowledging some positive value to the Jewishness of Paul. The Christ-event is that which liberates either gentiles or women from the constraints of the "bad," narrow Judaism.

As a result, the relevance of Paul's Judaism in relation to gender has only been considered by very few recent studies, mainly in general terms,[11] and there is a significant gap in gender-critical approaches to Paul in this respect. This is so despite the fact that there are inherent links between these two strands of interpretation, both at structural level with respect to Paul's way of arguing and theologizing, and in terms of content regarding Paul's explicit statements and activities in relation to women.[12]

Although questions concerning gender are not at the forefront in Paul's letters, there are some texts that address such concerns arising out of particular problems in an *ekklēsia*. Together with the women addressed, commended upon, or greeted in Paul's letters this indicates some interest in the question of gender in the *ekklēsiai*. Thus the statement that Paul was part of an inherently androcentric and kyriarchal social context requires further detailed assessment in light of relocating Paul in Judaism. Literary, epigraphic, and socio-historical evidence concerning the perception and role of women in first-century Judaism are decisive for understanding the Pauline discourse. Some of Paul's explicit statements about women (for example, 1 Cor. 7:1-16; 11:3-16; and 14:34-35) and his actual stance when it comes to co-workers for the gospel (Rom. 16:1-16) will be considered in the first part of this contribution. The question of gender and Paul's Judaism, however, is not confined to Paul's views and interaction with women. There are discourses like the

---

11. As, e.g., by Lopez in her *Apostle to the Conquered*, 119–37.
12. Cf. Kathy Ehrensperger, *That We May Be Mutually Encouraged: Feminism and the New Perspective in Pauline Studies* (London: T & T Clark, 2004), 27–42.

feminization of conquered peoples in Roman imperial propaganda that have rightly been considered in their importance; moreover, there are analogies between Paul within Judaism approaches and contemporary gender discourses. With regard to the latter, the emphasis on difference and particularity in identity formation are of specific importance and will be the focus of the second part of this contribution, followed by my conclusions.

"When You Come Together"—Women in the *Ekklēsia* in Corinth

The ambivalence of Paul's statements concerning women have been frequently noted, most explicitly those in 1 Corinthians. Whether one follows Antoinette Clark Wire's analysis and considers women prophets to be the problem that Paul addresses or not, a passage like 1 Corinthians 11:12-16 demonstrates that Paul was wavering between presupposing the unquestioned participation and active role of women in the gatherings of the *ekklēsia*, but at the same time, that he adheres in principle to a subordination paradigm that governs the relationship between men and women. The reasons provided for the necessity of women to have their head covered whilst prophesying, and for men not to cover their heads during the same activity, are based on a perceived hierarchical order of creation, with women clearly seen as subordinate to men.[13] The issue is complicated by the "rule" stated in 1 Corinthians 14:33-36, through which Paul seems to silence women in the assembly gatherings.

It has hardly ever been noted, however, that the fact that Paul discusses issues concerning the active role of women in the assemblies provides clear evidence that women were not only members of this messianic movement, but they were self-evidently part of the "assemblies," the actual gatherings of this movement, and they played

---

13. Cf., Ilan, *Silencing the Queen*, 4–19.

an active role in these gatherings! The mere fact that Paul considers it necessary to provide guidance to men *and* to women concerning the "orderly" way for "assembly meetings" to be conducted demonstrates that these were mixed gatherings wherein both men and women were active. In the context of Greek and Roman societies, in which gender segregation was the norm rather than the exception (certainly at the theoretical level), this is rather noteworthy, and the active role of women in such a mixed assembly even more so.[14] Paul never challenges the participation of women in the actual gatherings of the *ekklēsiai* in any way. What he does address is the conduct of both men and women on these occasions. Concerning this, as well as concerning the course of action when "married to an unbeliever" (1 Cor. 7:12-13), the Corinthians have sought Paul's advice and guidance (1 Cor. 7:1). They were concerned about these aspects, which could be an indication that such joint gatherings may not have been something they were familiar with from within their mainly non-Jewish contexts.[15] They could have had some knowledge from synagogue gatherings, but even though the gentile Christ-followers most likely also participated in these, and the *ekklēsiai tou theou* were closely associated with synagogue communities,[16] when they

14. This is not to deny that women could not be in influential positions and that in everyday life things were less clear than in theory. The numerous analogies between *ekklēsiai tou theou* and voluntary associations, cult groups, philosophical schools, and civic assemblies illuminate certain organizational aspects, but I am not aware that the fact that these *ekklēsiai* were mixed groups has been considered in any detail in recent studies. John S. Kloppenborg notes that, "Membership in professional guilds is likely to have been relatively homogenous not only with respect to the trade and the quarter of the city from which members were drawn, but also with respect to gender. Whereas domestic collegia clearly had women members, the evidence for the presence of women in the professional associations is ambiguous. There were of course, some collegia composed solely of women" (Kloppenborg, "Collegia and *Thiasoi*: Issues in Function, Taxonomy and Membership," in *Voluntary Associations in the Graeco-Roman World*, eds. John S. Kloppenborg and Stephen G. Wilson [London: Routledge, 1996], 16–30, 25). Considering this context, participation of men and women together in these assemblies seems rather exceptional and can best be explained by their analogy to Jewish synagogue communities.

15. I assume that Paul, as apostle to the nations, is addressing mainly members of the Christ-movement from the nations here, with Jewish members possibly present.

gathered as *ekklēsiai tou theou* the appropriate conduct in these may have required clarification.

The communication between Paul and the Corinthians is thus an example of the cultural translation process obviously required in order for these gentiles to understand what "turning to the true and living God" meant in practice. Paul was familiar with more than one culture and tradition—he was a bicultural/bilingual person, and his primary embeddedness in Judaism was in no ways diminished by his ability to relate meaningfully also to the world of Greeks, Galatians, and possibly Romans.[17] Thus, in light of Jewish tradition and practice, such mixed gatherings of people who worshipped the God of Israel would be considered normal by him, being common practice in synagogues throughout the empire. The fact that women were part of these gatherings is mentioned frequently, and there is no reason to doubt the respective literary sources. The presence of women (and children), as part of "all Israel," when the law is being read is attested frequently in biblical texts (Deut. 29:10-11; 31:11-12; Josh. 8:35; Neh. 8:2-3; 10:28; also 1 Esd. 9:40-41). That this is communal practice also in the synagogues of the first century is affirmed by Josephus, who in his report about the decree of Halicarnassus explicitly mentions men and women together as those who are granted the right to build a synagogue, assemble, and celebrate Sabbath (*Ant.* 14.258), and in the decree of the Sardians, their right to assemble according to their ancient legal tradition is affirmed by assigning the Jews a place to hold their assemblies that included

16. Cf. Mark D. Nanos, "The Churches within the Synagogues of Rome," in *Reading Paul's Letter to the Romans*, ed. Jerry L. Sumney (Atlanta: Society of Biblical Literature, 2010), 11–28, and William S. Campbell, "The Addressees of Paul's Letter to the Romans: Assemblies of God in House Churches or Synagogues?" in *Between Gospel and Election: Explorations in the Interpretation of Romans 9–11*, ed. J. Ross Wagner and Florian Wilk (Tübingen: Mohr Siebeck, 2010), 171–95.

17. See Ehrensperger, *Paul at the Crossroads of Cultures*, 113–21.

women and children (*Ant.* 14.260). Philo also has women included in the assembly as a matter of fact (*Decal.* 32).

The implications of this clear evidence of synagogue assemblies as mixed groups of men and women in the first century are significant. Given that the activities during these assemblies included the reading of the Scriptures and teaching as well as prayer,[18] this means that women were taught and participated in prayer alongside men. Neither Philo nor Josephus refer to an exclusion of women when it comes to learning the Scriptures.[19]

Paul's Pharisaism may shed further light on the inclusion of women not just as members of the movement but as participants in the actual gatherings of the *ekklēsiai*. Tal Ilan has presented convincing arguments that women were part of the Pharisaic movement as members in their own right.[20] She interprets *t. Demai* 2:16 as a clear reference to Pharisees. The verse stating that "A daughter of an *am-haaretz* married to a *haver*, a woman *am-haaretz* married to a *haver* . . . should undergo initiation (in order to be trustworthy),"[21] demonstrates that women were initiated into the movement as members in their own right. Based on this interpretation, Ilan argues that women were members of the Pharisaic movement, and

---

18. Josephus, *Ag. Ap.* 2.175; *Ant.* 16.43; Philo, *Legat.* 156 and 311-312; *Hypoth.* 7.12; *Somn.* 2.127; *Mos.* 2.215-216.

19. This is not to say that there was no separated seating during these assemblies, but the example of the *Therapeutae* cannot serve as illustration of a general practice. However, although the archaeological evidence does not provide any indication to that effect, it cannot be entirely excluded (cf. Bernadette Brooten, *Women Leaders in Ancient Synagogues: Inscriptional Evidence and Background Issues* [Chico, CA: Scholars, 1982]; Sarah L. Mattila, "Where Women Sat in Ancient Synagogues: The Archeological Evidence in Context," in *Voluntary Associations in the Graeco-Roman World*, 266–86. I am not excluding here the possibility that specific education of boys and men took place as well, but as far as the general synagogue meetings on the Sabbath are concerned, no gender specific teaching is mentioned in the sources.

20. Ilan, *Silencing the Queen*, 73–110.

21. *Haver* is understood to indicate a Pharisee, this being the self-designation of the group members preserved by the Tosefta, rather than the derogatory label "Pharisee," which is only rarely found in rabbinic literature (Ilan, *Silencing the Queen*, 98–105).

participated also in their communal meals.[22] If we follow her interpretation, this provides further evidence that Paul would have been familiar with, and would have taken it for granted that women were active members and participants in their own right in a subgroup of Judaism, and it should thus not come as a surprise that Paul would have considered the participation of women in the assemblies of the Christ-movement to represent nothing beyond that which was expected and normal.

Active participation in synagogue activities is presupposed also by Philo, who mentions male and female choirs in a tradition that depicts Miriam and Moses as choir leaders (*Mos.* 1.180; 2.256), most likely not merely for historical purposes. In his detailed report on the *Therapeutae,* the hymn singing of the male and female members in separate choirs figures prominently and leads to the question whether this activity should really have been confined to this particular group or was a more general communal activity.[23] Certainly the literary traditions refer to such male and female choirs (Ezra 2:65; Neh. 7:67, Ps. 148:12), or dancing and singing by women and men respectively (Jdt. 15:12-13). In addition, literature of the Second Temple period also envisages women as prophetesses (Judith in Jdt. 11:17-18; the daughters of Job, *T. Job* 47–53) and as leading the people in prayer (Jdt. 15:14—16:17). Esther and Judith are heroines who liberate their people or prevent their extinction, and in Pseudo-Philo's *Liber antiquitatum biblicarum,* Deborah, Jephtha's daughter, and Hannah, are portrayed as major characters in Israel's history. Deborah is a prophetess, but also a ruler over Israel and a teacher who enlightens all Israel (33:1). In light of this literary evidence, the active participation

---

22. Ilan, *Silencing the Queen,* 105–107.
23. E.g., Hengel maintains that this indicates wider communal practice; cf. Martin Hengel, "Proseuche und Synagoge," in *Judaica and Hellenistica: Kleine Schriften 1* (Tübingen: Mohr Siebeck, 1996), 171–95.

of women in the Jewish assemblies can hardly be doubted. The emergence of heroine stories and the emphasis on the significance of biblical female characters such as in *Liber antiquitatum biblicarum* provide clear indications that the presence of women in the *ekklēsiai tou theou* would likely have been assumed to be normal by Paul, rather than being an innovative or liberating move on the part of the Christ-movement.[24]

The clear evidence of mixed assemblies in synagogue communities, the participation of women in prayer and singing, and the high value attributed to prophets as well as prophetesses all indicate that the practice and guidance of Paul in 1 Corinthians 11:2-16 reflect his Judaism. He presupposes the joint participation of men and women, he presupposes that they both pray and prophesy, and he is concerned that this is being done in an orderly manner.

This observation does not of course exclude the perception that the relationship between men and women involved hierarchical relationships. Such a perception was shared in variations between the different traditions around the Mediterranean. I cannot discuss this aspect in any detail here, but the perception of the subordination of women was not a particularly Jewish tradition that Paul simply introduced to the Christ-movement. It is also not self-evident that the issues around head-coverings inherently bear the mark of hierarchy, although Paul presents them in that vein. The emphasis could also be understood as a mark of gender difference, and the request for the man not to pray with his head covered could actually be a mark of differentiation from Roman practice.[25]

24. Contra Wayne Meeks, *The First Urban Christians: The Social World of the Apostle Paul* (New Haven, CT: Yale University Press, 1993), 81. There may well have been tendencies to downgrade and restrict the role of women during the first century CE (cf., Sarah A. Brayford, "The Domestication of Sarah: From Jewish Matriarch to Hellenistic Matron," *Studies in Jewish Civilisation* 14 [2003]: 1–21). This may be evidence for the presence and significance of women in realms where restriction was argued, rather than for the opposite.

What is significant is that Paul, coherent with Jewish practice, assumes without question that women pray and prophesy in the meetings of the *ekklēsia tou theou*. The Corinthians are even commended by Paul in this respect (11:2), and it seems that his emphasis in 11:3-16 is on a deepened understanding of why women should pray and prophesy with their hair covered whilst men should not, rather than a dispute about whether women should have an active role during their meetings.

As noted above, the betrayal of this dynamic within the admonitions of 1 Corinthians 11:2-16 stands in tension with the statements in 14:33-35. If this is not an interpolation,[26] some explanation may again be found in Paul's Jewish tradition. If we trust Josephus and Philo in particular, then a distinction seems to have been made between women participating in the assemblies, being active in prayer, singing, and possibly prophesying, and the reading and interpretation of the Scriptures. Whilst information concerning the reading of the Scriptures is unclear and possibly may be performed by any member of the assembly (which might include women), Philo insists that interpretation and teaching is performed by a man of special knowledge, a leader, teacher, or "ruler" of the community.[27] During such expositions the assembly members listen in silence (*Mos.* 2.215; *Spec. Leg.* 2.62). It is evident that not everybody is considered to be qualified to explain the Scriptures, but only those "who are very learned explain to them what is of great importance and use. Lessons by which the whole of their lives may be improved" (*Spec. Leg.* 2.62). Silence is also the rule among the *Therapeutae* when the Scriptures are

---

25. Critical discussions concerning the veil are numerous and there is no consensus in sight about its rationale or function.

26. A number of feminist interpretations consider this most likely to be the case; cf. Luise Schottroff, *Der Erste Brief an die Gemeinde in Korinth* (Stuttgart: Kohlhammer, 2013), 280–85.

27. Thus also in the Essene communities; cf. 1QS 6:8-9; and Philo, *Prop.* 81–82.

read and explained (*Contempl.* 75), and the assembly is conducted in a clear and orderly manner (*Contempl.* 80).

Similarly, 1 Corinthians 14 deals with order during assembly meetings. Paul seems to be concerned that these meetings are conducted appropriately. The mutual up-building in the *ekklēsia* is at the center of his concern, but in order for this to be possible the members have to take turns when speaking (14:30-31). In some instances, Paul advises that silence is better than speaking, such as when there is nobody present who can interpret what is said "in tongue" (v. 28), or when "a revelation is made to someone sitting nearby," the first one should be silent (v. 30).

The issue of women talking is raised in this context, that is, not in a general vein. I think, given the context, women are not exclusively and generally told to be silent during the assembly meetings, but in relation to a particular aspect.[28] It seems that Paul does not refer to just any kind of talking but one that is specifically geared toward learning in relation to the Scriptures as indicated by the verb *mathein* (v. 35), and the reference to "the word of God" (v. 36).

Although I do not think that the reading and interpretation of the Scriptures was part of the *ekklēsia* meetings yet,[29] and teaching may refer to some oral traditions, Christ-centered or other, it could be that, in tune with some Jewish understanding, teaching was understood to be the domain of leading men, and thus anything related to it should not be raised by women during the assembly. If listening in silence generally was part of the practice of teaching, then the two aspects could have been combined by Paul here. Again, based on this evidence, this should not be seen as a reintroduction of a restrictive practice into a previously more liberating *ekklēsia*, but

---

28. Cf. Roy E. Ciampa and Brian S.Rosner, *The First Letter to the Corinthians* (Grand Rapids: Eerdmans, 2010), 720–23.

29. Exposure to such teaching was most likely in synagogue assemblies. See note 16 above.

most likely is part of the existing Jewish ethos of mixed assemblies with both men and women actively participating but in an "orderly manner," in analogy to synagogue or possibly other assemblies.[30] The mixed character of the *ekklēsiai* as well as the joint participation in worshipping, including the guidance about its proper order, are all based on, and developed in analogy to Jewish traditions and practice in which Paul was embedded.

Although some aspects of these assemblies and the guidance for proper conduct may have had analogies in the traditions with which those Christ-followers from the nations were familiar, Paul's perceptions and guidance are very much rooted in Jewish tradition. This is what should be expected since these *ekklēsiai* were called to turn to "the true and living God" through Christ. This is the God who had established his special bond with the people Israel; they are thus the ones who had received guidance for ways to live according to his will and for ways to worship him. Paul may have had significant knowledge and understanding of other traditions (Greek, Roman, Galatian, and so on), but the core of his message and the practice of life following from it was part of the Jewish social and symbolic universe. The uniqueness of what he was trying to do was to "translate" this message and practice so it could be applied to those from the nations without them becoming Jews.

Paul's Judaism, and more specifically his Pharisaism may also have been decisive for his advice concerning the question what Christ-followers should do "when married to an unbeliever" (1 Cor. 7:12-16). Tal Ilan has argued that as a Pharisee, Paul may well have been familiar with similar guidance, which she has identified as referring to Pharisees.[31] In *t. Demai* 2:17, referred to above, it is also asserted that, "A daughter of a *haver* married to an *am-haaretz*, the

---

30. As, e.g., that of the Therapeutae noted in Philo, *Contempl.*, 75–80.
31. Cf. note 19 above.

wife of a *haver* married to an *am-haaretz* . . . they remain trustworthy unless they become suspect." Ilan here sees a parallel to Paul's advice to those members of the Christ-movement who are married to an unbeliever. The status of the non-member does not affect the status of the member of the movement, Pharisaic or messianic respectively, as long as the member him or herself retains their own life according to the way of life of the Pharisaic or messianic community. Paul's guidance is thus seen as based on his experience as a Pharisee.[32]

These examples from 1 Corinthians demonstrate that Paul's guidance, which specifically addresses issues concerning women in the *ekklēsiai tou theou,* is consistent with and rooted in the Judaism of the Second Temple period. No differentiation between some narrow Jewish tradition and some liberating Jewish tradition, nor between any Jewish tradition and the Christ-movement could be discerned. Paul's guidance and way of arguing in relation to women is Jewish, although now applied to women from the nations who are in Christ. Paul is concerned with inducting these people from the nations into a way of life in relation to the God of Israel. Most naturally, such guidance would primarily orient itself on the way of life known by the Jewish people through their ancestral traditions, both scriptural and oral.

The leadership role of women in the early Christ-movement reveals similarly the Jewish imprint of Paul's practice rather than some new and thus liberating dimension in the Christ-movement, as Bernadette Brooten's analysis of epigraphic evidence demonstrates.[33] Female leadership was possible in Jewish tradition, as it was in Greek and particularly Roman tradition of the period.[34] It is beyond the

---

32. Ilan, *Silencing the Queen,* 107–10. Cf. also Caroline Johnson Hodge's article, which focuses on the dimension of holiness in this passage: "Married to an Unbeliever: Households, Hierarchies, and Holiness in 1 Corinthians 7:12-16," *Harvard Theological Review* 103 (2010): 1–25.

33. Brooten, *Women Leaders in the Ancient Synagogue.*

scope of this contribution to present a detailed analysis of Paul's perception of female leadership, but the evidence from Brooten's research demonstrates that such roles cohere with our analysis of Paul's statements and guidance concerning women in 1 Corinthians 11 and 14 as thoroughly Jewish. Paul's explicit references to women neither indicate his reactionary attitude nor his liberating stance; they cannot be attributed to some narrow or conservative Judaism or a liberating "in Christ" stance respectively. They are merely practical guidance and understanding from within Jewish tradition and practice now applied to non-Jews who join with Israel to worship God as theirs also.

Particularity and Difference in Paul's Discourse

As noted above, relocating Paul in Judaism in relation to questions of gender is not only relevant when women or issues specifically related to women are mentioned in his letters. Paul's own Jewish identity, and his insistence of the necessity to retain the particularity of identity in Christ have decisive implications in relation to gender sensitive approaches as well.

The Problem of Universalization

Universalizing interpretations of Paul, whether they are of the view that Paul has separated from Judaism wholesale, or differentiate as problematic one aspect of Judaism,[35] or whether they claim the identity of Israel for Christ-followers, all share the notion that there is something wrong with particular identities, or rather, to be precise, that there is something wrong with Jewish identity, including Paul's

---

34. See Susan Matthew, *Women in the Greetings of Romans 16.1-16* (London: T & T Clark, 2013), 54–64.
35. James D. G. Dunn, "Paul's Conversion: A Light to 20th Century Disputes," in *The New Perspective on Paul*, ed. James D. G. Dunn (Tübingen: Mohr Siebeck, 2005), 341–59.

Jewish identity. These approaches, albeit not identical with each other, share at a structural level the conflation/confusion of the universal scope of the message Paul proclaims with assimilation and sameness in terms of identity and practice.

Such perceptions are problematic also in light of gender perspectives. The ignoring, silencing, or use of women in a derogatory way as the other (and of men who did not conform to dominating notions of masculinity) in androcentric theologies, over centuries resonates, certainly at a structural level, with the universalizing notions of overcoming difference in some significant strands of Pauline interpretation. Although contemporary interpretation may be some distance away from advocating that in order for women to be saved they would have to become male,[36] the general notion that in Christ all differences are overcome negates ethnic diversity as well as gender and other diversities among human beings. If boundaries between "Jew and Greek" are supposed to be eradicated and their ethnic difference, including their respective traditions, are *adiaphora* the same must apply to gender difference. If the analogy is considered carefully this means that the particular identity of men and of women needs to be overcome in that only the "third dimension"—their humanity—is actually relevant in Christ. In parallel to the perception that in Christ the difference between Jews and Greeks is overcome since they are all "one" or "new" in Christ, the difference between men and women would need to be seen as overcome in Christ too, since they are all "one new man."[37] However, such a stance is hardly ever argued in New Testament

36. As the Gospel of Thomas assumes (*Gos. Thom.* 114).

37. The problem may be more accentuated in English as the term used for this common humanity is actually identical with the one used for the male human being, thus expressing quite clearly that the template of humanity is male. The German term *Mensch* for human being appears to express something beyond gender difference; but in both cases the terminology obscures the fact that human beings only exist in particular, concrete form.

interpretation and Paul does not seem to draw such a conclusion in Galatians 3:28, but clearly argues for the continued relevance of gender difference, as his arguments in, for example, 1 Corinthians 11 demonstrate.

Subsequent Christian tradition, however, continued to define the nature and function of women in Christ in the vein of the dominating androcentric discourses. In this perspective women were defined as the "other," that which the ideal "man" was not. Whoever did not cohere with this ideological perception was less than fully human, whether man or woman.[38] The supposed common humanity was the ideal of masculinity of the male dominating elite who declared this ideal to be actually universal.[39]

In a structurally similar vein, the perception that in Christ ethnic differences are overcome is a perception of those who eventually became the dominating force in the Christ-movement, that is, non-Jews. The true human being is not female, whereas the true Christian is not Jewish. With regard to the latter, however, an exclusivist claim to the heritage of Israel is made. A universalizing interpretation of Paul that advocates the overcoming of difference, and of Jewish difference in particular, as core to his gospel, results in parallel outcomes concerning the issue of "Jews and Greeks" in Christ as well as concerning women and men in Christ.

Israel and the Nations—Unity with a Difference

Reading the Pauline letters as documents of first-century Judaism and Paul's theologizing as part of an intra-Jewish discourse[40] rather

---

38. See, e.g., Jorunn Økland, *Women in their Place: Paul and the Corinthian Discourse of Space and Sanctuary Space* (London: T & T Clark, 2004), 15–20.

39. See my discussion of the Roman concept of "humanitas" in *Paul at the Crossroads of Cultures,* 89–90 and 97–101.

40. See, e.g., Mark D. Nanos, "Paul and Judaism: Why Not Paul's Judaism?" in *Paul Unbound: Other Perspectives on the Apostle,* ed. Mark Douglas Given (Peabody, MA: Hendrickson, 2010),

than as the documents of a former Jew,[41] a marginal Jew, or a Jewish apostate have wide-ranging implications. It means that the contextuality and embodiment of human life are taken seriously. Paul is recognized as located in a particular context and tradition, imprinted with a habitus, which although mutable, is nevertheless durable. His perception of the world of his time as well as his life are seen as decisively shaped by Jewish tradition, that is, the particular tradition of a particular people at a particular time.

This is a tradition for which the recognition of the particular identity of peoples, that is differentiation within diversity, is core to their understanding of God's good creation.[42] Paul's insistence on the diversity of peoples to be maintained within the movement, that is, the retention of the difference between "circumcision and uncircumcision" (1 Cor. 7:17-20) is rooted in the Jewish scriptural perception that Israel and the nations are different (e.g., Lev. 18:3-5). Israel's call to serve God establishes a specific bond between God and his people through the covenant. However, this does not isolate Israel from the world of other peoples. The genealogical narratives (Genesis 10) for instance indicate that in and with the particular bond between Israel and her God, there are inherent relations to other peoples, depicted in the form of kinship narratives (fictive or factual).[43] Difference and relatedness are not seen as being in contradiction with each other in Jewish tradition. This perception of the relationship between Israel and the nations is not always a

117–60; also Pamela Eisenbaum, *Paul Was Not a Christian: The Original Message of a Misunderstood Jew* (New York: HarperOne, 2009); William S. Campbell, *Paul and the Creation of Christian Identity* (London: T & T Clark, 2006); Magnus Zetterholm, "Paul and the Missing Messiah," in *The Messiah in Early Judaism and Christianity*, ed. Magnus Zetterholm (Minneapolis: Fortress Press, 2007), 33–54.

41. Love L. Sechrest, *A Former Jew: Paul and the Dialectics of Race* (London: T & T Clark, 2009).
42. See Beth A. Berkowitz, *Defining Jewish Difference: From Antiquity to the Present* (Cambridge: Cambridge University Press, 2012), 24–59.
43. Eric S. Gruen, *Rethinking the Other in Antiquity* (Princeton, NJ: Princeton University Press, 2011), 297–307.

happy one despite these inherent kinship ties, but visions of peaceful community between those who are and remain different are found in prophetic and other literature. The particular relationship of God with this people, through election, covenant, and guidance through the Torah, and the perception of "the other" as nevertheless part of God's creation and divine economy, are not seen as being in contradiction with each other in significant trajectories of this tradition. Terry Donaldson has affirmed "Jews could not tell their own national story without reference to the other nations, and if perhaps it was possible to narrate the story in such a way that the nations functioned simply as a foil for Israel, the story itself contained at least latent questions about the relationship between these other nations and the God who created them."[44]

There are numerous trajectories that envision non-Jews as joining themselves to the Lord as "others," rather than joining Israel, that is, a socio-ethnic group, through conversion. This differentiation is retained in visions of the future salvation, as, for example, in Zechariah 2:11-12, "Many nations (*goyim* – *ethnē*) shall join themselves to the Lord on that day, and shall be my people; and I will dwell in your midst. And you shall know that the Lord of hosts has sent me to you. The Lord will inherit Judah as his portion in the holy land, and will again choose Jerusalem." Similar traditions of a clear distinction between Israel and the nations can be found in Isaiah 56:6; 2:3; Micah 4:2; and Ezra 6:21.

These nations are not seen as becoming part of Israel, but they worship God as foreigners because God's house is now a house of prayer for all peoples (Isa. 56:7).[45] There are traditions in these

---

44. Terence L. Donaldson, *Judaism and the Gentiles: Jewish Patterns of Universalism (to 135 CE)* (Waco, TX: Baylor University Press, 2007), 2.
45. Joel Kaminsky, "Israel's Election and the Other in Biblical, Second Temple, and Rabbinic Thought" in *The "Other" in Second Temple Judaism: Essays in Honor of John J. Collins*, ed. Daniel C. Harlow, Karina Martin Hogan, and Mattew L. Goff (Grand Rapids: Eerdmans, 2011),

narratives that envision non-Jewish peoples joining in the praise of
the God of Israel without becoming members of the people Israel,
that is, without becoming like them. Their alterity is preserved.[46]
Trajectories of this scriptural tradition can be found in Second
Temple literature as well. Whilst it is not always clear whether the
distinction between Israel and the nations is envisaged as being
retained in such eschatological visions, some texts clearly presuppose
such a distinction, such as *T. Jud.* 25:5: "and the deer of Jacob shall
run with gladness; the eagles of Israel shall fly with joy; the impious
shall mourn and sinners shall weep, but all peoples (*ethnē*) shall glorify
God forever" (see also *1 En.* 90:30-38; *Pss. Sol.* 17:28, 34; *2 Bar.*
72:2-6). The distinctions between, and diversity of, nations/*ethnē* is
maintained and so is their specific way of life, possibly including
their way of relating to God. Whilst other traditions envisaged that
the nations would abandon their traditions and "turn to honouring
our laws alone" (Philo, *Mos.* 2.43-44), the Pauline insistence on the
retention of the particular identities of Israel and the nations is part
of one of the diverse continuous trajectories of Jewish tradition from
the Scriptures to Second Temple literature that envisage the unity
of Israel and the nations in their diversity.[47] It cannot be discerned
precisely which specific traditions of this narrative were influential
for Paul's understanding of his call to the nations, but it can hardly
be envisaged that such traditions were not of some importance for his

---

17–30, here 20, argues that even a text like Lev. 24:22, which refers to "one law for natives and
resident aliens" implies "that the group boundaries remain intact."

46. On alterity, see Emmanuel Levinas, *Totality and Infinity: An Essay on Exteriority* (Pittsburgh:
Duquesne University Press, 1969), 194–219, and also my discussion of Levinas and Paul in,
"Levinas, the Jewish Philosopher Meets Paul, the Jewish Apostle: Reading Romans in the Face
of the Other," in *Reading Romans with Contemporary Philosophers and Theologians*, ed. David
Odell-Scott (London: T & T Clark, 2007), 115–54.

47. For more details, see the discussion by Donaldson, *Judaism and the Gentiles*, 499–505; also
Ehrensperger, *Paul at the Crossroads of Cultures*, 154–60.

understanding of his call to bring about the obedience of faith among all the nations (Rom. 1:5).

Thus Paul does not consider particularity a problem that needs to be overcome. The identity, values, and commitment of particular people—Jews, Greeks, and barbarians—are not considered to be an obstacle for peace and reconciliation between people who are different, except that those from the nations have to "turn away from idols" (1 Thess. 1:9). Although the latter certainly had major implications at everyday level for those from the nations,[48] Paul consistently and repeatedly insists that Jews and "gentiles" retain their identity in Christ that they remain in the calling in which they were called (1 Cor. 7:17).[49]

It is a perception of unity that differs clearly from the prevalent perception of unity as enforced by imperial ideology, where acceptance and some respect by Rome for those who were different came at the price of assimilation to the way of life of the Roman (or Greek) elite.[50] Inherent to the recognition that Paul and the message he conveys are embedded in Judaism is the recognition of, and respect for, diversity and the different identities of Jews and non-Jews in Christ.

At the heart of the earliest Christ-movement, as in some traditions of Second Temple Judaism, there is thus not a hegemonic claim to sameness, but a recognition of unity and equality in difference. Neither Jew nor Greek have to assimilate to the identity of the other in order for unity and reconciliation to be possible in Christ. "Never to put a stumbling block or hindrance in the way of another" (Rom.

---

48. See Kathy Ehrensperger, "The Ministry to Jerusalem (Rom 15.31): Paul's Hopes and Fears," in *Erlesenes Jerusalem: Festschrift für Ekkehard W. Stegemann*, Lukas Kundert and Christina Tuor-Kurth eds. (Basel: Reinhardt Verlag 2013), 338–52.

49. William S. Campbell, *Unity and Diversity in Christ: Interpreting Paul in Context* (Eugene, OR: Cascade Books, 2013), 205–23; J. Brian Tucker, *Remain in Your Calling: Paul and the Continuation of Social Identity in 1 Corinthians 1–4* (Eugene, OR: Pickwick, 2011).

50. See Ehrensperger, *Paul at the Crossroads of Cultures*, 156–58.

14:13), not to injure one another (14:15), but accommodate one another (15:2), and welcome one another (15:7), are certainly not calls to assimilate to the identity of the other, and to become the same. The recognition and respect for the others in their difference is a prerequisite for understanding, reconciliation, and unity. Communication and community presuppose difference and plurality rather than sameness or uniformity.[51] Paul is trying to negotiate the recognition of "alterity" in relation to non-Jews in Christ, not at the expense of Jewish identity, but the opposite. Rather, the particular identities of both are being affirmed positively. It is these that are the building blocks of the unity in Christ rather than their eradication.

Such a recognition cannot be merely claimed for the Christ-followers from the nations, who are not required to become Jews and remain the "uncircumcision" but must also apply to the Jews who are not to become non-Jews but remain the "circumcision." The recognition of Paul's Jewishness is the recognition of particularity. It means to recognize that there is no such phenomenon as a universal human being in this earthly existence—there are only particular human beings in particular places at specific moments in time. Such particularity is claimed and positively asserted within Jewish tradition. As such the recognition of Paul's Jewishness should be a decisive aspect in any approaches that try to overcome universalizing hegemonic tendencies in contemporary interpretation, including in gender-critical approaches.

As I have argued above, the universalizing tendencies in interpretation not only denied recognition to Jewish identity but also continued to legitimize androcentric gender perceptions in that the ideal generic human being was conceptualized according to a dominating elitist template of masculinity.[52] Those who did not

---

51. Levinas, *Totality and Infinity*, 73; cf. also Ehrensperger, "Reading Romans in the Face of the Other."

conform to this image, whether men or women, would not be granted equal respect, as their difference was considered a hindrance to full humanity. This universalization of a particular male ideal had detrimental effects for women, and for peoples who eventually became subject to European colonization, as well as for men who did not conform to this image of masculinity. The universalization of a particular image of men as representing humanity as such imposed assimilation on those who were different or exposed them to contempt and humiliation.

The recognition of particularity as being at the center of the Christ-movement is thus an important step in light of a gender-critical perspective.

The Recognition of Particularity—Insights from Gender Studies

In contemporary contexts, the implications drawn from the recognition of Paul's Jewishness, including the recognition of particularity and diversity at the heart of his theologizing, can in my view be extended to issues concerning gender questions. It includes the recognition of the particularity of human beings per se, in the vein Hannah Arendt has formulated: "Plurality is the condition of human action because we are all the same, that is, human, in such a way that nobody is ever the same as anyone else who ever lived, lives, or will live."[53] The social, historical, cultural, and linguistic imprints of our contexts are durable dimensions of what it means to be human, and they include gender as well as other dimensions of our identity. I am not arguing an essentialist or individualistic stance here. I consider culture and social location to be constructed not in an individualistic sense but in a corporate sense, which means that individuals are born into existing cultures and societies, nurtured and corporately formed

---

52. For a detailed discussion see Ehrensperger, *That We May Be Mutually Encouraged*, 97–110.

53. Hannah Arendt, *The Human Condition* (Chicago: Chicago University Press, 1958), 8.

in a relational web that contributes to the formation of the "habitus."[54] Thus, men and women are socially conditioned in particular ways in action, reaction, and interaction in and with their contexts, and continue to be so in their respective walks of life.[55]

Largely through the influence of gender studies, the recognition of the embodied dimension of human beings has moved into the focus of attention in the social sciences and humanities.[56] Beate Krais is of the view that Pierre Bourdieu's concept of habitus provides the tool for "a systematic, analytical approach to the fundamental *bodiliness* of human action."[57] The body is a repository for social experience, constituting an essential part of the "habitus"[58] and as such it enacts what has been learned, "bringing it back to life. What is 'learned by the body' is not something one has, like knowledge . . .

54. Pierre Bourdieu has argued that this habitus, understood as dispositions, is imprinted durably in us and decisively shapes our ongoing interactions and reactions as we walk through life. It is thereby further formed and transformed by new contexts and experiences based on, and in relation to, the existing imprint.

55. Some feminist theorists have argued that this amounts to a deterministic inscription of gender, leaving no room for agency and change. See discussions in Lisa Adkins and Beverly Skeggs, eds., *Feminism after Bourdieu* (Oxford: Blackwell, 2004). Over against this, feminists from a poststructuralist perspective have argued for a radical constructivist stance in that gender is a performative discourse at the symbolic level of language, attributing the potential and power of agency to this level. However, this has been considered as a conflation of social reality with linguistic reality, and as dealing with issues of gender and other inequalities at an abstract level. In response to such theories, Bourdieu formulated that, "While it never does harm to point out that gender, nation, or ethnicity or race are social constructs, it is naïve, even dangerous, to suppose and suggest that one only has to 'deconstruct' these social artefacts, in a purely performative celebration of 'resistance,' in order to *destroy* them" (Pierre Bourdieu, *Pascalian Meditations* [Oxford: Polity, 2000], 108). I cannot discuss this debate here, but it is worth noting that feminist political theorist Lois McNay comments concerning poststructuralist feminism that "the imperialism of the universal that is implied in the over-extension of a linguistic model of identity formation is, in the final analysis, a form *par excellence* of symbolic violence perpetuated by 'enlightened' élites upon the practical activities of social actors" ("Agency and Experience: Gender as Lived Relation," in *Feminism after Bourdieu*, 175–90, here 181). She and other feminist theorists engage critically with Bourdieu's work and consider it relevant, albeit within limitations, for gender-critical approaches.

56. Including biblical studies, as Jennifer Glancy demonstrates in *Corporeal Knowledge: Early Christian Bodies* (New York: Oxford University Press, 2010).

57. Beate Krais, "Gender, Sociological Theory and Bourdieu's Sociology of Practice," *Theory, Culture, Society* 23, no. 6 (2006): 119–134, here 127. Emphasis in original.

58. Ibid., 127.

but something that one is."[59] Such learning is mediated in particular social contexts; it is both shaped by and contributes to how the context is shaped. Bourdieu thus argues that "the subject is not the instantaneous *ego* of a sort of individual *cogito*, but the individual trace of an entire collective history."[60] This collective contextuality is permeated by the omnipresence of gender in all social interactions and processes. In as much as there is no human existence apart from particular ethnic, linguistic, and cultural contexts, there is no human existence in a non-gendered form. However, this does not mean the same for everyone but should rather be considered in the vein of "variations of a theme."[61] Without resorting to essentialized or biological notions of gender in terms of characteristics, roles, or sexuality, the social and contextual dimension of human existence includes the embodiment of gender in various ways. Gender is not an abstraction but always concrete and thus particular, embodied or "inhabited" by men and women in particular ways within the contexts of their societies, who creatively shape, and are shaped by, this embodiment in interaction with other "players" in the multiple social fields of societies. Implicit to this recognition is the insight of the particularity of human existence.

An analogy can be drawn between the universalization of the image of the so-called ideal elite man as the template for being human, and the universalization of the non-Jewish way of life as the one and only way of life in Christ. Both are universalizations of particulars and thus are discourses of assimilating domination. To declare a particular embodiment or way of life universal means to ignore, eradicate, or delegitimize any other form or way of life, not just at the level of linguistic discourse but in actual reality. The

59. Pierre Bourdieu, *The Logic of Practice* (Cambridge: Polity, 1990), 73.
60. Ibid., 91.
61. See Krais, "Gender, Sociological Theory," 128.

contempt and at times violent oppression of women, Jews, non-elite men, and gay and lesbians are expressions of similar efficacies of universalizing notions and practices.

The recognition of Paul and his theologizing as Jewish, has significant implications in light of gender-critical perspectives since it resonates with the latter's emphasis on embodiment and the particularity of human experiences, practices, and perceptions. Paul himself did not draw out any implications of his emphasis on the retention of particular identities in Christ in relation to gender. This seemed to have been beyond his horizon. He was concerned about relationships between ethnically different peoples as constitutive of messianic communities. In order for particularity not to disintegrate into factionalism or superiority claims based on difference, the notion of equality is central in his theologizing. And although Paul does not apply his respective guidance explicitly to gender relations, there is no reason to not include these by analogy. Paul's stance against boasting can be seen as a test case in this regard.

Equality with a Difference

It is evident that Paul has a clear stance when it comes to expressions of superiority and humiliating behaviour within the Christ-following communities.[62] Although Paul clearly emphasizes the retention of Jewish and "gentile" identity in Christ, this is not an argument for negative stereotyping or any superiority claim by either of them. The particularity of "Jew and Greek" goes hand in hand with the emphasis on their equality in Christ. Neither Jews nor Christ-followers from the nations have any reason to boast over against each other (Rom.

---

62. Cf. also Kathy Ehrensperger, "'Called to be Saints' – the Identity-Shaping Dimension of Paul's Priestly Discourse in Romans," in *Reading Paul in Context: Explorations in Identity Formation: Essays in Honour of William S. Campbell,* ed. J. Brian Tucker and Kathy Ehrensperger, (London: T & T Clark, 2010), 90–109.

2:11, 17) . The only acceptable boasting in this movement is "in the Lord" (1 Cor. 1:31; Jer. 9:23).

It could be argued that this is merely another way of expressing superiority claims, and that by boasting in the Lord Paul claims authority and domination over the communites he had founded. It is possible to read respective passages in that vein.[63] But the Lord that Paul refers to here is not one of the heroes of Greek and Roman tradition but a God who taught Israel to walk and who lifted her like an infant to his cheek (Hos. 11:1-11), who called Israel, and now through Christ also calls those from the nations into a relationship with him, and does not force them into a connection with him in a dominating way. This indicates that "boasting in the Lord" can hardly have anything to do with superiority claims or an exercise of power in a dominating way. In order to teach a child to walk, nothing but tender, loving care and encouragement will help the child to trust in a steadfast, supportive hand, and eventually in his or her ability to walk. To respond to the call of this God means to live a way of life that corresponds to the One who called. It is a God who reminds his people that he freed them from slavery, which obliges them to care for those who are vulnerable in the community (Deut. 10:18-19; 24:17-18). Paul's Jewish tradition presents alternative perceptions to Greek and Roman notions of the use of power.[64]

---

63. Such readings are mainly rooted in male-stream theological perceptions of God as the absolute sovereign to whom humans owe submissive obedience. Such images of God have been challenged by feminist theologians as replications of patriarchal/kyriarchal paradigms of domination into the realm of the divine. Read through such frameworks Paul then is seen as replicating such paradigms and contributes to their stabilization. Feminist theologians such as Serene Jones and Joy Ann McDougall ("Sin – No More? A Feminist Re-Visioning of a Christian Theology of Sin," *Anglican Theological Review* 88, no. 2 [2006]: 215–35), have presented feminist approaches to the image of God and divine–human relation that emphasize interdependence and responsiveness as characteristics in this respect. However, they do not refer to Jewish tradition as actually the basis and root for such a perception of the divine-human relation. Based on feminist theories of power I have argued for a reading of the Pauline discourse of *hypakoē pisteōs* as a discourse of response-ability rooted in Judaism (*Paul and the Dynamics of Power*, 160–72).

There is a discourse of empowerment at the heart of this tradition, a discourse of trust in a God who hears the cries of those in need (e.g., Exod. 2:23-25; 3:7-9; Pss. 3:4; 9:12; 22:5; 32:7; 99:6; 106:44; 145:19; 1 Kgs. 8:51-53; Neh. 9:9; Isa. 19:20; 65:19). This tradition was alive in Second Temple Judaism in various forms, evident in clear echoes of the Exodus passages in *1 Enoch* 86:16ff., and when Philo tells of how Moses and Aaron told the people "how God had conceived pity and compassion for them, promised them freedom and a departure from thence to a better country, promising also that he himself would be their guide on their road" (*Mos.* 1.86). Josephus has Moses admonished to travel back to Egypt without delay, "but to make haste to Egypt, and to travel night and day, and not to draw out the time, and so make the slavery of the Hebrews and their sufferings to last the longer" (*Ant.* 2.274). According to the book of Judith, the prayers of the people in distress are heard: "The Lord heard their prayers and had regard for their distress; for the people fasted many days throughout Judea and in Jerusalem before the sanctuary of the Lord Almighty" (4:13); and Judith's own prayer expresses a strong trust that God will hear: "For your strength does not depend on number nor your might on the powerful. But you are the God of the lowly, helper of the oppressed, upholder of the weak, protector of the forsaken, savior of those without hope" (9:11).[65] It is in this Lord in whom Christ-followers shall boast, if they boast at all.[66] These

---

64. Cf. Augustus's report about the conquest of the Dacians: "an army of Dacians which crossed to the south of that river was, under my auspices, defeated and crushed, and afterwards my own army was led across the Danube and compelled the nations of the Dacians to submit to the rule of the Roman people" (*Res gestae* 30); or Pliny's report about Pompey's success: "Gnaeus Pompeius Magnus, Imperator, having completed a war of thirty years, routed, exiled, murdered, or accepted surrender of 183,000 people, sunk or captured 846 ships, received 1538 towns and forts in faith, subjugated lands from the Maetoinians to the Red Sea, rightly vows to Minerva" (*Nat.* 7.26.97). Numerous further examples of the Roman ideology of conquest that justified violence could be added here. Cf. also the discussion in David J. Mattingly, *Imperialism, Power, and Identity: Experiencing the Roman Empire* (Princeton, NJ: Princeton University Press, 2011), 125–45.

claims would need to orient themselves on the trust and faithfulness of God and the power exercised needs to be a power that respects and supports others in their particularity and difference.

Thus, this "anti-boasting" stance is not based on a notion of sameness. Paul affirms that there is an advantage in being Jewish when he asserts that they "were entrusted with the oracles of God" (Rom. 3:2), that to them "belong the adoption, the covenants, the giving of the law, the worship, and the promises" (Rom. 9:4). This clearly is an advantage, but it is not a reason for being superior to non-Jewish Christ-followers. To have an advantage and to be superior are not identical.[67] However, the advantage of the Jews provides also no reason for them to be treated more severely for their failure to remain faithful to the covenant, as, for example, an excellent theologian like J. Christiaan Beker could maintain.[68] Jews are affected by sin as are non-Jews, and in that sense they are equal with non-Jews, but they remain God's beloved *kata ten eklogen* (Rom. 11:28). Thus those from the nations who are now in Christ have no reason to boast over those Jews who are not convinced by the message of the gospel (Rom. 11:18),[69] or to consider the way of life of Jews in Christ as something that needs to be patiently accepted for the time being but that would eventually be rendered obsolete. Israel is called into existence by God through his covenant with them, the Torah is God's guidance for them to be Israel in an inhospitable

65. Cf. also Anathea Portier-Young, *Apocalypse Against Empire: Theologies of Resistance in Early Judaism* (Grand Rapids: Eerdmans, 2011), 354–55, who sees analogies to the Exodus narrative in the Enochic Book of Dreams (*1 En.* 83–90).

66. For a more detailed discussion, see Ehrensperger, *Paul and the Dynamics of Power*, 162–66.

67. Cf. Campbell, *Unity and Diversity*, 16, following Arland J. Hultgren, *Paul's Letter to the Romans* (Grand Rapids: Eerdmans, 2011), 133–39.

68. J. Christiaan Beker, *Paul, the Apostle: The Triumph of God in Life and Thought* (Edinburgh: T & T Clark, 1980), 81–82, makes statements such as "Paul wants to destroy the preeminently Jewish sin of boasting," and "The Jew highlights sin in its most demonic aspect."

69. Mark D. Nanos, "'Broken Branches': A Pauline Metaphor Gone Awry? (Romans 11:11-24)," in *Between Gospel and Election: Explorations in the Interpretation of Romans 9–11*, ed. J. Ross Wagner and Florian Wilk (Tübingen: Mohr Siebeck, 2010), 339–76.

world, and "the gifts and the calling of God are irrevocable" (11:19). This means that Israel's existence and identity are inherently linked with God's call and it is theologically inconceivable to argue that, if not immediately then eventually, Israel's way of life will be rendered obsolete in Christ.[70] This would mean that eventually Israel would actually cease to exist, rendering God's call revocable! This is certainly not Paul's conviction when he asserts that "all Israel will be saved" (Rom. 11:26). Equality does not "obliterate" difference. What Paul sees as being enabled in Christ is unity and reconciliation between those who are and remain different, Jews and Greeks, men and women, but who now can recognize each other as equals, that is, as brothers and sisters in Christ.

Conclusion

It has been demonstrated that there are significant analogies between gender-sensitive approaches and those that locate Paul firmly within Judaism. Taking Paul's Judaism seriously sheds new light on Paul's perception of women, on his actual guidance in relation to issues concerning women in particular, as well as on his recognition of them in their leadership roles. Rather than being an indication for a reactionary, innovative, or contradictory tendency, Paul's attitudes and relations to women are part of the way of life considered appropriate in relation to the God of Israel in Second Temple Judaism, applied by him now to those called from the nations.

Paul's specific and continued embeddedness in Judaism has been seen also in his insistence on the value and retention of particularity and differences in Christ. It leads him to practice a form of

---

70. As Troels Engberg-Petersen maintains in "'Everything is Clean' and 'Everything That is Not of Faith is Sin': The Logic of Pauline Casuistry in Romans 14.1–15.13," in *Paul, Grace, and Freedom: Essays in Honour of John K. Riches*, ed. Paul Middleton et al (London: T & T Clark, 2008), 22–38.

theologizing that is concrete and aware of the particularities and diversities of life. The overcoming of particularity and difference is not an option Paul could have advocated as it would have been inconsistent with the traditions of his ancestors also after the coming of Christ.

But difference cannot be a reason for superiority claims between those who are and remain different. Inherent to the advocacy for Jews and non-Jews to remain as called is the ruling out of any kind of boasting over one another. Any asymmetry between those called should lead to relationships of transformative power through which empowerment for life emerges.[71] Where such empowerment was blocked or hindered, whether in Rome or Galatia or at the Lord's Table in Corinth, Paul intervened. The calling of God initiates relationships, aiming at freeing those called from the constraints and burdens of sin, rather than from their particular identities, as Jews or nations, men or women. As those who are and remain different, they are those who are called and enabled to "shine forth the goodness of God . . . in and through . . . beneficent relations with others."[72] Relationality presupposes difference rather than overcoming it and recognition of, and respect for, those who are different is what actually enables community and understanding rather than a supposed notion of sameness.

Gender-critical approaches have raised awareness of the universalizing notions of traditional male-stream theologies and interpretations, and they have pioneered the necessity of critical reflection on the hermeneutical presuppositions at work in any interpreter's approach to biblical texts and theologies. This has transformative and at times radical implications for theologizing in

---

71. For a discussion of power in feminist perspective and its relevance for Pauline studies, see Ehrensperger, *Paul and the Dynamics of Power*, 24–34.

72. Kathryn Tanner, *Jesus, Humanity and the Trinity: A Brief Systematic Theology* (Minneapolis: Fortress Press, 2001), 69–70.

a gender-critical vein. The recognition of Paul's embeddedness in Judaism has similar although different transformative and radical implications for theologizing in a non-supersessionist vein. Thus the recognition of Paul and his theologizing in its concrete Jewish particularity should be a core dimension of gender-sensitive interpretative and theological approaches, in as much as gender-sensitive approaches should be included as a core aspect in Paul within Judaism studies. These approaches mutually resonate with each other in many ways, providing illuminating potential for each of them where the other is concerned.

9

Paul within Judaism: A Critical Evaluation from a "New Perspective" Perspective

Terence L. Donaldson

My assigned role in this project is to engage in a critical evaluation of the main chapters, as someone who is identified with the (now no longer quite so) New Perspective on Paul. I need to reserve most of the space that has been allotted to me for the task of critical engagement, rather than that of mapping the New Perspective or of promoting my own reading of Paul. Nevertheless, to provide a framework for my discussion of the preceding chapters, it seems appropriate to begin with a few comments about the New Perspective and my own approach.

As a category or label, "new perspective" has become increasingly problematical, in that it has come to be used in several different ways and thus is being applied to scholars whose interpretations of Paul differ from each other in significant aspects.[1] Popular use of the term goes back to a 1983 article by James Dunn,[2] where it was used to refer to the work of E. P. Sanders.[3] Since then, however, it has also come to be associated with Dunn's own attempts, along with those of N. T. Wright and others, to correct what they see as a deficiency in Sanders's argument (the correction centering on the idea that Paul's polemical discourse about "works of the law" is directed at misplaced Jewish confidence in ethnic "boundary markers" or "badges of membership"). In addition, the term is used more broadly and less precisely with reference to scholars who have not so much a shared position as a shared interest in a set of related questions stimulated by Sanders's trailblazing work.[4]

1. In a paper presented at a recent scholarly conference, I found myself sharing space in a list of New Perspective scholars with Neil Elliott, Lloyd Gaston, Richard Hays, Elizabeth Johnson, and Mark Nanos—congenial colleagues all, but hardly of the same mind on how to understand Paul.

2. James D. G. Dunn, "The New Perspective on Paul," *Bulletin of the John Rylands Library* 65 (1983): 95–122. Dunn has since pointed out, however, that it was used earlier by N. T. Wright, in Wright's article "The Paul of History and the Apostle of Faith," *Tyndale Bulletin* 29 (1978): 61–88. Wright, in turn, noted that the term had already appeared in Krister Stendahl's influential article, "The Apostle Paul and the Introspective Conscience of the West," *Harvard Theological Review* 56 (1963): 214; see N. T. Wright, *Justification: God's Plan and Paul's Vision* (Downers Grove, IL: IVP Academic, 2009), 28.

3. E. P. Sanders, *Paul and Palestinian Judaism* (Philadelphia: Fortress Press, 1977); Dunn also had access to the pre-publication manuscript of Sanders's *Paul, the Law, and the Jewish People* (Philadelphia: Fortress Press, 1983).

4. Included in this set of questions are: the nature of covenantal Judaism; the place of "Jews" and "gentiles" in Paul's structures of thought and activity; the nature of his "conversion" (his transformation from "zealot for the traditions of his ancestors" to "apostle to the gentiles"); the relationship of Paul's juridical language to other aspects of his discourse; the significance of Romans 9–11. See Magnus Zetterholm's chapter, "Paul as a First-Century Jew: The State of the Questions," in this volume for a more detailed account of the New Perspective and its place in the history of Pauline interpretation.

My 1997 monograph *Paul and the Gentiles*[5] was significantly influenced by the work of Sanders, though it was also an attempt to address a question that was left hanging in his seminal book *Paul and Palestinian Judaism*. While this means that my work is analogous in some respects to that of Dunn and Wright, I differ with them considerably in my sense of where Sanders needs to be corrected or supplemented.[6] Whether this qualifies me for a New Perspective badge of membership depends, I suppose, on how the boundary is drawn.

In the monograph just mentioned, I readily adopted, at least in broad terms, a number of Sanders's distinctive insights and arguments:

- his depiction of Judaism as characterized by what he termed "covenantal nomism";

- his argument that for Paul the "solution preceded the problem"—that is, that Christ represented not the solution to some already perceived failing or inadequacy in his own native Jewish "pattern of religion," but a new conviction;

- his insistence that interpreters of Paul need to make a distinction between surface rhetoric and underlying convictional structure—that is, between Paul's fundamental convictions and the arguments he used to defend them in specific contexts;

---

5. Terence L. Donaldson, *Paul and the Gentiles: Remapping the Apostle's Convictional World* (Minneapolis: Fortress Press, 1997); summaries of the position taken there can be found in Donaldson, "Israelite, Convert, Apostle to the Gentiles: The Origin of Paul's Gentile Mission," in *The Road from Damascus: The Impact of Paul's Conversion on His Life, Thought and Ministry*, ed. Richard N. Longenecker (Grand Rapids: Eerdmans, 1997), 62–84 and, to some extent, in Donaldson, "Introduction to the Pauline Corpus," in *The Oxford Bible Commentary*, ed. John Barton and John Muddiman (Oxford: Oxford University Press, 2001), 1062–83.

6. In addition to the material listed in the previous footnote, see Donaldson, "In Search of a Paul Neither Lutheran nor Idiosyncratic: James D. G. Dunn's *The Theology of Paul the Apostle*," *Critical Review of Books in Religion* 11 (1998): 35–55.

- as a particular instance of this, his insistence that Paul's juridical language (e.g., "justification by faith") should be seen not as a theological first principle or fundamental conviction, but as an argument used in certain circumstances to defend a fundamental conviction;

- his characterization of the "pattern of religion" that arises out of Paul's fundamental convictions as "participatory eschatology";

- and finally, his identification of Paul's most fundamental conviction as the belief that God has provided Christ as a means of salvation for all, gentiles as well as Jews, on equal terms.

It was this final item, however, that served as the point of departure for my own work. Sanders demonstrated to my satisfaction that, if we take this as Paul's governing conviction, we can make good sense of the often perplexing and apparently disjointed arguments that we encounter at the surface level of his letters. But he provided us with no real explanation of how Paul arrived at this conviction in the first place. Key elements of the conviction, namely "for all" and "on equal terms," are simply assumed. How are we to understand Paul's transition from "a zealot for the traditions of [his] ancestors" (Gal. 1:14)[7] to "the apostle to the gentiles"? As Dunn observed, in Sanders's reconstruction this transition appears to have been "arbitrary and irrational," the exchange of a "Lutheran Paul" for an "idiosyncratic Paul."[8] One might say that, for Sanders, this new conviction seemed

---

7. Since zeal generally refers to a willingness to use force to defend Torah-centered Judaism against a perceived threat, Paul's role as a zealous "persecutor of the church" (Phil. 3:6; cf. Gal. 1:14) means that he initially perceived the movement of Jewish Christ-believers as somehow outside the bounds of tolerance. While a distinction needs to be maintained between community discipline and exclusion, Paul's zeal-motivated opposition to Jewish Christ-believers needs to be accounted for in any account of this transition, and thus of any attempt to locate Paul the apostle "within Judaism."

8. "The Lutheran Paul has been replaced by an idiosyncratic Paul who in arbitrary and irrational manner turns his face against the glory and greatness of Judaism's covenant theology and

to have functioned as a kind of interpretive "black box," a theoretical construction that, while providing a convincing explanation of other things, is itself closed off from investigation.[9]

My approach, then, might be seen as an attempt to open up this black box—an attempt to reconstruct the cognitive dynamic by which Paul arrived at this new conviction. Implicit in Sanders's reconstruction, it seemed to me, especially in his theme "the solution as preceding the problem," is the idea that prior to his Damascus experience Paul had been fully at home in the world of covenantal nomism. The question, then, concerns Paul's transition from covenantal nomist (to use Sanders's term) to apostle to the gentiles. How are we to understand the shift of convictions involved in a transformation from covenantal nomist to preacher of this particular message—that is, that God has provided Christ as a means of salvation for all, gentile as well as Jew, on equal terms?

The search for an answer, I felt, needed to begin in Paul's native world, specifically in the range of Jewish conceptions about the religious status of non-Jews that I came to call "patterns of universalism." While the choice of term might require reconsideration,[10] I used it to refer to the various ways in which Jews were able to conceive of non-Jews as standing in a positive relationship with the God of Israel. In my earliest attempts to explore

abandons Judaism simply because it is not Christianity"; Dunn, "The New Perspective on Paul," 101.

9. A more generous way of putting it would be to say that it was not part of Sanders's purpose to reconstruct Paul's transition. His project was more synchronic and comparative—namely, as his subtitle indicates, to compare what he called "patterns of religion." In his follow-up book, however, he did take up the question of the origins of Paul's new convictions to some extent, in passing comments about eschatological traditions concerning the place of non-Jews in the age to come: "Paul's entire work, both evangelizing and collecting money, had its setting in the expected pilgrimage of the Gentiles to Mount Zion in the last days" (*Paul, the Law, and the Jewish People*, 171). In addition, in an ironic reversal of "solution" and "problem," he speculates about the possibility that, prior to his Christ-experience, Paul had experienced dissatisfaction with negative and exclusionary Jewish attitudes toward Gentiles (pp. 153–55).

10. Perhaps "patterns of inclusion" would be more appropriate.

Paul's concern for non-Jews, I thought that it could be understood as a fairly straightforward consequence of Jewish anticipations of the "eschatological pilgrimage of the nations" or, more generally, Jewish restoration eschatology.[11] Eventually, however, I found myself forced to abandon this approach in favor of a more complex reordering of Paul's convictional world.

This is not the place to attempt a description of this reordering as I came to understand it. Some of it will come into play in the critical engagement to follow, and what I have said to this point will be sufficient to set it into a clarifying context. Before turning to specific points of critical engagement, however, I want to express my appreciation to the editors for the project as a whole and to the individual authors for a set of bracing and invigorating essays. Reading them has provided me with a welcome opportunity not only to reexamine my previous thinking about Paul but also to refine it and move beyond it in some ways.

With respect to the project as a whole, I applaud wholeheartedly the desire to locate Paul "within Judaism," which here carries with it the shared perception that his mission among non-Jews is not to be set over against his Jewishness. Like many of his contemporaries within Judaism, Paul was concerned to locate his Judaism within the wider world—or, to draw on Paula Fredriksen's way of putting it, to locate the wider world within a map drawn with Israel at the center. While I will return to the issue later, looking more closely at the various dimensions of what the phrase might mean, I appreciate the insistence that Paul can be—is to be—seen as "within Judaism."

<hr/>

11. See Terence Donaldson, "The 'Curse of the Law' and the Inclusion of the Gentiles: Galatians 3.13-14," *New Testament Studies* 32 (1986): 94–112. While Jewish restoration eschatology does not always envisage the participation of non-Jews in end-time salvation, and while such participation is not always envisaged in terms of a pilgrimage to Zion, in what follows I will use these terms more or less interchangeably, without attempting to make any significant distinctions among them.

I also appreciate the attention that is given to terminological matters. Many of the terms and categories used in critical reconstructions of the past are laden with meanings and connotations that have accumulated through centuries of subsequent use, which readily leads to anachronisms, distortions, and false assumptions. As Krister Stendahl has observed, "Our vision is often more obstructed by what we think we know than by our lack of knowledge."[12] One aspect of the problem has to do with the terms "Christianity" and "Judaism" themselves, which are often used in essentializing and anachronistic ways to denote two "religions," clearly demarcated from each other by distinct and separate essences. The problem is explored in detail in Neil Elliott's chapter, "The Question of Politics: Paul as a Diaspora Jew under Roman Rule," and is addressed in helpful ways by others (Magnus Zetterholm, Caroline Johnson Hodge, Anders Runesson). Another aspect concerns the translation of terms that appear in our primary sources, several of which are subjected to fruitful examination in the volume, such as "church" for *ekklēsia* (Runesson) and "gentiles" for *ethnē* (Mark Nanos, Paula Fredriksen, Johnson Hodge). With respect to the latter, while I have for reasons of convenience used "gentile(s)" up to this point, for the rest of the paper I will use either *ethnē* itself or other formulations (non-Jews, non-Jewish nations, members of non-Jewish nations).[13]

Finally, I appreciate the way in which the chapters, taken cumulatively, serve to dislodge the question of "Paul and Judaism" from its traditional and tiresome location in a world of abstract concepts and rarified theological debates, and to place it squarely in the context of social realities and lived experiences—the practical decisions and situational accommodations that are part of everyday

12. Krister Stendahl, *Paul Among Jews and Gentiles* (Philadelphia: Fortress Press, 1976), 7.
13. See Terence Donaldson, "'Gentile Christianity' as a Category in the Study of Christian Origins," *Harvard Theological Review* 106, no. 4 (2013): 433–58.

life for the Torah observant (Karin Hedner Zetterholm); the omnipresence of gods and cult in the urban fabric (Fredriksen); the embodied realities of gender and ethnicity (Kathy Ehrensperger); and so on.

Turning from general appreciation to critical engagement, I will begin with two issues pertaining to Paul's convictions about the *ethnē* and then make some comments about ways in which the question "Paul within Judaism?" might be conceived.

Eschatological Inclusion of the *Ethnē*

To the extent that they address the question of the framework within which Paul conceived his mission to non-Jews, the contributors to this volume are unanimous: for Paul, his communities of non-Jewish Christ-believers represented the fulfillment of the Jewish expectation that in the end times the nations would abandon their idols, worship the God of Israel, and so share in the promised blessings of the age to come. So, for example:

> Paul allies himself here with the Jewish eschatological expectation that God will establish his kingdom for Israel and for favored nations. As the apostle to the gentiles, he sees himself in the tradition of the prophets who call gentiles to Jerusalem on the Day of the Lord, when "all the nations shall stream to [the Lord's house]" (Isa. 2:2). (Johnson Hodge)

> [These believing non-Jews] represented a population long anticipated within centuries of Jewish restoration theology: they were pagans-saved-at-the-End. (Fredriksen)

> Once such a vision made clear to him that God had raised the martyred Jesus from the dead—again, a realization that would have been intelligible within the bounds of Jewish apocalyptic experience—the consequences would have followed a thoroughly Jewish apocalyptic logic: "The vision would have confirmed to [Paul] that what the apocalypses promised God *would* do *someday*, God had in fact begun to do *now*." (Elliott)

... the chronometrical claim of the gospel that the time when the nations will worship God alongside of Israel has arrived. (Nanos)

In addition to this general claim that Paul's mission to non-Jews is to be accounted for in this way, the contributors are also unanimous in drawing on such eschatological pilgrimage expectations to account for a more specific aspect of Paul's gospel. For those who want to understand Paul from a location "within Judaism," his position with respect to the Torah and the *ethnē* presents a puzzle. Why was he adamantly opposed to any suggestion that non-Jews should become full Torah observers? As he says to his Galatian readers: "If you let yourself be circumcised," you will "have cut yourself off from Christ" (Gal. 5:2, 4). Why was it that Christ belief and full Torah observance were set out in such oppositional terms? On one hand, non-Jewish Christ-believers are worshippers of Israel's God, intimately linked with Israel's messiah (*en christō*) and qualified to view Abraham as their father; yet on the other, they are to remain as non-Jews, forbidden on pain of exclusion to become full Torah-observing proselytes. How are we to account for the distinctive profile that Paul imposes on his non-Jewish Christ-believers?

The answer, according to several of the contributors to this volume, is that this is a straightforward consequence of eschatological pilgrimage patterns of thought. As Johnson Hodge puts it:

For in Paul's view, God's larger plan requires gentiles to worship the God of Israel *as gentiles*, not as proselytes or something else. Paul allies himself here with the Jewish eschatological expectation that God will establish his kingdom for Israel and for favored nations. As the apostle to the gentiles, he sees himself in the tradition of the prophets who call gentiles to Jerusalem on the Day of the Lord, when "all the nations shall stream to [the Lord's house]" (Isa. 2:2). As Paula Fredriksen has argued, this eschatological pilgrimage tradition—both in Paul and in earlier Jewish literature—envisions gentiles turning to God as non-Jews, not as proselytes.

Similar arguments are put forward by Nanos,[14] Fredriksen,[15] Elliott[16] and Ehrensperger.[17]

As I have indicated already, I find this an appealing reading of Paul, and I continue to wish that I could find it persuasive. One of its appealing features is that it allows us to construct a smooth and non-disjunctive alignment between Paul's new gospel and his "former life in Judaism."[18] But two difficulties present themselves to me—one lighter, the other more fundamental. First, after spending a lot of time investigating the place of non-Jews in Jewish eschatological expectations, I remain unconvinced that the status of non-Jews in this material is as sharply delineated as has been made out here.[19] To be sure, there was a widespread expectation (albeit not universal) that non-Jews would share in the benefits of Israel's end-time redemption; in this I agree fully with the contributors under discussion here. But I am not as sure that these end-time pilgrims are necessarily expected to be categorically differentiated from Jews as far as Torah observance is concerned. Ehrensperger herself has observed, for example, that Philo anticipates a time when "each nation would abandon its

---

14. "Paul's argument here [Rom 3:29-31] revolves around the conviction that the awaited time of restoration of the nations as well as of Israel has begun, so that one need no longer be a member of the nation Israel to be reconciled to the God of all creation."

15. "Neither 'Jews' of a special sort (that is, *proselytoi*) nor 'normal' pagans (that is, people who showed respect to their own gods), they occupied a social and religious no-man's land. *Eschatologically*, however, they represented a population long anticipated within centuries of Jewish restoration theology: they were pagans-saved-at-the-End." Further, "these end-time pagans do not thereby 'become' Jews. Rather, they enter God's kingdom *as ethnē*, but they do not worship idols any more."

16. "In a variety of traditions, Jewish literature gives evidence of the expectation that at the last days, non-Jews would turn from idols to recognize the true God. That did not mean that they would stop being non-Jews."

17. "These people are not seen as becoming part of Israel, but they worship God as foreigners because God's house is now a house of prayer for all peoples (Isa. 56:7)."

18. As Elliott observes, "The consequence [of Paul's vision] would have been an abrupt about-face from persecuting the assemblies, but this turn would have been motivated and remains completely explicable within categories supplied by the Jewish apocalypses."

19. See Terence Donaldson, *Judaism and the Gentiles: Jewish Patterns of Universalism (to 135 CE)* (Waco, TX: Baylor University Press, 2007), 503–505.

peculiar ways, and, throwing overboard their ancestral customs, turn to honoring our laws alone" (*Mos.* 2.44). Similar expectations (i.e., of Torah-observing *ethnē* in the end times) are found in a number of other texts from the Second Temple period.[20] Given that one of the central biblical accounts of the end-time pilgrimage of the nations describes them as journeying to Jerusalem to learn God's ways, "for out of Zion shall go forth the law (*tôrāh*)" (Isa. 2:2-4),[21] this should not be surprising.

Now my intention here is not to argue the opposite case—that this material expects such participating non-Jews to become end-time proselytes, as it were. As I have pointed out elsewhere, there are a number of other texts that seem to imply that participating non-Jews would not become full Torah observers.[22] My point is that the pertinent material is ambiguous. Indeed, in most cases one gets the impression that the writers of this material were not very interested in the question.

If this is so, it makes it difficult to argue that anyone who (1) expected non-Jews to participate in end-time redemption, and (2) who believed that the age to come was beginning to dawn, would conclude, as a necessary inference, that (3) non-Jews who had turned to the God of Jacob should be forbidden to learn God's ways as they were set out in the Torah (to echo the language of Isa. 2:2-4). Of course, Paul (or anyone else "within Judaism") may have had his own reasons for interpreting Jewish restoration eschatology in this way. If so, however, these reasons would need to be identified and articulated. The "gospel that [he] proclaimed among the *ethnē*" (Gal.

---

20. *T. Levi* 18:9; *T. Naph.* 3:2; *Sib. Or.* 3:791, 757-758; 5:265.
21. If Johnson Hodge is right in saying that Paul "sees himself in the tradition of the prophets who call gentiles to Jerusalem on the Day of the Lord, when 'all the nations shall stream to [the Lord's house]' (Isa. 2:2)," one might readily expect him to encourage—rather than prohibit—full observance of the Torah that goes forth from Zion.
22. *Pss. Sol.* 17:28, 34; *Sib. Or.* 5:493; Tob. 14:5-7; *1 En.* 90:30-38; *2 Bar.* 72.

2:2) cannot be derived from eschatological pilgrimage traditions *tout court*; some intervening step would need to be added.

But is it even the case that Paul's gospel to the *ethnē* is to be accounted for on the basis of these particular eschatological expectations at all? This is the more fundamental question that I want to raise. Of course, eschatology has to be part of it. Paul sees Jesus as Israel's messiah, after all (Rom. 9:4-5); Christ-believers are those "on whom the ends of the ages has come" (1 Cor. 10:11); Christ's resurrection makes him "the first fruits of those who have fallen asleep" (1 Cor. 15:20); and so on. I have no quarrel with Nanos's "chronometrical gospel"[23] or Fredriksen's description of Paul and the other early apostles as "[k]nowing what time it was on God's clock (Rom. 13:11), racing in the (for all they knew) brief wrinkle in time between Christ's resurrection and his second coming (1 Cor. 15)." My question has to do with how Paul arrived at "the gospel that [he] proclaimed among the *ethnē*" (Gal. 2:2), with its peculiar profile, and whether his arrival point was determined by a route that went through the territory of Jewish restoration eschatology.

Given the importance of Romans 11 for contemporary endeavors to locate Paul "within Judaism," this is an appropriate place to start. How does Paul envisage the relationship between "Jewish restoration" and the inclusion of the *ethnē* in the eschatological scenario that is sketched out in the chapter? Several aspects are particularly striking.

First, Paul states—and repeats the statement two additional times for good measure—that the inclusion of the *ethnē* has been made possible by Israel's "stumbling," "defeat," or "rejection": through Israel's "stumbling" (*paraptōma*), "salvation has come to the *ethnē*" (v.

---

23. "The message in which they have believed involves the (chronometrical) propositional claim that the end of the ages has begun within the midst of the present age, initiating the reconciliation of the *kosmos*."

11); Israel's "defeat" (*hēttēma*) has produced "riches for the *ethnē*" (v. 12); Israel's "rejection" (*apobolē*) has brought about the "reconciliation of the world" (*katallagē kosmou*; v. 15). To be sure, in each case the emphasis lies elsewhere. In each case these statements form the protasis of a simple conditional sentence, the sentence as a whole carrying out an *a minore ad maius* form of argumentation. If Israel's current negative situation (stumbling / defeat / rejection) has produced such positive results (salvation / riches / reconciliation for the *ethnē* and the world), how much greater will be the results of the emergence of a more positive situation (Israel's "fullness" [*plērōma*; v. 12] / "acceptance" [*proslēmpsis*; v. 15]).[24] The way in which Paul states his argument in verses 11-15 indicates clearly that he fully expects the change in Israel's situation to take place. In other words, the emphasis falls not on present failure but on future blessing. This leads, however, to a second aspect.

In verses 25-26, Paul returns to this line of argument but takes it one step further. This time what has opened up the possibility of salvation for the *ethnē* is described as a situation of "hardening" (*pōrōsis*) that has come upon Israel (more precisely, "part of Israel"). Again, we find the expectation that Israel's current negative situation will be replaced by a positive one, though here stated more explicitly. Indeed, what comes into view here is a clear statement of Jewish restoration eschatology: "And so all Israel will be saved; as it is written: 'Out of Zion will come the Deliverer . . .'" This eschatological state of affairs has already been hinted at, in that in verse 15 the expected "how much greater" state of affairs seems to be the resurrection era itself ("life from the dead"). Taken together with the previous point, this seems to suggest that what made salvation possible for non-Jews was the postponement or delay of Israel's

24. For a more detailed analysis of this argument, see Donaldson, *Paul and the Gentiles*, 215–23.

restoration. If Israel had not stumbled, there would have been no opportunity for the *ethnē* to get in the race at all. Looked at from a different angle, it is when the "fullness (*plērōma*) of the *ethnē* has come in" that the salvation of Israel will take place. The achievement of the "fullness (*plērōma*) of the *ethnē*" serves to trigger the full appearance of the eschatological age.

This, in turn, leads to the third striking aspect of the scenario. Paul's identification of the eschatological trigger event as the "incoming" (*eiselthē*) of the "*fullness* of the *ethnē*" seems to suggest that at this point the period of gentile salvation will come to an end. In this point, at least, an aspect of the Romans 11 scenario finds its counterpart elsewhere in Paul's letters. It is those who are "of Christ" who will be made alive at his Parousia (1 Cor. 15:23); it is the "sons of light" who can anticipate salvation, while "sudden destruction" will come upon all others (1 Thess. 5:3-10); "now is the acceptable time, now is the day of salvation" (2 Cor. 6:2). Although Romans 11:11-26 seems to anticipate a future day of salvation for Israel, there is little indication, either in Romans or elsewhere, that Paul expects any grand pilgrimage of the nations on the other side of the Parousia.[25]

For present purposes, what is particularly striking about these three aspects is that, taken together, they represent an eschatological scenario that does not readily conform to the pattern of Jewish restoration eschatology. In the latter, the future inclusion of the *ethnē* is predicated on the restoration of Israel. The issue is not simply one of sequence, though it is that: the redemption of the *ethnē* follows

25. This is not to overlook Paul's universalist-sounding language (see, e.g., M. Eugene Boring, "The Language of Universal Salvation in Paul," *Journal of Biblical Literature* 105 [1986]: 269–92), although I do not think that it provides counter-evidence here. I do, however, recognize the force of Fredriksen's objection: "The resurrection of the dead, the transformation of the living, of history and of the cosmos, of heaven and of earth, all culminating in the redemption of, say, some three to four thousand people? It is possible, of course. But it is hard to imagine Paul's thinking so small, especially when we consider the traditions of Jewish restoration theology in which he stands."

the restoration of Israel (e.g., Tob. 14:6; *1 En.* 90:30-38).[26] Rather, it is precisely the restoration of Israel that brings about a change of heart among the *ethnē*. In Zechariah 8:20-23, for example, it is because "we have heard that God is with you" that "many peoples and strong nations" join them "to seek the Lord of hosts in Jerusalem." Likewise in *Sib. Or.* 3:702-723, it is precisely the divine preservation of the "sons of the great God" through a time of final judgment that leads "all islands and cities" to worship God at the temple and to "ponder the Law of the Most High God." Speaking in a different register, Philo suggests that, when the prospects of the Jews begin to flourish, "each nation [will] abandon its peculiar ways and . . . turn to honoring our laws alone" (*Mos.* 2.43-44).[27] In the strand of Jewish restoration eschatology that anticipated a positive place for the *ethnē*, then, the inclusion of the *ethnē* comes about as a result of the restoration of Israel. Paul's scenario, in which the inclusion of the *ethnē* is made possible by the failure of Israel[28] seems to turn this (eschato-)logic on its head.

Of course, the basic shape of early Jewish Christ-belief, with two eschatological focal points (resurrection and Parousia) in place of a more singular end-time restoration, would necessarily require some reformulation of Jewish restoration eschatology and the place of non-Jews within it. Still, the fact that Paul is prepared to predicate the inclusion of the *ethnē* not on Israel's restoration but on their rejection (albeit temporary)[29] means that any attempt to derive his gospel to the

26. Indeed, the sequence is readily apparent in virtually all the pertinent material; see the summary in Donaldson, *Judaism and the Gentiles*, 499-502.
27. On the eschatological underpinnings of this passage, see ibid., 231-35.
28. However this is to be understood. For a more detailed discussion of how Israel's "stumbling" (etc.) is to be understood, see Donaldson, *Paul and the Gentiles*, 219, and Donaldson, "Jewish Christianity, Israel's Stumbling and the *Sonderweg* Reading of Paul," *Journal for the Study of the New Testament* 29 (2006): 27-54.
29. Here one might also mention the fact that Paul is ready to see this scenario as a mystery (v. 25)—that is, something unknown in the past but recently revealed. His description of the

ethnē from Jewish restoration eschatology needs to argue the case, not simply assume it.

Here a point of clarification is in order. I am not necessarily wanting to argue that this scenario in anything like its form in Romans 11 predates the writing of the epistle or represents the framework within which he carried out his mission to the *ethnē* from the outset. I am fully prepared to see his argument here as a contingent formulation in the context of an occasional letter. My point has to do less with the surface of his argument and more with the underlying convictions that seem to shape and constrain it. That is, the logical moves that he is prepared to make in this chapter are not easily accounted for if one assumes that his convictions about the inclusion of the *ethnē* arise from Jewish restoration eschatology or end-time pilgrimage patterns of thought.

In addition to this point of clarification, a concession. There are places where Paul seems to be prepared to describe the blessings enjoyed by non-Jewish Christ-believers as somehow derived from, or a participation in, blessings that belong in the first instance to Jewish Christ-believers. One instance of this is his rationale for the collection project in Romans 15:25-27. This material gift to the saints in Jerusalem, he says, is an appropriate way for non-Jewish Christ-believers to acknowledge their indebtedness, since they as *ethnē*, "have come to share in their spiritual blessings." Another is the olive tree analogy of Romans 11:17-21, where the wild olive shoot (non-Jewish Christ-believers) have been grafted in to join the branches that remain[30] in their enjoyment of the tree's richness. Yet another is the statement in Galatians 3:13-14 that "Christ redeemed

mission to the *ethnē* as a *mustērion* makes it difficult to see it as a smooth and straightforward inference from Jewish restoration eschatology.

30. The key phrase in v. 17 is *en autois*; the NRSV rendering "in their place" (i.e., in place of the branches that have been cut off) is untenable.

us from the curse of the law . . . in order that the blessing of Abraham might come to the *ethnē*." The distinction that he makes at the outset of this section (2:15—3:29) between "we ourselves [who] are Jews by birth" and "sinners of the *ethnē*" (2:15) provides grounds for seeing a similar ethnic distinction in the "us" / *ethnē* contrast in 3:13-14.[31]

In each of these passages, then, the blessings currently experienced by non-Jewish Christ-believers are made possible in some way by blessings already bestowed on Jews. Such passages, together with the fact that Paul sees the existence of a Jewish "remnant" as significant (Rom. 11:1-10) and sees the "hardening" as applying only to "part" of Israel (11:25), might provide an opportunity to derive his mission to the *ethnē* from Jewish restoration patterns of thought. That is, the community of Jewish Christ-believers represents the "remnant" of Israel, the present "part" of the "all Israel" that will eventually experience salvation. Their present experience of the blessings of salvation thus represents (in this line of argument) the kind of "restoration of Israel" that opens the door to the inclusion of the *ethnē*. While I am not convinced that such an interpretation can be carried out in a thoroughgoing way, this is one aspect of Paul's discourse in which it might find some traction.

The *Ethnē* and the Fatherhood of Abraham

The second issue that I want to explore here has to do more directly with the distinctive profile that Paul imposes on his non-Jewish Christ-believers. One aspect of this has been touched on already: Paul's insistence that these non-Jewish believers are not to undergo circumcision or to take on any of the other aspects of the Torah that serve to differentiate Jews from non-Jews; that is, they are not to

---

31. Of course, this would also have the effect of seeing Jews as (also) under the "curse of the law," which may be problematical for some attempts to locate Paul within Judaism.

become proselytes. In the previous section I argued that this cannot be accounted for in any straightforward way from expectations about the inclusion of non-Jews in Jewish restoration eschatology. Here I want to pick up a second aspect of the profile—Paul's insistence that such uncircumcised believers can nevertheless call Abraham their father (*patera pantōn tōn pisteuontōn di'akrobustias*; Rom. 4:11).

Several contributors have commented on the distinctiveness of this profile, noting that it results in an ambiguous or even anomalous status for Paul's non-Jewish Christ-believers. Nanos, for one, speaks of their "anomalous identity." For Fredriksen, they "occupied a social and religious no-man's land." Johnson Hodge, in turn, describes Paul as "constructing an identity for these gentiles-in-Christ that resists classification. These gentiles occupy an in-between space, hovering around the borders of identities that they are not quite." As we have seen, there is a general agreement among the contributors that this status is to be understood as the appearance in the present of a category that originated as an expectation pertaining to the eschatological future. Nevertheless, there are differences among them as to the specific character of the anomaly.

In Fredriksen's characterization of Paul's perspective, the profile of these non-Jewish Christ-believers conforms neither to that of the proselyte nor to that of the god-fearer:

> It is on this point precisely that the radical novelty of the gospel message made itself socially felt. Yes, pagan culture—and Diaspora Jewish culture—were long familiar with "converts" and with god-fearers. But Paul's pagans fell into neither category. *Like* converts, his pagans made an exclusive commitment to the god of Israel; *unlike* converts, they did not assume Jewish ancestral practices (food ways, Sabbath, circumcision, and so on). *Like* god-fearers, Paul's people retained their native ethnicities; *unlike* god-fearers, they no longer worshiped their native gods. *Paul's pagans-in-Christ are neither converts nor god-fearers.*

For her part on the other hand, Johnson Hodge is prepared to align such "pagans-in-Christ" with "god-fearers": "Thus Paul's portrayal of gentiles-in-Christ fits into a larger trend among Jewish writers who tend to view the status of sympathetic gentiles as in-between." She adds to this, however, the fact that Paul is also prepared to see these believers as part of Abraham's "seed" (*sperma*). Noting that, in one strand of Jewish tradition (e.g., *Jubilees*), this idea is used to construct an identity for Israel as the "seed of Abraham" that categorically excludes the *ethnē*, she sees Paul as engaging in a different kind of identity construction, one in which "gentiles are actually included in the blessed lineage from the beginning." Nanos's description of Paul's non-Jewish believers in Christ as "neither guests nor proselytes but full members alongside of Jews" seems to be depicting the same sort of unprecedented and anomalous identity.

For my part, while I agree that there is an anomaly in Paul's categorization of the *ethnē*-in-Christ that deserves our attention, I remain unconvinced about Fredriksen's description of "god-fearers." To be sure, the material dealing with non-Jewish sympathizers reflects a considerable range; there certainly were those who associated with the Jewish community without ceasing to worship their own native gods—and, apparently, without any Jewish insistence that they do so.[32] At the same time, however, there is considerable evidence indicating that many did abandon polytheistic worship—those satirized by Juvenal, for example, who, without having yet undergone circumcision, "worship nothing but the clouds and the spirit of the sky" (*Satires* 14.96-106); or Izates, who like his mother had come "to worship God after the manner of the Jewish tradition" and for whom the only remaining step in becoming "genuinely a Jew" was circumcision (Josephus, *Ant.* 20.34-38).[33] In

---

32. See the evidence summarized in Donaldson, *Judaism and the Gentiles*, 473.

addition, one can also adduce the extended Jewish polemic against polytheism and "idol worship," especially in texts that at least envisage the possibility of non-Jews actually giving exclusive devotion to Israel's God yet without becoming full converts.[34] I remain unconvinced, then, that this combination (non-Jewish sympathizers who were not proselytes but who nevertheless gave exclusive devotion to Israel's God) represents an anomalous aspect in Paul's construction of identity. The combination was not the only acceptable option to be sure, but it certainly was not without precedent.

In my view, the truly anomalous aspect is Paul insistence that uncircumcised *ethnē*-in-Christ are at the same time full members of Abraham's "seed" (*sperma*). While Johnson Hodge has rightly called our attention to this, its significance has not been fully recognized.

In both Galatians and Romans, the climax of Paul's argument about the inclusion of non-Jews is that *ethnē* who are "in Christ" are *ipso facto* part of Abraham's "seed" (*sperma*; Gal. 3:29; also Rom. 4:13-18). Now most of Paul's argument in Galatians 3 and Romans 4 falls within the traditional structures of the discourse in Genesis about Abraham and the *ethnē*—Abraham as the "father of a multitude of *ethnē*" (Gen. 17:4-5); Abraham and his family being a source of blessing for "all the *ethnē*" (Gen. 22:18; cf. 12:3; 28:14); and so on. The Genesis narrative makes a sharp distinction, however, between these *ethnē* and Abraham's seed (*sperma* in Greek, rendering the Hebrew *zera'*). In Genesis 17, Abraham's "seed" is linked categorically with the covenant of circumcision: "This is my covenant, which you shall keep, between me and you and your seed after you: Every male

---

33. See also Shaye J. D. Cohen's category "Venerating the God of the Jews and denying or ignoring all other gods"; Cohen, *The Beginnings of Jewishness: Boundaries, Varieties, Uncertainties* (Berkeley: University of California Press, 1999), 150-54.
34. See, e.g., Philo *Virt.* 65; *Sib. Or.* 3:544-550, 624-629; and Donaldson, *Judaism and the Gentiles*, 493-98.

among you shall be circumcised. . . . Any uncircumcised male . . . shall be cut off from his people; he has broken my covenant" (vv. 10, 14).[35] While uncircumcised *ethnē* might be able to call Abraham "father," apart from the covenant of circumcision they are categorically excluded from Abraham's "seed."[36] In addition to the key passage in Genesis 17, *sperma, zera'* and equivalents are used consistently to denote Israel as a distinct covenant people, often in explicit contrast with *ethnē or goyim*.[37]

Paul could hardly have been unaware of the significance of *sperma*, given that he cites Genesis 17 in the context of an argument about Abraham's "seed" (in Rom. 4:17-18, where 17:5 is cited twice). What is striking, however, is that the passage he cites—"I have made you the father of many nations"—provided him with a much simpler way of identifying uncircumcised *ethnē*-in-Christ with Abraham and establishing their right to call him "father." He could simply have argued that Christ was the means by which the promises made to Abraham—that he would be the "father of a multitude of *ethnē*" and that "by [his] seed (*sperma*) all the nations of the earth shall gain blessing for themselves" (LXX Gen. 22:18; also 26:4)—was being fulfilled. Instead, he makes an exegetical move that lands him on untenable ground. He attempts to square the covenantal circle by applying to uncircumcised *ethnē* an identifier to which non-Jews were not entitled unless they ceased to be *ethnē* and became proselytes. The move seems not only to be one that could have been

---

35. *Sperma* appears seven times in LXX Genesis 17.

36. In LXX Gen. 22:18, for example, it is by Abraham's *sperma* that "all the nations of the earth [shall] gain blessing for themselves"; similarly LXX Gen. 26:4; 28:14.

37. *Sperma* appears in explicit contrast with the *ethnē* in LXX Gen. 26:4; Deut. 10:15; 1 Esd. 8:67; Ps. 105 (106): 27; Isa. 61:9; Wis 10:15; *Pss. Sol.* 9:9; presumably the same *zera' / goyim* binary underlies *Jub.* 2:20-21; 15:11-14; 16:16-18, 25-26. Where *sperma* appear without this explicit contrast to the *ethnē* (e.g., LXX Esther 9:27; Ps. 104 [105]:6; Isa. 41:8; Ezek. 20:5; 4 Macc. 18:1; *Pss. Sol.* 18:3; also *Jub.* 1:7-8), an implicit contrast is nevertheless present. Johnson Hodge has drawn our attention to the idea of the "holy seed" in Ezra and *Jubilees*.

easily avoided, but also one that Paul was determined to make: in both Romans 4 and Galatians 3 it comes as the climax or ultimate goal of his argument.[38] Why then did he choose such a difficult move when a simpler alternative was ready to hand? It is also worth noting in passing that this simpler alternative ("by [Abraham's] seed (*sperma*) all the nations of the earth shall gain blessing for themselves" [LXX Gen. 22:18]) readily lends itself to eschatological pilgrimage patterns of thought.

This is not the place to try to make sense of this puzzling aspect of the identity that Paul constructs for his *ethnē*-in-Christ. For present purposes it is sufficient to observe that the simpler option—that is, Christ as the means of fulfillment for the promise made to Abraham that he would be the father of many *ethnē*—would have provided a much more appropriate basis for any of the interpretations of Paul's project of identity construction that have been carried out in preceding chapters. To make the point more forcefully, the argument in these interpretations—that Paul's distinctive approach to the *ethnē* can be accounted for on the basis of an eschatological model that requires the distinction between non-Jews and Jews to be maintained—faces significant obstacles. It simply does not work, at least in any straightforward way. If this were Paul's starting point, why would he then ascribe an identity (*sperma Abraham*) that blurs this (supposedly essential) distinction in a fundamental way, especially when a simpler and more straightforward option was available? In short, to place Paul appropriately "within Judaism," I think more work needs to be done to make sense of his project of identity construction, a project that seems to have no real precedent or analogy within Judaism.[39]

---

38. It is probably also connected with his repeated assertions that, in some respects at least, there is "no distinction" (*ou gar estin diastolē*) between Jews and non-Jews (Rom. 3:22; 10:12; also Gal. 3:28).

Paul within Judaism

The preceding two sections have been engaged with the identity that Paul ascribes to his *ethnē*-in-Christ and its relationship with Jewish patterns of thought and expectation concerning the inclusion of non-Jews in the blessings of the age to come. I would like to conclude by placing this discussion within the more general question of what it might mean to talk about "Paul within Judaism."

To this end, it is apparent that a number of elements were intertwined in the preceding discussion that might helpfully be separated out. One distinction has to do with the conceptual and the sociological. The chapters themselves and my discussion here have dealt both with conceptual matters (symbolic universes, ethnic maps, eschatological scenarios) and with the lived experiences of human groups. In asking whether Paul and his mission to the *ethnē* can be located "within Judaism," are we asking about whether it is simply consistent with Jewish symbolic worlds, or about whether it took place in any real way within a Jewish social world? Another distinction is between Paul on one hand and his communities on the

39. My argument has been that prior to his Damascus experience Paul can be identified with a strand of Judaism that held that the only way in which non-Jews might have a portion in the age to come was to become proselytes in this age. In the terms of Galatians 5:11, he used to "preach circumcision" or, with reference to Josephus's account of King Izates, he used to play a role akin to that of Eleazar. The effect of his Damascus experience was to alter some of the convictional substance of his previous approach to the *ethnē*, but not its structure. That is, he continued to believe that for non-Jews to have a portion in the age to come they needed to become full members of Abraham's *sperma* in the present, and that this opportunity would come to an end with the future redemption of "all Israel." However, Christ had come to replace Torah as the means by which non-Jews could become incorporated into Abraham's *sperma*. For details, see Donaldson, *Paul and the Gentiles*. While this reconstruction continues to make sense to me, I realize that its primary value has to do with explaining how Paul might have arrived at his anomalous position about the status identity of his *ethnē*-in-Christ. It is not adequate in itself as an account of the position itself—how it played out on the ground; how it would have been perceived by others (Jewish and non-Jewish Christ-believers; Jewish and non-Jewish outsiders). In particular, while many of his later interpreters have understood Paul to be saying that in Christ any distinction between Jew and not-Jew was done away with, it is clear that for Paul *Ioudaioi* and *ethnē* continue to be distinct and fundamentally significant identity markers.

other. In asking whether Paul can be located "within Judaism," are we thinking just of Paul himself or are we asking about the location of his communities of *ethnē*-in-Christ as well?[40] Both options are complicated, but they are distinct. One could imagine, for example, a Paul who remained embedded within a Jewish world but communities of *ethnē*-in-Christ who existed quite apart from Jewish communities. A third distinction has to do with the perceiver. In asking whether Paul and his mission can be located "within Judaism," we need to ask who is doing the locating: Paul himself? The *ethnē*-in-Christ themselves? Jewish Christ-believers? Other Jews? Other *ethnē*? Modern scholars? One can well expect that perceptions will differ considerably from one to the next.

What emerges from this is a recognition that "Paul within Judaism" is a complex question, with sets of variables (or at least distinct points) arrayed along three axes:

1. *Domain*: If "Judaism" is a domain that someone can be "in," is it primarily (1.1) conceptual or (1.2) social?
2. *Entity*: What is it that might be located within this domain—(2.1) Paul or (2.2) his communities of *ethnē*-in-Christ?
3. *Perceiver*: From whose point of view is the determination of

40. In their chapters, K. Hedner Zetterholm and Runesson (who, because of the topics I wanted to explore in my response, regrettably did not come into my discussion to the same extent as the others) are interested both in Paul and in his congregations. Hedner Zetterholm's discussion of the practical realities of living in accordance with the Torah in concrete human situations probably pertains more to the Jewish Paul than to his non-Jewish congregations ("nothing in his reasoning seems to indicate that he had abandoned Jewish law"). Still, the congregations come into view in her discussion of 1 Corinthians 8–10, which is to be seen "an example of first-century Jewish halakah for Jesus-oriented gentiles" and not as a case of "a violation of Jewish law." Runesson's chapter represents preliminary ground-clearing work, as he demonstrates that use of the terms "Christianity" and "church" have the functional effect of locating Paul "outside Judaism" from the outset. By choosing to deal with "church" (in contrast to synagogue) as well as "Christianity" (in contrast to "Judaism"), he necessarily includes Paul's congregations within his purview: "Paul's use of *ekklēsia* indicates that as the 'apostle to the nations' he is inviting non-Jews to participate in specific Jewish institutional settings, where they may share with Jews the experience of living with the risen Messiah. . . ."

location being made—that of (3.1) Paul, (3.2) *ethnē*-in-Christ, (3.3) Jewish Christ-believers, (3.4) other Jews, (3.5) other *ethnē*, or (3.6) outside scholarly observers?[41]

Of course, the alternatives in each case are legitimate ones; there is no single "right choice" and all of the possible combinations are worth pursuing. At the risk of straying too far into the mathematical realm, then, one can say that the answer to the question is likewise complex, depending on the coordinates that result from choices made along the three axes.

Or perhaps there should be four, since both "Paul's mission" and "Judaism" were caught up in the flow of time. With respect to Paul's communities of *ethnē*-in-Christ at least, we must expect that their location with respect to the Jewish world was likewise in flux. What did the picture look like as we move from point to point along this axis—after Paul's death? After the destruction of Jerusalem? When the Pastoral Epistles were composed? At the time of Justin Martyr and Marcion? In other words, what was the fate of Paul's project throughout the process that led from "apostolic Judaism"[42] to "Christianity"?

41. This set of alternatives leads to another distinction, namely, between "categorization" (identities ascribed from without) and "group identification" (internally constructed self-definitions). For the distinction, see Richard Jenkins, *Social Identity* (London: Routledge, 2004), 20–22, and chapter 8 ("Groups and Categories"). Of course the two are not isolated but instead are integrally related in a dialectical process.
42. To use the term proposed by Nanos and Runesson.

Bibliography

Adkins, Lisa, and Beverly Skeggs, eds. *Feminism after Bourdieu*. Oxford: Blackwell, 2004.

Alcalay, Reuben. *The Complete Hebrew-English Dictionary*. 3 vols. Tel Aviv: Massada, 1990.

Arendt, Hannah. *The Human Condition*. Chicago: Chicago University Press, 1958.

Baird, William. *From Deism to Tübingen*. Vol. 1 of *History of New Testament Research*. Minneapolis: Fortress Press, 1992.

Barclay, J. M. G. *Jews in the Mediterranean Diaspora: From Alexander to Trajan (323 BCE–117 CE)*. Edinburgh: T&T Clark, 1996.

———. *Pauline Churches and Diaspora Jews*. Tübingen: Mohr Siebeck, 2011.

Barr, James. *The Semantics of Biblical Language*. Oxford: Oxford University Press, 1961.

Barret, Charles K. "Things Sacrificed to Idols." In *Essays on Paul*, 40–59. London: SPCK, 1982.

Baur, Ferdinand C. "Die Christuspartei in der korinthischen Gemeinde, der Gegensatz des petrinischen und paulinischen Christenthums in der ältesten Kirche, der Apostel Petrus in Rom." *Tübingen Zeitschrift für Theologie* 4 (1831): 61–206.

———. *Paul the Apostle of Jesus Christ*. 2 vols. Translated by E. Zeller. London: Williams & Norgate, 1876.

Beker, J. Christiaan. *Paul, the Apostle: The Triumph of God in Life and Thought.* Edinburgh: T & T Clark, 1980.

Berger, Peter L. *The Sacred Canopy: Elements of a Sociological Theory of Religion.* Garden City, NJ: Doubleday, 1969.

Berkovits, Eliezer. *Not in Heaven: The Nature and Function of Halakhah.* New York: Ktav, 1983.

Berkowitz, Beth A. *Defining Jewish Difference: From Antiquity to the Present.* Cambridge: Cambridge University Press, 2012.

Bernat, David A. *Sign of the Covenant: Circumcision in the Priestly Tradition.* Ancient Israel and Its Literature 3. Atlanta: Society of Biblical Literature, 2009.

Betz, Hans D. *The Sermon on the Mount: A Commentary on the Sermon on the Mount, Including the Sermon on the Plain.* Hermeneia. Minneapolis: Fortress Press, 1995.

Bhabha, Homi K. *The Location of Culture.* London: Routledge, 1994.

Bialik, Haim N. *Halachah and Aggadah.* Translated by Leon Simon. London: Education Department of the Zionist Federation of Great Britain and Ireland, 1944.

Binder, Donald D. *Into the Temple Courts: The Place of the Synagogues in the Second Temple Period.* Atlanta: Society of Biblical Literature, 1999.

Bloch, René. *Moses und der Mythos.* Leiden: Brill, 2010.

Blumenfeld, Bruno. *The Political Paul: Justice, Democracy and Kingship in a Hellenistic Framework.* Journal for the Study of the New Testament Supplement Series 210. Sheffield: Sheffield Academic Press, 2010.

Bodel, John, and Saul M. Olyan, eds. *Household and Family Religion.* Malden, MA: Blackwell, 2008.

Boer, Martinus de. "Paul's Mythologizing Program in Romans 5–8." In *Apocalyptic Paul: Cosmos and Anthropos in Romans 5–8*, edited by Beverly Roberts Gaventa, 1–20. Waco, TX: Baylor University Press, 2013.

Boring, M. Eugene. "The Language of Universal Salvation in Paul." *Journal of Biblical Literature* 105 (1986): 269–92.

Bourdieu, Pierre. *Pascalian Meditations*. Oxford: Polity, 2000.

Bousset, Wilhelm. *Die Religion des Judentums im neutestamentlichen Zeitalter*. Berlin: Reuther & Reichard, 1903.

Boyarin, Daniel. *A Radical Jew: Paul and the Politics of Identity*. Berkeley: University of California Press, 1994.

Brayford, Sarah A. "The Domestication of Sarah: From Jewish Matriarch to Hellenistic Matron." *Studies in Jewish Civilisation* 14 (2003): 1–21.

Brooten, Bernadette J. *Love Between Women: Early Christian Responses to Female Homoeroticism*. Chicago: University of Chicago Press, 1996.

———. *Women Leaders in Ancient Synagogues: Inscriptional Evidence and Background Issues*. Chico, CA: Scholars, 1982.

Brown, Francis, Samuel R. Driver, and Charles A. Briggs, eds. *A Hebrew-English Lexicon of the Old Testament*. Oxford: Clarendon, 1939.

Brown, Lesley, ed. *The New Shorter Oxford English Dictionary on Historical Principles*. Oxford: Clarendon, 1993.

Brubaker, Rogers. *Ethnicity Without Groups*. Cambridge, MA: Harvard University Press, 2004.

Brunt, John C. "Rejected, Ignored, or Misunderstood? The Fate of Paul's Approach to the Problem of Food Offered to Idols in Early Christianity." *New Testament Studies* 31 (1985): 113–24.

Bryan, Christopher. *Render to Caesar: Jesus, The Early Church, and the Roman Superpower*. New York: Oxford University Press, 2005.

Buell, Denise Kimber. *Why This New Race: Ethnic Reasoning in Early Christianity*. New York: Columbia University Press, 2005.

Campbell, William S. "The Addressees of Paul's Letter to the Romans: Assemblies of God in House Churches or Synagogues?" In *Between Gospel and Election: Explorations in the Interpretation of Romans 9–11*, edited by J. Ross Wagner and Florian Wilk, 171–95. Tübingen: Mohr Siebeck, 2010.

———. "'As Having and as Not Having': Paul, Circumcision, and Indifferent Things in 1 Corinthians 7:17-32a." In *Unity and Diversity in Christ: Interpreting Paul in Context: Collected Essays*, edited by William S. Campbell, 106–26. Eugene, OR: Cascade Books, 2013.

———. *Paul and the Creation of Christian Identity*. London: T & T Clark, 2006.

———. *Unity and Diversity in Christ: Interpreting Paul in Context*. Eugene, OR: Cascade Books, 2013.

Carson, D. A., Peter Thomas O'Brien, and Mark A. Seifrid, eds. *Justification and Variegated Nomism*. Vol. 2 of *The Paradoxes of Paul*. Tübingen: Mohr Siebeck, 2004.

Carter, Warren. *The Roman Empire and the New Testament*. Nashville: Abingdon, 2006.

Castelli, Elizabeth. *Imitating Paul: A Discourse of Power*. Louisville: Westminster John Knox, 1991.

Chaniotis, Angelos. "The Jews of Aphrodias: New Evidence and Old Problems." *Scripta Classica Israelica* 21 (2002): 209–42.

Charles, Ronald. *Paul and the Politics of Diaspora*. Minneapolis: Fortress Press, 2014.

Ciampa, Roy E., and Brian S. Rosner. *The First Letter to the Corinthians*. Grand Rapids: Eerdmans, 2010.

Cohen, Shaye J. D. *The Beginnings of Jewishness: Boundaries, Varieties, Uncertainties*. Hellenistic Culture and Society 31. Berkeley: University of California Press, 1999.

———. *Why Aren't Jewish Women Circumcised? Gender and Covenant in Judaism*. Berkeley: University of California Press, 2005.

Collins, Adela Yarbro. *Mark: A Commentary*. Hermeneia. Minneapolis: Fortress Press, 2007.

Concannon, Cavan W. *"When You Were Gentiles": Specters of Ethnicity in Roman Corinth and Paul's Corinthian Correspondence*. New Haven, CT: Yale University Press, 2014.

Deidun, Thomas. "James Dunn and John Ziesler on Romans in New Perspective." *Heythrop Journal* 33 (1992): 79–84.

Donaldson, Terence L. "The 'Curse of the Law' and the Inclusion of the Gentiles: Galatians 3.13-14." *New Testament Studies* 32 (1986): 94–112.

———. "'Gentile Christianity' as a Category in the Study of Christian Origins." *Harvard Theological Review* 106 (2013): 433–58.

———. "Introduction to the Pauline Corpus." In *The Oxford Bible Commentary*, edited by John Barton and John Muddiman, 1062–83. Oxford: Oxford University Press, 2001.

———. "Israelite, Convert, Apostle to the Gentiles: The Origin of Paul's Gentile Mission." In *The Road from Damascus: The Impact of Paul's Conversion on His Life, Thought and Ministry*, edited by Richard N. Longenecker, 62–84. Grand Rapids: Eerdmans, 1997.

———. "Jewish Christianity, Israel's Stumbling and the Sonderweg Reading of Paul." *Journal for the Study of the New Testament* 29 (2006): 27–54.

———. *Jews and Anti-Judaism in the New Testament: Decision Points and Divergent Interpretations.* Waco, TX: Baylor University Press, 2010.

———. *Judaism and the Gentiles: Jewish Patterns of Universalism* (to 135 CE). Waco, TX: Baylor University Press, 2007.

———. *Paul and the Gentiles: Remapping the Apostle's Convictional World.* Minneapolis: Fortress Press, 1997.

———. "In Search of a Paul Neither Lutheran nor Idiosyncratic: James D. G. Dunn's The Theology of Paul the Apostle." *Critical Review of Books in Religion* 11 (1998): 35–55.

Dorff, Elliot N. *For the Love of God and People: A Philosophy of Jewish Law.* Philadelphia: Jewish Publication Society, 2007.

———. *Matters of Life and Death: A Jewish Approach to Modern Medical Ethics.* Philadelphia: Jewish Publication Society, 1998.

———. "A Methodology for Jewish Medical Ethics." In *Contemporary Jewish Ethics and Morality: A Reader*, edited by Elliot N. Dorff and Louis E. Newman, 161–76. New York: Oxford University Press, 1995.

———. Daniel S. Nevins, and Avraham I. Reisner. "Homosexuality, Human Dignity, and Halakhah: A Combined Responsum for the Committee on Jewish Law and Standards," 2006, at http://www.rabbinicalassembly.org/sites/default/files/public/halakhah/teshuvot/20052010/dorff_nevins_reisner_dignity.pdf.

Dunn, James D. G. *A New Perspective in Jesus: What the Quest for the Historical Jesus Missed*. Grand Rapids: Baker Academic, 2005.

———. "The New Perspective on Paul." *Bulletin of the John Rylands Library* 65 (1983): 95–122.

———. *The New Perspective on Paul: Collected Essays*. Tübingen: Mohr Siebeck, 2005.

———. "Paul's Conversion: A Light to 20th Century Disputes." In *The New Perspective on Paul: Collected Essays*, edited by James D. G. Dunn, 341–59. Tübingen: Mohr Siebeck, 2005.

———. *The Theology of Paul the Apostle*. Grand Rapids: Eerdmans, 1998.

———. "Yet Once More – 'The Works of the Law,' A Response." In *The New Perspective on Paul: Collected Essays*, edited by James D. G. Dunn, 207–20. Tübingen: Mohr Siebeck, 2007.

Ehrensperger, Kathy. "'Called to be Saints' – the Identity-Shaping Dimension of Paul's Priestly Discourse in Romans." In *Reading Paul in Context: Explorations in Identity Formation: Essays in Honour of William S. Campbell*, edited by J. Brian Tucker and Kathy Ehrensperger, 90–109. London: T & T Clark, 2010.

———. "Levinas, the Jewish Philosopher Meets Paul, the Jewish Apostle: Reading Romans in the Face of the Other." In *Reading Romans with Contemporary Philosophers and Theologians*, edited by David Odell-Scott, 115–54. London: T & T Clark, 2007.

———. "The Ministry to Jerusalem (Rom 15.31): Paul's Hopes and Fears." In *Erlesenes Jerusalem: Festschrift für Ekkehard W. Stegemann*, edited by Lukas Kundert and Christina Tuor-Kurth, 338–52. Basel: Reinhardt Verlag 2013.

———. *Paul at the Crossroads of Cultures: Theologizing in the Space-Between.* London: Bloomsbury, 2013.

———. *Paul and the Dynamics of Power: Communication and Interaction in the Early Christ-Movement.* London: T & T Clark, 2007.

———. "Paul and Feminism." In *The Oxford Handbook of Pauline Studies*, edited by Barry Matlock. Oxford: Oxford University Press, forthcoming.

———. *That We May Be Mutually Encouraged: Feminism and the New Perspective in Pauline Studies.* London: T & T Clark, 2004.

Eisenbaum, Pamela. "Paul, Polemics, and the Problem of Essentialism." *Biblical Interpretation* 13 (2005): 224–38.

———. *Paul Was Not a Christian: The Original Message of a Misunderstood Apostle.* New York: HarperOne, 2009.

Ellenson, David H. "How to Draw Guidance from a Heritage: Jewish Approaches to Mortal Choices." In *Contemporary Jewish Ethics and Morality: A Reader*, edited by Elliot N. Dorff and Louis E. Newman, 129–39. New York: Oxford University Press, 1995.

Elliott, Neil. *The Arrogance of the Nations: Reading Romans in the Shadow of Empire.* Minneapolis: Fortress Press, 2008.

———. *Liberating Paul: The Justice of God and the Politics of the Apostle.* Maryknoll, NY: Orbis Books, 1994.

———. *The Rhetoric of Romans: Argumentative Constraint and Strategy and Paul's Dialogue with Judaism.* Journal for the Study of the New Testament Supplement Series 45. Sheffield: Sheffield Academic Press, 1990.

Engberg-Petersen, Troels. "'Everything is Clean' and 'Everything That is Not of Faith is Sin': The Logic of Pauline Casuistry in Romans 14.1—15.13." In *Paul, Grace, and Freedom: Essays in Honour of John K.*

Riches, edited by Paul Middleton et al, 22–38. London: T & T Clark, 2008.

Engberg-Pedersen, Troels, ed. *Paul Beyond the Judaism/Hellenism Divide*. Louisville: Westminster John Knox, 2001.

Esler, Philip F. *Conflict and Identity in Romans: The Social Setting of Paul's Letters*. Minneapolis: Fortress Press, 2003.

Feldman, Louis H. *Jew and Gentile in the Ancient World: Attitudes and Interactions from Alexander to Justinian*. Princeton, NJ: Princeton University Press, 1993.

Fisk, Bruce N. "Eating Meat Offered to Idols: Corinthian Behavior and Pauline Response in 1 Corinthians 8–10 (A Response to Gordon Fee)." *Trinity Journal* 10 (1989): 49–70.

Flusser, David. "The Ten Commandments and the New Testament." In *The Ten Commandments in History and Tradition*, edited by Ben-Zion Segal, 219–46. Jerusalem: Magnes, 1990, 219–46.

Fredriksen Paula. *Augustine and the Jews: A Christian Defense of Jews and Judaism*. New Haven, CT: Yale University Press, 2010.

———. *From Jesus to Christ: The Origins of the New Testament Images of Jesus*. New Haven, CT: Yale University Press, 1988.

———. "Judaism, the Circumcision of Gentiles, and Apocalyptic Hope." *Journal of Theological Studies* 42 1991: 558–64.

———. "Judaizing the Nations: The Ritual Demands of Paul's Gospel." *New Testament Studies* 56 (2010): 232–52.

———. "Mandatory Retirement: Ideas in the Study of Christian Origins Whose Time Has Come to Go." *Studies in Religion/Sciences Religieuses* 35 (2006): 231–46.

———. "Paul's Letter to the Romans, the Ten Commandments, and Pagan 'Justification by Faith'." *Journal of Biblical Literature* 133, no. 4 (2014): 801–8.

———. "Paul, Practical Pluralism, and the Invention of Religious Persecution in Roman Antiquity." In *Understanding Religious Pluralism: Perspectives from Religious Studies and Theology*, edited by Peter C. Phan and Jonathan Ray, 87–113. Eugene, OR: Wipf & Stock, 2014.

———. *Sin: The Early History of an Idea*. Princeton, NJ: Princeton University Press, 2012.

———. "What 'Parting of the Ways?'" In *The Ways That Never Parted*, edited by Adam Becker and Annette Y. Reed, 35–63. Tübingen: Mohr Siebeck, 2003.

———, and Oded Irshai. "Christian Anti-Judaism: Polemics and Policies, from the Second to the Seventh Centuries." Vol. 4 of *The Cambridge History of Judaism*, edited by Steven T. Katz, 997–1034. Cambridge: Cambridge University Press, 2006.

Frevel, Christian, ed. *Mixed Marriages: Intermarriage and Group Identity in the Second Temple Period*. New York: T & T Clark, 2011.

Frey, Jörg. "Paul's Jewish Identity." In *Jewish Identity in the Greco-Roman World*, edited by Jörg Frey, Daniel R. Schwartz, and Stephanie Gripentrog, 285–321. Leiden: Brill, 2007.

Gager, John G. *The Origins of Anti-Semitism: Attitudes Toward Judaism in Pagan and Christian Antiquity*. New York: Oxford University Press, 1985.

———. "Paul, the Apostle of Judaism." In *Jesus, Judaism, and Christian Anti-Judaism*, edited by Paula Fredriksen and Adele Reinhartz, 56–76. Louisville: Westminster John Knox, 2002.

Gaston, Lloyd. *Paul and the Torah*. Vancouver: University of British Columbia Press, 1987.

Gerdmar, Anders. *Roots of Theological Anti-Semitism: German Biblical Interpretation and the Jews, from Herder and Semler to Kittel and Bultmann*. Leiden: Brill, 2009.

Gilbert, Gary. "The Making of a Jew: 'God-Fearer' or Convert in the Story of Izates." *Union Seminary Quarterly Review* 44 (1991): 299–313.

Gill, Sam. "The Academic Study of Religion." *Journal of the American Academy of Religion* 62 (1994): 965–75.

Glancy, Jennifer. "Boasting of Beatings (2 Corinthians 11:23-25)." *Journal of Biblical Literature* 123 (2004): 99–135.

———. *Corporeal Knowledge: Early Christian Bodies*. New York: Oxford University Press, 2010.

Graf, Fritz. "Roman Festivals in Syria Palestina." In *The Talmud Yerushalmi and Graeco-Roman Culture*, edited by Peter Shäfer, 435–51. Tübingen: Mohr Siebeck, 2002.

Gruen, Eric S. *Diaspora: Jews Amidst Greeks and Romans*. Cambridge, MA: Harvard University Press, 2002.

———. "Jewish Perspectives on Greek Ethnicity." In *Ancient Perceptions of Greek Ethnicity*, edited by I. Malkin, 347–73. Cambridge, MA: Harvard University Press, 2001.

———. *Rethinking the Other in Antiquity*. Princeton, NJ: Princeton University Press, 2011.

Hafemann, Scott "Paul and His Interpreters." In *Dictionary of Paul and His Letters*, edited by Gerald F. Hawthorne and Ralph P. Martin, 666–79. Downers Grove, IL: InterVarsity, 1993.

Harland, Philip A. *Associations, Synagogues, and Congregations: Claiming a Place in Ancient Mediterranean Society*. Minneapolis: Fortress Press, 2003.

Harrison, James R. *Paul and the Imperial Authorities at Thessalonica and Rome*. WUNT 273. Tübingen: Mohr Siebeck, 2011.

Hayes, Christine. *Gentile Impurities and Jewish Identities: Intermarriage and Conversion from the Bible to the Talmud*. New York: Oxford University Press, 2002.

Hays, Richard B. *Echoes of Scripture in the Letters of Paul*. New Haven, CT: Yale University Press, 1989.

Hedner Zetterholm, Karin. "Alternative Visions of Judaism and Their Impact on the Formation of Rabbinic Judaism." *Journal of the Jesus Movement in its Jewish Setting* 1 (2014): 127–53, www.jjmjs.org.

Hengel, Martin. "Proseuche und Synagoge." In *Judaica and Hellenisica: Kleine Schriften 1*, 171–95. Tübingen: Mohr Siebeck, 1996.

Heschel, Abraham J. *God in Search of Man: A Philosophy of Judaism*. New York: Farrar, Straus & Giroux, 1989.

Hezser, Catherine. "Social Fragmentation, Plurality of Opinion, and Nonobservance of Halakhah: Rabbis and Community in Late Roman Palestine." *Jewish Studies Quarterly* 1 (1993): 234–51.

Hirshman, Marc. "Rabbinic Universalism in the Second and Third Centuries." *Harvard Theological Review* 93 (2000): 101–15.

Hitchens, Christopher. *God Is not Great: How Religion Poisons Everything*. London: Atlantic Books, 2008.

Hogg, Michael A., and Dominic Abrams. *Social Identifications: A Social Psychology of Intergroup Relations and Group Processes*. London: Routledge, 1988.

Horn, Friedrich W. "Paulus und die Herodianische Tempel." *New Testament Studies* 53 (2007): 184–203.

Horsley, Richard A. "Submerged Biblical Histories and Imperial Biblical Studies." In *The Postcolonial Bible*, edited by R. S. Sugirtharajah, 152–73. Sheffield: Sheffield Academic Press, 1998.

———, ed. *Paul and Empire: Religion and Power in Roman Imperial Society*. Harrisburg, PA: Trinity Press International, 1997.

———, ed. *Paul and Politics: Ekklesia, Israel, Imperium, Interpretation*. Harrisburg, PA: Trinity Press International, 2000.

———, ed. *Paul and the Roman Imperial Order*. Harrisburg, PA: Trinity Press International, 2004.

Horst, Pieter van der. "'Thou Shalt Not Revile the Gods': The LXX Translation of Exodus 22.28 (27), Its Background and Influence." *Studia Philonica* 5 (1993): 1–8.

Hultgren, Arland J. *Paul's Letter to the Romans*. Grand Rapids: Eerdmans, 2011.

Ilan, Tal. *Silencing the Queen: The Literary History of Shelomzion and Other Jewish Women*. Tübingen: Mohr Siebeck, 2006.

Isaac, Benjamin. *The Invention of Racism in Classical Antiquity*. Princeton, NJ: Princeton University Press, 2005.

Jenkins, Richard. *Social Identity*. London: Routledge, 2004.

Johnson Hodge, Caroline. "Apostle to the Gentiles: Constructions of Paul's Identity." *Biblical Interpretation* 13 (2005): 270–88.

———. *If Sons, Then Heirs: A Study of Kinship and Ethnicity in the Letters of Paul*. New York: Oxford University Press, 2007.

———. "Married to an Unbeliever: Households, Hierarchies and Holiness in 1 Corinthians 7:12-16." *Harvard Theological Review* 103 (2010): 1–25.

Johnson-DeBaufre, Melanie, and Laura Nasrallah. "Beyond the Heroic Paul: Toward a Feminist and Decolonizing Approach to the Letters of Paul." In *The Colonized Apostle: Paul Through Postcolonial Eyes*, edited by Christopher S. Stanley, 161–74. Minneapolis: Fortress Press, 2011.

Jones, Christopher P. *Kinship Diplomacy in the Ancient World*. Cambridge, MA: Harvard University Press, 1999.

Jones, Serene, and Joy Ann McDougall. "Sin – No More? A Feminist Re-Visioning of a Christian Theology of Sin." *Anglican Theological Review* 88 (2006): 215–35.

Kahl, Brigitte. *Galatians Rediscovered: Reading through the Eyes of the Vanquished*. Minneapolis: Fortress Press, 2011.

Kaminsky, Joel. "Israel's Election and the Other in Biblical, Second Temple, and Rabbinic Thought'" In *The "Other" in Second Temple Judaism: Essays in Honor of John J. Collins*, edited by Daniel C. Harlow, Karina Martin Hogan, and Mattew L. Goff, 17–30. Grand Rapids: Eerdmans, 2011.

Khamin, Alexei S. "Ignatius of Antioch: Performing Authority in the Early Church." PhD diss., Drew University, 2007.

Kittel, Gerhard., and Gerhard Friedrich, eds. *Theological Dictionary of the New Testament*. Translated by G. W. Bromiley. 10 vols. Grand Rapids: Eerdmans, 1964–1976.

Klawans, Jonathan. *Impurity and Sin in Ancient Judaism*. New York: Oxford University Press, 2000.

Kloppenborg, John S. "Collegia and Thiasoi: Issues in Function, Taxonomy and Membership." In *Voluntary Associations in the Graeco-Roman World*, edited by John S. Kloppenborg and Stephen G. Wilson, 16–30. London: Routledge, 1996.

Korner, Ralph. "Before 'Church': Political, Ethno-Religious and Theological Implications of the Collective Designation of Pauline Christ-Followers as *Ekklēsiai*." PhD diss., McMaster University, 2014.

Kraemer, Ross Shepard, and Mary Rose D'Angelo, eds. *Women and Christian Origins*. New York: Oxford University Press, 1999.

Kraemer, Ross Shepard. "Giving up the Godfearers." *Journal of Ancient Judaism 1* (forthcoming 2014).

———. *Unreliable Witnesses: Religion, Gender and History in the Greco-Roman Mediterranean*. New York: Oxford University Press, 2011.

Krais, Beate. "Gender, Sociological Theory and Bourdieu's Sociology of Practice." *Theory, Culture, Society* 23 (2006): 119–34.

Krause, Andrew. "The Nature of the First-Century Synagogue in Josephus: Aspects of Rhetoric and Historicity." PhD diss., McMaster University, forthcoming 2014.

Lamm, Norman. *The Shema: Spirituality and Law in Judaism as Exemplified in the Shema, the Most Important Passage in the Torah*. Philadelphia: Jewish Publication Society, 2000.

Langton, Daniel R. *The Apostle Paul in the Jewish Imagination: A Study in Modern Jewish–Christian Relations.* Cambridge: Cambridge University Press, 2010.

Leander, Hans. "Mark and Matthew after Edward Said." In *Mark and Matthew,* edited by Eve-Marie Becker and Anders Runesson, 2:289–309. Tübingen: Mohr Siebeck, 2013.

Levinas, Emmanuel. *Totality and Infinity: An Essay on Exteriority.* Pittsburgh: Duquesne University Press, 1969.

Levine, Lee I. *The Ancient Synagogue: The First Thousand Years.* 2nd ed. New Haven, CT: Yale University Press, 2005.

Levinskaya, Irina. *The Book of Acts in its Diaspora Setting.* Grand Rapids: Eerdmans, 1996.

Lieu, Judith. "The Race of the God-Fearers." *Journal of Theological Studies* 46 (1995): 483–501.

Liew, Tat-Siong Benny. *What Is Asian American Biblical Hermeneutics?: Reading the New Testament.* Honolulu: University of Hawaii Press, 2008.

Linder, Amnon. *Jews in the Legal Sources of the Early Middle Ages.* Detroit: Wayne State University Press, 1997.

———. *The Jews in Roman Imperial Legislation.* Detroit: Wayne State University Press, 1987.

Livesey, Nina. *Circumcision as a Malleable Symbol.* WUNT 2.295. Tübingen: Mohr Siebeck, 2010.

Lopez, Davina C. *Apostle to the Conquered.* Minneapolis: Fortress Press, 2008.

Luther, Martin. *Von den Jüden und iren Lügen.* Wittemberg: Hans Lufft, 1543.

MacDonald, Margaret Y. *Early Christian Women and Pagan Tradition: The Power of the Hysterical Woman.* Cambridge: Cambridge University Press, 1996.

Malina, Bruce J., and John J. Pilch. *Social-Science Commentary on the Letters of Paul.* Minneapolis: Fortress Press, 2006.

Martin, Dale B. *Sex and the Single Savior: Gender and Sexuality in Biblical Interpretation.* Louisville: Westminster John Knox, 2007.

———. "When Did Angels Become Demons?" *Journal of Biblical Literature* 129 (2010): 657–77.

Mason, Steve. "Jews, Judaeans, Judaizing, Judaism." *Journal for the Study of Judaism* (2007): 482–88.

Matthew, Susan. *Women in the Greetings of Romans 16.1-16.* London: T & T Clark, 2013.

Mattila, Sarah L. "Where Women Sat in Ancient Synagogues: The Archeological Evidence in Context." In *Voluntary Associations in the Graeco-Roman World,* edited by John S. Kloppenborg and Stephen G. Wilson, 266–86. London: Routledge, 1996.

Mattingly, David J. *Imperialism, Power, and Identity: Experiencing the Roman Empire.* Princeton, NJ: Princeton University Press, 2011.

McCutcheon, Russell T. "The Category 'Religion' in Recent Publications: A Critical Survey." *Numen* 42 (1995): 284–309.

McKnight, Scot, and Joseph B. Modica, eds. *Jesus Is Lord, Caesar Is Not: Evaluating Empire in New Testament Studies.* Downers Grove, IL: InterVarsity, 2013.

Meeks, Wayne. *The First Urban Christians: The Social World of the Apostle Paul.* New Haven, CT: Yale University Press, 1993.

Mitchell, Margaret M. *Paul and the Rhetoric of Reconciliation: An Exegetical Investigation of the Language and Composition of 1 Corinthians.* Louisville: Westminster John Knox Press, 1991.

Montefiore, Claude G. *Judaism and St Paul: Two Essays.* London: Goshen, 1914.

Moore, George F. "Christian Writers on Judaism" *Harvard Theological Review* 14 (1921): 197–254.

Moore, Stephen D. *Empire and Apocalypse: Postcolonialism and the New Testament.* Sheffield: Sheffield Phoenix, 2006.

———. and John C. Anderson. *New Testament Masculinities*. Atlanta: Society of Biblical Literature, 2003.

Muraoka, Takamitsu, ed. *A Greek-English Lexicon of the Septuagint*. Leuven: Peeters, 2009.

Murphy-O'Connor, Jerome. "Freedom or the Ghetto (1 Cor VIII:1–13, X:23–XI:1)." *Révue Biblique* 85 (1978): 541–74. Repr. in J. Murphy-O'Connor, *Keys to First Corinthians: Revisiting the Major Issues*. Oxford: Oxford University Press, 2009.

Murray, Michele. *Playing a Jewish Game: Gentile Christian Judaizing in the First and Second Centuries CE*. Waterloo, ON: Wilfred Laurier University Press, 2004.

Myllykoski, Matti. "'Christian Jews' and 'Jewish Christians': The Jewish Origins of Christianity in English Literature from Elizabeth I to Toland's *Nazarenus*." In *The Rediscovery of Jewish Christianity: From Toland to Baur*, edited by F. Stanley Jones, 3–41. Atlanta: Society of Biblical Literature, 2012.

Nanos, Mark D. "'Broken Branches': A Pauline Metaphor Gone Awry? (Romans 11:11-24)." In *Between Gospel and Election: Explorations in the Interpretation of Romans 9–11*, edited in J. Ross Wagner and Florian Wilk, 339–76. Tübingen: Mohr Siebeck, 2010.

———. "The Churches within the Synagogues of Rome." In *Reading Paul's Letter to the Romans*, edited by Jerry L. Sumney, 11–28. Atlanta: Society of Biblical Literature, 2010.

———. "Intruding 'Spies' and 'Pseudo-Brethren': The Jewish Intra-Group Politics of Paul's Jerusalem Meeting (Gal 2:1-10)." In *Paul and His Opponents*, edited by Stanley E. Porter, 59–97. Boston: Brill, 2005.

———. *The Irony of Galatians: Pauls' Letter in First Century Context*. Philadelphia: Fortress Press, 2001.

———. "The Letter of Paul to the Romans." In *The Jewish Annotated New Testament: New Revised Standard Version Bible Translation*, edited by Amy-

Jill Levine and Marc Zvi Brettler, 253–86. New York: Oxford University Press, 2011.

———. *The Mystery of Romans: The Jewish Context of Paul's Letter.* Minneapolis: Fortress Press, 1996.

———. "The Myth of the 'Law-Free' Paul Standing Between Christians and Jews." *Studies in Christian-Jewish Relations* 4 (2009): 1–21.

———. "Paul and the Jewish Tradition: The Ideology of the Shema." In *Celebrating Paul. Festschrift in Honor of Jerome Murphy-O'Connor, O.P., and Joseph A. Fitzmyer, S.J.*, edited by Peter Spitaler, 62–80. Washington, DC: Catholic Biblical Association of America, 2012.

———. "Paul and Judaism: Why Not Paul's Judaism?" In *Paul Unbound: Other Perspectives on the Apostle*, edited by Mark Douglas Given, 117–60. Peabody, MA: Hendrickson, 2010.

———. "Paul's Non-Jews Do Not Become 'Jews,' But Do They Become 'Jewish'?" *Journal of the Jesus Movement in its Jewish Setting* 1 (2014): 26–53, www.jjmjs.org.

———. "Paul's Relationship to Torah in Light of His Strategy 'to Become Everything to Everyone' (1 Corinthians 9:19–23)." In *Paul and Judaism: Crosscurrents in Pauline Exegesis and the Study of Jewish-Christian Relations*, edited by Didier Pollefeyt and Reimund Bieringer, 106–40. London: T & T Clark, 2012.

———. "The Polytheist Identity of the 'Weak,' and Paul's Strategy to 'Gain' Them: A New Reading of 1 Corinthians 8:1—11:1." In *Paul: Jew, Greek, and Roman*, edited by Stanley E. Porter, 179–210. Leiden: Brill, 2008.

———. "Romans 11 and Christian and Jewish Relations: Exegetical Options for Revisiting the Translation and Interpretation of this Central Text." *Criswell Theological Review* 9 (2012): 3–21.

———. "What Was at Stake in Peter's 'Eating with Gentiles' at Antioch?" In *The Galatians Debate: Contemporary Issues in Rhetorical and Historical Interpretation*, edited by Mark D. Nanos, 306–12. Peabody, MA: Hendrickson, 2002.

Nasrallah, Laura S. *An Ecstasy of Folly: Prophecy and Authority in Early Christianity.* Cambridge, MA: Harvard University Press, 2003.

Newman, Louis E. "Woodchppers and Respirators: The Problem of Interpretation in Contemporary Jewish Ethics." In *Contemporary Jewish Ethics and Morality: A Reader,* edited by Elliot N. Dorff and Louis E. Newman, 140–60. New York: Oxford University Press, 1995.

Nongbri, Brent. "Paul Without Religion: The Creation of a Category and the Search for an Apostle Beyond the New Perspective." PhD diss., Yale University, 2008.

Olyan, Saul M. "Purity Ideology in Ezra-Nehemiah as a Tool to Reconstitute the Community." *Journal for the Study of Judaism* 35 (2004): 1–16.

Overman, J. Andrew. *Matthew's Gospel and Formative Judaism: The Social World of the Matthean Community.* Minneapolis: Fortress Press, 1990.

Penner, Todd, and Caroline Vander Stichele. "Re-Assembling Jesus: Re-Thinking the Ethics of Gospel Studies." In *Mark and Matthew,* edited by Eve-Marie Becker and Anders Runesson, 2:311–34. Tübingen: Mohr Siebeck, 2013.

Peppard, Michael. *The Son of God in the Roman World.* New York: Oxford University Press, 2011.

Porter, Stanley E., and Cynthia Long Westfall, eds. *Empire in the New Testament: New Testament Studies.* Eugene, OR: Pickwick, 2011.

Portier-Young, Anathea. *Apocalypse Against Empire: Theologies of Resistance in Early Judaism.* Grand Rapids: Eerdmans, 2011.

Räisänen, Heikki. *Paul and the Law.* Philadelphia: Fortress Press, 1983.

———. *The Rise of Christian Beliefs: The Thought World of Early Christians.* Minneapolis: Fortress Press, 2010.

Rajak, Tessa. "The Parthians in Josephus." In *Das Partherreich und seine Zeugnisse: Beiträge des internationalen Colloquiums, Eutin (27. – 30 Juni 1996),* edited by J. Wiesehöfer, 309–24. Stuttgart: Franz Steiner, 1998.

Reed, Annette Y. *Fallen Angels and the History of Judaism and Christianity.* Cambridge: Cambridge University Press, 2005.

Richardson, Peter. *Building Jewish in the Roman East.* Waco, TX: Baylor University Press, 2004.

———. *Israel in the Apostolic Church.* London: Cambridge University Press, 1969.

Roth, Joel. "Homosexuality Revisited." 2006, at http://www.rabbinicalassembly.org/sites/default/files/public/halakhah/teshuvot/20052010/roth_revisited.pdf.

Rudolph, David J. *A Jew to the Jews: Jewish Contours of Pauline Flexibility in 1 Corinthians 9:19-23.* Tübingen: Mohr Siebeck, 2011.

Runesson, Anders, Donald D. Binder, and Birger Olsson, eds. *The Ancient Synagogue From its Origins to 200 C.E.: A Source Book.* Leiden: Brill, 2008.

———. "Behind the Gospel of Matthew: Radical Pharisees in Post-War Galilee?" *Currents in Theology and Mission* 37 (2010): 460–71.

———. "Inventing Christian Identity: Paul, Ignatius, and Theodosius I." In *Exploring Early Christian Identity*, edited by Bengt Holmberg, 59–92. Tübingen: Mohr Siebeck, 2008.

———. "Judging the Theological Tree by its Fruit: The Use of the Gospels of Mark and Matthew in Official Church Documents on Jewish-Christian Relations." In *Mark and Matthew*, edited by Eve-Marie Becker and Anders Runesson, 2:189–228. Tübingen: Mohr Siebeck, 2013.

———. *The Origins of the Synagogue: A Socio-Historical Study.* Stockholm: Almqvist & Wiksell, 2001.

———. "Paul's Rule in All the *Ekklēsiai* (1 Cor 7:17-24)." In *Introduction to Messianic Judaism: Its Ecclesial Context and Biblical Foundations*, edited by David Rudolph and Joel Willits, 214–23. Grand Rapids: Zondervan, 2013.

———. "Rethinking Early Jewish–Christian Relations: Matthean Community History as Pharisaic Intragroup Conflict." *Journal of Biblical Literature* 127 (2008): 95–132.

Runesson, Anna. *Exegesis in the Making: Postcolonialism and New Testament Studies.* Leiden: Brill, 2011.

Saldarini, Anthony J. *Matthew's Christian-Jewish Community.* Chicago: Chicago University Press, 1994.

Sanders, Edward P. *The Historical Figure of Jesus.* London: Penguin, 1993.

———. *Jewish Law from Jesus to the Mishnah: Five Studies.* London: SCM, 1990.

———. *Judaism: Practice and Belief, 63 BCE–66 CE.* Philadelphia: Trinity Press International, 1992.

———. "The Life of Jesus." In *Christianity and Rabbinic Judaism: A Parallel History of Their Origins and Early Development,* edited by Hershel Shanks, 41–83. Washington, DC: Biblical Archaeology Society, 1992.

———. "Paul's Jewishness." In *Paul's Jewish Matrix,* edited by T. G. Casey and Justin Taylor, 51–73. Rome: Gregorian & Biblical Press, 2011.

———. *Paul, the Law, and the Jewish People.* Minneapolis: Fortress Press, 1983.

———. *Paul and Palestinian Judaism: A Comparison of Patterns of Religion.* Philadelphia: Fortress Press, 1977.

———. *Paul: A Very Short Introduction.* Oxford: Oxford University Press, 1991.

Satlow, Michael L. *Jewish Marriage in Antiquity.* Princeton, NJ: Princeton University Press, 2001.

Scherman, Nosson. *The Complete Artscroll Siddur.* Brooklyn: Mesorah, 1988.

Schiffman, Lawrence H. "The Conversion of the Royal House of Abiabene [sp] Josephus and Rabbinic Sources." In *Josephus, Judaism, and Christianity,* edited by Louis H. Feldman and Gohei Hata, 293–312. Detroit: Wayne State University Press, 1987.

Schoedel, William R. *Ignatius of Antioch: A Commentary on the Letters of Ignatius of Antioch.* Hermeneia. Philadelphia: Fortress Press, 1985.

Schottroff, Luise. *Der Erste Brief an die Gemeinde in Korinth.* Stuttgart: Kohlhammer, 2013.

Schwartz, Daniel R. "God, Gentiles, and Jewish Law: On Acts 15 and Josephus's Adiabene Narrative." In *Geschichte—Tradition—Reflection: Festschrift für Martin Hengel zum 70. Geburtstag*, edited by Hubert Cancik, Hermann Lichtenberger, and Peter Schäfer, 263–82. Tübingen: Mohr Siebeck, 1996.

———. "'Judaean' or 'Jew'? How Should We Translate *Ioudaios* in Josephus?" In *Jewish Identity in the Greco-Roman World = Jüdische Identität in der griechischrämischen Welt*, edited by Jörg Frey, Daniel R. Schwartz, and Stephanie Gripentrog, 3–27. Leiden: Brill, 2007.

———. *Reading the First Century: On Reading Josephus and Studying Jewish History of the First Century*. WUNT 300. Tübingen: Mohr Siebeck, 2013.

Schürer, Emil. *Geschichte des jüdischen Volkes im Zeitalter Jesu Christi*. 2 vols. Leipzig: Hinrichs, 1886–1890.

———, and Geza Vermes et al. *History of the Jewish People in the Age of Jesus Christ*. 3 vols. Edinburgh: T & T Clark, 1973–87.

Schüssler Fiorenza, Elisabeth. *In Memory of Her: A Feminist Theological Reconstruction of Christian Origins*. New York: Crossroad, 1983.

———. *The Power of the Word: Scripture and the Rhetoric of Empire*. Minneapolis: Fortress Press, 2007.

Schwartz, Seth. "Gamaliel in Aphrodite's Bath: Palestinian Judaism and Urban Culture in the Third and Fourth Centuries." In *The Talmud Yerushalmi and Graeco-Roman Culture*, edited by Peter Schäfer, 203–17. Tübingen: Mohr Siebeck, 1998.

Scott, James M. "'And Then All Israel Will Be Saved' (Rom 11:26)." In *Restoration: Old Testament, Jewish, and Christian Perspectives*, edited by James M. Scott, 491–92. Supplements to the Journal for the Study of Judaism 72. Leiden: Brill, 2001.

———. *Paul and the Nations: The Old Testament and Jewish Background of Paul's Mission to the Nations with Special Reference to the Destination of Galatians*. Tübingen: Mohr Siebeck, 1995.

Sechrest, Love L. *A Former Jew: Paul and the Dialectics of Race*. London: T & T Clark, 2009.

Segal, Alan F. *Paul the Convert: The Apostolate and Apostasy of Saul the Pharisee*. New Haven, CT: Yale University Press, 1990.

Sim, David C. *The Gospel of Matthew and Christian Judaism: The History and Social Setting of the Matthean Community*. Edinburgh: T & T Clark, 1998.

Slingerland, H. Dixon. *Claudian Policymaking and the Early Imperial Repression of Judaism at Rome*. Atlanta: Scholars, 1997.

Smallwood, Mary. *The Jews Under Roman Rule from Pompey to Diocletian*. Leiden: Brill, 1976.

Smith, Jonathan Z. "Here, There, and Anywhere." In *Relating Religion: Essays in the Study of Religion*, 323–39. Chicago: University of Chicago Press, 2004.

———. "Religion, Religions, Religious." In *Critical Terms for Religious Studies*, edited by Mark C. Taylor, 269–84. Chicago: University of Chicago Press, 1998.

Smith, Morton, "Terminological Booby Traps and Real Problems in Second Temple Judaeo-Christian Studies." *Studies in the Cult of Yahweh*, edited by Shaye J. D. Cohen, 1:95–103. 2 vols. New York: Brill, 1996.

Stanley, Christopher D., ed. *The Colonized Apostle: Paul through Postcolonial Eyes*. Minneapolis: Fortress Press, 2011.

Stendahl, Krister. "The Apostle Paul and the Introspective Conscience of the West." *Harvard Theological Review* 56 (1963): 199–215.

———. *Final Account: Paul's Letter to the Romans*. Minneapolis: Fortress Press, 1995.

———. *Paul Among Jews and Gentiles, and Other Essays*. Philadelphia: Fortress Press, 1976.

Stern, Menachem. *Greek and Latin Authors on Jews and Judaism*. 3 vols. Jerusalem: Magnes, 1980.

Stowers, Stanley K. "The Concept of 'Community' and the History of Early Christianity." *Method and Theory in the Study of Religion* 23 (2011): 238–56.

———. *The Diatribe in Paul's Letter to the Romans.* Society of Biblical Literature Dissertation Series 57. Chico, CA: Scholars, 1981.

———. "Kinds of Myth, Meals, and Power: Paul and the Corinthians." In *Redescribing Paul and the Corinthians*, edited by Ron Cameron and Merrill Miller, 105–49. Atlanta: Society of Biblical Literature, 2011.

———. *A Rereading of Romans: Justice, Jews and Gentiles.* New Haven, CT: Yale University Press, 1994.

Tanner, Kathryn. *Jesus, Humanity and the Trinity: A Brief Systematic Theology.* Minneapolis: Fortress Press, 2001.

Taubes, Jacob. *The Political Theology of Paul.* Edited by Aleida Assmann et al. Translated by Dana Hollander. Stanford, CA: Stanford University Press, 2004.

Tellbe, Mikael. *Paul Between Synagogue and State: Christians, Jews, and Civic Authorities in 1 Thessalonians, Romans, and Philippians.* Stockholm: Almqvist & Wiksell, 2001.

Theissen, Matthew. *Contesting Conversion: Genealogy, Circumcision, and Identity in Ancient Judaism and Christianity.* New York: Oxford University Press, 2011.

Thiselton, Anthony C. *Hermeneutics: An Introduction.* Grand Rapids: Eerdmans, 2009.

Thomassen, Einar. "Some Notes on the Development of Christian Ideas about a Canon." In *Canon and Canonicity*, edited by Einar Thomassen, 9–28. Copenhagen: Museum Tusculanum Press, 2010.

Tomson, Peter J. *Paul and the Jewish Law: Halakha in the Letters of the Apostle to the Gentiles.* Assen: van Gorcum, 1990.

Tucker, Gordon. "Halakhic and Metahalakhic Arguments Concerning Judaism and Homosexuality." 2006, at http://www

.rabbinicalassembly.org/sites/default/files/public/halakhah/teshuvot/20052010/tucker_homosexuality.pdf.

Tucker, J. Brian. *"Remain in Your Calling": Paul and the Continuation of Social Identities in 1 Corinthians.* Eugene, OR: Pickwick, 2011.

———. *You Belong to Christ: Paul and the Formation of Social Identity in 1 Corinthians 1–4.* Eugene, OR: Pickwick, 2010.

Tzaferis, Vassilios. "Jewish Tombs at and near Giv'at ha-Mivtar." *Israel Exploration Journal* 20 (1970): 18–32.

Urbach, Ephraim. *The Sages.* Jerusalem: Magnes, 1975.

Wan, Sze-kar. "Does Diaspora Identity Imply Some Sort of Universality? An Asian-American Reading of Galatians." In *Interpreting Beyond Borders,* edited by Fernando F. Segovia, 107–31. Sheffield: Sheffield Academic Press, 2000.

Weber, Ferdinand. *System der altsynagogalen palästinischen Theologie aus Targum, Midrasch und Talmud.* Leipzig: Dörffling & Franke, 1880.

Welborn, Larry L. *An End to Enmity: Paul and the "Wrongdoer" of Second Corinthians.* BZNW 185. Berlin: de Gruyter, 2011.

Wiefel, Wolfgang. "The Jewish Community in Ancient Rome and the Origins of Roman Christianity. In *The Romans Debate,* edited by Karl P. Donfried, 85–101. Rev. ed. Peabody, MA: Hendrickson, 1991.

Williams, A. Lukyn, *Adversus Judaeos: A Bird's-Eye View of Christian Apologiae until the Renaissance.* Cambridge: Cambridge University Press, 2012 [1935].

Williams, Margaret. *Jews Among the Greeks and Romans: A Diasporan Sourcebook.* Baltimore: Johns Hopkins University Press, 1998.

Woolf, Greg, *Becoming Roman: The Origins of Provincial Civilization in Gaul.* Cambridge: Cambridge University Press, 1998.

———. "Becoming Roman, Staying Greek: Culture, Identity, and the Civilizing Process in Roman East." *Proceedings of the Cambridge Philological Society* 40 (1994): 116–43.

Wright, Nicolas T. *Justification: God's Plan and Paul's Vision.* Downers Grove, IL: IVP Academic, 2009.

———. *Paul and the Faithfulness of God.* Vol. 4 of *Christian Origins and the Question of God.* Minneapolis: Fortress Press, 2013.

———. "The Paul of History and the Apostle of Faith." *Tyndale Bulletin* 29 (1978): 61–88.

———. *The Resurrection of the Son of God.* Vol. 3 of *Christian Origins and the Question of God.* Minneapolis: Fortress Press, 2003.

Young, Frances. *Biblical Exegesis and the Formation of Christian Culture.* Cambridge: Cambridge University Press, 1997.

Zetterholm, Magnus. *Approaches to Paul: A Student's Guide to Recent Scholarship.* Minneapolis: Fortress Press, 2009.

———. *The Formation of Christianity in Antioch: A Social-Scientific Approach to the Separation Between Judaism and Christianity.* London: Routledge, 2003.

———. "Paul and the Missing Messiah." In *The Messiah in Early Judaism and Christianity*, edited by Magnus Zetterholm, 35–54. Minneapolis: Fortress Press, 2007.

———. "Purity and Anger: Gentiles and Idolatry in Antioch." *Interdisciplinary Journal of Research on Religion* 1 (2005): 3–24.

———. "'Will the Real Gentile-Christian Please Stand Up!': Torah and the Crisis of Identity Formation." In *The Making of Christianity: Conflicts, Contacts, and Constructions: Essays in Honor of Bengt Holmberg*, edited by Magnus Zetterholm and Samuel Byrskog, 373–93. Winona Lake, IN: Eisenbrauns, 2012.

Zias, J., and E. Sekeles. "The Crucified Man from Giv'at ha-Mitvar: A Reappraisal." *Israel Exploration Journal* 35 (1985): 22–27.

Økland, Jorunn. *Women in Their Place: Paul and the Corinthian Discourse of Gender and Sanctuary Space.* New York: T & T Clark, 2004.

Index of Modern Authors

Index of Biblical and Ancient References